Horace Walpole:
Memoirs and Portraits

Horace Walpole

Memoirs and Portraits

———————————— ◎ ————————————

Edited by

MATTHEW HODGART

The Macmillan Company

NEW YORK

*For copyright reasons, paperback copies of this
book may not be issued to the public, on loan or otherwise,
except in their original soft covers*

LIBRARY OF CONGRESS CATALOG CARD NUMBER: 17297

FIRST PUBLISHED 1822–45
REVISED EDITION © MATTHEW HODGART 1963

FIRST PUBLISHED IN THE UNITED STATES OF AMERICA
BY THE MACMILLAN COMPANY, 1963

Made and printed in Great Britain
by William Clowes and Sons, Limited, London and Beccles

Horace Walpole
Memoirs and Portraits

———————◎———————

Edited by
MATTHEW HODGART

The Macmillan Company
NEW YORK

*For copyright reasons, paperback copies of this
book may not be issued to the public, on loan or otherwise,
except in their original soft covers*

LIBRARY OF CONGRESS CATALOG CARD NUMBER: 17297

FIRST PUBLISHED 1822–45
REVISED EDITION © MATTHEW HODGART 1963

FIRST PUBLISHED IN THE UNITED STATES OF AMERICA
BY THE MACMILLAN COMPANY, 1963

Made and printed in Great Britain
by William Clowes and Sons, Limited, London and Beccles

Contents

LIST OF ILLUSTRATIONS   vii

ACKNOWLEDGMENT   viii

INTRODUCTION   ix

Memoirs and Portraits

1751	1
1752	38
1753	44
1754	45
1755	50
1756	54
1757	63
1758	77
1759	84
1760	92
1761	112
1762	123
1763	136
1764	149

CONTENTS

1765	156
1766	171
1767	176
1768	187
1769	205
1770	221
1771	238
APPENDIX	247
NOTES ON THE TEXT	250
EXPLANATORY NOTES	254
INDEX	260

List of Illustrations

facing page

Horace Walpole   72
From a portrait by Sir Joshua Reynolds, 1757

'Brother, Brother, we are both in the Wrong'   73
From a print of August 1756

'The Sturdy Beggar'   73
From a print of April 1757

George II   88
From the portrait by Robert Edge Pine, 1759

The Duke of Newcastle   89
From an engraving by Paton Thomson

The Duke of Bedford   89
From an engraving by Paton Thomson

The Prince of Wales and the Duke of Cumberland   89
*From an engraving by Paton Thomson after a drawing by
Richard Bentley*

'The State Quack'   152
From a print of September 1760

John Wilkes   153
Detail of a group portrait by Richard Houston, about 1768

George III   153
*Detail of a portrait from the studio of Allan Ramsay, about
1767*

Henry Pelham   168
*From an engraving by Paton Thomson after Richard
Bentley and an unknown artist*

William Pitt, Earl of Chatham   169
Detail of a portrait from the studio of Richard Brompton

The Duke of Argyll   169
Detail of a portrait by Allan Ramsay

Acknowledgment

The Editor wishes to thank the following for permission to reproduce extracts from manuscripts in their possession: the Earl Waldegrave; Mr W. S. Lewis; the Earl of Ilchester. He is also grateful for the help and advice given by Lord and Lady Waldegrave, Mr Lewis, and Patricia Hodgart.

The Editor and Publishers also wish to thank the following for permission to reproduce the illustrations appearing in this book:

The Trustees of the British Museum for the illustrations facing pages 73, 89, 152, and 168; the Marquess of Hertford and the City of Birmingham Museum and Art Gallery for page 72; the National Galleries of Scotland for page 169 (bottom); the National Portrait Gallery for pages 153 and 169 (top); and the Hon. Robin Neville and the Ministry of Public Building and Works for page 88.

Introduction

Horace Walpole exhibits the double face of his age. On the one hand, he is a romantic medievalist, the inventor of the Gothic novel, and the inspired decorator of Strawberry Hill: in his youth he wrote with feeling about the wild scenery of the Alps. On the other hand, he is rationalist, Stoic in ethics, neo-classical in many of his literary preferences, and an arch-Whig, with a strong dislike of enthusiasm in religion and politics. The first face is not to be dismissed as trivial: he was a serious student of medieval architecture, and, possessed of excellent taste himself, did much to shape English fashions for the next century. Did not Byron call him 'the father of the first romance and of the last tragedy' in English, and did not the Surrealists hail him as an ancestor? Nothing of this, however, will be seen in the pages that follow, where he appears as the unromantic chronicler of a political scene about which he had few illusions. 'Visions, you know,' he wrote to George Montagu in 1766, 'have always been my pasture; and so far from growing old enough to quarrel with their emptiness, I almost think there is no wisdom comparable to that of exchanging what is called the realities of life for dreams. Old castles, old pictures, old histories, and the babble of old people, make one live back into centuries that cannot disappoint one. One holds fast and surely what is past. The dead have exhausted their power of deceiving—one can trust Catherine of Medicis now.' Visions and dreams, however, whether of Italian castles or giant armour, were for the night watches of this tireless man; by day there was the teeming life of Court and Parliament, of the great country-houses and the muddy streets, to be recorded accurately and crisply in thousands of pages of letters and memoirs.

As historian of his century Horace Walpole had unique qualifications. He was the youngest son of Sir Robert Walpole, who was Prime Minister from 1721 to 1742 and whose greatness he contrasts with the decadent statesmen of the mid-century. Born in 1717, his godfathers were his uncle Horatio Walpole and the Duke of Grafton (whose son the Prime Minister figures extravagantly in the *Memoirs*); his godmother was his aunt Lady Townshend, married into another political dynasty. He had these and other family connections with the land-owning magnates who shared out the political power of the nation with the Court, to which he also had entry. Thus he knew personally almost everyone he describes in the *Memoirs*; and indeed the politics of the nation often read like a protracted family quarrel, observed acutely by a precocious younger cousin. He went to Eton at the normal age of ten, at 17 to King's College Cambridge, which was his father's college. While still an undergraduate he was presented with the first of his sinecures, which included the profitable positions of 'Usher of the Exchequer' and 'Controller of the Pipe and Clerk of the Estreats'; thanks to these and to legacies, he did not need to seek gainful employment at any time, and was rich enough to build, to collect, and to travel. After Cambridge came the Grand Tour. With his Eton and Cambridge friend Thomas Gray he crossed the Alps and spent the best part of two years in Italy; there was an estrangement with Gray, who returned alone, but they became firm friends again a few years later. While still out of England, Horace was 'elected' Member of Parliament for a Cornish rotten borough, which he later exchanged for King's Lynn; it was not until 1742 that he spoke for the first time in the House, but he remained as an eye-witness of many of the debates described in the *Memoirs* until his resignation 25 years later. The great torrent of letters began to flow in the thirties, and increased in the forties, when the main topics were high society, antiquarianism and to a lesser extent political scenes. In 1747 Walpole bought Strawberry Hill in Twickenham and began the long and delightful process of building, decorating, and furnishing that was to be the chief solace of his life. Even today it is a charming house, unjustly disparaged as gimcrack by critics who perhaps have never walked through its handsomely proportioned rooms.

When the *Memoirs* for the year 1751 were begun, apparently before the end of that year, Walpole was a popular and fashionable young man of 34, not evidently destined for high office but enjoying the confidence of many who held office, and consequently possessing an immense amount of political knowledge. This knowledge he decided to keep for posterity, but since the *Memoirs* remained private until after his death, let us first look at the rest of his public career. He was never so politically active as in 1757, when he 'used [his] utmost endeavours, but in vain, to save the unfortunate Admiral Byng',[1] an attempt which stands greatly to the credit of his warm heart, and led to his satirical pamphlet, *A Letter from Xo Ho, a Chinese Philosopher at London, to his Friend, Lien Chi, at Peking.* His next published works were his *Catalogue of Royal and Noble Authors* (1758) and his

---

[1] See *Short Notes*, p. 27, and below, pp. 60–70.

Anecdotes of Painting (1760). The accession of George III made little difference to the even tenor of Walpole's life, except that he withdrew little by little from the political hurly-burly, with one vain hope that his talents might be recognized by the first Rockingham administration. His imaginative life became more intense in his late forties: in 1764, inspired by a dream, he wrote *The Castle of Otranto* so quickly that it might almost be termed automatic writing; and in 1768 he finished his 'Jacobean' tragedy *The Mysterious Mother*, as well as *Historic Doubts on Richard III*. Though he became crippled with gout in hands as well as feet, the flow of good-natured and witty correspondence never ceased. His old friends died off; he found new ones to amuse, like the young Misses Berry. Unwillingly he became the 4th earl of Orford in 1791, and died a tolerably happy man in 1797, in his eightieth year.

Walpole's fame rests securely on his letters, which are among the finest in the English or perhaps any language. In eighteenth-century England, Walpole as a letter-writer was surpassed only by Thomas Gray (and some would say by William Cowper). But no-one else produced a comparable volume of correspondence on so many subjects, and with such unfailing sparkle. There survive over 4,000 letters to many correspondents, of which some 3,000 are in the unsatisfactory Toynbee edition. All, together with the letters addressed to Walpole, are being printed in the monumental Yale edition under the direction of Mr W. S. Lewis. Twenty-six large volumes, out of about 50, have appeared to date, each a model of accuracy and historical scholarship; and anyone who wants to know in detail about Walpole and about the people who figure in his *Memoirs* must consult this edition. But for the general reader this is out of the question: fortunately he may turn to some of the selections, which offer the best of the letters or the most striking passages from them. Among the editors of such works is Mr Lewis himself, who has thus set a precedent, to be followed in trepidation, for a shortened version of the *Memoirs*.

Walpole's letters often show a wonderful pictorial brilliance. His great set piece, the Funeral of George II (to George Montagu, 13 November 1760), shows a medievalist's interest in the background of Westminster Abbey, a painter's eye for the solemn procession, and a rich sense of the comic:

This grave scene was fully contrasted by the burlesque Duke of Newcastle—he fell into a fit of crying the moment he came into the chapel, and flung himself back in a stall, the Archbishop hovering over him with a smelling-bottle—but in two minutes his curiosity got the better of his hypocrisy and he ran about the chapel with his glass to spy who was or was not there, spying with one hand, and mopping his eyes with t'other. Then returned the fear of catching cold; and the Duke of Cumberland, who was sinking with heat, felt himself weighed down, and turning round, found it was the Duke of Newcastle standing upon his train, to avoid the chill of the marble. It was very theatric to look down into the vault, where the coffin lay, attended by mourners with lights.

There is a keener sense of place, time and people in this letter—more of life, in fact—than on almost any page of an eighteenth-century novelist. With hardly less remarkable skill and zest does he describe the execution of the Rebel Lords (to Sir Horace Mann, 21 August 1746), though on this occasion he was not an eye-witness, or an evening spent in the gardens of Vauxhall (to Montagu, 23 January 1750), or a house party at Stowe (to Montagu, 7 July 1770). His dramatic abilities appear at their best in his account of public scenes and riots: the Wilkes riots, the Gordon riots, the Cock Lane Ghost affair, peace celebrations, and the excitements about highwaymen are recounted with the greatest *sprezzatura*. (The account in the letters is usually more lively than the corresponding one in the *Memoirs*.) He catches almost everything on the surface of eighteenth-century life that has movement and glitter. Walpole has been compared to Dickens for descriptive power, and has earned Leslie Stephen's tribute: 'The history of England, throughout a very large segment of the eighteenth century, is simply a synonym for the works of Horace Walpole.... Turn over any of the proper decorous history books, mark every passage where, for a moment, we seem to be transported to the past ... and it will be safe to say that, on counting them up, a good half will turn out to be reflections from the illuminating flashes of Walpole.'

'This world is a comedy to those that think, a tragedy to those that feel', wrote Walpole to Lady Ossory in 1776, adding, 'this is the quintessence of all I have learned in fifty years.' He was then perhaps weary with completing the *Memoirs*, and, while granting him his mastery of the comic, we should not take his flippancy at its face value. Walpole had a generous heart, and showed active sympathy for victims of injustice, like Admiral Byng, and for just causes, like the

Americans'. His limitations are rather that he finds too many people ridiculous—even the great William Pitt appears as partly a charlatan —and that he protests his detachment and indifference too strongly for conviction. The less said about his literary tastes the better: admiring only Thomas Gray whole-heartedly, he saw Samuel Johnson merely as an absurdity and a political enemy. Despite these weaknesses, Walpole's intelligence and humanity are great enough to make the letters not only a vastly entertaining but a moving record.

In his correspondence Walpole had many purposes, but one of them was to include a political and social history of England. The letters to Sir Horace Mann, Ambassador to the court of Florence, are the closest to the *Memoirs* in matter and style: they provide a detailed commentary on affairs of state from the forties to the eighties, which Walpole called 'a correspondence of near half a century ... not to be paralleled in the annals of the Post-office!' In these letters Walpole wrote for posterity, showing what Mr W. S. Lewis calls a 'special attitude—half professional and half informal.' He retrieved and annotated several hundred of the letters, and took care to get his facts right. The same topics and the same incidents appear at length in the *Memoirs* and letters—the Seven Years' War, Byng, Wilkes, the Americans—often presented with more elegance and wit in the letters. The letters lack the minute account of Parliamentary affairs, which make the *Memoirs* as a whole not very approachable by the general reader; he will be put off especially by those of 1751, the first year covered, which are in part no more exciting to read than *Hansard*. But the letters also lack the glory of the *Memoirs*—the indiscreet, malicious, and highly perceptive 'characters' or 'portraits', which could *not* have been sent through the post, even to the most reliable friends. It is largely from these 'characters' that I have made this selection.

The tradition of inserting 'characters' into a narrative is an ancient one, and has been followed by many historians since Thucydides. Walpole was certainly familiar with the incisive, epigrammatic portraits by Tacitus, such as that of the Emperor Galba (*Histories* I, 49) which ends, 'et omnium consensu capax imperii nisi imperasset' ('by common consent capable of ruling, if only he had not ruled'). But in this art Walpole's masters were the English historians of the later seventeenth century, and above all Clarendon. Edward Hyde, Lord Clarendon (1609–1674), interspersed his great *History of the Rebellion and the Civil Wars* (published in 1704) with sharply defined portraits of the leading figures in his narrative, portraits that are themselves modelled on classical practice. Clarendon admired Tacitean paradox, and although avowedly partisan tried to give a just picture of a man's faults and merits, as in his character of Cromwell:

he was one of those men, *quos vituperare ne inimici quidem possent, nisi ut simul laudent* ('whom not even his enemies could blame, unless at the same time they praised'), for he could never have done half that mischief without great parts of courage and industry and judgment, and he must have had a wonderful understanding in the natures and humours of men, and as great a dexterity in applying them, who from a private and obscure birth (though of good family) without interest of estate, alliance, or friendships, could raise himself to such a height, and compound and knead such opposite and contradictory tempers, humours and interests into a consistence that contributed to his designs and to their own destruction, while himself grew powerful enough to cut off those by whom he had climbed in the instant that they projected to demolish their own building.

(The Latin tag, which Clarendon may have invented, could have been adopted by Walpole as his motto.) It has been pointed out that Clarendon was born into a great age of portrait-painting and that he may have tried to produce the verbal counterparts of the great Van Dycks he had seen in the palaces and country-houses of England. Walpole, with his interest in the fine arts, may have been similarly influenced; he is, however, less successful in revealing greatness or depravity. Lacking Clarendon's heroic view of life and sense of human dignity, his portraits create an inferior illusion of spiritual reality. On the other hand, he is often more successful than Clarendon in describing the externals of a man or a scene; he has more humour, and indeed his natural mode seems to be close to Hogarthian caricature. His prose, though sometimes careless, is more easily readable and freer from 'period' mannerisms than Clarendon's involved sentences, of which that on Cromwell is typical.

Walpole's devotion to Clarendon appears in small details, such as his frequent use of the words 'parts' (meaning 'capacities'). At one point we can perhaps catch a verbal echo: compare Clarendon's character of John Hampden:

He was a gentleman of good family in Buckinghamshire, and born to a fair fortune, and of a most civil and affable deportment. In his entrance into the world, he indulged to himself all the license in sports and exercises, and company, which was used by men of the most jolly conversation. . . .

with Walpole's character of John Wilkes, the affable and jolly Hampden of his day, which read in the first draft:

He was a gentleman of tolerable fortune in Buckinghamshire. . . .

Walpole had of course little or no sympathy with Clarendon's Tory politics. He must have read with greater approval of the sentiments, if with less admiration for the style, the Whig Gilbert Burnet (1643–1715). *Bishop Burnet's History of His Own Times*, published in 1723, is like Clarendon's, a history composed in great part of memoirs. Walpole certainly knew the more recent historian Laurence Echard, whose *History of England* (1707–1718) contains 'characters' in imitation of Clarendon's. Burnet and Echard were compared by Matthew Green in an Epigram which tells us some of the things that eighteenth-century readers, including Walpole, admired in historiography:

> *Gil's history appears to me*
> *Political anatomy,*
> *A case of skeletons well done,*
> *And malefactors every one.*
> *His sharp and strong incision pen*
> *Historically cuts up men,*
> *And does with lucid skill impart*
> *Their inward ails of head and heart.*
> *Laurence proceeds another way,*
> *And well-dress'd figures does display:*
> *His characters are all in flesh,*
> *Their hands are fair, their faces fresh;*
> *And from his sweetning art derive*
> *A better scent than when alive;*
> *He wax-work made to please the sons,*
> *Whose fathers were Gil's skeletons.*[1]

Walpole's reading of modern history was not confined to English: just as his model for letter-writing was Madame de Sévigné, so he may have learned something from the cynical Cardinal de Retz (1613–1679) whose *Mémoires* tell the story of the Fronde wittily but with less concern for accuracy than Walpole thought proper. (This may account

[1] Quoted by Bonamy Dobrée, *English Literature in the Early Eighteenth Century*, 1959, who gives an excellent account of these and other historians.

for Walpole's usual spelling of 'memoires'.) Walpole, unfortunately, did not know the greatest of early eighteenth-century memoirs, by the Duc de Saint-Simon (1675-1755), whose incomparable account of the last years of Louis XIV and of the Regency was not available[1]; the finest English achievement in this field, by John, Lord Hervey (1696-1743), was also published too late for Walpole.[2]

If Walpole is not quite the equal of Saint-Simon or Hervey in dramatic power or close observation, he is certainly their equal in accuracy. In his 'Postscript' to the memoirs for 1751, he claims that he is objective, impartial, and truthful:

> The reader has now seen these Memoires; and though some who know mankind, and the various follies, faults and virtues, that are blended in our imperfect natures, may smile with me at this free relation of what I have seen and known, yet I am aware that more will be offended at the liberty I have taken in painting men as they are; and that many, from private connections of party and family, will dislike meeting such unflattered portraits of their heroes or their relations. Yet this, I fear, must always be the case in any history written impartially by an eye witness; and eye witnesses have been generally allowed the properest historians.... Thus much I shall premise: if I had intended a romance, I would not have chosen real personages for the actors in it; few men can sit for patterns of perfect virtue. If I had intended a satire, I would not have amassed so many facts, which, if not true, would only tend to discredit the author, not those he may censure.

There is every reason to believe that Walpole got his facts right. The careful documenting of his letters by the Yale editors has proved how reliable he was; and in his own day he was admired as an accurate source. The Duke of Grafton said that there was no one from whom he 'received so just accounts of the schemes of the various factions' or that 'had so good means of getting the knowledge of what was passing'.[3] Walpole specifies in his 'Postscript' some of his excellent sources:

> For the facts, such as were not public, I received chiefly from my father and Mr. Fox, both men of veracity; and some from

---

[1] *Mémoires de Saint-Simon*, ed. A. de Boislisle, 42 volumes, Paris 1879-1928.

[2] *Memoirs of the Reign of King George II*, 1848; ed. Romney Sedgwick 1931, selected edition (Batsford) 1963.

[3] *Autobiography* (1898), pp. 140-41; cit. W. S. Lewis, *Horace Walpole*, 1960, p. 90.

communication with the Duke of Bedford at the very time they were in agitation. I am content to rest their authenticity on the sincerity of such men; at the same I beg it may be remembered, that I never assert anything positively unless from very good authority; and it may be observed, that where I am not certain, I always say, *it was said, it was believed, it was supposed*, or use some such phrase. The speeches, I can confirm, nay, of every one of them, to be still more authentic, as I took notes at the time, and have delivered the arguments just as I heard them....

His long accounts of the French Court are probably just as reliable. In a detailed account of Madame du Barry and the political repercussions of her becoming Louis XV's mistress in 1769—much longer than the version printed below, p. 218—he gives his sources specifically: chiefly his dear friend and correspondent Madame du Deffand, and the leading politicians and courtiers he met at her house.

In this situation were the politics of the court, when I left Paris Oct. 5 1769.... The authenticity of this narrative may be depended upon. I was witness to parts, & had all the rest from the first hands, & some from the chief persons of both parties.

Hor Walpole Oct. 17. 1769[1]

THE HISTORICAL SITUATION

When the Memoirs begin in 1751, George II was in the 34th year of his reign and the 68th of his life. It will be clear that for Walpole politics begin with the King, the Royal Family and the Court. George II and George III were not figure-head monarchs, but really ruled, although they were compelled to share their power with various ministers and with the political groupings, or connections, behind these ministers. Hence the importance given to the sudden death of Frederick, Prince of Wales, in 1751, which altered the Succession; and to the upbringing of the future George III. George III's mother, the 'Princess Dowager', hardly gets a mention in the history text-books, but to Walpole she was a sinister influence on Court policy and on national affairs. Walpole's detestation of George III was almost as whole-hearted; again his judgment is at variance with the more sympathetic approach of most modern historians.

Walpole's judgment of the leading ministers is hardly more friendly.

[1] From an unpublished MS in the possession of Mr W. S. Lewis.

Many of those prominent in 1751 had been his father's enemies, or false friends; notably the Pelhams, who continued to hold power until the end of George II's reign. Henry Pelham was First Lord of the Treasury until his death in 1754; he was succeeded by his brother the 'burlesque' Duke of Newcastle. Walpole always calls these men and their successors Prime Ministers, although the term had no strict constitutional meaning and is often avoided by modern historians. The Seven Years' War began in 1756: in that year Newcastle lost power temporarily and then shared it with William Pitt. Pitt, though only a Secretary of State, was responsible for the successful prosecution of the war; and to him alone Walpole was willing to allow a measure of greatness. 1759 was the Annus Mirabilis, with the great victories of Quebec, Lagos, and Minden, about which little is said in this selection, though much in the full text of the Memoirs and the letters. When George III came to the throne in 1760, everyone expected changes to be made, and Walpole at first thought it quite proper that some of the King's friends should receive their reward. Lord Bute, always referred to as 'the Favourite', was appointed the other Secretary of State in 1761, which led to the resignation of Pitt; and in the following year Bute succeeded Newcastle as First Lord of the Treasury. As much through inefficiency as unpopularity Bute had to resign in April 1763. The next Ministry, under George Grenville, had to cope with the demagogic attacks of John Wilkes, which are described at some length by Walpole, and the first serious trouble with the American colonies. In 1765 the King had his first fit of madness, and Grenville was succeeded by a largely anti-Court Ministry under the Whig Lord Rockingham. Rockingham had neither the energy nor the talent to survive for long, and in 1766 the Duke of Grafton formed a Cabinet, which included for a time William Pitt, now Lord Chatham. Walpole, because of family connections, knew Grafton best of all these Prime Ministers; hence the detailed and scandalous anecdotes, now printed here for the first time, which are intended to explain why Grafton, a man of intelligence, could not give his mind sufficiently to the problems of the day. The American situation grew more critical, and the return of Wilkes led to fresh agitation against the Court and Government, culminating in the Letters of Junius. In 1770 Lord North began his long and disastrous administration, during which he acted more as the agent of George III than any other Prime Minister had done. In 1771, when these Memoirs end, the 'present discontents', as Burke called them, were no nearer to being allayed than they had been in 1763.

The background for the first five Ministries of George III is one of turbulence and even incipient revolution. Neither Wilkes nor his supporters had any clear notions of what they were up to in their attacks on the King and Court; but Walpole did not understand them any better. It is perhaps best to regard this period as a crisis of the *ancien régime*, which affected England, America and France equally strongly, although the symptoms differed. The old political system, which Walpole understood so well, was cracking under the strain of political and social changes, which few at the time understood. Worse was to come: in 1781, towards the end of the American War, Walpole was reduced to despair. But the system survived, thanks to the growing prosperity of the country, and thanks to the unbounded energies of landlords, farmers, merchants, soldiers, sailors, administrators, and orators, and the people of England. It is with such people that these selections from the *Memoirs* are concerned.

DATES OF THE MEMOIRS

The earliest surviving memoirs of Horace Walpole are called 'Mémoires from the Declaration of the War with Spain': from this title, they should begin with the events of 1744, but only the portions covering the years 1746–1750 are extant. These are in an unpublished MS in the possession of Mr W. S. Lewis; since they are largely in the form of notes, they have not been included in this selection. Walpole made virtually a new start in 1751: in his 'Short Notes' on his own life he records under that year, 'About this time I began to write my *Memoirs*. At first, I intended only to write the history of one year.' The *Memoirs* for 1751 (which in fact mention events that took place late in 1750) were finished on 28 May, 1752. That Walpole once thought of publishing them as a separate book appears from 'The Author's Postscript to these Memoirs', which is wrongly placed in the printed editions as a preface to the whole of 'George II': this passage contains general reflections on the writing of history, but the only specific events referred to are those of 1751. It begins 'The reader has now seen these Memoirs' and the entries for 1751, more detailed than for any subsequent year, are long enough to make a small book in themselves. I do not know when Walpole abandoned this idea.

His next plan was evidently to continue with the entries for each year after 1751, writing up a finished literary work from notes and jottings made earlier; each year continued to make a separate unit but now contained less full accounts of the debates in the House of Commons. From the 'Short Notes' on his own life, and from dates written in the MS, we can establish when many parts of the rough draft (Chewton MS 'First Copy') were written.[1] The memoirs for a given year were drafted sometimes within a few months after it had finished, and sometimes as much as six years later. Walpole also incorporated set pieces and 'characters', which he had written earlier, into memoirs of a later date: for example, 'The Parallel of Sir Robert Walpole and Mr. Pelham', included under 1751 (see below p. 34) was written in 1747.

Walpole then prepared a fair copy (Chewton MS 'Second Copy'—a fuller description of these MSS will be found below, p. xxix); this is neatly written in his own hand, with revisions and with additional footnotes. At some time he evidently considered publishing the memoirs of 1751 to 1755 as a separate book: Lord Holland wrote in 1822 that there was also a third copy for those years, written by Walpole's secretary but corrected in Walpole's own hand, which looked as if it had been carefully prepared for the press. This plan was also dropped, but Walpole seems to have continued to prepare his memoirs for posthumous publication, making a fair copy of every year's entries up to the end of 1770. We do not know the dates of these fair copies, since Walpole did not enter them in the MS; but it is fairly certain, from the revisions of Lord North's 'character' which I discuss later, that the fair copy of 1770 was written as late as 1782.

For the year 1771 only one MS is extant, which seems to be the rough draft, and that is the end of the *Memoirs* proper. Walpole wrote in his 'Short Notes': '20 April 1772, finished my Memoirs, which conclude with the year 1771; intending for the future only to carry on a journal.' This Journal he kept up till 1791, making one copy only: the section from 1772 to 1783 has been published, and is generally known as the 'Last Journals'; the section from 1784 to 1791, in the possession of Mr W. S. Lewis, has never been published. In general the 'Last Journals' are rather inferior in style and content, although

---

[1] Memoirs for 1755 and 1756, begun 26 December 1755; for 1756, begun 8 August 1758; for 1757, begun 9 October 1758; for 1758, begun 17 August 1759, finished 28 October 1759; for 1759, begun 10 October 1763, finished 28 October 1763; for 1760 to the end of the reign of George II, begun 29 October 1763, finished 9 November 1763; for the beginning of the reign of George III in 1760, begun 18 August 1766; for 1765, finished July 1769; for 1766, finished August 1769; for 1767, begun October 1769, finished 1 December 1769; those for 1768, 1769, and 1770 were written in 1771; and the Memoirs for 1771 were begun on 7 January and finished 20 April 1772.

they contain striking passages about Charles James Fox and the Prince of Wales: they have not been included in this selection.

REVISIONS

Walpole's revisions have been the subject of some discussion. He has been attacked by historians like Carl Becker, who 'have decided that Walpole doctored the *Memoirs* after he wrote them to conform to his changed opinions of people and views of government'[1] and he has been warmly defended by Mr Lewis. Walpole certainly did make many slight changes in his second draft, and a few more serious ones. Some of the more interesting examples are given in the Textual Notes at the end of this volume. In the first place, there are deletions of over-bitter or hasty judgments. Thus he erased the following comment on the Duke of Cumberland: 'It is uncertain whether his inordinate passion for war proceeded from brutal courage, from love of rule, or from love of blood; for he was as cruel as if he had been a coward; it is certain that it did not proceed from love of glory.' For this he substituted the more flattering sentence, 'With the most heroic bravery, he had all the severity that levels valour to cowardice, and seemed to love war for itself, without feeling the passions that it gratifies' (see p. 14). The deletions occur mainly in the earlier part of 'George II'; later there are far more additions. Walpole inserted some seven lines in a comment on Pitt (see p. 78) which begin 'but his passion for fame and the grandeur of his ideas compensated for his defects'. Elsewhere Walpole seems to have felt that he had been unfair to Pitt's greatness; to another passage he added in the second copy a eulogy on Pitt's 'prodigality unhappily copied in the next reign, throughout the American war, by men who imitated Mr Pitt in nothing else, and who had none of his genius, ambition, patriotism, activity, nor even his lofty ideas' (p. 88). This addition drew a comment from his editor Lord Holland, which I quote in the notes; yet there is nothing disingenuous about Walpole's addition, since its later date would be obvious to his readers.

A more complex case is presented by the 'Character of Lord North' (p. 225), which exists in three drafts. The earliest, presumably written in 1770, just after North became First Lord of the Treasury, is in an unpublished MS belonging to Mr W. S. Lewis, which I quote with his permission; the next is in the 'First Copy' of the Chewton MSS;

[1] W. S. Lewis, *Horace Walpole*, 1960, p. 83.

and the third, printed here, is in the 'Second Copy' of the Chewton MSS. The first twenty or so lines, with the striking description of North's appearance, down to 'attain the rank of Prime Minister' are very nearly the same in all three drafts, although Walpole deleted from the list of North's qualities 'boldness' and added 'yet was not avaricious' (Chewton MS 'First Copy'). But the earliest version continues:

> He felt the importance of the moment, & profited of it like a man. His knowledge supplied what the Bedford faction wanted most, the science of revenue—& his activity and indefatigable industry promised them a more serviceable agent than they had found in the Duke of Grafton. He had no party to balance their power, nor any squeamishness to clash with their intrigues. He had no stains on his character, but the very common facility of a politician, & no faction could reproach him with more doublings than every faction had been guilty of themselves. He was more likely to be a useful minister than an obnoxious one. His passions disposed him to no personal blackness, & shoud his administration prove violent, or iniquitous, he was pretty sure that the public woud do him so much justice as to believe that his associates the Bedfords were the instigators of his faults.

There the draft ends, apparently looking to the future. Some time during the next year (the memoirs for 1770 were written in 1771) Walpole rewrote this 'character', deleting the above-quoted passage and substituting the following (Chewton MS 'First Copy'), which seems to look back at some experience of North's administration:

> He had knowledge, and though fond of his amusement, seemed to have necessary activity till he reached the summit. To the Court he was agreable from being connected with no party, and from having no glaring fault or vice, was not unwelcome to the nation. He appeared in no light but that of a useful minister: yet one great singularity came out in his character, which was that no man was more ready for violent extremes under the Administration of others, no man was more temperate than Lord North during his own.

In the latest version (Chewton MS 'Second Copy') he kept the first of these sentences ('He had knowledge...the summit') in its place, and worked in part of the last sentence ('One singularity...during his own') into a later position; but expanded the 'character' to twice the length, as can be seen in the version printed below. This version, which mentions 'the American war' (1775) and 'the additional war with

France' (1778), seems to have been written after North's fall from power in March 1782, giving an account of the whole of his administration. But since the references to the war are overt, there is no question of duplicity. Walpole is frankly rewriting his opinions in the light of history. He can be blamed only for failing to indicate in his latest text the dates of his revisions and additions.

EDITIONS

The editing of Walpole's *Memoirs* is a strange and romantic story which has by no means reached its conclusion. It begins with a Memorandum which Walpole wrote in 1793, three years before his death: 'In the round library of books of prints up two pair of stairs in my house at Strawberry Hill there is a large wainscot chest marked on the outside lid with a great A. As soon as I am dead, I solemnly desire and enjoin my executrix to see it strongly corded up without being opened, and the cords to be sealed with her own seal; and I desire her to deposit the key of the chest with the church plate in the church at Houghton in Norfolk, and to take a receipt for it from the vicar and every succeeding vicar with a solemn promise not to deliver the said key until the first Earl of Waldegrave that shall attain the age of thirty-five years shall demand it.' Only an Earl Waldegrave who was also 'Master of Strawberry Hill should take possession of the great chest marked A'. This Memorandum enjoined that the contents of the chest should never pass out of the possession of the Waldegrave family and also that they should not be published. It should be remembered that Walpole's niece Maria had married the 2nd Earl Waldegrave; and that one of their daughters had married her cousin the 4th Earl Waldegrave, who had died in 1789. Their eldest son the 5th Earl was alive when the above Memorandum was written but in the following year he was accidentally drowned at the age of ten, while a schoolboy at Eton; the title then passed to his brother John James, 6th Earl (1785–1835), who duly became master of Strawberry Hill and the owner of Horace Walpole's box.

Walpole had also written a letter to the infant 5th Earl (undated, but later than 1789) which seems to prohibit publication:

My dear Lord,

When you shall have time to read over the mass of papers contained in this box, you will find they are not proper to be seen by anyone at present; and therefore I trust you will not mention the contents to anybody at present, but reserve them in your own custody. They are most imperfect both at the beginning and end; nor do I ever wish to have them published; but as they contain a great deal of curious matter, you may like to have them preserved in your family, but I am sure will give strong injunctions against their being made public in any manner. I have so high an opinion both of your good sense and honour, that I trust them entirely to your discretion.[1]

This memorandum and perhaps the letter was three years later superseded by another one, which was endorsed 'Not to be opened till after my Will.'

In my Library at Strawberry Hill are two wainscot chests or boxes, the larger marked with an A, the lesser with a B. I desire, that as soon as I am dead, my Executor and Executrix will cord up strongly and seal the larger box, marked A, and deliver it to the Honourable Hugh Conway Seymour, to be kept by him unopened and unsealed till the eldest son of Lady Waldegrave, or whichever of her sons, being Earl of Waldegrave, shall attain the age of twenty-five years; when the said chest, with whatever it contains, shall be delivered to him for his own. And I beg that the Honourable Hugh Conway Seymour, when he shall receive the said chest, will give a promise in writing, signed by him, to Lady Waldegrave, that he or his Representatives will deliver the said chest unopened and unsealed, by my Executor and Executrix, to the first son of Lady Waldegrave who shall attain the age of twenty-five years. The key of the said chest is in one of the cupboards of the Green Closet, within the Blue Breakfast Room, at Strawberry Hill, and that key, I desire, may be delivered to Laura, Lady Waldegrave, to be kept by her till her son shall receive the chest.

(Signed) Hor. Walpole Earl of Orford.

August 19, 1796

In this Memorandum there is nothing about forbidding publication. The box was duly delivered to its new owner, who became 25 in 1810; but it is not certain that he opened the box until 1813.[2] The young

[1] Letter in the possession of the Earl Waldegrave, printed by his permission.
[2] The Earl of Ilchester, 'Some pages torn from the Last Journals of Horace Walpole', *Studies in Art and Literature for Belle da Costa Greene*, edited by Dorothy Miner, Princeton 1954, pp. 449–58. To this article I owe many of the facts about the editing of the Memoirs.

Earl turned over the box to his friend Henry Richard Fox, 3rd Baron Holland, a classical scholar and literary man (1773–1840), who kept it at Holland House for several years before deciding to edit the journals. He began to do so about 1820, probably with the help of Sir James Mackintosh, the historian; and chose for first publication Walpole's 'George II', together with a memoir of the years 1754–58 written by James, 2nd Earl Waldegrave. Both of these works were sold for £2,500 to the publisher Murray, who brought out the Waldegrave memoir in 1821, and 'George II' in 1822.

Lord Holland and Lord Waldegrave had evidently agreed that Walpole's text should not be published in its entirety, for reasons given in the Preface to 'George II'. Lord Waldegrave had begun by mutilating a page, and Lord Holland continued this treatment of the manuscripts, confining it almost entirely to the second or fair copy: there are, fortunately, only a very few mutilations of the first or rough draft. One or both of them went right through 'George II', 'George III' and the 'Last Journals': from the 'Last Journals' whole pages were removed, in particular some dealing with Charles James Fox, Lord Holland's distinguished uncle (see p. xxxi). As well as physical cuts, there are erasures, not always successful: the long story about the Duke of Grafton and Nancy Parsons (see p. 194) is smeared over in ink but can be read fairly easily with the aid of the rough draft, which is almost untouched. In addition, passages of 'George III' were marked in red crayon: most but not all of these were omitted in the printed text. Other omissions were indicated to the printer presumably by written instructions. Lord Holland carefully preserved the excerpted fragments but kept them at Holland House. The manuscripts of 'George II' were probably sent direct to the printer, and Lord Holland proceeded to do most of his editorial work from the proofs.

The proofs of Lord Holland's edition have survived, bound into one large volume, which has a Holland House book-plate and is now in the possession of the Earl of Ilchester. It contains many notes written by Lord Holland in red pencil, proof-corrections in ink, marginal captions, additional notes, written both on the pages and on inserted sheets, instructions to the printer, and occasional queries from the printer addressed to Lord Holland. Most of it consists of first proof, not quite a complete set, but there are also some sheets of revised proof, which provide interesting evidence about Lord Holland's editorial methods. For example, Lord Holland not only made deletions in the manuscript that he sent to the printers but made further cuts in the proofs. A passage of Volume I, p. 39, (not included in this selection) reads in proof, following the manuscript: 'Nugent had set out ill in virtue, by marrying a rich widow, to the impoverishment of her son, and had lost the reputation of a great poet....' The instruction in the margin reads: 'dele to had lost put some three or four stars in place of words left out.' The printer did it wrongly and a second proof was required before the text read, 'Nugent *   *   *   * had lost the reputation of a great poet.' On p. 104 of the same volume Walpole's text read in proof: 'Lord Talbot, a lord of good parts, only that they had rather more bias to madness than sense.' Lord Holland altered 'madness' to 'extravagance' and wrote at the foot of the page: 'Mem. Where it is ventured from delicacy to the publick or to families to soften an expression, great care must be taken to place the word substituted for that omitted between inverted commas '—' or brackets ( ) as the Editor must in the preface apprize the reader of these little variations from the original & the reader be enabled to judge of their insignificance.' Lord Holland, however, was not always scrupulous about showing where he had made cuts: for example, there are many alterations in the passage about Lord Hartington and the Duke of Devonshire (see this selection, p. 28) which are not indicated in the printed text. There are also silent cuts in the 'characters' of the Second Duke of Grafton, Princess Emily and Lord Holderness (see below pp. 24, 25 and 29), and a total of about two dozen deletions in the proofs of 'George II'.

Lord Holland also altered in proof the passage in his Preface (Vol. I, p. xxxi) where he discusses his editorial methods. This originally read:

> With respect to omissions, it is right to inform the reader, that one gross, indelicate and ill-authenticated story had been cut out by Lord Waldegrave before the manuscript was delivered to the publisher; [*amended to* editor] but the editor has been assured that the facts related in it rested on no authority but mere rumour. Some, though very few, coarse expressions have been altered or [*last two words deleted*] suppressed by the editor; [*inserted* and the vacant spaces filled up by asterisks] and two or three passages, affecting the private character of private persons, and nowise connected with any political event, or illustrative of any great public character, have been omitted. Sarcasms on mere bodily infirmity, in which the author was too apt to indulge, have in some instances been expunged; and where love intrigues were either alluded to or mentioned on the scandalous reports of the day, the name of

the lady has been left out, unless the anecdote had been in print before, or was so intimately connected with some event of importance, that it could not be suppressed without injury to historical truth. These liberties, which would be still more indispensable if the remaining historical works of Lord Orford were ever published, the Editor thought himself justified to use, as the work, though evidently written for publication, was left by the Author, without instructions how to dispose of it, entirely at the discretion of those by whose authority it is now given to the public.

The passage from 'and where love intrigues...' to '...how to dispose of it' gave Lord Holland much trouble: after trying various emendations he rewrote the passage, as it stands in the printed text, on a separate sheet. The sense is the same, but there are such changes as 'love intrigues' to 'private amours'. All this may make a later editor feel like a cad for mentioning a lady's name; yet restore the names he must, to avoid 'injury to historical truth'.

Lord Holland was much bothered, as this editor has been, by the vagaries of Horace Walpole's spelling; and his attempts to regularize it have in general been followed in this text. At one point Walpole quotes a letter from Henry Fox with the words 'I must loose no time': Lord Holland exclaims in the margin, 'The puppy may write it with two oo if he likes it but he has no right to make my grandfather an accomplice'! This irritation, which is shown elsewhere, springs not only from spelling trouble but also from Horace Walpole's many jabs at the Fox family; and it evidently caused Lord Holland to make more serious omissions and mutilations of later parts of the manuscript, particularly of passages dealing with Charles James Fox.

Lord Holland did not continue, as he had planned, with the editing of 'George III', apparently because of political work and poor health. Lord Waldegrave died in 1835 and it was decided by his executors that the editing of the next series should be entrusted to Sir Denis Le Marchant, a Whig politician and writer. 'George III' (1760–1771), edited in the same bowdlerized fashion but with rather fuller historical notes was published by Richard Bentley in 1845. In 1859 Bentley published the 'Last Journals' (1772–1783), which were edited by Dr. John Doran, an Irish man of letters. Doran did a rather poor job: he was far less accurate than the two previous editors in transcribing the text or proof-reading it, and he included cuttings from newspapers and other printed material, which Walpole had pasted into his journals, without indicating that these were not written by Walpole. The later editions of 'George III' by Barker and of the 'Last Journals' by Steuart added little to the notes and nothing to the bowdlerized text except fresh errors: the manuscripts, which had been returned to the Waldegrave family, were not consulted.

Holland House, with its heirlooms, passed to the Earl of Ilchester, and was destroyed by an air raid early in the 1939–1945 war. After the war the 6th Earl of Ilchester discovered among the Holland House Papers some fragments excerpted from the Waldegrave MSS. He published in the article listed below as B.7 some of the missing pages, concerning Charles James Fox, together with an indignant memorandum by the 3rd Lord Holland, the original editor, contradicting many of Horace Walpole's statements. After Lord Ilchester's death in 1959 the Holland House MSS were acquired by the British Museum, where eight fragments are preserved. The latest chapter in this story is the discovery in 1962 by the 7th Earl of Ilchester of the proofs of 'George II', which are described above.

This selection contains extracts from the Memoirs of George II and George III only, covering the years 1750 to 1771. Because the 'Last Journals' are less interesting as literature and as history, and because their text cannot yet be restored to a satisfactory state, it has been decided not to include any extracts from them here. The text of this selection is based on the Second or Fair Copy of the Chewton MSS: where gaps exist in this MS, the text has been supplied from the First Copy or rough draft, and this has been indicated in the textual notes. Some of the more important variations between the two copies are also given in the textual notes: this is not of course offered as a full scholarly edition, but I have tried to provide a more accurate text than can be found in the printed editions. Walpole's spelling has been partially modernized.

The extracts are given in chronological order. The text has been broken up and titled: there are no silent omissions from the text, but an extract may begin or end in the middle of one of Walpole's paragraphs. Many of Walpole's footnotes have been omitted and a few explanatory notes have been added.

SOURCES

The Chewton MSS are in the possession of the Earl Waldegrave at Chewton House, Chewton Mendip, Bath, Somerset; other MSS mentioned below are in the possession of Mr W. S. Lewis at Farmington, Connecticut; of the Earl of Ilchester at Melbury House, Dorchester; and of the British Museum (Holland House papers).

A MANUSCRIPTS

1 'Memoires from the Declaration of the War with Spain'. These early memoirs, which end in 1750, are in Mr Lewis's collection; they have not yet been printed, and are not included in this selection.

2 'George II', 1751–1760. 'First Copy' or rough draft in Walpole's hand. Chewton MSS.

3 'George II', 1751–1760. 'Second Copy' or fair copy, also in Walpole's hand, with revisions and additions including notes. Chewton MSS. Wherever possible, this text has been used here.

4 'George II' 1751–1755. The 'Third Copy', described by Lord Holland in his Preface to his edition of 1822 as follows:

> ...and this third or last copy extending to the end of 1755, is written by his [Walpole's] secretary or amanuensis, Mr. Kirkgate, with some corrections by himself, and the notes on the blank pages, opposite to the fair copy, entirely in his own hand. This last copy was bound into two regular volumes, with etchings from designs furnished by Bentley and Muntz, to serve as a frontispiece to the whole work, and as headpieces for each chapter, explanations of which were subjoined at the end.

Mr W. S. Lewis owns the original drawings mentioned above, together, he informs me, 'with bits and pieces of the MS that appear above or below the drawings'. The location of the rest of the MS, if it survives, is not known. There are good reasons for believing that its text does not differ significantly from that of the 'Second Copy'.

5 'George III', 1760–1770. 'First Copy' or rough draft. Chewton MSS; similar to (2) above.

6 'George III', 1760–1771. 'Second Copy' or fair copy. Chewton MSS; similar to (3) above. This is the only Chewton MS for the year 1771; this is bound up with the 'Second Copy', but appears to be similar to the 'First Copy', containing like the other rough drafts several inserted sheets.

7 'George III', 1769, a 'journal' 'which preceded the foul copy of the *Memoirs* for those years'. (W. S. Lewis, *Horace Walpole*, 1960, p. 83, n. 25.) In the possession of Mr Lewis, who has kindly transcribed extracts for me; not used in this selection, since it consists of notes which were greatly expanded in the first draft.

8 'Last Journals', 1771–1783. Chewton MS, one copy only. Not used for this selection.

9 Fragments and leaves cut out or torn out from the Chewton MSS by Lord Holland about 1820. The Holland House papers, British Museum, include eight of these fragments, cut out of the *Memoirs* for 1751 and 1752. See also B.7 below.

10 'Journals', 1783–1791, 'still unpublished; they were acquired by Richard Bentley from Mary Berry, and were sold to Mr W. S. Lewis in 1937 by the present Mrs. Bentley.' (A. T. Hazen, *A Bibliography of Horace Walpole*, 1948, p. 93.) In Mr Lewis's collection; not included in this selection.

11 Other MSS in the possession of Mr Lewis: 'some of the "characters" inserted by Walpole in his transcribed copies of the published *Memoirs*, Bentley's drawings for them [see above A.4], and many preliminary notes and jottings on odds and ends of paper.' (*Horace Walpole*, 1960, p. 83, n. 25). Of these, this selection includes the hitherto unpublished 'characters' of George III and of Lord Mansfield (pp. 247 and 248). The others are an early draft of the 'characters' of Lord North, one of the Duke of Devonshire (written in 1780 or later) and a long account of the story of Madame du Barry, dated October 17th 1769, of which another version is given below (p. 20).

12 Proofs of *Memoires of the last ten years of the reign of George the Second*, 1822, edited by Lord Holland, with corrections and additions, including interleaved sheets, in the hand of Lord Holland. In the possession of the Earl of Ilchester.

B PRINTED EDITIONS

1 *Memoires of the last ten years of the reign of George the Second*, 2 vols., 1822. Edited by Lord Holland. Also issued as vols. 7 and 8 of Horace Walpole's *Works* (1798–1825); contains plates from Bentley and others, mentioned in A.4 above.

2 New edition of the above, in 3 vols., 1846; reprinted 1847.

3 *Memoirs of the reign of King George the Third*, 4 vols., 1845. Edited by Sir Denis le Marchant. Reprinted Philadelphia 1845, London 1851.

4 New edition of the above, edited by G. R. F. Barker, 1894.

5 *Journal of ... George III from 1771 to 1783*, 2 vols., 1859. Edited by Dr. John Doran.

6 New edition of the above, *The Last Journals of Horace Walpole*, 2 vols., 1910. Edited by A. Francis Steuart.

7 The Earl of Ilchester, 'Some pages torn from the Last Journals of Horace Walpole,' *Studies in Art and Literature for Belle da Costa Greene*. Edited by Dorothy Miner, Princeton 1954, pp. 449–58. Includes the first printing of one of the fragments referred to in A.9 above.

George II

HORACE WALPOLE BEGINS HIS MEMOIRS, JANUARY 1751

It had been much expected that on the King's return from Hanover several changes would be made in the Ministry. The Duke of New-castle had for some time before his attending the King thither, dis-agreed with the other Secretary of State, the Duke of Bedford, not only because he had brought the latter into the Ministry (his incessant motive of jealousy,) nor from the impetuosity of the Duke of Bedford's temper, but from the intimate connections that Lord Sandwich had contracted with the Duke. Lord Sandwich had been hoisted to the head of the Admiralty by the weight of the Duke of Bedford, into whose affection he had worked himself by intrigues, cricket-matches, and acting plays, and whom he had almost persuaded to resign the Seals in his favour. There had been a time when he had almost obtained the Duke of Newcastle's concurrence; and if he could have balanced himself between the Duke and the Duke of Newcastle, one may, without wronging the delicacy of his political character, suspect that he would have dropped the Duke of Bedford's confidence. But a blind devotion to the Duke's inclinations, which he studied in all the nego-tiations of the war and the peace, protracting the one to flatter his command, and hurrying on the other when no part of Flanders was left for the Duke's army, and himself was impatient to come over to advance his interest in the Cabinet, this had embroiled him with the Duke of Newcastle, and consequently cemented his old attachments.

Mr. Pelham had, according to his manner, tried to soothe where his brother provoked, been convinced by trifles that his brother's jealousy was solidly grounded, adopted his resentments, and promoted them. While the Court was at Hanover, Lord Sandwich had drawn a great concourse of the young men of fashion to Huntingdon races, and then carried them to Woburn to cricket-matches made there for the enter-tainment of the Duke. These *dangerous* practices opened Mr. Pelham's eyes; and a love-affair between one of his daughters and a younger brother of the Duchess of Bedford fixed his aversion to that family. At this period the Duke of Richmond died, who besides the Duchess and his own dignity, loved the Duke of Newcastle—the only man who ever did. The Pelhams immediately offered the Mastership of the Horse to the Duke of Bedford, which he would have accepted, had they left him the nomination of Lord Sandwich for his successor.

The King came over; but though the brothers were resolved to dis-agree with their associates in the Ministry, they could not resolve to remove them; none of the great offices were filled up but the Lieutenancy of Ireland, from which Lord Harrington was removed in the most unworthy manner. He had raised himself from a younger brother's fortune to the first posts in the Government, without either the talent of speaking in Parliament, or any interest there. He had steered through all the difficulties of the Court and changes of Ministry, with great dexterity, till in the year 1746, notwithstanding all his personal obliga-tions to the King, he was the first man who broke into his closet at the head of those insulting and disloyal resignations that were calculated and set on foot by the Pelhams, in the very heat of the rebellion, to force their master, by a general desertion of his servants, to abandon Lord Granville, whom he was recalling into the Ministry. The King had brooded over this ingratitude, not with much hope of revenging it, but as he sometimes resented such indignities enough to mention them, the Pelhams sacrificed Lord Harrington to their master, astonished at their complaisance, in order to bargain for other victims on his part, which they would have forced, not purchased, if there had been any price necessary but their own ingratitude. Lord Harrington was re-moved, and the Lieutenancy of Ireland again heaped on the Duke of Dorset, then President of the Council.

Richard Lyttelton and George Townshend

The Mutiny Bill was likely to pass with less noise; when Colonel Richard Lyttelton, intending mischief though without seeing half way into the storm he was raising, took notice of the extraordinary novelties and severity of these modern regulations. He was a younger brother of the pious George Lyttelton, with less appearance of, but with not much more real integrity. He was grown a favourite of the Prince of Wales by a forwardness of flattery that had revolted even the Duke, at whose expense on some disobligations he was now paying court to the elder brother.

He was seconded by Colonel George Townshend, eldest son of my Lord Townshend, a very particular young man, who, with much oddness, some humour, no knowledge, great fickleness, greater want

2

of judgment, and with still more disposition to ridicule, had once or twice promised to make a good speaker. He was governed by his mother, the famous Lady Townshend, who having been neglected by the Duke,[1] after some overtures of civility to him, had dipped into all the excess of Scotch Jacobitism, and employed all her wit and malice, the latter of which, without any derogation to the former, had vastly the ascendant, to propagate the Duke's unpopularity.

Henry Seymour Conway

.... Colonel Henry Conway, the latter a young officer, who having set out upon a plan of unfashionable virtue, had provoked the King and Duke by voting against the Army at the beginning of the war. He was soon after, by the interest of a near relation of his, placed in the Duke's family, where he grew a chief favourite, not only by a steady defence of military measures on all occasions, but by most distinguished bravery in the battles of Fontenoy and Laffelt (in the latter of which he was taken prisoner), by a very superior understanding, and by being one of the most agreeable and solid speakers in Parliament, to which the beauty of his person, and the harmony of his voice, did remarkably contribute.

Lord Chesterfield

The same day, Lord Chesterfield brought a Bill into the House of Lords for reforming our style according to the Gregorean account, which had not yet been admitted in England, as if it were matter of heresy to receive a Kalendar amended by a Pope. He was seconded by Lord Macclesfield, a mathematical Lord, in a speech soon after printed, and the Bill passed easily through both Houses. Lord Chesterfield had made no noise since he gave up the Seals in 1748, when he published his Apology for that resignation. It was supposed to be drawn up by Lord Marchmont, under his direction, and was very well written; but to my Lord Chesterfield's great surprise, neither his book nor his retirement produced the least consequence. From that time he had lived at White's, gaming, and pronouncing witticisms among the boys of quality.

[1] The Duke of Cumberland.

He had early in his life announced his claim to wit, and the women believed in it. He had besides given himself out for a man of great intrigue, with as slender pretensions; yet the women believed in that too—one should have thought they had been more competent judges of merit in that particular! It was not his fault if he had not wit; nothing exceeded his efforts in that point; and though they were far from producing the wit, they at least amply yielded the applause he aimed at. He was so accustomed to see people laugh at the most trifling things he said, that he would be disappointed at finding nobody smile before they knew what he was going to say. His speeches were fine, but as much laboured as his extempore sayings. His writings were— everybody's: that is, whatever came out good was given to him, and he was too humble ever to refuse the gift. But besides the passive enjoyment of all good productions in the present age, he had another art of reputation, which was, either to disapprove the greatest authors of other times, or to patronize and commend whatever was too bad to be ascribed to himself. He did his admirers the justice to believe that they would applaud upon his authority every simple book that was published, and every bad actor that appeared upon the stage.

His first public character was Ambassador to Holland, where he courted the good opinion of that economical people by losing immense sums at play. On his return he attached himself to Lord Townshend, who was then breaking with Sir Robert Walpole, and did himself no good by that connection: but what pinned down his disgrace, was the Queen's seeing him one Twelfth Night, after winning a large sum of money at hazard, cross St. James's Court, to deposit it with my Lady Suffolk till next morning:—the Queen never pardoned an intimacy there. He continued in Opposition for the remainder of Sir Robert Walpole's Ministry, and after the ineffectual motion in 1740 for removing that Minister, Lord Chesterfield was dispatched to Avignon by the party to solicit, by the Duke of Ormond's means, an order from the Pretender to the Jacobites, to concur roundly in any measure for Sir Robert's destruction: they had retired without voting on the question abovementioned. Lord Chesterfield had accepted no employment till the removal of Lord Granville, when he was sent again to Holland, and then made Lord Lieutenant of Ireland, and became the most popular Governor they ever had. Nothing was cried up but his integrity, though he would have laughed at any man who really had any confidence in his morality: and how little he repented his negotiations at Avignon would appear, if a story told of him is authentic (which I do

4

not vouch), that being at Dublin in the height of the Rebellion, a zealous Bishop came to him one morning before he was out of bed, and told him he had great grounds to believe the Jacobites were going to rise. The Lord Lieutenant coolly looked at his watch, and replied, 'I fancy they are, my Lord, for it is nine o'clock.'

He had married the Duchess of Kendal's niece, designing to become heir to her aunt, but had not the address to succeed; yet, miscarrying with the late King's mistress, he was rewarded by old Marlborough among the rest of the legatees, whom she had selected for the prejudice they had done to the Royal Family. She was scarce cold before he returned to the King's service. In short, my Lord Chesterfield's being the instrument to introduce this new era into our computation of time will probably preserve his name in almanacs and chronologies, when the wit that he had but laboured too much, and the gallantry that he could scarce ever execute, will be no more remembered.

Bishop Secker

March 10th.—The King would not go to Chapel, because Secker, Bishop of Oxford, was to preach before him. The Ministers did not insist upon his hearing the sermon, as they had lately upon his making him Dean of St. Paul's. Character and popularity do not always depend upon the circumstances that ought to compose either. This Bishop, who had been bred a Presbyterian and Man-midwife, which sect and profession he had dropt for a season, while he *was* President of a very free thinking club,[1] had been converted by Bishop Talbot, whose relation he married, and his faith settled in a Prebend of Durham: from thence he was transplanted, at the recommendation of Dr. Bland, by the Queen, and advanced by her (who had no aversion to a medley of religions, which she always compounded into a scheme of heresy of her own), to the living of St. James's, vacant by the death of her favourite Arian, Dr. Clarke, and afterwards to the Bishoprics of Bristol and Oxford.[2] It is incredible how popular he grew in his parish, and how much some of his former qualifications contributed to heighten his present doctrines. His discourses from the pulpit, which, by a

[1] Here is my evidence. Mr Robyns said he had known him an atheist, and he advised him against talking so openly in coffee houses. Mr. Stevens, a mathematician who lives much in the house with Earl Powlett, says Secker made him an atheist at Leyden, where the club was established. [H.W.]

[2] He was nominated to the Archbishopric of Canterbury, 28 March 1758. [H.W.]

fashion that he introduced, were a kind of moral essays, were as clear from quotations of Scripture, as when he presided in a less Christian society; but what they wanted of Gospel, was made up by a tone of fanaticism that he still retained; and if he no longer exercised his function of bringing Christians into the world with his own hands, he laboured truly for the encouragement of the good cause, and was a noted promoter of holy wedlock. He had made a match between a daughter of the late Duke of Kent, who was nothing less than a monster, and a Doctor Gregory, whose talents would have been extremely thrown away in any priesthood, where celibacy was one of the injunctions. He had been presented with a noble service of plate for procuring a marriage between the heiress of the same Duke of Kent and the Chancellor's son, and was now forced upon the King by the gratitude of the same Minister, though he had long been in disgrace for having laid his plan for Canterbury in the interest he had cultivated at the Prince's Court. But even the Church had its renegades in politics, and the King was obliged to fling open his asylum to all kinds of deserters; content with not speaking to them at his levee, or listening to them in the pulpit!

The Prince of Wales

The Prince of Wales had been ill of a pleurisy, but was so well recovered as to attend the King to the House of Lords on the 12th, where he was very hot. He went to Carlton-house to unrobe, put on only a light frock, and went to Kew, where he walked some time, and returning to Carlton-house, laid down upon a couch for three hours in a ground room next to the garden, caught a fresh cold, and relapsed that night. He had had a blow upon his stomach in the summer by a fall, from which he had often felt great pains. Dr. Wilmot, Taylor, and Leigh attended him, and Hawkins the Surgeon. On Monday, 18th, a thrush appeared; however, he was thought better. On Wednesday night, between nine and ten o'clock, Wilmot and Hawkins were with him; he had a fit of coughing. Wilmot said, 'Sir, you have brought up all the phlegm; I hope this will be over in a quarter of an hour, and that your Royal Highness will have a good night.' Hawkins went out of the room, and said, 'Here is something I don't like.' The cough continued; the Prince laid his hand upon his stomach, and said, *'Je sens la mort.'* Pavonarius, his favourite German valet-de-chambre, who was holding him up, felt him shiver, and cried, "Good God! the Prince is going!' The Princess, who was at the feet of the bed, snatched up a candle, but before she got to him, he was dead! An imposthume had broken, which, on his body being opened, the Physicians were of opinion had not been occasioned by the fall, but from a blow of a tennis-ball three years before.

Thus died Frederick Prince of Wales! having resembled his pattern the Black Prince in nothing but dying before his father. Indeed it was not his fault if he had not distinguished himself by any warlike achievements. He had solicited the command of the Army in Scotland during the last Rebellion; though that ambition was ascribed rather to his jealousy of his brother than to his courage. A hard judgment! for what he could he did! When the Royal Army lay before Carlisle, the Prince at a great supper that he gave to his Court and his favourites, as was his custom when the Princess laid in, had ordered for the dessert the representation of the citadel of Carlisle in paste, which he in person and the Maids of Honour bombarded with sugar plums. He had disagreed with the King and Queen early after his coming to England; not entirely by his own fault. The King had refused to pay what debts he had left at Hanover; and it ran a little in the blood of the family to hate the eldest son: the Prince himself had so far not degenerated, though a better natured man, and a much better father, as to be fondest of his second son, Prince Edward. The Queen had exerted more authority, joined to a narrow prying into his conduct, than he liked; and Princess Emily, who had been admitted into his greatest confidence, had not forfeited her duty to the Queen by concealing any of his secrets that might do him prejudice.

Lord Bolingbroke, who had sowed a division in the Pretender's Court, by the scheme for the father's resigning his claim to the eldest boy, repeated the same plan of discord here, on the first notice of the Prince's disgusts; and the whole Opposition was instructed to offer their services to the Heir Apparent against the Crown and the Minister. The Prince was sensible of flattery, and had a sort of parts that made him relish the sort of parts of Lord Chesterfield, Doddington, and Lyttelton, the latter of whom being introduced by Doddington, had wrought the disgrace of his protector. Whoever was unwelcome at St. James's was sure of countenance at the Prince's apartments there. He was in vain reprimanded for this want of respect. At last, having hurried the Princess from Hampton Court, when she was in actual labour, to the imminent danger of hers and the child's life, without

7

acquainting either King or Queen, the formal breach ensued; he
having added to this insult, a total silence to his mother on her
arriving immediately to visit the Princess, and while he led her to her
coach; but as soon as he came in sight of the populace, he knelt down
in the dirt and kissed her hand with the most respectful show of
duty. He immediately went all lengths of opposition and popularity
till the fall of Sir Robert Walpole, when he was reconciled to, though
never after spoken to, by the King.

On Lord Granville's disgrace, he again grew out of humour; but
after having been betrayed and deserted by all he had obliged, he
did not erect a new standard of opposition, till the Pelhams had
bought off every man of any genius that might have promoted his
views. Indeed, his attachment to his followers was not stronger than
theirs to him. Being angry with Lord Doneraile for not speaking
oftener in the House of Commons, he said 'Does he think I will
support him, unless he does as I would have him? Does not he consider
that whoever are my Ministers, I must be King?" His chief passion
was women, but like the rest of his race, beauty was not a necessary
ingredient. Miss Vane, whom he had debauched without loving, and
who had been debauched without loving him so well as either Lord
Harrington or Lord Hervey, who both pretended to her first favours,
had no other charms than of being a Maid of Honour, who was willing
to cease to be so upon the first opportunity.

Of his favourite mistresses, Lady Archibald Hamilton had been
neither young nor handsome within his memory. Lady Middlesex
was very short, very plain, and very yellow: a vain girl, full of Greek
and Latin, and music, and painting, but neither mischievous nor
political. Lady Archibald was very agreeable and artful, but had lost
his heart, by giving him William Pitt for a rival. But though these
mistresses were pretty much declared, he was a good husband, and
the quiet inoffensive good sense of the Princess (who had never said
a foolish thing, or done a disobliging one since her arrival, though
in very difficult situations, young, uninstructed, and besieged by the
Queen, Princess Emily, and Lady Archibald's creatures, and very jar-
ring interests), was likely to have always preserved a chief ascendant
over him.

Gaming was another of his passions, but his style of play did him
less honour than the amusement. He carried this dexterity into practice
in more essential commerce, and was vain of it! One day at Kensington
that he had just borrowed five thousand pounds of Doddington, seeing

him pass under his window, he said to Hedges his Secretary, 'That man is reckoned one of the most sensible men in England, yet with all his parts, I have just nicked him out of five thousand pounds.' He was really childish, affectedly a protector of arts and sciences, fond of displaying what he knew: a mimic, the Lord knows what a mimic! —of the celebrated Duke of Orleans, in imitation of whom he wrote two or three silly French songs. His best quality was generosity; his worst, insincerity, and indifference to truth, which appeared so early, that Earl Stanhope wrote to Lord Sunderland from Hanover, what I conclude his character with, 'He has his father's head, and his mother's heart.'

The Princess stayed four hours in the room after he was dead, before she could be quite convinced of it. At six in the morning they put her to bed; but she rose again at eight, and sent for Dr. Lee, and burnt, or said she burnt, all the Prince's papers. As soon as he was dead, Lord North was sent to notify it to the King, who was playing at cards. He immediately went down to Lady Yarmouth, looking extremely pale and shocked, and only said *Il est mort!* He sent a very kind message to the Princess, and another the next morning in writing by the Lord in Waiting, Lord Lincoln. She received him alone, sitting with her eyes fixed; thanked the King much, and said she would write as soon as she was able; in the meantime, recommended her miserable self and children to him.

The King and she both took their parts at once; she, of flinging herself entirely into his hands, and studying nothing but his pleasure, but with winding what interest she got with him to the advantage of her own and the Prince's friends: the King of acting the tender grandfather; which he, who had never acted the tender father, grew so pleased with representing, that he soon became it in earnest. When he was called the morning after the Prince's death, they found him drest, walking about his room, and extremely silent. Princess Emily, who had no great reason to flatter herself with much favour if her brother had lived to be King, sent immediately for the Duke from Windsor, who, on receiving the news, said to Lord Sandwich with a sneer, 'It is a great blow to this country, but I hope it will recover it in time!' He little thought that he himself was to receive the greatest shock from it! He sent a compliment by Lord Cathcart to Prince George, who cried extremely. As soon as the Prince's death was published, elegies were cried about the streets, to which they added, 'Oh, that it was but his brother!' and upon Change and in the City,

9

'Oh, that it was but the butcher!' In short, the consternation that spread on the apprehensions that the Duke would at least be Regent on the King's death, and have the sole power in the mean time, was near as strong as what was occasioned by the notice of the Rebels being at Derby.

Prince George's Governor and Preceptors

The King went again to see the Princess, and settled with her the new Governor and Preceptors for the children. Lord North had lately been entrusted with the care of Prince George, with the promise of an Earldom; an amiable worthy man, of no great genius, unless compared with his successor. The Pelhams, who had now laid a plan of perpetuating that power, which by so many accidents had dropped into their hands, determined to beset the young Prince entirely with their own creatures. Lord North was removed to make way for Lord Harcourt, who wanted a Governor himself, as much as the Duke of Newcastle was likely to do by parting with Stone, who was to be the real engine of their policy, while Lord Harcourt, who was civil and sheepish, did not threaten them with traversing their scheme, or teaching the young Prince other arts than what he knew himself— hunting and drinking. Stone, lately grown a personal favourite with the King during the journeys to Hanover, was a dark, proud man, very able and very mercenary. The other Preceptor was Hayter, Bishop of Norwich, a sensible, well-bred man, natural son of Blackbourn, the jolly old Archbishop of York, who had all the manners of a man of quality, though he had been a buccaneer and was a clergyman; but he retained nothing of his first profession except his seraglio. Lord Hartington had been offered the government of the Prince, but declined it.

The Late Prince's Friends

The late Prince's debts, which were supposed very great, were extremely denied, and concealed as carefully as they would have been vaunted by those who had laid that foundation of their future advancement, if he had lived to be King. The Hanoverians, who were said to have lent him considerable sums, took care not to be the most clamorous for repayment. All who had flattered themselves with rising in his reign, by being so insignificant at present as to have no other support, were extremely disappointed at losing their only prospect. Some Peerages were still-born, more First-ministerships, and sundry regiments and inferior posts. Drax, his Secretary, who could not write his own name; Lord Baltimore, who, with a great deal of mistaken knowledge, could not spell; and Sir William Irby, the Princess's Polonius, were to be Barons. Doddington, it is said, had actually kissed his hand for the reversion of a Dukedom. This man, with great knowledge of business, much wit, and great parts, had, by mere absurdity of judgment, and a disposition to finesse, thrown himself out of all estimation, and out of all the great views which his large fortune and abilities could not have failed to promote, if he had but preserved the least shadow of steadiness. He had two or three times alternately gone all lengths of flattery with Sir Robert Walpole and the Prince of Wales. The latter and he had met again at last in a necessary connection, for no party would have anything to do with either.

Lord Chief Justice Willes

Lord Chief Justice Willes was designed for Chancellor. He had been raised by Sir Robert Walpole, though always brow-beaten by haughty Yorke, and hated by the Pelhams, for that very attachment to their own patron. As Willes's nature was more open, he returned their aversion with little reserve. He was not wont to disguise any of his passions. That for gaming was notorious; for women, unbounded. There was a remarkable story current of a grave person's coming to reprove the scandal he gave, and to tell him that the world talked of one of his maid servants being with child. Willes said, 'What is that to me?' The monitor answered, 'Oh! but they say that it is by your Lordship.' 'And what is that to you?' He had great quickness of wit, and a merit that would atone for many foibles, his severity to, and discouragement of that pest of society, attorneys: hence his Court was deserted by them; and all the business they could transport, carried into the Chancery, where Yorke's filial piety would not refuse an asylum to his father's profession.

Dr. Lee

Dr. Lee was made Treasurer to the Princess, against the inclination of the Pelhams; but the Duke of Newcastle soon began to pay such court to him, and he to be so pleased with it, that they were satisfied. He was a man of great integrity, and had preserved it through all the late changes. His election to be Chairman of the Committee of Privileges and Elections was the first instance of Sir Robert Walpole's declining power; he had been made a Lord of the Admiralty by Lord Granville and Lord Bath, and had resigned with the former, notwithstanding great offers from his antagonists. The Prince had designed him for Chancellor of the Exchequer, a post for which he was little qualified; for though he was a speaker of great weight in Parliament, which was set off with a solemn harmonious voice, and something severe in his style, his business of civilian had confined him to too narrow a sphere for the extensive knowledge of men that is requisite to a Prime Minister.

William Pitt and Henry Fox

Pitt was undoubtedly one of the greatest masters of ornamental eloquence. His language was amazingly fine and flowing; his voice admirable; his action most expressive; his figure genteel and commanding. Bitter satire was his forte: when he attempted ridicule, which was very seldom, he succeeded happily; when he attempted to reason, poorly. But where he chiefly shone, was in exposing his own conduct: having waded through the most notorious apostasy in politics, he treated it with an impudent confidence, that made all reflections upon him poor and spiritless, when worded by any other man. Out of the House of Commons he was far from being this shining character. His conversation was affected and unnatural, his manner not engaging, nor his talents adapted to a country where Ministers must court, if they would be courted.

Fox, with a great hesitation in his elocution, and a barrenness of expression, had conquered these impediments and the prejudices they had raised against his speaking, by a vehemence of reasoning, and closeness of argument, that beat all the orators of the time. His spirit, his steadiness, and humanity procured him strong attachments, which the more jealous he grew of Pitt, the more he cultivated. Fox always spoke to the question, Pitt to the passions: Fox, to carry the question; Pitt, to raise himself: Fox pointed out, Pitt lashed the errors of his antagonists: Pitt's talents were likely to make him soonest, Fox's to keep him First Minister longest.

Lord Middlesex and the Duke of Dorset

The King offered the Princess a Master of Horse, but told her it must be a nobleman, and there was one to whom he had an objection: this was Lord Middlesex. She desired none; if she had been disposed to contend, it would not have been of all men in favour of the Lord in question. His figure, which was handsome, had all the reserve of his family, and all the dignity of his ancestors. He was a poet, too, because they had been poets. As little as he came near them in this talent, it was what he most resembled them in, and in what he best supported their honour. His passion was the direction of operas, in which he had not only wasted immense sums, but had stood lawsuits in Westminster Hall with some of those poor devils for their salaries. The Duke of Dorset had often paid his debts, but never could work upon his affections; and he had at last carried his disobedience so far, in complaisance to, and in imitation of the Prince, as to oppose his father in his own boroughs. That Duke, with the greatest dignity in his appearance, was in private the greatest lover of low humour and buffoonery. He had early lost the hearts of the Whigs by some indirect connections with Lord Oxford in the end of Queen Anne's reign; and he was never thought to have wanted a tendency to power, in whatever hands it was, or was likely to be lodged.

The Duke of Cumberland

The Duke had broke entirely with the Duke of Newcastle towards the end of the war, when Lord Sandwich having been ordered to communicate a new plan to Count Kaunitz, had desired to be excused, but the orders being repeated, he had obeyed artfully. The Duke thought him in the wrong, and had received his consent to say everything that might reconcile him to the Duke of Newcastle, but that he thought himself in the wrong. The Duke of Newcastle had neither accepted nor refused the Duke's mediation, who was not apt to pardon slighter offences than contempt. He loved indiscriminate submission; flattery did not come up to his ideas of obedience, and consequently he overlooked it: but the least opposition he never forgave. With the most heroic bravery, he had all the severity that levels valour to cowardice, and seemed to love war for itself, without feeling the passions that it gratifies.

It is certain that his martial genius did not proceed from love of glory, nor much from ambition. Glory he despised, saying, 'That when he was most popular, the satisfaction was allayed, by thinking on Admiral Vernon!' and he had taken every step to make himself unpopular both with the people and the Army; and thought it so much beneath his rank to have any share in the Ministry, that he would not be of the Cabinet Council, and even when desired to attend their consultations for the expedition to Port L'Orient, he would not vouchsafe to give his opinion, but confined himself to answering their questions. His strongest principle was the dignity of the Blood Royal, and his maxim to bear anything from his brother if he had lived to be King, rather than set an example of disobedience to the royal authority. These prejudices and this pride were the swellings of his heart and temper, not the errors of his head, for his understanding was strong, judicious, and penetrating, though incapable of resisting partialities and piques, of which he was susceptible from the slightest merit, or most trifling offence. He was as angry at an officer's transgressing the minutest precept of the military rubric as at deserting his post, and was as intent on establishing the form of spatter-dashes, or the pattern of cockades, as on taking a town, or securing an advantageous situation.

The misfortunes the nation had suffered from his inexperience while he commanded in Flanders had been amply atoned by his defeating the Rebels in Scotland; but that victory made him in the end more unpopular than all his defeats; for the Scotch, the Jacobites, and his brother's jealousy never rested till they had propagated such stories of his tyranny and severity, as entirely lost him the hearts of the nation. He bore that hatred mildly, and said, 'That so far from resenting it (though he did not know, since he came from Flanders, that he had deserved either praise or blame) he should always with gratitude remember the behaviour of the English, who received him with transports after the battle of Laffelt, instead of impeaching him.' It is said, that after the loss of that day, an English captive telling a French officer, that they had been very near taking the Duke prisoner, the Frenchman replied, 'We took care of that; he does us more service at the head of your Army.' General Legonier, who, by an action of the most desperate gallantry, had prevented the total destruction of our troops in that battle, and almost made Marshal Saxe doubt of his victory, was never kindly treated by the Duke afterwards. Hawley, his executioner, who had been beat at Falkirk by his own arrogance and obstinacy, was always in his favour. He despised money, fame, and politics; loved gaming, women, and his own favourites, and yet had not one sociable virtue.

William Pulteney, Lord Bath

Lord Bath is so known a character, that it is almost needless to draw him. Who does not know that Mr. Pulteney was the great rival of Sir Robert Walpole, whose power he so long opposed, at last overturned, and was undone with it? Who does not know that his virtue failed the moment his inveteracy was gratified? Who does not know that all the patriot's private vices which his party would not see while he led them, were exposed, and, if possible, magnified by them the instant he deserted them? Who does not know that he had not judgment or resolution enough to engross the power, which he had forfeited his credit and character to obtain? and who does not know that his ambition, treachery, irresolution, timidity, and want of judgment were baffled and made advantage of by a man who had all those vices and deficiencies in a stronger proportion—for who does not know the Duke of Newcastle?

Speaker Onslow

The Speaker was master of an honesty, which though it would bend very much upon most occasions, especially when its warping would prop its reputation, was tough and steady when pushed to an extremity: and he would sometimes see that extremity as soon in trifles as in materials. His disinterestedness was remarkable, and he was fond of exerting it. Popularity was his great aim, impartiality his professed means, universal adulation and partiality to whatever was popular, his real means of acquiring it. He was bigotted to the power of the House of Commons; and, like all zealots, ardent for his own authority, as intimately connected with the interests of his idol. He had much devotion from the House, few friends in it, for he was too pompous to be loved, though too ridiculous to be hated; had too much knowledge not to be regarded; too much dignity in his appearance not to be admired; and was too fond of applause not to miss it.

Horace Walpole the Elder

Horace Walpole was still one of the busiest men in Parliament; generally bustling for the Ministry to get a Peerage, and even zealous for them when he could not get so much as their thanks. With the King he had long been in disgrace, on disputing a point of German genealogy with him (in which his Majesty's chief strength lay), whose the succession of some Principality would be, if eleven or twelve persons then living should die without issue. He knew something of everything but how to hold his tongue, or how to apply his knowledge. As interest was in all his actions, treaties were in all his speeches. Whatever the subject was, he never lost sight of the Peace of Utrecht, Lord Bolingbroke, and the Norwich manufactures; but his language and oratory were only adapted to manufacturers. He was a dead weight on his brother's Ministry; the first to take off that load on his brother's fall; yet nobody so intemperately abusive on all who connected with his brother's enemies; nobody so ready to connect with them for the least flattery, which he loved next to money—indeed he never entirely forgave Lord Bath for being richer. His mind was a strange mixture of sense alloyed by absurdity, wit by mimicry, knowledge by buffoonery, bravery by meanness, honesty by selfishness, impertinence by nothing. His body was more uniform, for that was throughout burlesque and uncouth.

Various Churchmen

But religious animosities were out of date; the public had no turn for controversy; the Church had no writers to make them fond of it again. This had lately appeared; Dr. Middleton, the best writer of the age, had overturned the Fathers, and exploded some visions of the Bishop of London, without a tolerable answer being made in defence of either. Of the prelates, the Archbishop was a harmless good man, inclined to much moderation, and of little zeal for the tinsel of religion. Hutton, the other Archbishop, was well bred and devoted to the Ministry. Honest old Hoadley, who, to the honour of his times, had, though the champion of Liberty, risen to the rich Bishopric of Winchester, was in a manner superannuated. Sherlock of London, almost as able a combatant for the power and the doctrines of the Church, was past his strength, and still fonder of the politics of the Government than of the honour of the Keys. The Bishop of Durham had been wafted to that See in a cloud of metaphysics, and remained absorbed in it. Gooch of Ely, the highest Churchman in his heart, had risen to his present greatness in the Church by shifting his politics. The rest were men neither of note nor temper to give the Ministry any disturbance.

Lord Hardwicke

Sir Philip Yorke, Baron of Hardwicke and Lord Chancellor, was a man of low birth and of lower principles. He was a creature of the Duke of Newcastle, and by him introduced to Sir Robert Walpole, who contributed to his grandeur and baseness, in giving him an opportunity of displaying the extent of the latter, by raising him to the height of the former. He had good parts, which he laid out so entirely upon the Law in the first part of his life, that they were of little use to him afterwards, when he would have applied them to more general views. He was Attorney-General, and when the Solicitor Talbot was, after a contest, preferred to him for the Chancellorship (the contest lay between their precedence, for Talbot was as able a man, and an honest one), Sir Robert Walpole made Yorke Chief Justice for life, and greatly increased the salary. Talbot dying in a short time after his advancement, to the great grief of all good men, Yorke succeeded. In his Chief-Justiceship he had gained the reputation of humanity, by some solemn speeches made on the Circuit, at the condemnation of wretches for low crimes; a character he lost with some when he sat as Lord High Steward at the trials of the Scotch Lords, the meanness of his birth breaking out in insolent acrimony. On his promotion, he flung himself into politics; but as he had no knowledge of foreign affairs, but what were whispered to him by Newcastle, he made a very poor figure.

In the House of Lords, he was laughed at; in the Cabinet, despised. On the Queen's death, he went deep into the Duke's shallow scheme of governing the King by the Princess Emily; for this cabal thought that he must necessarily be ruled by a woman, because the Queen was one, not considering it was because she was a wise one. This scheme was to be built on the ruin of Sir Robert Walpole, who had no other trouble to make it miscarry than in making the King say 'Pho!' to the first advice this Junto gave him. Their next plot was deeper laid, and had more effect: by a confederacy with the chiefs of the Opposition, they overturned Sir Robert Walpole; and in a little time, the few of their associates that they had admitted to share the spoils. When Yorke had left none but his friends in the Ministry, he was easily the most eminent for abilities. His exceeding parsimony was qualified by his severity to and discouragement of usurers and gamesters; at least, he endeavoured to suppress that species of avarice that exists by supplying and encouraging extravagance. The best thing that can be remembered of the Chancellor is his fidelity to his patron; for let the Duke of Newcastle betray whom he would, the Chancellor always stuck to him in his perfidy and was only not false to the falsest of mankind.

The Duke of Newcastle

He succeeded young to an estate of about thirty thousand pounds a year, and to great influence and interest in several counties. This account in reality contains his whole character as a Minister; for to the weight of this fortune he solely owed his every-other-way most unwarrantable elevation. His being heir to his uncle, the old Duke of Newcastle, obtained from the Crown a new creation of the title in his person; and, though he was far from having parts to procure him a Peerage, his Peerage and vast income procured him the first posts in the Government. His person was not naturally despicable; his incapacity, his mean soul, and the general low opinion of him, grew to make it appear ridiculous. A constant hurry in his walk, a restlessness of place, a borrowed importance, and real insignificance, gave him the perpetual air of a solicitor, though he was perpetually solicited; for he never conferred a favour till it was wrested from him, but often omitted doing what he most wished done. This disquiet and habit of never finishing, which, too, proceeded frequently from his beginning everything twenty times over, gave rise to a famous *bon mot* of Lord Wilmington—a man as unapt to attempt saying a good thing, as to say one. He said, 'the Duke of Newcastle always loses half an hour in the morning, which he is running after the rest of the day without being able to overtake it.'

He early distinguished himself for the House of Hanover, and in the last years of Queen Anne retained a great mob of people to halloo in that cause. He and his brother Harry raised a troop for King George on the Preston Rebellion, where the latter gave proofs of personal courage. The Duke was rewarded with the Garter, and some time after made Lord Chamberlain. The late King chose him for the honour of being Godfather to a new-born son of the Prince of Wales, which his Royal Highness much disapproving, was the immediate cause of that famous breach in the Royal Family, when the Prince and Princess left the palace very late at night. On Lord Carteret's being sent into honourable banishment, as Lord Lieutenant of Ireland, by the power of Lord Townshend and Sir Robert Walpole, the latter proposed to make the Duke of Newcastle Secretary of State, having experienced how troublesome a man of parts was in that office. The Viscount's first wife having been the Duke's sister was another reason for their depending the more on his attachment to them; but that very relation had given Lord Townshend too many opportunities of discovering how little he was to be trusted, particularly from his having betrayed Lord Sunderland, his first patron, to Lord Townshend, who earnestly objected to the choice of him, and endeavoured to convince Sir Robert Walpole how much his falsehood would give an edge to his incapacity. As the disagreement increased between those two Ministers, the Duke in every instance betrayed his brother-in-law to Sir Robert. The Viscount was not of Walpole's forgiving temper, and was immediately for discarding the Duke. He pressed both King and Queen to it; exclaimed against his childishness and weakness, and insisted upon his dismission as the only terms of reconciliation with Sir Robert. The King, who always hated him, easily yielded to make Sir Paul Methuen Secretary of State in his room; but the greater power of Sir Robert with the Queen (whose policy had long been employed in keeping open the breach, in order to govern both), saved the Duke for future scenes of perfidy and ingratitude. . . .

The Duke of Newcastle had no pride, though infinite self-love: jealousy was the great source of all his faults. He always caressed his enemies, to list them against his friends; there was no service he would not do for either, till either was above being served by him: then he would suspect they did not love him enough; for the moment they had every reason to love him, he took every method to obtain their hate, by exerting all his power for their ruin. There was no expense to which he was not addicted, but generosity. His houses, gardens, table, and equipage, swallowed immense treasures: the sums he owed were only exceeded by those he wasted. He loved business immoderately, yet was only always doing it, never did it. His speeches in Council and Parliament were flowing and copious of words, but empty and unmeaning: his professions extravagant, for he would profess intentions of doing more service to many men, than he even did hurt to others. Always inquisitive to know what was said of him, he wasted in curiosity the time in which he might have earned praise. He aimed at everything; endeavoured nothing. Fear, a ridiculous fear, was predominant in him; he would venture the overthrow of the Government, and hazard his life and fortunes rather than dare to open a letter that might discover a plot. He was a Secretary of State without intelligence, a Duke without money, a man of infinite intrigue without secrecy or policy, and a Minister despised and hated by his master, by all parties and Ministers, without being turned out by any!

Henry Pelham

It may appear extraordinary that Mr. Pelham, who had not so much levity in his character, should consent to be an accomplice in his brother's treacheries, especially as upon every interval of rivalship, the Duke grew jealous of him. The truth was, that Mr. Pelham, who had as much envy in his temper, and still more fondness for power, was willing to take advantage of his brother's fickleness, and reaped all the emolument without incurring the odium of it. He had lived in friendship with Sir Robert Walpole, Lord Chesterfield, and the Duke of Bedford; while his brother was notoriously betraying them shrugged up his shoulders, condemned the Duke, tried to make peace, but never failed to profit of their ruin the moment it was accomplished. The falsehood and frivolousness of their behaviour can never appear in a stronger light than it did in the present instance, and in all the transactions that relate to Lord Granville. That Lord had hurried into power on Sir Robert Walpole's disgrace, and declared he would be a Page of the Back Stairs rather than ever quit the Court again. He had no sooner quitted his party, who had long suspected him, than he openly declared himself a protector of Sir Robert Walpole; and to give the finishing stroke to his interest with the King, drove deep into all his Majesty's Hanoverian politics, persuaded, in spite of the recent instance before his eyes, that whoever governed the King, must govern the kingdom.

Lord Granville

His person was handsome, open, and engaging; his eloquence at once rapid and pompous, and by the mixture, a little bombast. He was an extensive scholar, master of classic criticism, and of all modern politics. He was precipitate in his manner, and rash in his projects; but though there was nothing he would not attempt, he scarce ever took any measures necessary to the accomplishment. He would profess amply, provoke indiscriminately, oblige seldom. It is difficult to say whether he was oftener intoxicated by wine or ambition: in fits of the former, he showed contempt for everybody; in rants of the latter, for truth. His genius was magnificent and lofty; his heart without gall or friendship, for he never tried to be revenged on his enemies, or to serve his friends.

Thomas Winnington

The King sent for Winnington, and commissioned him to invite the deserters to return to their posts. Winnington had been bred a Tory, but had left them in the height of Sir Robert Walpole's power: when that Minister sunk, he had injudiciously, and to please my Lady Townshend, who had then the greatest influence over him, declined visiting him in a manner to offend the steady old Whigs; and his jolly way of laughing at his own want of principles had revolted all the graver sort, who thought deficiency of honesty too sacred and profitable a commodity to be profaned and turned into ridicule. He had infinitely more wit than any man I ever knew, and it was as ready and quick as it was constant and unmeditated. His style was a little brutal; his courage not at all so; his good-humour inexhaustible: it was impossible to hate or to trust him. He died soon after by the ignorance of a quack, when he stood in the fairest point of rising, to the great satisfaction of Mr. Pelham, whom he rivalled and despised.

George the Second

The King had fewer sensations of revenge, or at least knew how to hoard them better than any man who ever sat upon a throne. The insults he experienced from his own, and those obliged servants, never provoked him enough to make him venture the repose of his people, or his own. If any object of his hate fell in his way, he did not pique himself upon heroic forgiveness, but would indulge it at the expense of his integrity, though not of his safety. He was reckoned strictly honest; but the burning of his father's will must be an indelible blot upon his memory; as a much later instance of his refusing to pardon a young man who had been condemned at Oxford for a most trifling forgery, contrary to all example when recommended to mercy by the Judge; merely because Willes, who was attached to the Prince of Wales, had tried him, and assured him his pardon, will stamp his name with cruelty, though in general his disposition was merciful, if the offence was not murder. His avarice was much less equivocal than his courage: he had distinguished the latter early; it grew more doubtful afterwards: the former he distinguished very near as soon, and never deviated from it. His understanding was not near so deficient as it was imagined; but though his character changed extremely in the world, it was without foundation; for if he deserved to be so much ridiculed as he had been in the former part of his reign, or so respected as in the latter, he was consistent in himself, and uniformly meritorious or absurd.

His other passions were Germany, the Army, and women. Both the latter had a mixture of parade in his pursuit of them; he kept my Lady Suffolk,[1] and afterwards Lady Yarmouth, as his mistresses, while

[1] Henrietta, daughter of Sir Henry Hobart, was first married to Colonel Henry Howard, afterwards Earl of Suffolk, by whom she had an only son, Henry, who succeeded his father, but died a young man. Mr. Howard and she travelled in very mean circumstances to Hanover before the accession of that family to the Crown; and after it, she was made a Woman of the Bedchamber to the Princess; and being *confidante* of the Prince's passion for, who was in love with Mrs. Ballenden and soon after privately married to Colonel Campbell, Mrs. Howard had the address to divert the channel of his inclination to herself. Her husband bore it very ill, and attempted to force her from St. James's, but was at last quieted with a pension of £1200 per annum. Yet Mrs. Howard had little interest with the King. The Queen persecuted whoever courted her; and Sir R. Walpole directing all his worship to the uncommonly-powerful wife, Mrs. Howard naturally became his enemy, and as naturally attached herself to Lord Bolingbroke; the more

he admired only the Queen[1]; and never described what he thought a handsome woman, but he drew her picture. Lady Suffolk was sensible, artful, and agreeable, but had neither sense nor art enough to make him think her so agreeable as his wife. When she had left him, tired of acting the mistress, while she had in reality all the slights of a wife, and no interest with him, the Opposition affected to cry up her virtue, and the obligations the King had to her for consenting to seem his mistress, while in reality she had confined him to mere friendship—a ridiculous pretence, as he was the last man in the world to have taste for talking sentiments, and that with a woman who was deaf! Lady Yarmouth was inoffensive, and attentive only to pleasing him, and to selling Peerages whenever she had an opportunity. The Queen had been admired and happy for governing him by address; it was not then known how easily he was to be governed by fear.

Indeed there were few arts by which he was not governed at some time or other of his life; for not to mention the late Duke of Argyle, who grew a favourite by imposing himself upon him for brave; nor

---

intimate connection of which intercourse, carelessly concealed by a mistress that was tired, and eagerly hunted out by a wife still jealous, was unravelled by the Princess Emily at the Bath, and at last laid open by the cautious Queen; the King stormed; the mistress was glad he did, left him in his moods, and married George Berkeley, brother to the late Earl, by whom she was again left a widow in 1746. [H.W.]

[1] He has often, when Mrs. Howard, his mistress, was dressing the Queen, come into the room, and snatched the handkerchief off, and cried, 'Because you have an ugly neck yourself, you love to hide the Queen's!' Her Majesty (all the while calling her 'My good Howard') took great joy in employing her in the most servile offices about her person. The King was so communicative to his wife, that one day Mrs. Selwyn, another of the Bedchamber Women, told him he should be the last man with whom she would have an intrigue, because he always told the Queen. Their letters, whenever he was at Hanover, were so long, that he has complained when she has written to him but nineteen pages; and in his, at the beginning of his amour with Lady Yarmouth, he frequently said, 'I know you will love the Walmoden, *because she loves me.*' Old Blackbourn, the Archbishop of York, told her one day, 'That he had been talking to her Minister Walpole about the new mistress, and was glad to find that her Majesty was so sensible a woman as to like her husband should divert himself.' Yet with the affectation of content, it made her most miserable: she dreaded Lady Yarmouth's arrival, and repented not having been able to resist the temptation of driving away Lady Suffolk the first instant she had an opportunity, though a rival so powerless, and so little formidable. The King was the most regular man in his hours: his time of going down to Lady Suffolk's apartment was seven in the evening: he would frequently walk up and down the gallery, looking at his watch, for a quarter of an hour before seven, but would not go till the clock struck. . . . The King had another *passager amour* (between the disgrace of Lady Suffolk and the arrival of Lady Yarmouth) with the Countess Dowager of Deloraine, Governess to the two youngest Princesses; a pretty idiot, with most of the vices of her own sex, and the additional one of ours, drinking. Yet this thing of convenience, on the arrival of Lady Yarmouth, put on all that dignity of passion, which even revolts real inclination. [H.W.]

23

Lord Wilmington, who imposed himself upon him for the Lord knows what; the Queen governed him by dissimulation, by affected tenderness and deference: Sir Robert Walpole by abilities and influence in the House of Commons; Lord Granville by flattering him in his German politics; the Duke of Newcastle by teazing and betraying him; Mr. Pelham by bullying him—the only man by whom Mr. Pelham was not bullied himself. Who indeed had not sometimes weight with the King, except his children and his mistresses? With them he maintained all the reserve and majesty of his rank. He had the haughtiness of Henry the Eighth, without his spirit; the avarice of Henry the Seventh, without his exactions; the indignities of Charles the First, without his bigotry for his prerogative; the vexations of King William, with as little skill in the management of parties; and the gross gallantry of his father, without his goodnature or his honesty:—he might, perhaps, have been honest, if he had never hated his father, or had ever loved his son.

The Second Duke of Grafton

The Duke of Grafton was a very extraordinary man; with very good common sense and knowledge of mankind, he contrived to be generally thought a fool, and by being thought so, contrived to be always well at Court, and to have it not remarked that he was so: yet he would sometimes boast of having been a short time in Opposition, and of having early resolved never to be so again. He had a lofty person, with great dignity; great slowness in his delivery, which he managed with humour. He had the greatest penetration in finding out the foibles of men that ever I knew, and wit in teazing them. He was insensible to misfortunes of his own or of his friends: understood the Court perfectly, and looking upon himself as of the Blood Royal, he thought nothing ought to affect him, but what touched them: as he had no opportunity of forsaking them for a family to which he was more nearly related, one must not say he would have forsaken them: betraying was never his talent; he was content to be ungrateful, when his benefactors were grown unhappy. He was careless of his fortune, and provided against nothing but a storm that might remove him from his station. An instance once broke out of his having ambition to something more than barely adorning the Court. On the Queen's death, whom he always hated, teazed, yet praised to the King,

24

he was imprudent enough in a private conversation with Sir Robert Walpole and the Duke of Newcastle, to dispute with the latter, whose the power should be, both silently agreeing, fools as they were, in his very presence, that it was no longer to be Sir Robert's. Grafton thinking to honour him enough by letting him act under him, said at last in a great passion to t'other Duke 'My Lord, sole Minister I am not capable of being; first Minister, by God, I will be.' The foundation of either's hopes lay in their credit with Princess Emily, who was suspected of having been as kind to Grafton's love, as she would have been unkind in yielding to Newcastle's, who made exceeding bustle about her, but was always bad at executing all business. The Queen, who was suspected of indulging her daughter to prevent her indulging herself, had in reality a thorough aversion to the Duke of Grafton for the liberties he took with one of her great blood; and if she had not been prevented by Sir Robert Walpole, would one night have complained to the King, when the Princess and the Duke, who hunted two or three times a week together, had stayed out unusually late, lost their attendants, and gone together to a private house in Windsor Forest. The Queen hated him too for letting her see he knew her. He always teazed her, and insisted that she loved nobody. He had got a story of some Prince in Germany, that she had been in love with before her marriage: 'God, madam,' he used to say, 'I wish I could have seen that man that you *could* love!' 'Why,' replied she, 'do you think I don't love the King?' 'God, I wish I was King of France, and I would be sure whether you do or not!'

Princess Emily

Princess Emily, whether from the Duke of Grafton's growing old, or from any new passion, detached herself from that cabal, and united with her brother the Duke and the Bedfords. She was meanly inquisitive into what did not relate to her, and foolishly communicative of what was below her to know: false without trying to please, mischievous with more design, impertinent even where she had no resentment; and insolent, though she had lost her beauty, and acquired no power. After her father's death, she lived with great dignity; but being entirely slighted by her nephew, who was afraid of her frankness, she soon forbore going to Court or to keep a Drawing-room herself, on pretence of her increased deafness. She was extremely deaf, and very short-sighted; yet had so much quickness and conception, that she seemed to hear and see more readily than others. She was an excellent mistress to her servants, steady to her favourites, and nobly generous and charitable.

The Duke of Newcastle

The Duke of Newcastle, who had conquered every obstacle to power but the aversion of his master, began to think he might as well add his favour to the other attributes of a Minister; and having over-turned Lord Granville for his German adulation, was so equitable as to make the King amends by giving in to all excess of it himself. There was one impediment; he had never been out of England, and dreaded the sea. After having consulted his numerous band of physicians and apothecaries, he at last ventured; and himself and his gold plate, and his mad Duchess, under a thousand various convoys, treated Europe with a more ridiculous spectacle than any it had seen since Caligula's cockle-shell triumph.

The Duke of Bedford

He was a man of inflexible honesty, and good-will to his country: his great economy was called avarice; if it was so, it was blended with more generosity and goodness than that passion will commonly unite with. His parts were certainly far from shining, and yet he spoke readily, and upon trade, well: his foible was speaking upon every subject, and imagining he understood it, as he must have done, by inspiration. He was always governed generally by the Duchess, though un-measurably obstinate, when once he had formed or had an opinion instilled into him. His manner was impetuous, of which he was so little sensible, that being told Lord Halifax was to succeed him, he said, 'He is too warm and overbearing; the King will never endure him.' If the Duke of Bedford could have thought less well of himself, the world would probably have thought better of him.

Lord Sandwich

His friend Lord Sandwich was of a very different character; in nothing more than in the inflexibility of his honesty. The Duke of Bedford loved money, to use it sensibly and with kindness to others;

Lord Sandwich was rapacious, but extravagant when it was to promote his own designs. His industry to carry any point he had in view was so remarkable, that for a long time the world mistook it for abilities; but as his manner was most awkward and unpolished, so his talents were but slight, when it was necessary to exert them in any higher light than in art and intrigue. The King had never forgiven him his indecent reflections upon the Electorate when he was in Opposition, and as soon as ever he found his Ministers would permit him to show his resentment, he took all occasions to pay his court to them by treating Lord Sandwich ill, particularly by talking to Lord Anson before him on all matters relating to the fleet. An incident (one should have thought quite foreign to the Administration) contributed to give the King a new handle to use Lord Sandwich with indignity: the Bedfords had transacted a marriage between one of the Duchess's sisters and Colonel Waldegrave, against the consent of her father, Lord Gower; and Lord Sandwich had been so imprudent as to let the ceremony be performed at his apartments at the Admiralty. The Pelhams, who always inoculated private quarrels on affairs of State, dispatched my Lord Gower to ask a formal audience of the King, and complain of Lord Sandwich's contributing to steal his daughter. Lord Gower was a comely man of form, had never had any sense, and was now superannuated. He had been educated a stiff Jacobite, elected their chief on his first coming into the King's service, and had twice taken the Privy Seal before he could determine to change his principles. The King entered into his quarrel; and the Pelhams by this artifice detached him from his family, and persuaded him that to resign with them would be sacrificing himself in the cause of Lord Sandwich, who had offered him such an indignity.

Mr. Legge

Legge was a younger son of Lord Dartmouth, who had early turned him into the world to make his fortune, which he pursued with an uncommon assiduity of duty. Avarice or flattery, application or ingratitude, nothing came amiss that might raise him on the ruins of either friends or enemies; indeed, neither were so to him, but by the proportion of their power. He had been introduced to Sir Robert Walpole by his second son, and soon grew an unmeasurable favourite, till endeavouring to steal his patron's daughter, at which in truth Sir Robert's partiality for him had seemed to connive, he was discarded entirely; yet taken care of in the very last hours of that Minister's power; and though removed from the Secretaryship of the Treasury, being particularly obnoxious to Lord Bath, he obtained a profitable employment by the grossest supplications to the Duke of Bedford; and was soon after admitted into the Admiralty by as gross court paid to Lord Winchelsea, whom he used ill the moment he found it necessary to worship that less intense but more surely-rising sun, Mr. Pelham. He had a peculiarity of wit and very shrewd parts, but was a dry and generally an indifferent speaker. On a chosen embassy to the King of Prussia, Legge was duped and ill-treated by him. Having shuffled for some time between Mr. Pelham, Pitt, the Duke of Bedford, and Lord Sandwich, and wriggled through the interest of all into the Treasury, and then to the Treasurership of the Navy, he submitted to break his connections with the two latter by being the indecent messenger of Lord Sandwich's disgrace.

The Duke of Devonshire and Lord Hartington

Lord Hartington and his father the Duke of Devonshire were the fashionable models of goodness, though if it were necessary for the good man to be perfect like the Stoic's wise man, their want of sense and generosity would have rendered their titles disputable. Indeed their chief merit was a habit of caution. The Duke's outside was unpolished, his inside unpolishable. He loved gaming, drinking, and the ugliest woman in England, his Duchess, on whose account he had resigned his employments to retire with her after having parted with her and turned her head, by breaking a promise he had given her of not marrying his son to Lady Burlington's daughter. The Marquis was more fashioned, but with an impatience to do everything and a fear to do anything, he was always in a hurry to do nothing. His discretion was so great that he would sooner whisper to a man's prejudice, than openly deliver a harmless opinion; and these whispers had the more effect as he was too civil ever to own himself an enemy. Nor was this all malice; if he had had reflection enough to design all the mischief he did he would have been less capable of doing it. They are the tales of the gentle and the good that stab. Perhaps he thought that what was discreetly related, secured the aspersed as well as the aspersor. Sir Robert Walpole had set up the father as the standard of Whiggism; in gratitude, he was constantly bigotted to whoever passed for the head of the Whigs: but the dexterity of raising his son to so eminent a post as Master of the Horse during his own life, and obtaining a peerage for his son-in-law by retiring from power himself, extremely lessened the value of the rough diamond that he had hitherto contrived to be thought.

Lord Holderness

On 18th [June] appeared the last and greatest phenomenon, Lord Holderness, who had been fetched from his Embassy in Holland to be Secretary of State. In reality, he did justice to himself and his patrons, for he seemed ashamed of being made so considerable, for no reason but because he was so inconsiderable. He had a formality in his manner that would have given an air of truth to what he said, if he would but have assisted it with the least regard to probability; but this made his narrations more harmless than Lord Egremont's, for they were totally incredible. His passion for directing operas and masquerades was rather thought a contradiction to his gravity, than below his understanding, which was so very moderate, at the same time that his face being overspread with a hideous humour made his appearance offensive, that no relations of his own exploits would not a little time before have been sooner credited, than two events that really came to pass, his being made Secretary of State, and having his wife, a very pretty woman, jealous of him—but indeed, these only proved that there was nothing but what women and the Duke of Newcastle could grow to admire. What contributed a little to make the King consent to this wonderful promotion was his mother, Lady Fitzwalter, being distantly related to the Royal Family. The Queen and the Princesses always talked to her in French, though she had never been out of England, because her ancestors came originally from Germany.

George Lyttelton

Absurdity was predominant in Lyttelton's composition: it entered equally into his politics, his apologies, his public pretences, his private conversations. With the figure of a spectre, and the gesticulations of a puppet, he talked heroics through his nose, made declamations at a visit, and played at cards with scraps of history, or sentences of Pindar. He had set out on a poetical love plan, though with nothing of a lover but absence of mind, and nothing of poet but absence of meaning; yet he was far from wanting parts; spoke well when he had studied his speeches; and loved to reward and promote merit in others. His political apostasy was as flagrant as Pitt's: the latter gloried in it: but Lyttelton, when he had been forced to quit virtue, took up religion, and endeavoured to persuade mankind that he had just fixed his views on heaven, when he had gone the greatest lengths to promote his earthly interest; and so finished was his absurdity, that he was capable of believing himself honest and agreeable.

Sir Charles Hanbury Williams

Sir Charles Hanbury Williams had been attached to Mr. Winnington, and was the particular friend of Fox. Towards the end of Sir Robert Walpole's power, they, Lord Hervey and Lord Ilchester, had forced the last into the Secretaryship of the Treasury, against the inclination of the Minister; an instance at that time unparalleled; much copied since, as the Government has fallen into weaker hands. Sir Charles remained a steady friend to Walpole, and persecuted his rival, Lord Bath, in a succession of satiric odes, that did more execution in six months, than *The Craftsman* had done in twice the number of years; for the Minister only lost his power, but the patriot his character. If Sir Charles had many superiors in poetry, he had none in the wit of his poetry. In conversation he was less natural, and overbearing: hated with the greatest good-nature, and the most disinterested generosity; for fools dreaded his satire—few forgave his vanity. He had thrown up his place on some disgusts; the loss of Mr. Winnington, and a quarrel with the Irish, occasioned by an ode he wrote on the marriage of the Duchess of Manchester and Mr. Hussey, fomented by Lord Bath and his enemies, and supported with too little spirit, had driven him to shelter his discontents in a foreign Embassy, where he displayed great talents for negotiation, and pleased as much by his letters, as he had formerly by his poetry.

The Prince and Princess of Orange

On the 13th [August], an express arrived of the death of the Prince of Orange, who, having been at Aix la Chapelle, caught a fever on his return, and died in five days.

He had long been kept out of all share in the government, like his predecessor, King William; like him, lifted to it in a tumultuous manner, on his country being overrun by the French; and the Stadholdership made hereditary in his family before they had time to experience how little he was qualified to re-establish their affairs. Not that he wanted genius, but he was vain and positive, a trifling lover of show, and not master of the great lights in which he stood. The Princess Royal was more positive, and though passionately imperious, had dashed all opportunities that presented for the Prince's distinguishing himself, from immoderate jealousy and fondness for his person. Yet the Mars who was locked in the arms of this Venus, was a monster so deformed, that when the King had chosen him for his son-in-law, he could not help, in the honesty of his heart, and the coarseness of his expression, telling the Princess how hideous a bridegroom she was to expect, and even gave her permission to refuse him. She replied, she would marry him if he was a baboon. 'Well, then,' said the King, 'there is baboon enough for you!'

The Princess immediately took the oaths as *Gouvernante* to her son, and all orders of men submitted to her as quietly as in a monarchy of the most established duration; though the opposite faction was numerous, and she herself lethargic and in a very precarious state of health. Lord Holderness was sent to condole and advise her. She, who had long been on ill terms with, and now dreaded the appearance of being governed by her father, received the Ambassador and three letters written with the King's own hand, in the haughtiest and most slighting manner. Lord Holderness was recalled in anger. The Princess, equally unfit to govern, or to be governed, threw herself into the arms of France, by the management of one Dubacq, a little Secretary, who had long been instilling advice into her, to draw her husband from the influence of Monsieur Bentinck and the Greffier, the known partizans of England; the former of whom, immediately after the death of the Prince, refused to admit Dubacq to a Council, to which

31

she had called him, with the chiefs of the Republic, at the House in the Wood.

The Princess Royal was accomplished in languages, painting, and particularly music; the Queen, and the King too, before their rupture, had great opinion of her understanding; but the pride of her race, and the violence of her passions had left but a scanty sphere for her judgment to exert itself.

Lord Bolingbroke

The 12th [of December] died Lord Bolingbroke; a man who will not be seen in less extraordinary lights by posterity than he was by his cotemporaries, though for very different reasons. His own age regarded him either as the greatest statesman oppressed by faction, and the greatest genius persecuted by envy; or as the most consummate villain preserved by clemency, and the most treacherous politician abandoned by all parties whom he had successively betrayed. Posterity will look on him as the greatest philosopher from Pope's writings; or as an author of a bounded genius from his own. To see him in a true light, they must neither regard all the incense offered to him by Tories, nor credit all the opprobrium cast on him by Whigs. They must see him compounded of all those vices and virtues that so often enter into the nature of a great genius, who is not one of the greatest.

Was it being master of no talents to have acted the second part, when little more than a youth, in overturning such a Ministry, and stemming such a tide of glory, as Lord Godolphin's and the Duke of Marlborough's? Were there no abilities, after his return from banishment, in holding such a power as Sir Robert Walpole's at bay for so many years, even when excluded from the favourable opportunity of exerting his eloquence in either House of Parliament? Was there no triumph in having chiefly contributed to the fall of that Minister? Was there no glory in directing the councils and operations of such men as Sir William Windham, Lord Bath, and Lord Granville? And was there no art in persuading the self-fondest and greatest of poets, that the writer of *Craftsmen* was a more exalted genius than the author of the *Dunciad*? Has he shown no address in palliating the exploded treaty of Utrecht? Has he not, in his letters on that event, contrived to make assertions and hypothesis almost balance stubborn facts? To cover his own guilt, has he not diverted our attention towards pity for the great enemy, in whose service he betrayed his own country?

On the other hand, what infamy to have sold the conqueror to the conquered! What ingratitude in labouring the ruin of a Minister, who had repealed his sentence of banishment! What repeated treasons to the Queen, whom he served; to the Pretender, who had received and countenanced him; to the late King, who had recalled him! What ineffectual arts to acquire the confidence of the late King by means of the Duchess of Kendal, and of the present King by Lady Suffolk! What unwearied ambition, even at seventy years of age, in laying a plan of future power in the favour of the Prince of Wales! What deficience in the very parts that had given success to the Opposition, to have left him alone excluded from reaping the harvest of so many labours! What blackness in disclosing the dirtiness of Pope, who had deified him! And what philosophy was that which had been initiated in the ruin of the Catalans; had employed its meridian in labouring the restoration of Popery and arbitrary power; and busied the end of its career, first in planning factions in the Pretender's Court, by the scheme of the father's resigning his claim to the son; and then in sowing the seeds of division between a King and a Prince, who had pardoned all his treasons!

Sir Robert Walpole and Lord Bolingbroke had set out rivals at school, lived a life of competition, and died much in the same manner, provoked at being killed by empirics; but with the same difference in their manner of dying as had appeared in the temper of their lives: the first with a calmness that was habitual philosophy; the other with a rage that his affected philosophy could not disguise. The one had seen his early ambition dashed with imprisonment, from which he had shot into the sphere of his rival, who was exiled, sentenced, recalled; while Walpole rose gradually to the height of temperate power, maintained it by the force of his single talents against Bolingbroke, assisted by all the considerable geniuses of England; and when driven from it at last, resigned it without a stain or a censure, and retired to a private life, without an attempt to re-establish himself—almost without a regret for what he had lost. The other, unquiet, unsteady, shocked to owe his return to his enemy, more shocked to find his return was not to power, incapable of tasting the retirement which he made delightful to all who partook it, died at last with the mortification of owing his greatest reputation to the studies he had cultivated to distress his antagonist. Both were beloved in private life; Sir Robert from the

33

humanity and the frankness of his nature; Bolingbroke from his politeness of turn and elegance of understanding. Both were fond of women; Walpole with little delicacy; Bolingbroke to enjoy the delicacy of pleasure. Both were extravagant; and the Patriot who accused, and the Minister who had been accused of rapine, died poor or in debt. Walpole was more amiable in his virtues; Bolingbroke more agreeable in his vices.

The Queen of Denmark

About the middle of this month [December], died his Majesty's youngest daughter, the Queen of Denmark, a Princess of great spirit and sense, and in the flower of her age. Her death, which was terrible, and after an operation that lasted an hour, resembled her mother's— a slight rupture which she concealed, and had been occasioned by stooping when she was seven months gone with her first child. The Queen had in a manner prophesied to her when she was expiring herself: 'Louisa, remember I die by being giddy, and obstinate in having kept my disorder a secret!' Her fate, too, had borne a resemblance to her mother's; for the King of Denmark, though passionately fond of her, to prevent the appearance of being governed, had kept a mistress, and given her great uneasiness: yet she never mentioned it in her confidential letters to her own family. The Duke said, she had always told them, that if she was unhappy, they should never know it. In her last moments, she wrote a moving letter to the King, the Duke, and her sisters, to take leave of them. This letter, and the similitude of hers and her mother's death, struck the King in the sharpest manner, and made him break out into warm expressions of passion and tenderness. He said, 'This has been a fatal year to my family! I lost my eldest son—but I am glad of it;—then the Prince of Orange died, and left everything in confusion. Poor little Edward has been cut open (for an imposthume in his side), and now the Queen of Denmark is gone! I know I did not love my children when they were young; I hated to have them running into my room; but now I love them as well as most fathers.'

Mr. Pelham and Sir Robert Walpole

But it is time to conclude the history of this extraordinary year, all the chief events of which having terminated in confirming the power of Mr. Pelham, it will be proper, before I take leave of the reader, to add this person's portrait to those of the under-actors; and the better to illustrate it, I shall take the liberty of examining his and his master Sir Robert Walpole's characters together, though it is difficult to compare two Ministers, when on one side genius must be entirely left out of the question: nor could anything draw on a parallel between a man of genius and a man of none, but the singular case of the latter having affected what the former could not—I mean power without unpopularity.

When Elijah was hurried to heaven, he left his cloak to Elisha with a *double* portion of his spirit: but that legacy in no sense happened to Mr. Pelham, who was as much inferior to Sir Robert Walpole in political courage as in abilities. Sir Robert Walpole was bold, open, steady, never dejected; he would attempt for honest ends where strict morality did not countenance his opinion; he always disclosed his arts after they had effected his purpose; and sometimes defeated them by too early discovery. He never gave up his party to serve himself, though he has departed from his own opinion to please his friends, who were serving themselves; nor did he ever lose his cheerfulness, though he had hurt himself against his opinion.

Mr. Pelham was timorous, reserved, fickle, apt to despair. He would often not attempt when he was convinced it would be right; would sooner hurt himself by not telling his mind, than attain his aim by being communicative; and often gave up his party, indeed not to serve himself but his enemies, and frequently disappointed himself of success, by never expecting to succeed. Presumption made Sir Robert Walpole many enemies; want of confidence in himself kept from Mr. Pelham many friends. Sir Robert Walpole was content to have one great honest view, and would overlook or trample upon the intermediate degrees. Mr. Pelham could never reach a great view, by stumbling at little ones; he would scruple to give an hundred pounds to one opponent, and to buy off another would give up a question that might endanger the nation. Sir Robert Walpole loved power so much, that he would not endure a rival; Mr. Pelham loved it so well, that he would endure anything. The one would risk his Administration, by driving every considerable man from Court, rather than venture their being well there; the other would employ any means to take able men out of the Opposition, though he ventured their engrossing his authority and outshining his capacity; but he dreaded abuse more than competition, and always bought off his enemies to avoid their satire, rather than to

35

acquire their support: whereas, Sir Robert Walpole never trading but for numbers, and despising invectives, and dreading rivals, gained but weak, uncertain assistance, and always kept up a formidable Opposition. His apprehension of competitors was founded on prudence, because great part of his authority depended upon the King's favour: Mr. Pelham owing nothing to that, had the less reason to fear losing it; as he maintained himself in the Ministry in spite of the King's partiality to abler men, he had no reason to be jealous of their getting interest at Court.

Sir Robert Walpole raised himself to the head of the Administration, without interest, without fortune, without alliances, and in defiance of the chiefs of his own party: he rose by the House of Commons, he fell by it. Mr. Pelham found himself next upon the list, and was recommended to a strong party by their leader. He would never have risen, had he had no other foundation than the House of Commons, and would fall tomorrow if he had no other support; for he must be undone whenever his safety depends upon himself. Sir Robert Walpole's eloquence was made for use, and he never could shine but when it was necessary he should. He wanted art when he had no occasion for it; and never pleased, but when he did more than please. I am not going to contrast this part of their characters, nor to say that Mr. Pelham only shone upon trifling and unnecessary occasions, for he did not do even that; he was obscure upon the most trivial occurrences, perplexed even when he had but one idea, and whenever he spoke well, it was owing to his being heated; he must lose his temper before he could exert his reason. Sir Robert Walpole palliated too little, Mr. Pelham too much. The one would defend his errors by a majority; the other with a greater majority would excuse his merit, and would sooner obscure and depreciate his meaning when right and clear of itself, than not apologize for it. Sir Robert Walpole could not deviate but with openness and sincerity; the other degraded truth by timidity, sense by mystery, and right by asking pardon for it.

The one was honoured by his enemies, the other at best pitied by his friends. His most prejudiced opponents often grew convinced that the former was in the right: the heartiest friends of the latter knew he meant to be so, but never found stronger reasons to confirm them in their opinion. The one durst do right and durst do wrong too; the other dared either so little, that it generally ended in his doing the latter. Sir Robert Walpole never professed honesty, but followed it; Mr. Pelham always professed it, and kept his word, when nothing happened to make him break it; and then he broke it for some other honest end, though perhaps far from being equally cogent.

Sir Robert Walpole's mastery was understanding his own country, and his foible, inattention to every other country, by which it was impossible he could thoroughly understand his own. Mr. Pelham understood more of his own country than of others, though he would have made a better Minister for any other nation; for as he would not have met with opposition or contradiction, two things his nature could not bear, and as he meant exceedingly well, he would have served the country that employed him to the best of his understanding, and that might have cleared up as well as his temper, when he had nothing to perplex it. In the knowledge of the Revenue, he and all other men must yield to Sir R. Walpole, though he and all other men make the same use of that knowledge, which is to find new funds for the necessities of the Government, and for the occasions of the Administration: by those occasions, I mean corruption, in which I believe Mr. Pelham would never have wet his finger, if Sir Robert Walpole had not dipped up to the elbow; but as he did dip, and as Mr. Pelham was persuaded that it was as necessary for him to be Minister as it was for Sir Robert Walpole, he plunged as deep. The difference was, that Mr. Pelham always bribed more largely as he had more power; for whenever it tottered, he the less ventured to prop it by those means, as he was the more afraid of being called to account for putting them in practice.

Sir Robert Walpole, with the greatest confidence of himself, had no pride; Mr. Pelham had the most, with the least self-sufficience. Both were loved in private life. Sir Robert Walpole loved magnificence, and was generous to a fault: the other had neither ostentation nor avarice, and yet had little generosity. The one was profuse to his family and his friends, liberal indiscriminately, unbounded to his tools and spies: the other loved his family and his friends, and enriched them as often as he could steal an opportunity from his extravagant bounty to his enemies and antagonists. Indifferent people were too indifferent to him; and for intelligence, it was one of the greatest blemishes of his Administration, he wanted it so entirely—not resolution more! Sir Robert Walpole's friendships were chiefly confined to persons much below him; Mr. Pelham's were almost all founded on birth and rank: the one was too familiar, the other never so. Sir Robert Walpole was forgiving to a fault, if forgiveness can be faulty; Mr. Pelham never forgave, but when he durst not resent. Sir Robert Walpole met with much ingratitude; Mr.

Pelham was guilty of much. Both were frequently betrayed: Sir Robert Walpole without being deceived; Mr. Pelham not half so often as he suspected it. The one was most depreciated while he was Minister; the other will be most when he ceases to be Minister. All men thought Mr. Pelham honest till he was in power; the other never was thought so till he was out.

Both were fortunate in themselves, unhappy in their brothers. With unbounded thirst for politics, the Duke of Newcastle and Horace Walpole were wretched politicians: each inferior to their brothers in everything laudable; each assuming and jealous of their own credit though neither the Duke nor Horace could ever have been considerable, but by the fortune of their brothers. The one childish and extravagant, the other a buffoon and avaricious; Horace sunk into contempt when his brother fell with honour; the Duke was often on the point of dragging his brother down, and was the object of all contempt, even where his brother had still power and honour. Mr. Pelham maintained his inferiority to Sir Robert Walpole even in the worthlessness of his brother.

Memoires of the year 1752

I sit down to resume a task, for which I fear posterity will condemn the author, at the same time that they feel their curiosity gratified. On reviewing the first part of these Memoires, I find the truth rigidly told. And even since they were written, I have often been struck with the censures which are passed on such historians as have fairly displayed the faulty sides of the characters they exhibit. Theopompus is called a satirist: Timæus was so severe, as to be nicknamed Epitimæus, the Blamer. Some of our own annalists, as Wilson, Weldon, Osborn, (though frequently quoted) are seldom mentioned without reproach. I defend them not: if their representations are exaggerated, they not only deserve reproach, but discredit.

On the other hand, I examined the candid authors. Two of our own, who deal wonderfully in panegyric, Clarendon and Echard, I find to have dispensed invectives with a liberal hand on men of parties opposite to their own—does then the province of praise and censure depend on the felicity of choosing one's party? *That* shall never influence me—I would as soon wish to be rejected for flattering one

38

party, as for blaming another. Nor can I, on the strictest consideration, determine to write like biographers and authors of Peerages and Compendiums, who sink all executions in a family, all blots in a 'scutcheon, and lay out their personages as fair as if they wrote epitaphs, not history. Does any noble family extinguish? One should grieve, on reading their genealogies, that such a succession of heroes, statesmen, patriots, should ever fail; if a little knowledge of mankind did not call forth the blemishes, which these varnishers have slubbered over. If I write, I must write facts. The times I describe have neither been glorious nor fortunate. Have our affairs gone ill, and yet were our Governors wise? Have Parliaments been venal, servile, and yet individuals upright? If I paint the battle of Dettingen in prosperous colours, am I an admired historian? If I mention hostages sent to France, am I an abusive one? Are there no shades, no degrees of vices and misconduct? Must no Princes be blamed, till they are Neros? Must Vespasian's avarice pass unnoticed, because he did not set fire to the city—because he did not burn the means of gratifying his exactions?

Suppose I were to comply with this indulgent taste, and write thus:—George the Second was the most glorious Monarch that ever sat on the English Throne; his victories over the united arms of Spain and France will illustrate our annals till time is no more; and his condescension and generosity will conspire to raise his private character to a level with his public. The Duke of Newcastle was a prodigy of sincerity, steadiness, and abilities. Mr. Pelham was the humblest man, the bravest Minister, the heartiest friend, the openest enemy. The Earl of Holderness the most graceful dancer that ever trod the stage of business since the days of Chancellor Hatton—avaunt, Flattery! tell the truth, my pen!

The miscarriage of the Rebellion had silenced Jacobitism; the death of the Prince of Wales had quashed opposition; and the removal of the Duke of Bedford and Lord Sandwich had put an end to factions in the Ministry. The ascendant of the Pelhams drew the attention of the disaffected, who began to see a prospect of the restoration, if not of the Stuarts, at least of absolute power; and this union was not a little cemented by the harmony of hatred, in which both the Pelhams and the Jacobites concurred against the Duke and the Duke of Bedford; neither the one nor the other were disposed at this juncture to stem the torrent. The Duke was determined not to give the Pelhams so fair an opportunity of mischief, as by setting up the standard of opposition during his father's life; and the treasures which he expected at the King's death, and would not risk losing, he knew would indemnify the delay of his revenge. The Duke of Bedford, who had been driven into contention, not sought it himself, did not feel resentment enough for the loss of power, which he had never much coveted, to make him eager in returning ill-usage; and as he thought himself distinguished by the King's esteem, he affected gratitude to the Master, more than revenge to the Ministers. Pitt and his little faction were rather unsatisfied, than in possession of any title to complaint; and yet from that quarter seemed to lour the first small cloud that might at all obscure the present halcyon season.

The Duke of Argyll

Archibald Campbell, Earl of Isla, was younger brother of the admired John, Duke of Argyle, whom he succeeded in the title, and with whom he had little in common, but the love of command. The elder brother was graceful in his figure, ostentatious in his behaviour, impetuous in his passions; prompt to insult, even where he had wit to wound and eloquence to confound; and what is seldomer seen, a miser as early as a hero. Lord Isla was slovenly in his person, mysterious, not to say with an air of guilt in his deportment, slow, steady where suppleness did not better answer his purpose, revengeful, and if artful, at least not ingratiating. He loved power too well to hazard it by ostentation, and money so little, that he neither spared it to gain friends or to serve them. He attained the sole authority in Scotland, by making himself useful to Sir Robert Walpole, and preserved it by being formidable to the Pelhams. The former had disgusted the zealous Whigs in Scotland by throwing himself into the arms of a man of such equivocal principles; the Earl pretended to return it, by breaking with his brother when that Duke quarrelled with Sir Robert: yet one chief cause of Walpole's fall was attributed to Lord Isla's betraying to his brother the Scotch boroughs entrusted to his management in 1741. It must be told, that Sir Robert Walpole always said, he did not accuse him. Lord Isla's power received a little shock by Lord Tweedale's and Lord Stair's return to Court on that Minister's retreat; but like other of Lord Orford's chief associates, Lord Isla soon recovered his share of the spoils of that Administration. He had been ill with the Queen (of whom he knew he was sure while he was sure of Sir

Robert Walpole) from his attachment to Lady Suffolk: he connected with Lord Granville, while Lord Granville had any sway; and as easily united with the Pelhams, when power was their common pursuit, and the humiliation of the Duke and the Duke of Bedford the object of their common resentment; for common it was, though the very cause that naturally presented them to the Duke of Argyle's hatred, their zeal and services, ought at least to have endeared them to the brothers.

By a succession of these intrigues, the Duke of Argyle had risen to supreme authority in Scotland: the only instance wherein he declined the full exertion of it was, when it might have been of service to the master who delegated it, in the time of the Rebellion: at that juncture he posted to London: the King was to see that he was not in Rebellion; the Rebels, that he was not in arms. But when this double conduct was too gross not to be censured, he urged a Scotch law in force against taking up arms without legal authority; so scrupulously attached did he pretend to be to the constitution of his country, that he would not arm in defence of the essence of its laws against the letter of them. In his private life he had more merit, except in the case of his wife, whom having been deluded into marrying without a fortune, he punished by rigorous and unrelaxed confinement in Scotland. He had a great thirst for books; a head admirably turned to mechanics; was a patron of ingenious men, a promoter of discoveries, and one of the first great encouragers of planting in England; most of the curious exotics which have been familiarized to this climate being introduced by him. But perhaps too much has been said on the subject of a man, who, though at the head of his country for several years, had so little great either in himself or in his views, and consequently contributed so little to any great events, that posterity will probably interest themselves very slightly in the history of his fortunes.

The Pretender's Family and Court

The English Court at Rome was as little free from intestine divisions as the Hanoverian Court at London. The Cardinal of York, whose devotion preserved him from disobedience to his father as little as his princely character had preserved him from devotion, had entirely abandoned himself to the government of an Abbé, who soon grew displeasing to the old Pretender. Commands, remonstrances, requests, had no effect on the obstinacy of the young Cardinal. The father, whose genius never veered towards compliance, insisted on the dismission of the Abbé. Instead of parting with his favourite, the young Cardinal with his minion left Rome abruptly, and with little regard to the dignity of his Purple. The Holy See, which was sunk to having few more important negotiations to manage, interested itself in the reconciliation, and the haughty young Eminence of York was induced to return to his father, but without being obliged to sacrifice his Abbé. As I shall not often have occasion to mention this imaginary Court, I will here give a cursory picture of it.

The Chevalier de St. George is tall, meagre, melancholy in his aspect. Enthusiasm and disappointment have stamped a solemnity on his person, which rather creates pity than respect: he seems the phantom, which good-nature, divested of reflection, conjures up, when we think on the misfortunes, without the demerits, of Charles the First. Without the particular features of any Stuart, the Chevalier has the strong lines and fatality of air peculiar to them all. From the first moment I saw him, I never doubted the legitimacy of his birth—a belief not likely to occasion any scruples in one whose principles directly tend to approve dethroning the most genuine Prince, whose religion, and whose maxims of government are incompatible with the liberty of his country.

He never gave the world very favourable impressions of him: in Scotland, his behaviour was far from heroic. At Rome, where to be a good Roman Catholic it is by no means necessary to be very religious, they have little esteem for him: it is not at home that they are fond of martyrs and confessors. But it was his ill-treatment of the Princess Sobieski, his wife, that originally disgusted the Papal Court. She, who to zeal for Popery had united all its policy, who was lively, insinuating, agreeable, and enterprising, was fervently supported by that Court, when she could no longer endure the mortifications that were offered to her by Hay and his wife, the titular Counts of Inverness, to whom the Chevalier had entirely resigned himself. The Pretender retired to Bologna, but was obliged to sacrifice his favourites, before he could re-establish himself at Rome. His next Prime Minister was Murray, nominal Earl of Dunbar, brother of the Viscount Stormont, and of the celebrated Solicitor-General. He was a man of artful abilities, graceful in his person and manner, and very attentive to please. He had distinguished himself before he was of age, in the last Parliament of Queen Anne, and chose to attach himself to the unsuccessful party abroad, and for whose re-establishment he had co-operated. He was, when still very young, appointed Governor to the young Princes, but growing suspected by the warm Jacobites of some correspondence with Sir Robert Walpole, and not entering into the favourite project of Prince Charles's expedition to Scotland, he thought fit to leave that Court, and retire to Avignon, where, while he was regarded as lukewarm to the cause, from his connection with the Solicitor-General here, the latter was not at all less suspected of devotion to a Court where his brother had so long been First Minister.

The characters of the Pretender's sons are hitherto imperfectly known; yet both have sufficiently worn the characteristics of the house of Stuart, bigotry and obstinacy and want of judgment. The eldest set out with a resolution of being very resolute, but it soon terminated in his being only wrong-headed.

The most apparent merit of the Chevalier's Court is the great regularity of his finances, and the economy of his exchequer. His income before the Rebellion was about £23,000 a year, arising chiefly from pensions from the Pope and from Spain, from contributions from England, and some irregular donations from other Courts. Yet his payments were not only most exact, but he had saved a large sum of money, which was squandered on the unfortunate attempt in Scotland. Besides the loss of a Crown, to which he thought he had a just title, besides a series of disappointments from his birth, besides that mortifying rotation of friends, to which his situation has constantly exposed him, as often as faction and piques and baffled ambition have driven the great men of England to apply to or desert his forlorn hopes, he has, in the latter part of his life, seen his own little Court and his parental affections torn to pieces, and tortured by the seeds of faction, sown by that master-hand of sedition, the famous Bolingbroke, who insinuated into their councils a project for the Chevalier's resigning his pretensions to his eldest son, as more likely to conciliate the affections of the English to his family. The father and the ancient Jacobites never could be induced to relish this scheme. The boy and his adherents embraced it as eagerly as if the father had really a Crown to resign. Slender as their Cabinet was, these parties divided it; and when I was at Rome, Lord Winton was a patriot at that Court, and the ragged type of a minority which was comprehended in his single person.

1753
Louis XV

By the very loyal, consequences equally threatening were feared from a new amour of the King of France, who had taken a mistress of Irish extraction, the daughter of a shoemaker, formerly a life-guardman: her name, Murphy, and of signal beauty. Madame Pompadour was a friend to peace and England. This deviation in the Monarch's constancy was, however, of transitory duration. With scarce complaisance, with no affection, he had for many years confined himself to his homely, elderly, unattractive queen. All the intrigues of a gallant Court, or of interested factions, had not been able to undermine his conjugal regularity, for it was no more. Accident threw him into the arms of Madame de Mailly, a sensible woman, a fine figure, but very plain; he demanded not beauty, and became as regular as with the Queen. To engage him more, that is, to govern him, Madame de Mailly associated to their suppers her sister, Madame de Vintimille, a woman of great wit, but exceedingly ill-proportioned with beauty—a great oversight in an ugly woman who had dispossessed an ugly one. The coadjutrix soon displaced her introductress; but died in labour; of poison, as the state of intrigues would of course suppose. The Monarch hankered about the same family, and took a third sister, who was gloriously beautiful, and whom he created Duchesse de Chateauroux. In the triumph of her concubinage, the King fell ill at Metz. Fitzjames, Bishop of Soissons, attacked a frightened piety, which was natural and only subdued by constitution. The mistress was not only discarded, but publicly affronted, the Monarch permitting it; and the Queen, who was sent for, made a foolish triumphal entry to thank the Lord for the recovery of the King's soul and body—but as soon as the latter was re-established, the Queen was sent to her prayers, the Bishop to his diocese, and the Duchess was recalled—but died suddenly. Though a jealous sister may be supposed to dispatch a rival, can one believe that Bishops and Confessors poison?

Madame Pompadour, the wife of a *fermier général*, succeeded: grace, beauty, address, art, ambition, all met in that charming woman. She governed him more than he had ever been governed but by Cardinal Fleury: she engaged in all politics, she gave life and agreeableness to all; she amassed vast treasures herself, she was the cause of squandering vast treasures, in varying scenes of pleasure to divert the gloom of a temper which was verging nearer to the age of devotion. The Clergy hated her, for she countenanced the Parliament; the people imputed oppressions to her; the Dauphin, who was a bigot, and who loved his mother, affected to shock her: yet the King, who was the best father in the world, bore with great mildness so unpleasant an attack on royal and parental authority.

Archibald Cameron

[June] 7th. Dr. Archibald Cameron suffered death at Tyburn. He had been forced into the Rebellion by his brother Lochiel, whom he had tried to confine, to prevent his engaging in it: not that Lochiel had taken arms voluntarily: he was a man of great parts, but could not resist the desperate honour which he thought the Pretender did him, in throwing himself into his arms, and demanding his sword and interest. The Doctor, who was a man of learning and very valuable humanity, which he had displayed in endeavours to civilize that part of a barbarous country, and in offices of benevolence to the soldiers employed on the Highland roads, and to the mine-adventurers established at Strontean, was torn from these sweet duties, from his profession, from a beloved and large family, and attended his rash brother at Prestonpans and Falkirk, escaped with him, and was appointed physician to Lochiel's regiment in the French service. He ventured back, was taken as mentioned above, and underwent a forced death with as much composure as a philosopher could affect at dying a natural one.

1754

Mr. Pelham

These were the last occurrences in the life of that fortunate Minister, Henry Pelham, who had surmounted every difficulty, but the unhappiness of his own temper. The fullness of his power had only contributed to heighten his peevishness. He supplied the deficiencies of genius by affected virtue; he had removed superiors by treachery, and those of whom he was jealous, by pretexting, or administering to the jealousies of his brother: but the little arts by which he had circumvented greater objects, were not applicable even to his own little passions. He enjoyed the plenitude of his Ministry but a short time, and that short period was a scene of fretfulness. He had made a journey to Scarborough in the summer for scorbutic complaints, but receiving little benefit from a short stay, and being banqueted much on the road, he returned with his blood more disordered. It produced a dangerous boil, which was once thought cured; but he relapsed on the third of March, and died on the sixth, aged near sixty-one.

It would be superfluous to add much to the character already given of him in the former part of these memoires. Thus much may be said with propriety: his abilities, I mean, parliamentary, and his eloquence cleared up, and shone with much greater force, after his power was established. He laid aside his doubling plausibility, which had at once raised and depreciated him, and assumed a spirit and authority that became him well. Considering how much he had made it a point to be Minister, and how much his partizans had proclaimed him the only man worthy of being Minister, he ought to have conferred greater benefits on his country. He had reduced interest and a part of the National Debt; these were his services. He had raised the name of the King, but he had wounded his authority. He concluded an ignominious peace; but the circumstances of the times made it be thought, and perhaps it was, desirable. The desertion of the King in the height of a Rebellion, from jealousy of a man with whom he soon after associated against some of the very men who had deserted with him, will be a lasting blot on his name—let it be remembered as long, that, though he first taught or experienced universal servility in Englishmen, yet he lived without abusing his power, and died poor.

The Writing of History

Having never proposed to write a regular history, but to throw together some anecdotes and characters which might cast a light on the times in which I have lived, and might lead some future and more assiduous historian to an intimate knowledge of the men whose counsels or actions he shall record, I had determined to lay down my pen at the death of that Minister, whose fortune, situation, and genius had superinduced a very new complexion over his country, and who had composed a system of lethargic acquiescence, in which the spirit of Britain, agitated for so many centuries, seemed willingly to repose. But as the numbness of that enchantment has been dispelled by the evanition of the talisman, though so many of its mischievous principles survive, I shall once again endeavour to trace the stream of events to their secret source, though with a pen more unequal than ever to the task. A monkish writer may be qualified to record an age of barbarity and ignorance; Sallust alone was worthy to snatch the rapid episode of Catiline from oblivion; Tacitus, to paint monsters whose lives surpassed caricatura; Livy, to embrace whole ages of patriots and heroes. Though no Catiline, I trust, will rise in my pages, to deform his country by his horrid glory; though our present Minister, notwithstanding he has the monkey disposition of Heliogabalus, is happily without his youth or lusts, and by the character of the age that disposition is systematized into little mischiefs and unbloody treacheries; though we have no succession of incorrupt senators; yet the times beginning to wear in some lights a more respectable face, it will require a steadier hand, and more dignified conceptions, than served to seize and to sketch out the littlenesses and trifles that had characterized the foregoing period.

The style, therefore, of the following sheets will perhaps wear a more serious aspect than I have used before: yet shall I not check a smile now and then at transient follies; nor, as much appropriated as gravity is to an historian, can I conceive how history can always be faithful, if always solemn. Is a palace a perpetual shrine of virtue, or incessantly a tribunal of severity? do not follies predominate in mankind over either virtues or vices? and whoever has been conversant in a Court, does he not know how strongly the cast of it verges towards ridiculous? Besides, I am no historian: I write casual memoires, I draw characters; I preserve anecdotes, which my superiors, the historians of Britain, may enchase into their weighty annals, or pass over at their pleasure. In one point I shall not vary from the style I have assumed, but shall honestly continue to relate the blemishes of material personages as they enter upon the scene: and whoever knows the interior of affairs, must be sensible to how many more events the faults of statesmen give birth, than are produced by their good intentions.

If I do not forbid myself censure, at least I shall shun that frequent poison of histories, flattery. How has it preponderated in most writers! My Lord Bacon was almost as profuse of his incense on the memory of dead Kings, as he was infamous for clouding the living with it. In the reign of Henry the Seventh, the whole strain of his panegyric (and it is more justly to be called so than Pliny's, whose patron was really a good Prince), is to erect that sordid Monarch's tyranny into prudence, nay, his very knavery into policy! Comines, an honester writer, though I fear by the masters whom he pleased, not a much less servile courtier, says, that the virtues of Louis the Eleventh preponderated over his vices! Even Voltaire, who feels for Liberty more than almost any French did, has in a manner purified the dross of adulation, which cotemporary authors had squandered on Louis the Fourteenth, by adopting and refining it after the tyrant was dead. In his war of 1741, he paints that phantom of Royalty, the present King, extinguishing at Metz, with as much energy of concern, as if he was describing the death-bed of a Titus or an Antonine.

But how unpardonable is a flattering history!—if anything can shock one of those mortal divinities (and they must be shocked before they will be corrected), it would be to find that the truth will be related of them at last. Nay, is it not cruel to them to hallow their bad memories? one is sure they will never *hear* truth; shall they not even have a chance for *reading* it?

It may be wondered that I, who know and have drawn the emptiness of present Royalty, should, in the exordium to a new period, in which surely the effulgence of Majesty has not been displayed with any new lustre, detain the reader with reflections on a pageant which has so little operation on the reality of the drama. But I must be pardoned: though I now behold only a withering King, good, as far as acquiescing to whatever is the emergent humour of his people, and by no means the object of jealousy to his subjects, yet I am sensible that, from the prostitution of patriotism, from the art of Ministers who have had the address to exalt the semblance while they depressed the reality of Royalty, and from the bent of the education of the young Nobility, which verges to French maxims and to a military spirit, nay, from the ascendant which the Nobility itself acquires each day in this country, from all these reflections, I am sensible, that prerogative and power have been exceedingly fortified of late within the circle of the Palace; and though fluctuating Ministries by turns exercise the deposit, yet there it is; and whenever a Prince of design and spirit shall sit in the Regal Chair, he will find a bank, a hoard of power, which he may play off most fatally against this constitution. That evil I dread—the steps to that authority, that torrent which I should in vain extend a feeble arm to stem, those steps I mean to follow and record.

My reflections led me early towards, I cannot quite say Republicanism, but to most limited Monarchy; a principle as much ridiculed ever since I came into the world, as the profligacy of false patriots has made patriotism—and from much the same cause. Republicans professed to be saints, and from successful sainthood became usurpers: yet Republicanism, as it tends to promote Liberty, and Patriotism as far as it tends to preserve or restore it, are still godlike principles. A Republican who should be mad, should be execrable enough to endeavour to imbrue his country in blood merely to remove the name of a Monarch, deserves to excite horror; a quiet Republican, who does not dislike to see the shadow of Monarchy, like Banquo's ghost, fill the empty chair of state, that the ambitious, the murderer, the tyrant may not aspire to it; in short, who approves the name of a King, when it excludes the essence; a man of such principles, I hope, may be a good man and an honest; and if he is that, what matters if he is ridiculous? A Republican, who sees monarchy realizing, who observes all orders of men tending to exalt higher what all orders had concurred to depress; who has found that the attempts of the greatest men to divert the torrent, have been turned afterwards to swell it; who knows the inefficacy of all endeavours to thwart the bent of a nation, and who is but too sensible how unequal his own capacity and virtue would be to so heroic a character; such a man may be pardoned, I hope, if he contents himself with the silent suffrage and wishes of his heart, though he has not the parade of martyrs, nor the courage of a Roman, in as un-Roman—(why should it be beneath the dignity of history to say?) in as un-British an age as ever was.

George Washington

In August came news of the defeat of Major Washington in the Great Meadows on the western borders of Virginia: a trifling action, but remarkable for giving date to the war. The encroachments of the French have been already mentioned; but in May they had proceeded to open hostilities. Major Washington with about fifty men attacked one of their parties, and slew the commanding officer. In this skirmish he was supported by an Indian half-king and *twelve* of his subjects, who in the Virginian accounts is called a very considerable monarch.

49

On the third of July, the French being reinforced to the number of nine hundred fell on Washington in a small fort, which they took, but dismissed the Commander with military honours, being willing, as they expressed it in the capitulation, to show that they treated them like friends! In the express which Major Washington dispatched on his preceding little victory, he concluded with these words; 'I heard the bullets whistle, and believe me, there is something charming in the sound.' On hearing of this letter, the King said sensibly, 'He would not say so, if he had been used to hear many.' However, this brave braggart learned to blush for his rodomontade, and desiring to serve General Braddock as Aide-de-camp, acquitted himself nobly.

Lord Gower and Lord Albemarle

At the conclusion of the year deceased two men in great offices, whose deaths made remarked what their lives might have done; how little they were worthy of their exaltation. The one, Lord Gower, Lord Privy Seal, had indeed a large fortune, and commanded boroughs. Lord Albemarle, the other, died suddenly at Paris, where his mistress sold him to that Court. Yet the French Ministry had little to vaunt; while they were purchasing the instructions of our Ambassador, attentive only to acquire the emptiest of their accomplishments, they employed at our Court a man too empty to learn even the dullest of ours. Lord Albemarle made great proficience in the study of their manners, while Monsieur de Mirepoix could not learn even to pronounce the names of one or two of our games at cards, which, however, engaged most of the hours of his negotiation. Our Colonies were to be protected by the copy of a *Petit Maître*; we were to be bullied out of them by an apprentice to whisk! How serious a science, Politics!

1755

Parliamentary Orators

But if this traffic for a partial revolution in a system, still upheld, was scandalously inglorious, at least it called forth a display of abilities that revived the lustre of the House of Commons, and in the point of

eloquence carried it to a height it perhaps had never known. After
so long a dose of genius, there at once appeared near thirty men, of
whom one was undoubtedly a real orator, a few were most masterly,
many very able, not one was a despicable speaker. Pitt, Fox, Murray,
Hume Campbell, Charles Townshend, Lord George Sackville, Henry
Conway, Legge, Sir George Lyttelton, Oswald, George Grenville, Lord
Egmont, Nugent, Doddington, the Lord Advocate of Scotland, Lord
Strange, Beckford, Elliot, Lord Barrington, Sir George Lee, Martin,
Dr. Hay, Northey, Potter, Ellis, Lord Hilsborough, Lord Duplin, and
Sir Francis Dashwood, these men, perhaps, in their several degrees,
comprehended all the various powers of eloquence, art, reasoning,
satire, learning, persuasion, wit, business, spirit, and plain common
sense. Eloquence as an art was but little studied but by Pitt: the
beauties of language were a little and but a little more cultivated,
except by him and his family. Yet the grace and force of words were
so natural to him, that when he avoided them, he almost lost all
excellence. As set speeches were no longer in vogue, except on intro-
ductory or very solemn occasions, the pomp and artful resources of
oratory were in a great measure banished; and the inconveniences
attending long and unpremeditated discourses, must (as I have delivered
them faithfully,) take off from, though they ought to add to, their
merit. Let those who hear me extol, and at the same time find Mr.
Pitt's oration not answer to my encomiums, reflect how bright his
talents would shine, if we saw none of his, but which, like the productions of ancient great masters, had been prepared for his audience,
and had been polished by himself for the admiration of ages! Similes,
and quotations, and metaphors were fallen into disrepute, deservedly:
even the parallels from old story, which, during the virulence against
Sir Robert Walpole, had been so much encouraged, were exhausted
and disregarded. It was not the same case with invectives; in that
respect eloquence was little more chastened. Debates, where no personali-
ties broke out, engaged too little attention. Yet, upon the whole, the
style that prevailed was plain, manly, argumentative; and the liberty
of discussion of all topics in a government so free, and the very newspapers and pamphlets that skimmed or expatiated on all those subjects, and which the most idle and most illiterate could not avoid
perusing, gave an air of knowledge and information to the most
trifling speakers.

I shall not enter into a detail of all the various talents of the men I
mentioned; the genius and characters of many of them have been

marked already in different parts of this work. Most of them were more or less imperfect; I pretend to consider the whole number but as different shades of oratory. Northey saw clearly, but it was for a very little way. Lord Strange was the most absurd man that ever existed with a very clear head: his distinctions were seized as rapidly as others advance positions. Nugent's assertions would have made everybody angry, if they had not made everybody laugh; but he had a debonair jollity that pleased, and though a bombast speaker, was rather extravagant from his vociferation, than from his arguments, which were often very solid. Dr. Hay's manner and voice resembled Lord Granville's, not his matter; Lord Granville was novelty itself; Dr. Hay seldom said anything new; his speeches were fair editions of the thoughts of other men: he should always have opened a debate! Oswald overflowed with a torrent of sense and logic: Doddington was always searching for wit; and what was surprising, generally found it. Oswald hurried argument along with him; Doddington teased it to accompany him. Sir George Lyttelton and Legge were as opposite in their manners; the latter concise and pointed; the former, diffuse and majestic. Legge's speeches seemed the heads of chapters to Sir George Lyttelton's dissertations. Sir Robert Walpole said of Legge that he had no rubbish in his head. Lord Duplin aimed at nothing but understanding business and explaining it. Sir Francis Dashwood, who loved to know, and who cultivated a roughness of speech, affected to know no more than what he had learned from an unadorned understanding. George Grenville and Hume Campbell were tragic speakers of very different kinds; the latter far the superior. Grenville's were tautologous lamentations; Campbell's bold reprehensions. Had they been engaged in a conspiracy, Grenville, like Brutus, would have struck and wept; Campbell would have rated him for weeping. The six other chief speakers may, from their ages and rank in the House, be properly thrown into two classes.

Mr. Conway soothed and persuaded; Lord George Sackville informed and convinced; Charles Townshend astonished; but was too severe to persuade, and too bold to convince. Conway seemed to speak only because he thought his opinion might be of service; Lord George because he knew that others misled, or were misled; Charles Townshend, neither caring whether himself or others were in the right, only spoke to show how well he could adorn a bad cause, or demolish a good one. It was frequent with him, as soon as he had done speaking, to run to the opposite side of the House, and laugh with those he had attacked, at those who had defended. One loved the first, one feared the second, one admired the last without the least mixture of esteem. Mr. Conway had a cold reserve, which seemed only to veil goodness: Lord George, with a frankness in his speech, had a mystery in his conduct, which was far from inviting. Charles Townshend had such openness in all his behaviour, that he seemed to think duplicity the simplest conduct: he made the innocence of others look like art. But what superiority does integrity contract, when even uniformity of acting could exalt so many men above the most conspicuous talents that appeared in so rhetorical an age! Mr. Townshend was perhaps the only man who had ever genius enough to preserve reason and argument in a torrent of epigrams, satire, and antithesis!

The other Parliamentary chiefs were as variously distinguished by their abilities. Pitt, illustrious as he was in the House of Commons, would have shone still more in an assembly of inferior capacity: his talents for dazzling were exposed to whoever did not fear his sword and abuse, or could detect the weakness of his arguments. Fox was ready for both. Murray, who, at the beginning of the session, was awed by Pitt, finding himself supported by Fox, surmounted his fears, and convinced the House, and Pitt too, of his superior abilities: he grew most uneasy to the latter. Pitt could only attack, Murray only defend: Fox, the boldest and ablest champion, was still more formed to worry: but the keenness of his sabre was blunted by the difficulty with which he drew it from the scabbard; I mean, the hesitation and ungracefulness of his delivery took off from the force of his arguments. Murray, the brightest genius of the three, had too much and too little of the lawyer: he refined too much, and could wrangle too little for a popular assembly. Pitt's figure was commanding; Murray's engaging from a decent openness; Fox's dark and troubled—yet the latter was the only agreeable man: Pitt could not unbend; Murray in private was inelegant; Fox was cheerful, social, communicative. In conversation, none of them had wit; Murray never had: Fox had in his speeches from clearness of head and asperity of argument: Pitt's wit was genuine, not tortured into the service, like the quaintnesses of my Lord Chesterfield.

I have endeavoured in this book (and consequently shall be much more concise in others, on Parliamentary Debates,) to give an idea of the manner and genius of our chief orators, particularly of Mr. Pitt, the most celebrated: his greatest failure was in argument, which made him, contrary to the rule of great speakers, almost always commence the Debate: he spoke too often, and he spoke too long. Of the above-recorded speeches, his first, on the Address, was sublime and various; on the Army, at once florid and alarming; on the Militia, clear, un-adorned, and like a man of business: that against Hume Campbell, most bitter; the last, full of wit; but being hurt at the reflections on his pomp and invective, he took up in the rest of that session a style of plain and scarce elevated conversation, that had not one merit of any of his preceding harangues.

1756

Lord Bute and the Princess Dowager

June 4th.—The Prince of Wales attained the age prescribed for his majority; by which the Regency Bill remains only a dangerous precedent of power to posterity—no longer so to us, for whose sub-jections it was artfully, though, by the grace of God, vainly calculated! This epoch, however, brought to light the secrets of a Court, where hitherto everything had been transacted with mysterious decency. The Princess had conducted herself with great respect to the King, with appearance of impartiality to Ministers and factions. If she was not cordial to the Duke, or was averse to his friends, it had been imputed less to any hatred adopted from her husband's prejudices, than to jealousy of the government of her son: if the world should choose to ascribe her attention for him to maternal affection, they were at liberty; she courted and watched him neither more nor less for their conjectures. It now at last appeared that paternal tenderness or ambition were not the sole passions that engrossed her thoughts. It had already been whispered that the assiduity of Lord Bute at Leicester House, and his still more frequent attendance in the gardens at Kew and Carlton House, were less addressed to the Prince of Wales than to his mother. The eagerness of the Pages of the Backstairs to let her know whenever Lord Bute arrived, a mellowness in her German accent as often as she spoke to him, and that was often and long, and a more than usual swimmingness in her eyes, contributed to dispel the ideas that had been conceived of the rigour of her widow-hood. On the other hand, the favoured personage, naturally ostentatious of his person, and of haughty carriage, seemed by no means desirous of concealing his conquest. His bows grew more theatric, his graces contracted some meaning, and the veins in the calf of his leg were constantly displayed in the eyes of the poor captivated Princess, and of a Court, who maliciously affected to wonder that they preserved so much roundness. Indeed, the nice observers of the Court-thermometer, who often foresee a change of weather before it actually happens, had long thought that her Royal Highness, susceptible of warmer sensations, was likely to choose younger Ministers than that formal piece of empty mystery, Cresset; or the matron-like decorum of Sir George Lee.

Her eyes had often twinkled intelligibly enough at her countryman, Prince Lobkowitz: yet perhaps she had never passed the critical barrier, if her simple husband, when he took up the character of the Regent's gallantry, had not forced an air of intrigue even upon his wife. When he affected to retire into gloomy *allées* with Lady Middlesex, he used to bid the Princess walk with Lord Bute. As soon as the Prince was dead, they walked more and more, in honour of his memory.

The favour of Lord Bute was scarce sooner known, than the connections of Pitt and Legge with him. The mystery of Pitt's breach with Fox was at once unravelled; and a Court secret of that nature was not likely long to escape the penetration of Legge, who wormed himself into every intrigue where his industry and subservience could recommend him—yet Legge had not more application to power, than Newcastle's jealousy of it. Such an entrenchment round the successor alarmed him. It was determined in his little council that the moment the Prince of Wales should be of age, he should be taken from his mother; but the secret evaporating, intimations by various channels were conveyed to the Duke of Newcastle and to the Chancellor, how much the Prince would resent any such advice being given to the King, and that it would not be easy to carry it into execution. The Prince lived shut up with his mother and Lord Bute; and must have thrown them under some difficulties: their connection was not easily reconcileable to the devotion which they had infused into the Prince; the Princess could not wish him always present, and yet dreaded his being out of her sight. His brother Edward, who received a thousand mortifications, was seldom suffered to be with him; and Lady Augusta, now a woman, was, to facilitate some privacy for the Princess, dismissed from supping with her mother, and sent back to cheesecakes with her little sister Elizabeth, on pretence that meat at night would fatten her too much.

The Ministers, too apt to yield when in the right, were now obstinate in the wrong place; and without knowing how to draw the King out of the difficulty into which they were pushing him, advised this extraordinary step. On May 31st, Lord Waldegrave, as the last act of his office of Governor, was sent with letters of the same tenor to the Prince and to his mother, to acquaint them that the Prince, being now of age, the King, who had ever shown the greatest kindness and affection for him, had determined to give him £40,000 a year, would settle an establishment for him, of the particulars of which he should be informed, and that his Majesty had ordered the apartments of the late Prince at Kensington and of the Queen at St. James's to be fitted up for him: that the King would take Prince Edward too, and give him an allowance of £5,000 a year.

After a little consult in their small cabinet, both Prince and Princess sent answers in writing, drawn up, as was believed, by Legge, and so artfully worded, that the supposition was probable. The Prince described himself as penetrated by the goodness of his Majesty, and receiving with the greatest gratitude what his Majesty in his parental affection was pleased to settle on him; but he entreated his Majesty not to divide him from his mother, which would be a most sensible affliction to both. The answer of the Princess marked, that she had observed with the greatest satisfaction the impression which his Majesty's *consideration* of the Prince had made on him; and she expressed much sensibility of all the King's kindness to her. On the article of the separation she said not a word.

What now was the King to do? The Prince had accepted the allowance as *given*; and had refused to leave his mother, which had not been made a *condition* of the gift. Was the gift to be revoked, because the Prince had natural affection? Was the whole message to be carried into execution, and a young man, of age by Act of Parliament, to be taken by force, and detained a prisoner in the palace? What law would justify such violence? Who would be the agents of such violence? His Majesty himself, and the late Prince of Wales, had furnished the Prince with precedents of mutinying against the Crown with impunity. How little the Ministers, who had planned the first step, knew what to advise for the second, was plain, from their giving no further advice for above a month; and from the advice which they did give then, and from the perplexity in which they remained for two months more, and from the ignominious result of the whole transaction, both to the King and to themselves at last.

Minorca: Richelieu and Blakeney

During these agitations of the Court, which were little known, and less talked of, the attention of the public was directed to Minorca. Sixteen thousand French had landed there without opposition; no part of the island, indeed, was capable of defence, but Fort St. Philip. The inhabitants received the invaders even with alacrity, though their privileges had been preserved under the English Government, and though they enjoyed all the folly of their religion without the tyranny of it. The Jews and Greeks established there behaved with more gratitude: of the natives, sixteen only adhered to the English. The magistrates hurried to take new oaths, and to welcome the singular personage sent to be a conqueror. This was the Duc de Richelieu; a man, who had early surprised the fashionable world by his adventures, had imposed on it by his affectations, had dictated to it by his wit and insolent agreeableness, had often tried to govern it by his intrigues, and who would be the hero of the age, if histories were novels, or women wrote history. His first campaign was hiding himself at fourteen under the Duchess of Burgundy's bed, from whence he was led to the Bastille, and whither he had returned four several times. A genius so enterprising could not fail to captivate the ladies: the Duchess of Modena, the Regent's daughter, would fain have preferred him to the *triste* glory of reigning over an acre of territory with a dismal Italian husband. Richelieu was soon after sent to, and as soon recalled from Vienna, for carrying a black lamb in his state-coach at midnight to sacrifice to the moon, in order to obtain a recruit of vigour. The very exploit gained him as many hearts as if the boon had been granted. Yet, with an advantageous person and adventurous disposition, he was supposed to want the two heroic attributes that generally compose a woman's Alexander. So much was his courage questioned, that he was driven to fight and kill the Prince of Lixin in the trenches at Philipsbourg.

Ruling the female world, and growing exhausted with the fatigues of his government, he at last thought of reposing himself on the lesser care of the French Monarchy: and making himself necessary to the pleasure of the mistresses, the Duchesse de Chateauroux and Madame Pompadour, he attained considerable weight in a Government where trifling qualities are no disrecommendation. Embarking with all the luxurious pomp of an Asiatic grandee, this genteel but wrinkled Adonis sailed to besiege a rock, and to attack a rough veteran, who was supposed to think that he had little business left but to do his duty and die. His name was Blakeney: he had passed through all the steps of his profession, and had only attained the sweets of it by living to be past the enjoyment of them. He was remarkably generous and disinterested, and of great bravery, which had been but little remarked. Having the government of the Castle of Stirling in the last Rebellion, he was summoned to give it up as soon as the King's troops were defeated at Falkirk: but he replied, the loss of that battle made no alteration in his orders—yet he had then provision but for three weeks. This gallantry, which had been overlooked for his sake, was now recollected and extolled for our own: the most sanguine hopes were conceived—Minorca was regarded as the nation's possession, Scotland as the King's: if the former was lost, it passed to an enemy—Stirling would only have gone to another *friend*. As every day brought out the weakness of the garrison of Mahon, all hope was contracted to the person of Blakeney: yet in no neglect were the Ministry more culpable, for he proved to be superannuated.

The French covered the siege with a fleet of twelve men-of-war. Accounts were impatiently expected here of the arrival of Admiral Byng in those seas with his squadron, and with succours which he was ordered to take in at Gibraltar, and which it was hoped he would be able to fling into St. Philip's. If he could effect that service, and disperse or demolish the French fleet, there was no doubt but the troops on the island must remain prisoners of war, or be the victims of their attempt; for as yet they had made little progress. Having landed on the opposite side of the island, they found the roads almost impracticably rocky; and if cut off from supplies from the continent, they must have perished by hunger, Minorca by no means supplying the natives with superabundance. The heats, too, were now coming on, which would be insupportable to new constitutions, to the natural impatience of the French, and still more to an effeminate General. Hitherto their transports had passed and repassed in full security. The Mediterranean, where we so long had reigned, seemed abandoned by the English.

The truth was, the clamours of the merchants, sometimes reasonable, always self-interested, terrified the Duke of Newcastle; and while, to prevent their outcries in the City of London, he minced the Navy of England into cruisers and convoys, every other service was neglected.

I say it with truth (I say it with concern, considering who was his associate), this was the year of the worst Administration that I have seen in England; for now Newcastle's incapacity was left to its full play. While conjoined with Sir Robert Walpole, the attention of the latter to the security of the House of Brunswick, and to the preservation of public tranquillity, prevented the mischiefs that the Duke's insufficience might have occasioned. If Lord Granville, his next coadjutor, was rash and dangerous, yet he ventured with spirit, and had great ideas and purposes in view. He provided not the means of execution, but an heroic plan was not wanting; and if he improperly provoked some allies, he stuck at nothing to engross the whole cooperation of others. Mr. Pelham was too timorous not to provide against complaint: his life was employed in gathering up the slips of his brother. But now Fox was called in to support a Government, from a share in which it was determined he should be excluded, and every part of which, where he had influence, it was a measure with Newcastle to weaken, the consequences could not but be fatal—and fatal they were! Indeed, Fox himself was not totally excusable. He came in, despairing of the prosperity of his country; and neither conversant in, nor attentive to the province allotted to him; he thought too much of wresting the remains of power from his competitors. He had neither the patriotism which forms a virtuous character, nor the love of fame which composes a shining one, and often supplies the place of the other. His natural bent was the love of power, with a soul generous and profuse; but growing a fond father, he became a provident father—and from a provident father to a rapacious man, the transition was but too easy!

The Age

As I shall soon be obliged to open a blacker scene than what has hitherto employed my pen, I will take leave of the preceding period with these few remarks. Considering how seldom the world is blessed with a government really good, and that the best are generally but negatively good, I am inclined to pronounce the times of which I have been writing, happy. Every art and system that brings advantage to the country was *permitted*: commerce was in no shape checked: liberty, not being wanton, nay, being complaisant, was not restrained. The Church was moderate, and, when the Ministry required it, yielding. If the Chancellor was ravenous, and arbitrary, and ambitious, he moved too deliberately and too gravely, to bring on any eminent mischief. If the Duke of Newcastle was fond of power, and capricious, and fickle, and false, they were the whims of a child: he circumscribed the exertion of his pomp to laying perhaps the first stone of a building at Cambridge, for a benefaction to which he was forced to borrow a hundred pounds. His jealousy was not of the privileges of Parliament, but lest some second among his favourites should pay more court to his first favourite than to him; and if he shifted his confidence, and raised but to depress, and was communicative but to betray, he moved in a narrow circle, and the only victims of his whims were men who had shifted and betrayed as often, and who deserved no better fortune. If the Duke was haughty and rigorous, he was satisfied with acting within the sphere of the Army, and was content to govern it, not to govern by it. If the King was too partial to Hanover, and was unnecessarily profuse of subsidies to Germany, perhaps it was the only onerous grievance; and the King, who did no more harm, and the Ministers who by vailing to this passion, purchased the power of doing no more harm, certainly constituted no very bad Government. The occasions of war called forth another complexion—but we must proceed with a little regularity.

Admiral Byng

July 26th.—The prisoners arrived at Portsmouth; Mr. Byng was immediately committed to close confinement. His younger brother who went to meet him, was so struck with the abuse he found wherever he passed, that he fell ill on the first sight of the Admiral, and died next day in convulsions. Byng himself expressed no emotions but of surprise at the rigour of his treatment, persisting in declarations of having beaten the French. West, whose behaviour had been most gallant, was soon distinguished from his chief, and was carried to Court by Lord Anson. The King said to West, 'I am glad to hear you have done your duty so well; I wish every body else had!' Anson himself did not escape so honourably: his incapacity grew the general topic of ridicule; and he was joined in all the satiric prints with his father-in-law, Newcastle, and Fox. A new species of this manufacture now first appeared, invented by George Townshend: they were caricaturas on cards. The original one, which had amazing vent, was of

Newcastle and Fox, looking at each other, and crying, with Peachum, in the Beggar's Opera, *'Brother, brother, we are both in the wrong.'* On the Royal Exchange a paper was affixed, advertising, *'Three king-doms to be let; inquire of Andrew Stone, broker, in Lincoln's-Inn-fields.'*

From Portsmouth, Byng, strictly guarded, at once to secure him from the mob and inflame their resentment, was transferred to Green-wich. His behaviour continued so cheerfully firm and unconcerned, that those who thought most moderately of his conduct, thought full as moderately of his understanding. Yet, if *he* could be allowed a judge, Lord Anson had, in the year 1755, given the strongest testimonial in Byng's favour, recommending him particularly for an essential service, as one whose head and heart would always answer. As a forerunner to the doom of the Admiral, so much demanded from, and so much intended by the Ministry, General Fowke was brought to his trial for disobedience of orders in refusing the regiment for Minorca. He pleaded the latitude and discretion allowed to him by his orders, and the imminent danger of his important government. Though the danger of that was increased by the probability that France would either offer Minorca to purchase the alliance of Spain, or assistance to recover Gibraltar, yet Fowke found neither efficient to save him; no, nor the diversity of opinions in his Judges; yet it was plain from their sentence, that they by no means thought he came under the rigour of the law, condemning him only to be suspended for a year, for having mistaken his orders. When a man is tried for an absolute breach of orders, and appears only to have mistaken them, in equity one should think that punishment ought to fall on those who gave the orders. However, as the mob was to be satiated with victims, that the real guilty might escape, Fowke was broken by the King, and his regiment given to Jefferies.

The next symptom of discontent was an address to the King from Dorsetshire, demanding an inquiry into the loss of Minorca, and justice on the culpable. This flame spread: the counties of Huntingdon, Buck-ingham, Bedford, Suffolk, Shropshire, Surrey, Somerset, and Lan-cashire, with the great towns, as Bristol, Cheshire, Leominster, and others, followed the example, and directed their members to promote the inquiry. But the strongest and most dictatorial was that presented from the City of London; to which the trembling Ministers persuaded the King to pledge his royal word that he would save no delinquent from justice. A promise that, being dictated by men secure of the Parliament, plainly indicated on what class of criminals punishment was not designed to be inflicted. The Duke of Newcastle, indeed, could with more propriety than the rest engage the King in a promise, seemingly indefinite, he, who with a volubility of timorous folly, when a deputation of the city had made representations to him against the Admiral, blurted out, 'Oh! indeed he shall be tried immediately, he shall be hanged directly.'

The Czarina Elizabeth

The Czarina was an amiable woman of no great capacity. She had been deprived of a throne to which she had pretensions, and had passed her youth in the terror which must accompany such a claim in a despotic empire, where, if civilized manners were stealing in, humanity to a competitor was one of the last arts of which they were likely to find or adopt a pattern. Yet she had been treated with great lenity, and, which perhaps was still more extraordinary, as the addition of gratitude, another virtue, made the imitation still more difficult, returned it. Her first transport on her rapid elevation was devout mercy; she made a vow never to put any person to death, and adhered to it; Siberia and the prisons, during her reign, were crowded with criminals, tortured, but never executed. She not only spared the little dethroned Czar, John, and had him educated with great care but was as indulgent as she could be with safety to her rival, the Princess Anne, his mother. With so much tenderness of heart, it was not wonderful that her heart was entirely tender—and how slight was that unbounded abuse of power, which only tended to gratify an unbounded inclination! Let us compare the daughters of two ferocious men, and see which was the sovereign of a civilized nation, which of a barbarous one. Both were Elizabeths. The daughter of Peter was absolute, yet spared a competitor and a rival; and thought the person of an Empress had sufficient allurements for as many of her subjects as she chose to honour with the communication. Elizabeth of England could neither forgive the claim of Mary Stuart nor her charms, but ungenerously imprisoned her when imploring protection, and without the sanction of either despotism or law sacrificed Mary to her great and little jealousy. Yet this Elizabeth piqued herself on chastity; and while she practised every ridiculous art of coquetry to be admired at an unseemly age, kept off lovers whom she encouraged, and neither gratified her own desires nor their ambition—who can help preferring the honest, open-hearted, barbarian Empress?

The Duke of Newcastle

When all was adjusted, the Duke of Newcastle resigned, November 11th. As he retired *without terrors* and *with parade*, it was easy to penetrate his hopes of returning to Court. It was assiduously propagated in all the public papers, that he departed without place or pension; and his enormous estate, which he had sunk from thirty to thirteen thousand pounds a year, by every ostentatious vanity, and on every womanish panic, between cooks, mobs, and apothecaries, was now represented by his tools as wasted in the cause of the Government. To show how *unrewarded* he chose to relinquish the Administration, this was the catalogue of his disinterestedness. His Dukedom was entailed on his nephew, Lord Lincoln; the only one conferred by George the Second. Another nephew, Mr. Shelley, had the reversion of the Pipe Office. His cousin, young T. Pelham, already of the Board of Trade, got another reversion in the Custom House. His creature, Sir George Lyttelton, was indemnified with a Peerage. His secretary, Mr. West, was rewarded with a reversion for himself and son. Jones, a favourite clerk, and nephew of the Chancellor, had another reversion. An Irish Earldom was given to Mr. O'Brien.

All this being granted, his Grace retired to Claremont, where, for about a fortnight, he played at being a country gentleman. Guns and green frocks were bought, and at past sixty he affected to turn sportsman; but getting wet in his feet, he hurried back to London in a fright, and his country was once more blessed with his assistance.

1757

Damiens

A century had now passed since reason had begun to attain that ascendant in the affairs of the world, to conduct which it had been granted to man six thousand years ago. If religions and governments were still domineered by prejudices, if creeds that contradict logic, or tyrannies that enslave multitudes to the caprice of one, were not yet exploded, novel absurdities at least were not broached; or if propagated, produced neither persecutors nor martyrs. Methodism made fools, but they did not arrive to be saints; and the histories of past ages describing massacres and murders, public executions of violence, and the more private though not less horrid arts of poison and daggers, began to be regarded almost as romances. Caesar Borgia seemed little less fabulous than Orlando; and whimsical tenures of manors were not more in disuse, than sanguinary methods of preserving or acquiring empires. No Prime Ministers perished on a scaffold, no heretics in the flames; a Russian Princess spared her competitor; even in Turkey the bow-string had been relaxed—alas! frenzy revived in France the credibility of assassination; guilt renewed in England machinations of scarce a whiter dye.

The contests between the Parliament and the Clergy about the Bull *Unigenitus* were still carried on in France. The conduct of the former was such a happy composition of good sense and temper, that they neither deserted their duty under oppression, nor sought to inflame the populace to support them against their oppressors. Even the Clergy were blessed with more moderation than is usual in such contentions; and, what was as lucky, had no able heads to direct them. The Court of Rome, instead of profiting of these divisions, had used its influence to compose them. Benedict the Fourteenth then sat in the Apostolic Chair; a man in whom were united all the amiable qualities of a Prince and a Pastor: he had too much sense to govern the Church by words, too much goodness to rule his dominions by force. Amid the pomp of Popery he laughed at form, and by the mildness of his virtue made fanaticism, of whatever sect, odious. Yet this venerable Pontiff, now sinking under the weight of fourscore years, was at last surprised into, or perhaps never knew that his name was used in, issuing a Bull to enforce, under pain of damnation, the acceptance of the Bull *Unigenitus*. Louis the Fifteenth was persuaded to use that most solemn act of their government, a Bed of Justice, to compel the Parliament to register the Papal Ordinance. The greater part of the members preferred resigning their employments. The King had taken this step in one of those relapses into weakness which his constitution furnished, rather than a want of understanding. The Dauphin was a far more uniform bigot. It is related of him, that about a year before this period, reading the life of Nero, he said, '*Ma foi, c'étoit le plus grand scélérat du monde! il ne lui manquoit que d'être Janseniste.*' And he had even gone so far as to tell his father, 'that were he King, and the Pope should bid him lay down his Crown, he would obey.' The King, with a tender shrewdness, said 'and if he should bid you take mine from me, would you?'

The King not being constant in such steady obedience to the Clergy, they had much aspersed him, and traduced his life and government. The partizans of the Parliament loved him as little; and when he passed through Paris to hold his Bed of Justice, he was received with sullen coldness. One woman alone crying *Vive le Roi!* was thrown down and trampled to death by the mob. In such a disposition, it was almost extraordinary that no fanatic was found to lift the arm of violence; a madman supplied the part, without inviting Heaven to an association of murder.

January 5th.—Between five and six in the evening the King was getting into his coach to go to Trianon. A man, who had lurked about the colonnades for two days, pushed up to the coach, jostled the Dauphin, and stabbed the King under the right arm with a long knife; but the King having two thick coats, the blade did not penetrate deep. The King was surprised, but thinking the man had only pushed against him, said, *'Le coquin m'a donné un furieux coup de poing'*— but putting his hand to his side and feeling blood, he said, *'Il m'a blessé; qu'on le saississe, et qu'on ne lui fasse point de mal.'* The King was carried to bed; the wound proved neither mortal nor dangerous; but strong impressions, and not easily to be eradicated, must have been made on a mind gloomy and superstitious. The title of *Well-beloved* could but faintly balance the ideas of Henry the Third stabbed, of Henry the Fourth stabbed, of enraged Jesuits, and an actual wound. Yet all the satisfaction that the most minute investigation of circumstances could give, and that tortures could wrest from the assassin, was obtained.

Damiens, the criminal, appeared clearly to be mad. He had been footman to several persons, had fled for a robbery, had returned to Paris from a dark and restless habit of mind; and from some preposterous avidity of horrid fame, and from one of those wonderful contradictions of the human mind, a man aspired to renown that had descended to theft. Yet in this dreadful complication of guilt and frenzy, there was room for compassion. The unfortunate wretch was sensible of the predominance of his black temperament; and the very morning of the assassination, asked for a surgeon to let him blood; and to the last gasp of being, persisted that he should not have committed his crime, if he had been blooded. What the miserable man suffered is not to be described. When first seized, and carried into the guard-chamber, the Garde-des-sceaux and the Duc d'Ayen ordered the tongs to be heated, and pieces of flesh torn from his legs, to make him declare his accomplices. The industrious art used to preserve his life was not less than the refinement of torture by which they meaned to take it away. The inventions to form the bed on which he lay, (as the wounds on his leg prevented him standing,) that his health might in no shape be affected, equalled what a refining tyrant would have sought to indulge his own luxury.

When carried to his dungeon, Damiens was wrapped up in mattresses, lest despair might tempt him to dash his brains out—but his madness was no longer precipitate. He even sported, horridly sported, with indicating variety of innocent persons as his accomplices; and sometimes, more harmlessly, with playing the fool with his judges. In no instance he sunk either under terror or anguish. The very morning on which he was to endure the question, when told of it, he said with the coolest intrepidity, *'La journée sera rude'*—after it, insisted on wine with his water, saying, *'Il faut ici de la force,'* and at the accomplishment of his tragedy, studied and prolonged on the precedent of Ravaillac's, he supported all with unrelaxed firmness; and even unremitted torture of four hours, which succeeded to his being two hours and a half under the question, forced from him but some momentary yells —a lamentable spectacle; and perhaps a blameable one. Too severe pains cannot be used to eradicate the infernal crime of holy assassination; but what punishments can prevent madness? Would not one rather stifle under a feather bed, than draw out on the rack a being infected with a frenzy of guilt and heroism?

King George ordered Mr. Pitt to send a compliment on the French King's escape, which was conveyed by the Spanish Minister, and was handsomely received and answered.

Admiral Byng

Accordingly, January 29th, Mr. Byng was summoned to hear his sentence. He went with that increase of animated tranquillity which a man must feel who sees a period to his sufferings, and the rays of truth and justice bursting in at last upon his innocence. His Judges were so aware of the grounds he had for this presumption, that they did permit a momentary notice to be given him, that the sentence was unfavourable. A friend was ordered to prepare him—and felt too much of the friend to give the hint sufficient edge; but by too tenderly blunting the stroke, contributed to illustrate the honour and firmness of the Admiral's mind. He started, and cried, 'Why, they have not put a slur on me, have they?' fearing they had censured him for cowardice. The bitterness of the sentence being explained, and being satisfied that his courage was not stigmatized, his countenance resumed its serenity, and he directly went with the utmost composure to hear the law pronounced. For a moment he had been alarmed with shame; death, exchanged for that, was the next good to an acquittal.

I have spoke of Admiral Byng, not as a man who thought himself innocent, but as of one marked for sacrifice by a set of Ministers, who meant to divert on him the vengeance of a betrayed and enraged nation. I have spoken, and shall speak of him as of a man most unjustly and wickedly put to death; and as this was the moment from which my opinion sprung, however lamentably confirmed by the event, it is necessary in my own vindication to say a few words, lest prejudice against the persecutors, or for the persecuted, should be suspected of having influenced my narrative. I can appeal to God that I never spoke to Mr. Byng in my life, nor had the most distant acquaintance with any one of his family. The man I never saw but in the street, or in the House of Commons, and there I thought his carriage haughty and disgusting. From report, I had formed a mean opinion of his understanding; and from the clamours of the world, I was carried away with the multitude in believing he had not done his duty; and in thinking his behaviour under *his* circumstances weak and arrogant. I never interested myself enough about him to inquire whether this opinion was well or ill founded. When his pamphlet appeared, I read it, and found he had been cruelly and scandalously treated. I knew enough not to wonder at this conduct in *some* of his persecutors— yet it concerned not me; and I thought no more about it till the sentence, and the behaviour of his Judges which accompanied it, struck me with astonishment! I could not conceive, how men could acquit honourably and condemn to death with the same breath! How men could feel so much, and be so insensible at the same instant; and from the prejudice of education which had told me that the law of England understood that its ministers of justice should always be Counsel *for* the prisoner, I could not comprehend how the members of the Court-Martial came to think that a small corner of a law ought to preponderate for rigour, against a whole body of the same law which they understood directed them to mercy; and I was still more startled to hear men urge that their consciences were bound by an oath, which their consciences told them would lead them to murder....

February 16th.—The day after the Judges had given their opinion on the sentence, the King in Council referred that opinion to the Admiralty. The King signs no sentence himself: where he does not interpose his prerogative of pardon, execution follows of course. In naval affairs, the Lords of the Admiralty sign the warrant. Lord Temple had dropped hints to the King in favour of Byng, but with more reserve with regard to the prisoner, than towards the majesty of the sovereign, to whom at one time he said in his closet, with a contemptuous sneer, 'And if he dies well, what will *you* say then?'. It was applied so *ad hominem,* that the King interpreted it as reflection on his own courage. The Admiralty thus pushed, and weighing on one hand the unpopularity of a direct refusal to sign, and on the other the authority of the Judges, which had been given at their request, determined to comply. That very night Lord Temple, Dr. Hay, and Elliot, signed the sentence, and sent it to Portsmouth, ordering execution on the 28th. Admiral Forbes, in every part of his conduct uniformly amiable and upright, refused peremptorily to sign it.

While Mr. Byng was thus pursued or given up by his countrymen, our enemies acted a very different part. Voltaire, hearing of the Admiral's trial, sent from Switzerland to the Court-Martial, a letter which he had casually received some time before from Marshal Richelieu, in which the latter spoke with encomiums on the behaviour of the English commander:—but they, who had been so ready to censure Mr. Byng on the dispatch of his antagonist La Galissonière, were far from being equally forward to give any weight to Richelieu's testimonial in his favour.

* * *

As the day approached for the execution of the Admiral, symptoms of an extraordinary nature discovered themselves. Lord Hardwicke had forgot to make the Clergy declare murder innocent, as the lawyers had been induced to find law in what no man else could find sense. Lord Anson himself, in midnight fits of weakness and wine, held forth at Arthur's on his anxiety to have Mr. Byng spared; and even went so far as to break forth abruptly to Lord Halifax, the Admiral's relation by marriage, 'Good God! my Lord, what shall we do to save poor Mr. Byng?' The Earl replied, 'My Lord, if you really mean it, no man can do so much towards it as yourself.' Keppel, a friend of Anson, and one of the Judges, grew restless with remorse. Lest these aches of conscience should be contagious, the King was plied with antidotes. Papers were posted up with paltry rhymes, saying,

> *'Hang Byng,*
> *Or take care of your King.'*

Anonymous letters were sent to terrify him if he pardoned; and, what could not be charged, too, on mob-libellists, he was threatened, that unless Mr. Byng was shot, the City would refuse to raise the money for Hanover.

*   *   *

The fatal morning arrived, but was by no means met by the Admiral with reluctance. The whole tenor of his behaviour had been cheerful, steady, dignified, sensible. While he felt like a victim, he acted like a hero. Indeed, he was the only man whom his enemies had had no power to bend to their purposes. He always received with indignation any proposal from his friends of practising an escape; an advantage he scorned to lend to clamour. Of his fate he talked with indifference; and neither shunned to hear the requisite dispositions, nor affected parade in them. For the last fortnight he constantly declared that he would not suffer a handkerchief over his face, that it might be seen whether he betrayed the least symptom of fear; and when the minute arrived, adhered to his purpose. He took an easy leave of his friends, detained the officers not a moment, went directly to the deck, and placed himself in a chair with neither ceremony nor lightness. Some of the more humane officers represented to him, that his face being uncovered might throw reluctance into the executioners; and besought him to suffer a handkerchief. He replied, with the same unconcern, 'If it will frighten *them*, let it be done: they would not frighten me.' His eyes were bound; they shot, and he fell at once.

It has often been remarked that whoever dies in public, dies well. Perhaps those, who, trembling most, maintain a dignity in their fate, are the bravest: resolution on reflection is real courage. It is less condemnable than a melancholy vainglory, when some men are ostentatious at their death. But surely a man who can adjust the circumstances of his execution beforehand; who can say, 'Thus I will do, and thus'; who can sustain the determined part, and throws in no unnecessary pomp, that man does not fear—can it be probable he ever did fear? I say nothing of Mr. Byng's duels; cowards have ventured life for reputation: I say nothing of his having been a warm persecutor of Admiral Matthews: cowards, like other guilty persons, are often severe against failings, which they hope to conceal in themselves by condemning in others: it was the uniformity of Mr. Byng's behaviour from the outset of his persecution to his catastrophe, from whence I conclude that he was aspersed as unjustly, as I am sure that he was devoted maliciously, and put to death contrary to all equity and precedent.

Archbishop Herring

[March] On the 13th, died Dr. Herring, Archbishop of Canterbury, a very amiable man, to whom no fault was objected; though perhaps the gentleness of his principles, his great merit, was thought one. During the Rebellion he had taken up arms to defend from oppression *that* religion, which he abhorred making an instrument of oppression. He was succeeded by Dr. Hutton, Archbishop of York, a finer gentleman, except where money was in question. The Duke of Newcastle, to pay court to Leicester-house, had promised York to Dr. Thomas of Peterborough, the Prince's Preceptor: but though he had been raised by the King himself, his Majesty (to thwart the Princess, who had indulged the Bishop in no weight with her son, and was consequently indifferent about him) refused to confirm the grant, and bestowed the Archbishopric on Gilbert of Salisbury, who had formerly shed courtly tears in a sermon on the Queen. Gilbert was composed of that common mixture, ignorance, meanness, and arrogance. Having once pronounced that Dr. King ought to be expelled Oxford for disaffection, the latter said he would consent to expulsion, provided Gilbert would propose it in Convocation—the motion must have been in Latin. Thomas was permitted to succeed to Salisbury. On the news of Gilbert's promotion, they rung the bells at York backwards, in detestation of him. He opened a great table there, and in six months they thought him the most Christian Prelate that had ever sat in that See.

General Conway and Others

The measure was settled in July; but it was the 8th of September before the Fleet sailed. The French, though they did not learn the specific spot of destination, had ample time for preparation; and having a chain of garrisons along the coast, and being never totally destitute of supernumerary troops, hoped to be able to draw together a sufficient body wherever the storm should fall. As the event occasioned much discourse, I shall be excusable for detailing it; yet I shall do it with brevity; and, as much proceeded from the personal characters of the commanders, I shall describe them shortly, and with the more satisfaction, as their faults flowed from no want of courage; on the contrary, they possessed amongst them most of the various shades of that qualification. Mordaunt, as I have said, had a sort of alacrity in daring, but from ill health was grown more indifferent to it. He affected not Mr. Pitt, and from not loving the projector, was more careless than he should have been of the success of the project, presuming, unfortunately for himself, that if it should appear impracticable, the original mover would bear the blame.

Conway, secure of his own intrepidity, and of no ostentation, could not help foreseeing that from the superiority of his talents to those of Mordaunt, the good conduct of the expedition would be expected from him. The more answerable he thought himself, the more he guarded against objections. Cold in his deportment, and with a dignity of soul that kept him too much above familiarity, he missed that affection from his brother officers, which his unsullied virtues and humanity deserved; for he wanted the extrinsic of merit. Added to these little failings, he had a natural indecision in his temper, weighing with too much minuteness and too much fluctuation whatever depended on his own judgment. Cornwallis was a man of a very different complexion: as cool as Conway, and as brave, he was indifferent to everything but to being in the right. He held fame cheap, and smiled at reproach. General Howard was one of those sort of characters who are only to be distinguished by having no peculiarity of character. Under these was Wolfe, a young officer who had contracted reputation from his intelligence of discipline, and from the perfection to which he had brought his own regiment. The world could not expect more from him than he thought himself capable of performing. He looked on danger as the favourable moment that would call forth his talents.

Sir Edward Hawke commanded the fleet—a man of steady courage, of fair appearance, and who even did not want a plausible kind of sense; but he was really weak, and childishly abandoned to the guidance of a Scotch secretary. The next was Knowles, a vain man, of more parade than real bravery. Howe, brother of the Lord of that name, was the third on the naval list. He was undaunted as a rock, and as silent; the characteristics of his whole race. He and Wolfe soon contracted a friendship like the union of a cannon and gunpowder.

The Duke of Cumberland

The Duke of Cumberland, after the battle of Hastenbecke, had retired with his army towards Stade, and was followed by the French. The Duchies of Bremen and Verden were at the eve of falling into their hands, and the King expected that they would be given back to Sweden. The Hanoverian Ministry did not doubt but the Duke's high spirit would venture the Army being cut to pieces rather than surrender them prisoners, and they complained of the scanty assistance afforded by England. Lady Yarmouth even said to Lord Hertford, 'Que peut on faire, mylord! le Ministère Anglois ne nous a voulu donner que quelques tonneaux de farine.' The truth was, the King, to avoid expense, had neglected to raise the Militia of Hanover, though they had implored it, and might have given a decisive turn to the battle in his favour. Both the Sovereign and his German Council were determined at all events to save the Duchies and the troops, and the most positive orders were dispatched to the Duke in consequence of those resolutions. Yet, not trusting to what conditions his son, however obedient, might obtain, his Majesty prevailed on his son-in-law, the King of Denmark, to interpose his good offices, and accordingly, on the 7th of September, Count Lynar, Governor of Oldenburgh, arrived in the Duke's camp as mediator, and a passport being demanded for him from Marshal Richelieu, the latter sent it with an escort of a hundred horse, and by the next day a convention was obtained and signed, by which Stade and the district round it was left to the Hanoverians, with permission to the rest of those troops to repass the Elbe, observing a strict neutrality. The troops of Hesse, Brunswick, Saxe-Gotha &c., in the King's pay, were to retire to their several countries.

When the news of this suspension of arms arrived at Kensington, it occasioned the greatest surprise, the greatest clamour—for even the Monarch acted surprise! The Foreign Ministers acquainted those of England that it was concluded, or certainly would be. The English with great truth disavowed all knowledge, and protested entire disbelief of it. They not only had not been entrusted with the secret, but saw their master affect equal indignation, and encouraged by that dissimulation, ventured to insist on his permitting them to write to

Horace Walpole

From a portrait by Sir Joshua Reynolds, 1757

'Brother, Brother, we are both in the Wrong'
From a print of August 1756: see page 61

'The Sturdy Beggar'
Henry Fox, his sons Stephen and Charles James, and Bubb Dodington
(Fox had obtained for himself and his sons the reversion of Dodington's place as
Clerk of the Pells in Ireland)
From a print of April 1757

foreign Courts that he disavowed the transaction. Even this he granted. He went further: he told Dabreu, the Spanish Minister, that he would show him the rough draft of a letter which he had prepared to send to his son, with a positive command to fight. It was true, he had written such a letter; it is no less true that he never sent it.

As the Dictator of the Convention disavowed it, as the father disclaimed the son, it was natural for those who suffered by the act, and for those who hated the actor, to break out against both. The King of Prussia said we had undone him, without mending our own situation. The Princess of Wales, Lord Hardwicke, and Legge, threw the strongest reflections on the Duke; the last, indeed, with appearance of reason, being extremely hampered, as Chancellor of the Exchequer, by this transaction. How should he be able, he said, next winter to propose the Hessian troops, whose hands were now tied up from assisting us, or must he waive the subsidy to them, when they were starving in our cause? The others went further; they called his Royal Highness's Generalship in question; he was brave indeed, but that was all; he had wasted a good Army; had beaten the French, and did not know it.

But the most indecent in personal invectives was Baron Munchausen, the Hanoverian Minister in England—a man reckoned one of their ablest heads, and who had hitherto always comported himself with civility and inoffensively. He went so far as to call for a Council to examine the Duke's behaviour; and Lord Hardwicke, to extend the insult, or to divide it amongst many, desired the whole Cabinet Council, not merely the Junto, might meet: the affair was too serious. Thither Munchausen brought copies of his own letters to the Duke, to prove that his Royal Highness had acted without authority. Mr. Pitt observed, that they proved the direct contrary; and he, who certainly had never managed the Duke, nor stood on any good terms with him, acted a part nobly honest: when the King told him that he had given his son no orders for this treaty, Pitt replied with firmness, 'But *full powers*, Sir; very *full powers*.'

Yet this sincerity in a foe could infuse none into a father. Two messengers were dispatched to recall the Duke, and, October 12th, he arrived at Kensington. It was in the evening, and he retired to his own apartment, where Mr. Fox and his servants were attending. He thanked Mr. Fox for being there, and said, 'You see me well both in body and mind. I have written orders in my pocket for everything I did.' (He afterwards said, his orders had been so strong, that he had not expected to obtain such good conditions.) He then dismissed Fox, saying he would send for him again. (The shortness of this interview, he afterwards told Mr. Fox, had proceeded from his determination of seeing nobody alone who could be supposed to advise him, till he had taken the step he meditated.) At nine, the hour the King punctually goes to play in the apartment of Princess Emily, the Duke went to her. The King, who was there, had ordered the Princess not to leave them alone, received him with extreme coldness; and when his Royal Highness went afterwards into the other room where the King was at cards, his Majesty said aloud, 'Here is my son, who has ruined me and disgraced himself,'—and unless this was speaking to him, spoke not a word. At eleven, when the cards were over, the Duke went down to Lady Yarmouth, and told her the King had left him but one favour to ask, which he was come to solicit by her interposition, as he wished to make it as little disagreeable to the King as possible—it was to desire leave to resign everything, the post of Captain-General, and his regiment. The Countess was in great concern at the request, and said, 'Pray, Sir, don't determine this at once.' He replied, he begged her pardon; he was not come for advice; he had had time to think, and was determined. 'Then, Sir,' said she, 'I have nothing left but to obey.'

The King received the notification with as much real agitation as he had counterfeited before. The next morning he ordered the Cabinet Council to wait on the Duke, and pay their respects to him. Lord Holderness went in first, and kissed his hand, but was not spoken to. Pitt followed; and of him his Royal Highness took most notice, speaking to him at different reprisals with kindness, to mark his satisfaction with Pitt's behaviour. He said a little to the Duke of Newcastle, Lord Granville, and Lord Anson. Lord Hardwicke was out of town. The Duke of Devonshire was sent to the Duke in private, to persuade him not to resign. He was inflexible. Devonshire was sent again to ask from the King as a favour that he would at least retain his regiment; he need not do the duty; but his Majesty should not think himself safe in any other hands; yet even this counterfeit of confidence was an aggravation of the cruelty. The Duke learned that this solicitude about the regiment proceeded solely from the King's averseness to give it to Prince Edward, as would be expected—and he was not softened by such duplicity. He even determined never to be employed under his father again, telling Fox, that no collusion about the treaty should be imputed to him, by his resuming his command. To Conway, he said, he could not, did not hope that the King would do what was necessary to justify him, it was therefore necessary to do all he could to justify himself. The next day, the Duke visited the Princess, and beginning to mention his resolution of resigning, she rung the bell, and asked him if he would not see the children.

When the King found his son's resentment inflexible, he thought of nothing but making it as little uncomfortable to himself as possible: provided the interior face of the palace was not discomposed, he cared little about justifying himself or making any reparation to his son; who, he thought, might as easily forget in the ceremonies of the Drawing-room what he had suffered, as his Majesty drowned all sensibility in the parade of that narrow sphere. He insisted that the Duke should appear as usual at Court, and come to him in a morning. The Duke acquiesced, saying, he should always show the utmost respect to the King as his father, but never could serve him more. When these *essential* forms were adjusted, the Duke sent for Munchausen, and said, 'Mr. Privy-councillor, I hear the King has sent for opinions of Hanoverian Generals on my conduct; here are the opinions of the Hessian Generals, and of the Duke of Wolfenbuttle. As the King has ordered the former to be deposited among the archives of Hanover, I hope he will do me the justice to let these be registered with them. Take them, and bring them back to me to-morrow.' Munchausen returned with them the next day, and with a message from the King that his Majesty had been better informed, and thought better of his Royal Highness than he had done; and then Munchausen falling prostrate to kiss the lappet of his coat, the Duke with dignity and anger checked him, and said, 'Mr. Privy-councillor, confine yourself to that office; and take care what you say, even though the words you repeat should be my father's; I have all possible deference for him, but I know how to punish anybody else that presumes to speak improperly of me.'

On the 15th, the Duke resigned all his commands.

I have dwelt minutely on the circumstances of this history, having learned from the best authorities, and being sure that few transactions deserve more to be remembered. A young Prince, warm, greedy of military glory, yet resigning all his passions to the interested dictates of a father's pleasure, and then loaded with the imputation of having acted basely without authority: hurt with unmerited disgrace, yet never breaking out into the least unguarded expression; preserving dignity under oppression, and the utmost tenderness of duty under the utmost delicacy of honour—this an uncommon picture—for the sake of human nature, I hope the conduct of the father is uncommon too! When the Duke could tear himself from his favourite passion, the Army, one may judge how sharply he must have been wounded. When afterwards the King, perfidiously enough, broke that famous convention, mankind were so equitable as to impute it to the same unworthy politics, not to the disapprobation he had pretended to feel on its being made. In a former part of this history I have said with regard to his eldest, that the King might have been an honest man, if he had never hated his father, or had ever loved his son—what double force has this truth, when it is again applied to him on his treachery to the best son that ever lived! Considering with what freedom I have spoken of the Duke's faults in other parts of this work, I may be believed in the just praise bestowed on him here.

Colley Cibber

Colley Cibber, that good-humoured and honest veteran, so unworthily aspersed by Pope, and whose Memoires, with one or two of his comedies, will secure his fame, in spite of all the abuse of his cotemporaries, dying about this time at a very great age, the Duke of Devonshire bestowed the laurel on Mr. Whithead, a man of a placid genius. His Grace had first designed it for Gray, then for Mason, but was told that both would decline it. In truth, it was not Cibber's silly odes that disgraced the employment, but an annual panegyric venally extorted for whatever King, and with or without occasion, that debased the office. Gray, crowned with the noblest wreaths of Parnassus, could not stoop to be dubbed poet by a Lord Chamberlain; and Mason, though he had not then displayed all the powers of his genius, had too much sense and spirit to owe his literary fame to anything but his own merit.

Princess Caroline

On the 28th of December died the King's third daughter, Princess Caroline. She had been the favourite of the Queen, who preferred her understanding to those of all her other daughters, and whose partiality she returned with duty, gratitude, affection, and concern. Being in ill health at the time of her mother's death, the Queen told her she would follow her in less than a year. The Princess received the notice as a prophecy; and though she lived many years after it had proved a vain one, she quitted the world, and persevered in the closest retreat, and in constant and religious preparation for the grave; a moment she so eagerly desired, that when something was once proposed to her, to which she was averse, she said, 'I would not do it to die!" To this impression of melancholy had contributed the loss of Lord Hervey, for whom she had conceived an unalterable passion, constantly marked afterwards by all kind and generous offices to his children. For many years she was totally an invalid, and shut herself up in two chambers in the inner part of St. James's, from whence she could not see a single object. In this monastic retirement, with no company but of the King, the Duke, Princess Emily, and a few of the most intimate of the Court, she led, not an unblameable life only, but a meritorious one: her whole income was dispensed between generosity and charity; and, till her death by shutting up the current discovered the source, the jails of London did not suspect that the best support of their wretched inhabitants was issued from the Palace.

From the last Sunday to the Wednesday on which she died, she declined seeing her family; and when the mortification began, and the pain ceased, she said, 'I feared I should not have died of this!'

1758

Pitt and other Great Men

Pitt was now arrived at undisturbed possession of that influence in affairs at which his ambition had aimed, and which his presumption had made him flatter himself he could exert like those men of superior genius, whose talents have been called forth by some crisis to retrieve a sinking nation. He had said the last year to the Duke of Devonshire, 'My Lord, I am sure I can save this country, and nobody else can.' It were ingratitude to him to say that he did not give such a reverberation to our stagnating councils, as exceedingly altered the appearance of our fortune. He warded off the evil hour that seemed approaching; he infused vigour into our arms; he taught the nation to speak again as England used to speak to Foreign Powers; and so far from dreading invasions from France, he affected to turn us into invaders—indeed, those efforts were so puny, so ill-concerted, so ineffectual to any essential purpose, that France looked down with scorn on such boyish flippancies, which Pitt deemed heroic, which Europe thought ridiculous, and which humanity saw were only wasteful of lives, and precedents of a more barbarous warfare than France had hitherto been authorized to carry on. In fact, Pitt had neither all the talents he supposed in himself, nor which he seemed to possess from the vacancy of great men around him. Thinly, very thinly, were great men sown in my remembrance: I can pretend to have seen but five; the Duke of Cumberland, Sir Robert Walpole, Lord Granville, Lord Mansfield, and Pitt. I have expatiated on all their characters separately; and yet I am inclined to say a few words more in the light of comparison. It is by setting the same characters in different oppositions and points of view, that nearer acquaintance with them may be struck out.

Lord Granville was most a genius of the five: he conceived, knew, expressed whatever he pleased. The state of Europe and the state of literature were equally familiar to him. His eloquence was rapid, and flowed from a source of wit, grandeur, and knowledge. So far from premeditated, he allowed no reflection to chasten it. It was entertaining, it was sublime, it was hyperbole, it was ridiculous, according as the profusion of ideas crowded from him. He embraced systems like a legislator, but was capable of none of the detail of a magistrate. Sir Robert Walpole was much the reverse: he knew mankind, not their writings; he consulted their interests, not their systems; he intended their happiness, not their grandeur. Whatever was beyond common sense, he disregarded. Lord Mansfield, without the elevation of Lord Granville, had great powers of eloquence. It was a most accurate understanding, and yet capable of shining in whatever it was applied to. He was as free from vice as Pitt, more unaffected, and formed to convince, even where Pitt had dazzled. The Duke of Cumberland had most expressive sense, but with that connection between his sense and sensibility, that you must mortify his pride before you could call out the radiance of his understanding. Being placed at the head of armies without the shortest apprenticeship, no wonder he miscarried: it is cruel to have no other master than one's own faults. Pitt's was an unfinished greatness: considering how much of it depended on his words, one may almost call his an artificial greatness; but his passion for fame and the grandeur of his ideas compensated for his defects. He aspired to redeem the honour of his country, and to place it in a point of giving law to nations. His ambition was to be the most illustrious man of the first country in Europe; and he thought that the eminence of glory could not be sullied by the steps to it being passed irregularly. He wished to aggrandize Britain in general, but thought not of obliging or benefitting individuals.

Lord Granville you loved till you knew him; Sir Robert Walpole, the more you knew him: you would have loved the Duke, if you had not feared him. Pitt liked the dignity of despotism; Lord Mansfield the reality: yet the latter would have served the cause of power, without sharing it: Pitt would have set the world free, if he might not command it. Lord Granville would have preferred doing right, if he had not thought it more convenient to do wrong: Sir Robert Walpole meant to serve mankind, though he knew how little they deserved it; and this principle is at once the most meritorious in oneself and to the world. I beg pardon for this digression.

Various Churchmen

Before I quit the affairs of [Ireland], I must mention a spiritual business that made some noise there. Dr. Clayton, Bishop of Clogher, had already distinguished himself as a man of parts and a free-thinker. His Essay on Spirit, which seemed to accord with Clarke's esoteric doctrine, had more the address of an heresiarch than the plain-dealing simplicity of a Christian pastor. He now published a vindication of the Testament, which seemed calculated for doing anything with the Testament rather than supporting it. Yet the man was believed sincere in his opinions—and so a man ought to be who thinks it worth his while to expose himself by exploding any common prejudices. He even aspired to sufferings for his zeal in propagating counterband metaphysics among illiterate Irish. But the Bishops, his brethren, taking the alarm, and intending a meeting with their *orthodox* Primate, in order to prepare an application to the Crown for a royal visitation, Clayton died suddenly of a panic, though possessed of a good private estate, and ambitious of martyrdom!

This little flame was soon extinguished; in fact, there were no religious combustibles in the temper of the times. Popery and Protestantism seemed at a stand. The modes of Christianity were exhausted, and could not furnish novelty enough to fix attention. Zinzendorffe plied his Moravians with nudities, yet made few enthusiasts. Whitfield and the Methodists made more money than disturbances; his largest

crop of proselytes lay among servant-maids; and his warmest devotees
went to Bedlam without going to war. Bower, whom some thought
they had detected as a Jesuit, and who at most was but detected as
an impostor, had laid open the practices of the Catholics, and detailed
the establishments of the Jesuits in the very heart of London, without
occasioning either alarm or murmur against those Fathers. His History
of the Popes, one of the ablest performances we have, was decried,
because, to recommend a work of truth and utility, he had embroidered
his own story with some marvellous legends. Yet, uninflammable as
the times were, they carried a great mixture of superstition. Masquerades
had been abolished, because there had been an earthquake at Lisbon;
and when the last Jubilee-masquerade was exhibited at Ranelagh,
the ale-houses and roads to Chelsea were crowded with drunken
people, who assembled to denounce the judgments of God on persons
of fashion, whose greatest sin was dressing themselves ridiculously.

A more inconvenient reformation, and not a more sensible one, was
set on foot by societies of tradesmen, who denounced to the magistrate
all bakers that baked or sold bread on Sundays. Alum, and the
variety of spurious ingredients with which bread and indeed all wares
were come to be adulterated all the week round, gave not half so much
offence as the vent of the chief necessary of life on the seventh day.
Indecent prints were prohibited: the Chief-Justice Mansfield caused to
be seized at an auction a well-known tale, called 'The Woman of
Pleasure', a work that simplified novels to their original intention.
Some of the Elders, too, of our own Church, seeing what harvests
were brought into the tabernacles of Whitfield and Wesley by familiarizing God's word to the vulgar, and by elevating vulgar language, had
the discretion to apply the same call to their own lost sheep, and
tinkled back their old women by sounding the brass of the Methodists.
One Ashton, a quaint and fashionable preacher of the Orthodox, talked
to the people in a phrase compounded of cant and politics: he reproved
them for not coming to church, where *God keeps a day, but sees
little company*; and informed them that *our ancestors loved powder
and ball, and so did our Generals; but the latter loved them for their
hair and hands.* Yet to do justice to better principles, the age had
made some estimable improvements. Prize-fighting, in which we had
horribly resembled the most barbarous and most polite nations, was
suppressed by the Legislature. Hogarth had undertaken the cause of
humanity, and painted satires on all species of cruelty. From France
and Italy, we had adopted hospitals for foundlings; and from the

dictates of nature, all manner of hospitals. Our stage grew chaste; indecency dared not show its face in a modern comedy, though it still remained in possession of the old ones; and what is remarkable, having been tolerated when women went to the theatre in masks, preserved its hold, now they went without them.

The House of Lords

Let us, before we pass to the discussion of the Bill, anticipate the behaviour of all these persons and bodies of men, all engaged by common interest and common honour to support the charter, for which they had violated other inferior ties; but almost all swayed by private and separate interests to abandon the cause. The King talked openly at his Levée against the Bill; and it was understood to be offensive to him to vote for the extension of it. He was King; he did not desire to reduce the prerogative lower than it had been delivered to him. The Lords were become so much more considerable than they had been before the Revolution, that they were in no danger from the Crown; and when they do not fear it, they will always be ready to uphold it. They look on themselves as distinct from the rest of the nation; and at best, leave the people to be taken care of by their representatives, the Commons. As jealous of, and as fond of their privileges, as the King of his prerogative, they are attentive to maintain them, and deem the rights of the people rather encroachments than a common interest. Added to this general description, they were, at the time I write of, a tame, subservient, incapable set of men, governed entirely by the Duke of Newcastle, and the two lawyers, Hardwicke and Mansfield. Those lawyers were instances of the discrimination that ought to be made between the spirit of the laws and the profession of them. Nobody better read in them, nobody more warm to enforce them, nobody less actuated by the essence of them. If either of them ever took the side of liberty, or the side of mildness, I am willing to be thought to asperse them. The conduct of the Prelates had for so many years been so uniformly supple, that no man expected anything from them but complaisance for the Court—and they deceived no man! The Hierarchy behaved so nobly in the reign of James the Second, and has behaved so poorly ever since, that they seem to know no medium between a mitre and a crown of martyrdom. If the clergy are not called to the latter, they never deviate from the pursuit of the former. One would think their motto was, *Canterbury or Smithfield*.

Character of the Author

At this stage I shall make a pause in my work, uncertain whether ever to be resumed, though I am rather inclined to prolong it to the conclusion of the war. I warn my readers, however, not to expect as much intelligence and information in any subsequent pages of these Memoires as may have appeared in the preceding. During the former period I lived in the centre of business, was intimately connected with many of the chief actors, was eager in politics, indefatigable in heaping up knowledge and materials for my work. Now, detached from those busy scenes, with many political connections dropped or dissolved, indifferent to events, and indolent, I shall have fewer opportunities of informing myself of others. And here perhaps it may not be improper, or unwelcome to the reader, if I say some words on the author of these Memoires: the frankness of the manner will prove it flows from no vainglory; yet to take off all such appearance, and to avoid a nauseous egotism, I shall make use of the third person.

Horace Walpole, without the least tincture of ambition, had a propensity to faction, and looked on the mischief of civil disturbance as a lively amusement. Indignation at the persecution raised against his father, and prejudices contracted by himself, conspired with his natural impetuosity of temper to nourish this passion. But coming into the world when the world was growing weary of faction, and some of the objects dying or being removed, against whom his warmth had been principally directed, maturity of reason and sparks of virtue extinguished this culpable ardour. Balanced for a few years between right and wrong, happily for him virtue preponderated early enough to leave him some merit in the option. Arts, books, painting, architecture, antiquities, and those amiable employments of a tranquil life, to which in the warmest of his political hours he had been fondly addicted, assumed an entire empire over him. The circumstances too of the times contributed to make him withdraw from the scene of business. With Newcastle he had determined never to connect: Fox's behaviour on the case of Mr. Byng had rooted out his esteem, and the coldness discovered by Fox on Walpole's refusing to concur in all his politics, had in a manner dissolved their friendship. Of Pitt he retained the best opinion; but the wanton exposure of so many lives at the affair of St. Cas, and in those other visionary attempts on the coast of France, had painted Pitt on his mind as a man whose thirst of glory was inconsistent with humanity; and being himself strongly tinctured with tenderness, he avoided any further intercourse with a Minister, who was Great with so little reluctance.

Thus without disgrace, disappointment, or personal disgust, Walpole, at the age of forty-one, abandoned the theatre of affairs; and retaining neither resentment to warp, nor friendship to bias him, he thinks himself qualified to give some account of transactions, which few men have known better, and of which scarce any can speak with equal impartiality. He has not falsified a circumstance to load any man; he has not denied a wrong act to excuse himself. Yet lest even this unreserve should not be thought sufficient, lest some secret motives should be supposed to have influenced his opinions, at least his narrative, he will lay open to the reader his nearest sentiments. Severity in some of the characters will be the most striking objection. His dislike to a few persons probably sharpened his eyes to their faults, but he hopes never blinded him to their virtues—lest it should have done, especially in so inflammable a nature, he admonishes the reader of his greatest prejudices, as far as they could have risen from any provocation. From the Duke of Cumberland, Mr. Pelham, and Lord Hardwicke, he had received trifling offence. To the two last he avows he had strong aversion. From Mr. Fox, as I have said, he had felt coldness and ingratitude. By his uncle and the Duke of Devonshire he had been injured—by the former basely betrayed; yet of none of these has he omitted to speak with praise when he could find occasion. Of Lord Hardwicke had he known a virtue, he would have told it: for now, when his passions are subsided, when affection and veneration for truth and justice preponderate above all other considerations, would he sacrifice the integrity of these Memoires, his favourite labour, to a little revenge that he shall never taste? No; let his narration be measured by this standard, and it will be found that the unamiableness of the characters he blames imprinted those dislikes, as well as private distaste to some of them. The King, the Duke of Newcastle, and others, who do not appear in these writings with any signal advantage, never gave him the most distant cause of dissatisfaction.

How far his own character may have concurred towards forming his opinions may be calculated from the following picture, impartial as far as a man can know himself.

Walpole had a warm conception, vehement attachments, strong aversions; with an apparent contradiction in his temper, for he had numerous caprices, and invincible perseverance. His principles tended to Republicanism, but without any of its austerity; his love of faction was unmixed with any aspiring. He had great sense of honour, but not great enough, for he had too much weakness to resist doing wrong, though too much sensibility not to feel it in others. He had a great measure of pride, equally apt to resent neglect, and scorning to stoop to any meanness or flattery. A boundless friend; a bitter, but a placable enemy. His humour was satiric, though accompanied with a most compassionate heart. Indiscreet and abandoned to his passions, it seemed as if he despised or could bear no constraint; yet this want of government of himself was the more blameable, as nobody had greater command of resolution whenever he made a point of it. This appeared in his person: naturally very delicate, and educated with too fond a tenderness, by unrelaxed temperance and braving all inclemency of weathers, he formed and enjoyed the firmest and unabated health. One virtue he possessed in a singular degree, disinterestedness and contempt of money, if one may call that a virtue, which really was a passion. In short, such was his promptness to dislike superiors, such his humanity to inferiors, that, considering how few men are of so firm a texture as not to be influenced by their situation, he thinks, if he may be allowed to judge of himself, that had either extreme of fortune been his lot, he should have made a good prince, but not a very honest slave.

1759

William Pitt and General Wolfe

On his [Moyston's] waiving Martinico, Pitt carried a list of names to the King, who selected Hopson—a choice not consonant to Mr. Pitt's practice, who considering that our ancient officers had grown old on a very small portion of experience, which by no means compensated for the decay of fire and vigour, chose to trust his plans to the alertness and hopes of younger men. This appeared particularly in the nomination of Wolfe for the enterprise on Quebec. Ambition, activity, industry, passion for the service, were conspicuous in Wolfe. He seemed to breathe for nothing but fame, and lost no moments in qualifying himself to compass his object. He had studied for his purpose, and wrote well. Presumption on himself was necessary to such a character; and he had it. He was formed to execute the designs of such a master as Pitt, till risen to an eminence, whence he might choose to thwart his master. To Wolfe was associated George Townshend, whose proud and sullen and contemptuous temper never suffered him to wait for thwarting his superiors till risen to a level with them. He saw everything in an ill-natured and ridiculous light—a sure prevention of ever being seen himself in a great or favourable one. The haughtiness of the Duke of Cumberland, the talents or blemishes of Fox, the ardour of Wolfe, the virtue of Conway, all were alike the objects of Townshend's spleen and contradiction—but Wolfe was not a man to waive his preeminence from fear of caricatures. He felt his superior knowledge and power, and had spirit enough to make Townshend sensible at least of the latter—a confidence in himself that was fortunate for his country—but we must pass to the other events of the year which preceded the decision of that attempt.

Mr. Pitt, on entering upon Administration, had found the nation at the lowest ebb in point of power and reputation. His predecessors, now his coadjutors, wanted genius, spirit, and system. The Fleet had many able officers; but the Army, which, since the resignation of the Duke of Cumberland, had lost sight of discipline, was destitute of Generals in whom either the nation or the soldiery had any confidence. France, who meaned to be feared, was feared heartily; and the heavy debt of the nation, which was above fourscore millions, served as an excuse to those who understood nothing but little temporary expedients to preach up our impossibility of making an effectual stand. They were willing to trust that France would be so good as to ruin us by inches.

Pitt had roused us from this ignoble lethargy: he had asserted that our resources were still prodigious—he found them so in the intrepidity of our troops and navies—but he went farther, and perhaps too far. He staked our revenues with as little management as he played with the lives of the subjects; and as if we could never have another war to wage, or as if he meant, which was impracticable, that his Administration should decide which alone should exist as a nation, Britain or France, he lavished the last treasures of this country with a prodigality beyond example and beyond excuse; yet even that profusion was not so blameable as his negligence. Ignorant of the whole circle of finance, and consequently averse from corresponding with financiers, a plain set of men, who are never to be paid with words instead of figures, he kept aloof from all details, drew magnificent plans, and left others to find the magnificent means. Disdaining, too, to descend into the operations of an office which he did not fill, he affected to throw on the Treasury the execution of measures which he dictated, but for which he thus held himself not responsible. The conduct was artful, new, and grand; and to him proved most advantageous. Secluded from all eyes, his orders were received as oracles; and their success, of consequence, was imputed to his inspiration. Misfortunes and miscarriages fell to the account of the more human agents: corruption and waste were charged on the subordinate priests. They indeed were charmed with this dispensation.

As Mr. Pitt neither granted suits nor received them, Newcastle revelled in a boundless power of appointing agents, commissaries, victuallers, and the whole train of leeches, and even paid his court to Pitt by heaping extravagance on extravagance; for the more money was thrown away, the greater idea Pitt conceived of his system's grandeur. But none flattered this ostentatious prodigality like the Germans. From the King of Prussia and Prince Ferdinand to the lowest victualler in the camp, all made advantage of English easiness and dissipation. As the Minister was proud of such pensioners, they were not coy in begging his alms. Fox, too, was not wanting to himself during this harvest, to which his office of Paymaster opened so commodious an inlet. Depressed, annihilated as a statesman, he sat silent, indemnifying himself by every opportunity of gain which his rival's want of economy threw in his way. The larger and more numerous are subsidies, the more troops are in commission, the more are on service abroad, the ampler means has the Paymaster of enriching himself. An unfortunate campaign, or an unpopular peace might shake the Minister's establishment—but till this vision of expensive glory should be dissipated, Fox was determined to take no part. But thence, from that inattention on one hand, and rapacity on the other, started up those prodigious private fortunes which we have seen suddenly come forth—and thence we remained with a debt of an hundred and forty millions!

The admirers of Mr. Pitt extol the reverberation he gave to our councils, the despondence he banished, the spirit he infused, the conquests he made, the security he affixed to our trade and plantations, the humiliation of France, the glory of Britain carried, under his Administration, to a pitch at which it never had arrived—and all this is exactly true. When they add, that all this could not be purchased too dearly, and that there was no option between this conduct and tame submission to the yoke of France—even this is just in a degree; but a material objection still remains, not depreciating a grain from this bill of merits, which must be gratefully acknowledged by whoever calls himself Englishman—yet very derogatory from Mr. Pitt's character, as virtually trusted with the revenues, the property of his country. A few plain words will explain my meaning, and comprehend the force of the question. All this was done—but might have been done for many millions less—the next war will state this objection more fully.

Posterity, this is an impartial picture. I am neither dazzled by the blaze of the times in which I have lived, nor, if there are spots in the sun, do I deny that I see them. It is a man I am describing, and one whose greatness will bear to have his blemishes fairly delivered to you—not from a love of censure in me, but of truth; and because it is history I am writing, not romance. I pursue my subject.

Lord Granby and Lord Sackville

With Fitzroy came over the Duke of Richmond; and they, particularly the latter, disclosed a passage, which soon threw the nation into a flame. Lord George Sackville, by his weight with Mr. Pitt, and in Parliament, had insisted on going to Germany, and had gone without the King's approbation, and even without waiting on his Majesty. Lord Granby was next to Lord George in command, and so popular, that when he set out for the Army, fifty-two young officers had solicited to be his Aides-de-camp. Between these two Lords a coolness soon ensued, and divided the Army, if it can be called *division*, where almost every heart sided with Lord Granby. He was open, honest, affable, and of such unbounded good-nature and generosity, that it was impossible to say which principle actuated him in the distribution of the prodigious sums that he spent and flung away.

Lord George Sackville was haughty, reserved but to a few, and those chiefly Scotch; and with no pre-eminence over his rival, but what his rank in command gave him, and his great talents, in which there could be not the smallest competition; and yet with those superior talents, Lord George never had the art of conciliating affection. He had thwarted Prince Ferdinand, and disgusted him, in the preceding campaign; and was now in the Army against the Prince's inclination. The latter, with equal haughtiness, but with far more art and address, could not fail of fomenting a breach that tended so much to mortify Lord George, and to promote his own views. Lord Granby was tractable, unsuspicious, and not likely to pry into or control the amazing impositions of the German agents, which Lord George had too honestly, too indiscreetly, or too insultingly let Prince Ferdinand see had not escaped his observation, instead of remonstrating or withstanding such dissipation, as he should have done, at home—though it is questionable whether his representations would have been listened to by Mr. Pitt, who cared not what he lavished on whoever would carry on his glorious sketches, or rather adventurous darings—a prodigality unhappily copied in the next reign, throughout the American war, by men who imitated Mr. Pitt in nothing else, and who had none of his genius, ambition, patriotism, activity, nor even his lofty ideas.

General Waldegrave

A promotion of Lieutenants-General was immediately made, in order to include and hasten the rank to General Waldegrave, to whom the success of the battle had in great measure been owing. The six English regiments, who sustained the whole effort of the French, had begun the engagement with less promise of valour. At first they began to give way. Waldegrave, affecting not to perceive that their motion tended towards a retreat, cried out, 'Wheel to the right!'— they did, and recovered the day. Waldegrave was a man who united much frankness with steady attention to his interest. His parts were never taken notice of but on this occasion: but such an occasion is immortality.

The Spanish Royal Family

While the war seemed drawing towards a conclusion in the North, it looked as if fate was opening a new source of calamities to mankind. Ferdinand King of Spain died; a Prince of no abilities, and lately of disordered intellects. His want of issue had formerly been imputed to drugs administered to him by the practices of his mother-in-law, Elizabeth Farnese, the politic Queen-dowager. Men of a suspicious cast might attribute his frenzy to the same cause; but a more

George II

From the portrait by Robert Edge Pine, painted without the King's knowledge, 1759

The Duke of Newcastle   The Duke of Bedford

Both from engravings by Paton Thomson

The Prince of Wales   The Duke of Cumberland

From an engraving by Paton Thomson after a drawing by Richard Bentley commissioned by Walpole

pregnant reason might be assigned. His father, who certainly was far from being afflicted with any bodily debility, had been equally disturbed in his understanding. Ferdinand's Queen, who had great ascendant over him, had kept his madness within bounds. On her death nobody had any influence with him. His disorder, thus left to itself, increased and put an end to his life about a year after the decease of his Queen.

The Queen-dowager, though not absolute directress of affairs during the life of her son-in-law, had yet, from her intrigues, bribes, and dependents, and still more from the visible and approaching prospect of her own son's succession, acquired much authority, though not enough to throw the kingdom, as she wished, into direct connection with France. The probability of the weight she would have with her son Don Carlos; the power his own Queen, who was a daughter of Saxony, was known to have with him; and the subjection in which we had held him while only King of Naples—all these motives concurred to lead him into French measures. Naples, by the peace of Aix-la-Chapelle, had been destined to his brother the Duke of Parma. Don Carlos, indeed, had never given his consent to that disposition: he was less inclined to conform to it when the forces of Spain enabled him to dispute it. Accordingly, on obtaining the Spanish Crown, he destined that of Naples to one of his younger sons. The eldest, called Duke of Calabria, and heir-apparent of Spain, inherited the weakness of mind of his grandfather and uncle. Him, therefore, it was determined totally to set aside. Solemnity was used in proceeding to that rejection. The young Prince, then thirteen, was formally examined by physicians. One of them was so honest as to refuse to sign his persuasion of the Prince's incapacity, though at length he too yielded. The case was novel and striking. Just, undoubtedly, to the people who were to be governed: but many favours of hereditary right—that is, men who think that no want of talents or virtues ought to exclude a Prince from exercising that office which requires the noblest share of both, and hold that mankind, like land, ought to be the property of birth—will not be pleased with the reasons which the Neapolitan physicians were of opinion disqualified the Prince for the throne of Spain.

'He was short, his joints were contracted, he stooped, looked down, squinted, was sometimes indifferent to things convenient for him, at others too warm and impetuous. His passions not restrained by reason; he had an obstinate aversion to sweetmeats; was disturbed by all sorts of noise; pain or pleasure made no lasting impressions on him; he was utterly unacquainted with good-breeding; had not the least idea of the mysteries of their holy religion; loved childish amusements, the most boisterous the best; and was continually shifting from one thing to another.'

If these defects were disqualifications, hard would be the fate of most sovereigns! how seldom would an eldest son succeed his father! Would not one think that the faculty of physic at Naples had rather been describing a Monarch than dispossessing him? One thing is evident—it must have been a King who selected *such* criterions for judging whether his son was capable of governing a great nation. 'Ask him,' we must suppose, said his Neapolitan Majesty, 'whether he loves sweetmeats! if he does not, he is unworthy of filling the throne of his ancestors.' The Prince's ignorance of good-breeding and of his religion seems rather imputable to his parents and preceptors than to him. If it was the mysteries of the Roman Catholic faith which he was incapable of comprehending, I should suspect the Prince was a sensible lad. Perhaps the honest physician thought as I do—at least, I do not doubt but, if permitted, he would have asked the Prince other questions.

Voltaire, who, I do not know why, thinks Princes are always to be mentioned with strict decorum, could hardly persuade any man to refrain from laughing at this absurd catalogue of royal deficiencies. The Prince really was an idiot; nor was it likely that a father would wish to disinherit his own child, especially who was not old enough to have given him jealousy, unless the incapacity had been glaring and hopeless—but one would think the whole Cabinet of Naples had been idiots likewise, when they could find no better colours to dress up a notorious fact. Indeed, the Spanish as well as Portuguese statesmen have been woefully defective in composition in this age, as often as they have attempted to lay the grounds of their proceedings before the rest of Europe. The most barbarous periods of monkish ignorance and despotism produced nothing more despicable than several manifestos of those Crowns.

The Prince was set aside in consequence of the decision of the physicians. The second son was carried to Spain and declared Prince of Asturias. To the third was actually resigned the Crown of Naples, though too young to have it known whether he was more fit to reign than his eldest brother—but a baby is never thought disqualified. The tranquillity, however, of that child's reign depended so much on preserving the friendship of England, that the new King of Spain was not impatient to hurry into French councils. His wife too had prepossessed him with apprehensions of being governed by his mother. The Crown of Naples, which he had owed entirely to her intrigues, could not induce him to put that of Spain under her direction. She could not even obtain to see him alone—a mortifying return from a darling son, who had been absent from her thirty years! But if the new Queen in that instance showed her influence, she lost it in every other. The King was extremely weak, but unmeasurably obstinate. The Crown of Spain, or probably some Spanish Minister, infused into him higher thoughts of himself. He grew jealous of his wife's ascendant, sent away a Neapolitan Duchess who governed her, and took a resolution of deciding everything by his own judgment. He could not have chosen a worse counsellor. The disgraces that soon attended his measures made the true Spaniards wish that the Neapolitan doctors had been consulted on more cases than one.

The Lady Elizabeth

The death of King Ferdinand was followed (September 4) by that of the Lady Elizabeth of England, second daughter of Frederic, Prince of Wales, in her eighteenth year. She had the quickest parts of any of his children, but was extremely deformed and homely. She died at Kew, of an inflammation in her bowels, having been ill but two days.

Bishop Warburton

Pitt, in contradiction to the House of Manners, who solicited for Dr. Ewer, to Newcastle, who stickled for a Cambridge man, and to the opposition of the Episcopal Bench, made Warburton Bishop of Gloucester; whose doubtful Christianity, whose writings and turbulent arrogance, made him generally obnoxious. Warburton, inquiring of a friend what the Clergy thought of his promotion, and being told how much it offended them, said, 'Tell them it was well for their cause that I did not embrace any other profession.'

1760

Lord Ferrers

While this affair was depending, a more atrocious criminal appeared on the stage. Lawrence, Earl Ferrers, had been parted from his wife, and an allowance settled on her by Parliament out of his estate, for his causeless ill-usage of her. A receiver of his rents, too, had been appointed, but the nomination left to the Earl, who named one Johnson, his own steward. That honest man not proving so tractable as his Lordship expected, had fallen under his displeasure. The Earl lived at his own seat in Leicestershire with a former mistress, whom he had taken again on being separated from his wife, and by whom he had four children. In that retirement there appeared many symptoms of a phrenzy incident to his family, as had also during his cohabitation with his lady; and frequent drunkenness inflamed the disorder. In that mood of madness and revenge he sent for Johnson, having artfully dispatched his family and servants different ways on various pretences. The poor man was no sooner alone with him, than the Earl locking the door, and holding a pistol to his breast, would have obliged Johnson to sign a paper, avowing himself a villain. While the unhappy man, kneeling at his feet, hesitated to sign, Lord Ferrers shot him in the body. The wound was mortal, but not instantly so. Remorse or fear seized on the murderer, for he was then sober. He sent for a surgeon, and wished to have Johnson saved. Those sentiments soon vanished, or were expelled by drink; for the Earl passed the remaining hours of that horrid day between his bottle and the chamber of the expiring man, sometimes in promises to his daughter, whom he had summoned to her father, oftener in transports of insult, threats and cruelty to the victim himself, who languished till the next morning. At first the Peer prepared to defend himself from being seized; but his courage failed him, as it had on former occasions. He was apprehended by the populace, and lodged in Leicester jail. Thence he was brought to town, and carried before the House of Lords, where his behaviour was cool and sensible. The Lords committed him to the Tower.

Tobias Smollett

In February was tried a criminal of a still different complexion. Dr. Smollett was convicted in the King's Bench of publishing scurrilous abuse on Admiral Knollys in *The Critical Review*. Smollett was a worthless man, and only mentioned here because author of a History of England, of the errors in which posterity ought to be warned. Smollett was bred a sea-surgeon, and turned author. He wrote a tragedy, and sent it to Lord Lyttelton, with whom he was not acquainted. Lord Lyttelton, not caring to point out its defects, civilly advised him to try comedy. He wrote one, and solicited the same Lord to recommend it to the stage. The latter excused himself, but promised, if it should be acted, to do all the service in his power for the author. Smollett's return was drawing an abusive portrait of Lord Lyttelton in *Roderick Random*, a novel; of which sort he published two or three. His next attempt was on the History of England; a work in which he engaged for booksellers, and finished, though four volumes in quarto, in two years; yet an easy task, as being pilfered from other histories. Accordingly, it was little noticed till it came down to the present time: then, though compiled from the libels of the age and the most paltry materials, yet being heightened by personal invectives, strong Jacobitism, and the worst representation of the Duke of Cumberland's conduct in Scotland, the sale was prodigious. Eleven thousand copies of that trash were instantly sold, while at the same time the University of Oxford ventured to print but two thousand of that inimitable work, Lord Clarendon's *Life*! A reflection on the age sad to mention, yet too true to be suppressed! Smollett's work was again printed, and again tasted: it was adorned with wretched prints, except two or three by Strange, who could not refuse his admirable graver to the service of the Jacobite cause.

Smollett then engaged in a monthly magazine, called *The Critical Review*, the scope of which was to decry any work that appeared favourable to the principles of the Revolution. Nor was he single in that measure. The Scotch in the heart of London assumed a dictatorial power of reviling every book that censured the Stuarts, or upheld the Revolution—a provocation they ought to have remembered when the tide rolled back upon them. Smollett, while in prison, undertook a new magazine; and notwithstanding the notoriety of his disaffection,

WALPOLE: MEMOIRS AND PORTRAITS

obtained the King's patent for it by the interest of Mr. Pitt, to whom he had dedicated his history. In the following reign he was hired to write a scurrilous paper, called *The Briton*, against that very patron, Mr. Pitt.

Lord Ferrers

The trial of Lord Ferrers had more solemn conclusion. To one man his crimes were advantageous. Sir Robert Henley, Lord Keeper, had been hoisted to that eminence by circumstances of faction; which, however, could not give weight to his decisions in Chancery. Those, as he complained, were often reversed before his face by the House of Lords without his being empowered to defend them, he not being a Peer. It was proper to appoint him Lord High Steward for the trial of Lord Ferrers; and it was requisite, to fill that office, that he should be a Peer. Henley was accordingly created a Baron; but as the Seals had not taught him more law, a Coronet and White Staff contributed as little to give him more dignity. He despised form, even where he had little to do but to be formal. He did not want sense, and spirit still less; but he could not, or would not, stoop to so easy a lesson as that of ceremonial.

Nothing is more awful than the trial of a British Peer; yet, the mean appearance of the prisoner, and the vulgar awkwardness of the Chief Judge, made the present trial as little imposing as possible. The Earl's behaviour conciliated no favour to him: it was somewhat sullen, and his defence contemptible, endeavouring to protract the time, though without address. At length he pleaded madness—unwillingly, but in compliance with the entreaties of his family. The audience was touched at the appearance of his two brothers, reduced to depose to the lunacy in their blood. But those impressions were effaced, and gave way to horror, when it appeared to the Court that the Earl had gloried in his shocking deed. Being easily convicted, he begged pardon of his Judges for having used the plea of madness. But if his life was odious, and during his life his cowardice notorious, he showed at his death that he did not want sense, resolution, or temper. He bore the ignominy of his fate like a philosopher, and went to meet it with the ease of a gentleman. In the tedious passage of his conveyance from the Tower to Tyburn, which was impeded by the crowds that assembled round his coach, he dropped not a rash word, nor one that had not sense

94

and thought in it. Little was wanting to grace his catastrophe but less resentment to his wife, the peculiarity of being executed in his wedding habit too strongly marking that he imputed his calamity to that source. His relation, Lady Huntingdon, the Metropolitan of the Methodists, had laboured much in his last hours to profit of his fears for the honour of her sect; but, having renounced the plea of madness, he did not choose to resign his intellects to folly. So impudent, however, were those knavish zealots, that one Loyd, a Methodist, having been robbed by his coachman, a Methodist too, Whitfield appeared at the trial before the Lord Mayor, and read an excommunication that he had pronounced against the coachman. They would have accepted a murderer, if a proselyte from the Established Church; and flattered themselves that they could shake off the infamy of a house-breaker by casting him out from their own—so brief and effectual do enthusiasts hold their own legerdemain.

The Duke of Cumberland

While the theatre of war was thus open to men so formed to shine on it, another hero, who had been excluded from the scene, was in a melancholy condition. The Duke of Cumberland in the summer had a stroke of palsy. He soon recovered both his speech and limbs; but the grossness of his constitution, and other disorders, made his friends apprehend he would not long survive it. Himself treated it with indifference, and with the same philosophy with which his high spirit had supported misfortunes to him more sensible.

Lord Clanrickard

The martial temper of the age called forth a champion of dissimilar[1] complexion. There was in Ireland an Earl of Clanrickard, who, even in this country, where singular characters are not uncommon, had been reckoned more than ordinarily extravagant. The Duke of Bedford had refused to let him raise a regiment. To prove his valour, he challenged the Lord-Lieutenant, who contemning so improper an adversary, the Earl printed in the public papers a letter to the Duke,

[1] To the Duke of Cumberland.

reproaching him with rejecting the challenge, and reflecting both on his Grace and his secretary, whose bones he threatened to break. Such an insult on the chief governor of a kingdom was atrocious. The Privy Council of England ordered the Attorney-General to commence a prosecution against the Earl. Mr. Rigby, whose spirit was more question-less than the Earl's, returned a challenge for himself; but the Earl thought it safest to confine his prowess to the master, and forbore coming to England. Three years afterwards, when Rigby went to Ireland to qualify for a place, the Privy Council of that kingdom obliged Lord Clanrickard to give security for his good behaviour; and the matter was compromised.

George the Second

These were the last events in the long and memorable reign of George the Second—a reign that had produced as great statesmen, orators, and heroes as dignify the annals of whatever country. His thirteen first years were stamped with every blessing of peace, but unanimity—if disagreement is an evil to a free country, to which jealousy is perhaps essential. A Rebellion and two wars called forth all our resources: the disgrace that attended the councils and prosecution of the first war served but to illustrate the abilities of the nation, which, reviving from its ignominy and calamities, carried the glory of our arms and measures to a height unknown in our story. The Prince himself was neither accessory to the one or to the other. His greatest merit was bearing either fortune with calmness. Triumphant as Elizabeth and Anne, he neither presumed on the zeal of his subjects like the first, nor was so like the last as to concur in or behold an ignominious peace, that tarnished such conspicuous victories, and squandered such irrecoverable advantages. Full of years and glory, he died without a pang, and without a reverse. He left his family firmly established on a long-disputed throne, and was taken away in the moment that approaching extinction of sight and hearing made loss of life the only blessing that remained desirable.

On the 25th of October he rose as usual at six, and drank his chocolate; for all his actions were invariably methodic. A quarter after seven he went into a little closet. His German *valet de chambre* in waiting, heard a noise, and running in, found the King dead on the floor. In falling, he had cut his face against the corner of a bureau.

He was laid on a bed, and blooded, but not a drop followed: the ventricle of his heart had burst. Princess Amalie was called, and told the King wanted her. She went immediately, and thought him in a fit. Being deaf herself, she saw nothing in the chamber that indicated his being dead; and putting her face close to his, to hear if he spoke to her, she then perceived he was lifeless.

The character of this Prince has been so amply displayed in the course of this work, that it were tautology to recapitulate it. His faults were more the blemishes of a private man than of a King. The affection and tenderness he invariably showed to a people over whom he had unbounded rule, forbid our wondering that he used circumscribed power with moderation. Often situated in humiliating circumstances, his resentments seldom operated when the power of revenge returned. He bore the ascendant of his Ministers, who seldom were his favourites, with more patience than he suffered any encroachment on his will from his mistresses. Content to bargain for the gratification of his two predominant passions, Hanover and money, he was almost indifferent to the rest of his royal authority, provided exterior observance was not wanting; for he comforted himself if he did not perceive the diminution of Majesty, though it was notorious to all the rest of the world. Yet he was not so totally careless of the affections and interests of this country as his father had been. George the First possessed a sounder understanding and a better temper: yet George the Second gained more by being compared with his eldest son, than he lost if paralleled with his father. His treatment of his second son, to whose valour he was indebted for the preservation of his Crown, and to the silence and tenderness of whose duty he owed the preservation of his honour, was punished by the ingratitude of the Princess of Wales.

Bookish men have censured his neglect of literature—a reflection that at least is evidence that public utility is not the sole purport of their labours. But the advantages resulting to their country from authors must be better ascertained, before the imputation becomes a grave one. Had he pensioned half a dozen poets, and reaped their incense, the world had heard of nothing but his liberality. Let Kings prefer a Tillotson or a Seneca, nay, a Bacon or a Newton—if Bacon or Seneca will not forget their philosophy. Let them enrich such angelic men, when there are such angelic men, as Dr. Hales: but money is as well hoarded as squandered on Boileaus and Benserades, on Atterburys and Drydens. In truth, I believe King George would have preferred a guinea to a composition as perfect as Alexander's Feast. He certainly

did not spare rewards to those who served their country. The profusion of favours which he suffered the Duke of Newcastle to shower
on the University of Cambridge ought to disculpate the King from
the charge of neglecting literature—it was the fault of that body if
they were not learned.

If dying but moderately rich were as good a proof that he had not
been avaricious, one of the greatest stains of his character would be
effaced. By his will he gave fifty thousand pounds between his three
surviving children, the Duke, Princess Amalie, and Mary, Princess of
Hesse: a strong box, not to be opened, to Lady Yarmouth. The rest
of his private fortune he had given by a deed, executed soon after the
battle of Culloden, and unrevoked, to the Duke of Cumberland;
who thence became heir to his jewels (sold afterwards to the successor
for about fifty thousand pounds), and to his mortgages in Germany,
amounting to about an hundred and fourscore thousand more:—a
scanty pittance, if compared with what he must have amassed in a
reign of three and thirty years. For part of that term he had received
yearly to his own use an hundred thousand pounds from the Civil List,
and never less than fifty thousand; relinquishing the rest to the disposal
of his Ministers for necessary services! At his accession he was worth
three hundred thousand pounds. The revenues of Hanover exceeded
five hundred thousand pounds a year; a sum he by no means expended.
Reduce his savings to the lowest, discount his purchases, and swell
Lady Yarmouth's legacy, which was given out to be ten thousand
pounds, to four times that sum; and allow two millions, which his
last war is said to have cost him in defence of Hanover; it will still
be difficult to believe that he did not die worth three hundred and
fifty thousand pounds—what became of the rest, or how concealed if
there was more, I pretend not to determine, nor even to guess.

The King himself had stated his late expenses for Hanover still
higher than I have set down. Mr. Onslow, the Speaker, showed me
a remarkable paper, which had been brought to him at the King's
command, in the year 1758, by Baron Munchausen, with whom Mr.
Onslow had no acquaintance. In that memorandum, the King declared
that he had then expended on the war £2,500,000, the savings of
thirty years; that he had borrowed above £200,000, here in England,
as much more in Germany, and that the Hanoverian Chancery of
war owed 200,000 rix dollars. 'The King', concluded the paper, 'can
do no more himself towards the war.'—If he did more in the two
following years, and it has never been pretended that he stopped

his hand in 1758, his remaining ability to go on induces a suspicion
that there was as little exactness observed in stating the rest of the
account. On the envelope of Munchausen's paper Mr. Onslow had
written, 'I could send no answer to this.'

The morning after the King's death, the Duke of Cumberland sent
for Lord Waldegrave, and told him, that if, as Lady Yarmouth
believed, no new will had been made since that in Princess Amalie's
hands, his father had done greatly for him—not, however, so largely
as he had once purposed; he had said to the Duke, 'William, I see
you will never marry; it is in vain to think of making a great establishment of a new branch through you: I shall do well for you for your
life; yet not so large as I should have done in that case.' This certainly
intimated a project of leaving his purchased Principalities in Germany
to the Duke.

Lord Waldegrave in return showed his Royal Highness an *extraordinary* piece; it was endorsed, *very private paper*, and was a letter
from the Duke of Newcastle to the first Earl of Waldegrave; in which
his Grace informed the Earl, that he had received by the messenger
the copy of the will and codicil of George the First; that he had
delivered it to his Majesty, who put it into the fire without opening
it—'so,' adds the Duke, 'we do not know whether it confirms the
other or not:' and he proceeds to say, 'I dispatch a messenger to the
Duke of Wolfenbuttle with the treaty, in which is granted all he
desires; and we expect by the return of the messenger the original
will from him.' George the First had left two wills; one in the
hands of Dr. Wake, Archbishop of Canterbury, the other with the
Duke of Wolfenbuttle. The Archbishop, on news of the King's death,
carried his copy to the Privy Council, and, without the precaution of
opening it before them, which the poor man could not apprehend
would be so necessary as it proved, gave it into the new King's hands,
who, to the Prelate's great surprise, carried it from the Council
unopened. The letter I have quoted above shows what was the fate
of the other copy: the honest Duke of Wolfenbuttle sold it for a
subsidy! George the First had been in the right to take these precautions: he himself had burned his wife's testament,[1] and her father's,

[1] This fact I learned from Henrietta, Countess of Suffolk, mistress of George the
Second. The Electress of Hanover liked the famous Count Konigsmark, while her
husband was at the Army. The old Elector, father of George the First, ordered
him away. The Electress, then Hereditary Princess, was persuaded to let him kiss
her hand before his departure. She saw him in bed — he retired, and was never
heard of more. When George the Second went first to Hanover after his father's

the Duke of Zell, both of whom had made George the Second their heir—a palliative of the latter's obliquity, if justice would allow of any violation.

End of the reign of King George the Second.

MEMOIRES OF THE REIGN OF KING GEORGE THE THIRD

Whoever has taken the trouble of reading my Memoires, which relate the transactions during the last ten years of King George the Second, will have seen that I had taken a resolution of interfering no

---

death, and made some alterations in the palace, the body of Konigsmark was found under the floor of the chamber next to the Electress's chamber. He had been strangled immediately on leaving her, by the old Elector's order, and buried under the floor. This fact Queen Caroline related to my father, Sir Robert Walpole. George the Second told it to his wife, but never to his mistress, Lady Suffolk, who had never heard it till I told it to her many years after. The Electress was separated from George I on that amour, and was called Duchess of Halle; and he married the Duchess of Kendal with his left hand. When the French threatened Hanover in Queen Anne's war, the Duchess of Halle was sent to her parents, the Duke and Duchess of Zell, who doted on her their only child, and she stayed a year with them; but though they were most earnest to retain her, she was forced to return to her confinement, in which she died the year before her husband. Some French prophetess, as supposed hired by the Duke of Zell, warned George I to take care of his wife, for he would not long outlive her. As the Germans are very superstitious, he believed the prophecy; and when he took leave of his son and the Princess of Wales, Caroline, he told them he should never see them more. George II, who hated his father, and was very fond of his mother, meant, if she had survived her husband, to bring her over, and declare her Queen Dowager. Lady Suffolk told me, that the morning after the news of the death of George I arrived, when she went, as Woman of the Bedchamber, to the new Queen, she found a whole and half-length portraits of the Electress hung up in the apartment; George II had had them locked up, but had not dared to produce them. Princess Amalie has the half-length at her house in Cavendish-square. George I told the Duchess of Kendal, that if he could, he would appear to her after his death. Soon after that event, a large bird, I forget of what sort, flew into her window. She believed it was the King's soul, and took the utmost care of it. George II was not less credulous; he believed in vampires. His son Frederic affected the same contradictory fondness for his grandfather, and erected the statue of George I in Leicester-fields; and intended, if he had come to the crown, to place a monument to his memory in St Paul's.

George I, besides the Duchess of Kendal, had several other mistresses, particularly one whom he brought over and created Countess of Darlington; by whom he was father of Charlotte, Viscountess Howe, though she was not publicly avowed. In the last year or two of his life he had another mistress, Miss Anne Brett, daughter, by her second husband, Colonel Brett, of the famous divorced Countess of Maccles-field, mother of Savage, the poet. Miss Brett had an apartment given to her in the palace at St James's, and was to have been created a Countess, if the King had returned. She afterwards married Sir William Leman. [H.W.]

more in public affairs. It was no ambition, or spirit of faction, that engaged me in them again. Inconstancy, or weariness of retirement, were as little the motives of my return to action. I am going to set forth the true causes; and if I am obliged to make more frequent mention of myself than I should wish to do, it will be from the necessity I am under of unfolding the secret springs of many events in which I was unwillingly a considerable actor. It is to gratify no vanity that I relate them: my portion was not brilliant: and though my counsels might have been more serviceable to my country and to my friends if they had been more followed, they were calculated to produce neither glory nor profit to myself, and were much oftener neglected than listened to. Nor should they be remembered here, if many miscarriages had not accrued from the neglect of them, as was felt and confessed by those to whom they had been suggested.

How far I have been in the right or in the wrong, I leave to the judgment of posterity, who shall be impartially informed; and who may draw some benefit from the knowledge of what I have seen; though few persons, I believe, profit much from history. Times seldom resemble one another enough to be very applicable; and if they do, the characters of the actors are very different. They, too, who read history most, are seldom performers in the political drama. Yet they who have performed any part of it, are at least able to give the best account of it, though still an imperfect one. No man is acquainted with the whole plot; as no man knows all the secret springs of the actions of others. His passions and prejudices warp his judgment, and cast a mist before the most penetrating sagacity. Yet, partial as the narratives of the actors must be, they will certainly approach nearer to truth than those of spectators, who, beholding nothing but events, pretend to account for them from causes which they can but suppose, and which frequently never existed. It is this assistance to history which I now offer, and by which I may explain some passages, which might otherwise never be cleared up.

I have a new reason for repeating here what I have said in former pages, that these are memoires, not history. The inequality, and perhaps even the contradictory opinions which may appear in them from being written at different periods, forbid this work to aim at the regular march of history. As I knew men more, I may have altered my sentiments of them—they themselves may have changed. If I had any personal causes for changing my opinion, I have told them fairly that the fault may be imputed to my passions, rather than to those I speak of. The actions of the persons must determine whether they altered, or I was prejudiced. But, though this dissonance may cast unequal colours on my work, I choose to leave it as I wrote it, having at each period spoken truth as it appeared to me. I might have made it more uniform by correction; but the natural colouring would have been lost; and I should rather have composed than written a history. As it stands an original sketch, it is at least a picture of my own mind and opinions. That sketch may be valuable to a few who study human nature even in a single character.

But I will make no further apology for a work which I am sensible has many faults; which I again declare I do not give as a history; and to which, if it has not merits sufficient to atone for its blemishes, I desire no quarter may be given. Remember, reader, I offer you no more than the memoires of men who had many faults, written by a man who had many himself; and who writes to inform you, not to engross your admiration. Had he given you a perfect history, and a flattering picture of himself, his work would have been a romance, and he an impostor. He lived with a contempt of hypocrisy; and writes as he lived.

Accession of George the Third

George the Second, contradicting the silly presages drawn from parallels, which had furnished opposition with names of unfortunate Princes, who were the second of their name, as Edward, Richard, Charles, and James, terminated his career with glory both to himself and his people. He died, crowned with years and honours, and respected from success, which with the multitude is the same as being beloved. He left a successor in the vigour of youth, ready to take the reins, and a ministry universally applauded, united, and unembarrassed by opponents.

No British monarch has ascended the throne with so many advantages as George the Third. Being the first of his line born in England, the prejudice against his family as foreigners ceased in his person. Hanover was no longer the native soil of our Princes; consequently, attachment to the Electorate was not likely to govern our councils, as it had done in the last two reigns. This circumstance, too, of his birth, shifted the unpopularity of foreign extraction from the House of Brunswick to the Stuarts. In the flower and bloom of youth, George had a handsome, open, and honest countenance; and with the favour that attends the outward accomplishments of his age, he had none of the vices that fall under the censure of those who are past enjoying them themselves.

The moment of his accession was fortunate beyond example. The extinction of parties had not waited for, but preceded, the dawn of his reign. Thus it was not a race of factions running to offer themselves, as is common, to a new Prince, bidding for his favour, and ready each to be disgusted if their antagonists were received with more grace; but a natural devolution of duty from all men to the uncontroverted heir of the Crown, who had no occasion to court the love of his subjects, nor could fear interrupting established harmony but by making any change in a system so well compacted. The Administration was firm, in good harmony with one another, and headed by the most successful genius that ever presided over our councils. Conquests had crowned our arms with wonderful circumstances of glory and fortune; and the young King seemed to have the option of extending our victories and acquisitions, or of giving peace to the world, by finding himself in a situation so favourable, that neither his ambition nor moderation could have been equitably reprehended. The designs and offences of France would have justified a fuller measure of revenge; moderation could want no excuse.

A passionate, domineering woman, and a Favourite without talents, soon drew a cloud over this shining prospect.

Without anticipating events too hastily, let it suffice to say that the measure of war was pushed, without even a desire that it should be successful; and that, although successful, it was unnaturally checked by a peace, too precipitate, too indigested, and too shameful, to merit the coldest eulogy of moderation.

The first moment of this new reign afforded a symptom of the Prince's character; of that cool dissimulation in which he had been so well initiated by his mother, and which comprehended almost the whole of what she had taught him. Princess Amalie, as soon as she was certain of her father's death, sent an account of it to the Prince of Wales; but he had already been apprised of it. He was riding, and received a note from a German *valet-de-chambre*, attendant on the late King, with a private mark agreed upon between them, which certified him of the event. Without surprise or emotion, without dropping a word that indicated what had happened, he said his horse was lame, and turned back to Kew. At dismounting he said to the groom, 'I have said this horse is lame; I forbid you to say the contrary.'

Mr. Pitt was the first who arrived at Kensington, and went to Princess Amailie for her orders. She told him nobody could give him better counsel than his own. He asked if he ought not to go to the Prince? She replied she could not advise him; but thought it would be right. He went. I mention these little circumstances because they show, from Mr. Pitt's uncertainty, that he was possessed with none of the confidence and ardour of a man who thinks himself a favourite.

From Kew the new King went directly to Carleton House, which belonged to the Princess Dowager; ordering his servants and the Privy Council to wait for him at Saville House, then his own residence; and adjoining to Leicester House, where the Princess usually lived. The Duke of Cumberland went to Leicester House, and waited two hours; but was sent for, as soon as the King knew it, to Carleton House, where he determined to stay, and avoid the parade and acclamation of passing through the streets: at the same time dismissing the guards, and ordering them to attend the body of his grandfather.

To the Duke of Cumberland he marked great kindness, and told him it had not been common in their family to live well together; but he was determined to live well with all his family. And he carried this attention so far as to take notice to the Duke after Council, that his friend Mr. Fox looked in great health. And again, when the Privy Council had made their address to his Majesty by the mouth of the Archbishop, it not being thought decent that the compliment on the death of his father should be uttered by the Duke, the King remarked it, and expressed an apprehension that they had put a slight upon his uncle. Nor would he suffer the name of his brother, the Duke of York, to be mentioned in the public prayers, because it must have taken place of that of the Duke of Cumberland.

At that first Council, the King spoke to nobody in particular but his former governor, Lord Waldegrave. His speech to them he made with dignity and propriety. In whatever related to his predecessor he behaved with singular attention and decency, refusing at first to give the word to the guard; and then only renewing what the late King had given. He sent to Princess Amalie to know where her father's will was deposited. She said one copy had been entrusted to her eight or nine years before; but thinking the King had forgotten it, she had lately put him in mind of it. He had replied, 'Did not she know, that when a new will was made, it cancelled all preceding?' No curiosity, no eagerness, no haste was expressed by the new King on that head; nor the smallest impediment thrown in the way of his grandfather's intentions. A Gentleman of the Bedchamber was immediately dismissed, who refused to sit up with the body, as is usual. Wilmot and Ranby, the late King's physician and surgeon, acquainted the King with two requests of their master, which were punctually complied with. They were, that his body might be embalmed as soon as possible, and a double quantity of perfumes used; and that the side of the late Queen's coffin, left loose on purpose, might be taken away and his body laid close to hers.

In his first Council the King named his brother the Duke of York, and Lord Bute, of the Cabinet. As no notice was taken of Lord Huntingdon, it indicated an uncertainty whether he, who had been Master of the Horse to the King when Prince, or Lord Gower, who had held that office under the late King, should fill the post. To the Speaker of the House of Commons, the King said it should not be his fault if that assembly did not go upon business earlier in the day than they had done of late; a flattering speech to an old man attached to old forms.

The King's speech to his Council afforded matter of remark, and gave early specimen of who was to be the confidential minister, and what measures were to be pursued: for it was drawn by Lord Bute, and communicated to none of the King's servants. It talked *of a bloody and expensive war, and of obtaining an honourable and lasting peace.* Thus was it delivered; but Mr. Pitt went to Lord Bute that evening, and, after an altercation of three hours, prevailed that in the printed copy the words should be changed to *an expensive but just and necessary war*; and that after the words *honourable peace* should be inserted, *in concert with our allies.* Lord Mansfield and others counselled these palliatives too; but it was two o'clock of the following afternoon before the King would yield to the alteration. Whether, that the private Junto could not digest the correction, or whether to give an idea of his Majesty's firmness, I know not; but great pains were taken to imprint an idea of the latter, as characteristic of the new reign; and it was sedulously whispered by the creatures of the Favourite and the Mother, that it was the plan to retain all the late King's ministers, but that his Majesty would not be governed by them, as his grandfather had been. In confirmation of part of this advertisement, the King told the Duke of Newcastle and Mr. Pitt that he knew their attachment to the Crown, and should expect theirs, and the assistance of all honest men.

Mr. Pitt was too quick-sighted not to perceive what would be the

complexion of the new reign. His favourite war was already struck at.
He himself had for some time been on the coldest terms with Lord
Bute; for possession of power, and reversion of power could not fail
to make two natures so haughty, incompatible. It was said, and I
believe with truth, that an outset so unpromising to his darling
measures made Mr. Pitt propose to the Duke of Newcastle a firm
union against the Favourite; but the Duke loved intrigues and new
allies too well to embrace it. And from that refusal has been dated
Mr. Pitt's animosity to Newcastle; though the part the latter
took more openly and more hostilely against him afterwards was
sufficient cause for that resentment. Whether these two men, so
powerful in Parliament and in the nation, could have balanced the
headlong affection that attends every new young Prince, is uncertain.
I think they could. A war so triumphant had captivated the whole
country. The Favourite was unknown, ungracious, and a Scot: his
connection with the Princess, an object of scandal. He had no declared
party; and what he had was insignificant. Nor would he probably
have dared to stem such a body of force as would have appeared
against him. At least the union of Pitt and Newcastle would have
checked the torrent, which soon carried everything in favour of
Prerogative. Newcastle's time-serving undermined Mr. Pitt, was destruc-
tive to himself, threw away all the advantages of the war, and brought
the country to the brink of ruin.

Yet this veteran, so busy, so selfish, and still so fond of power,
for a few days acted the part he ought to have adopted in earnest.
He waited on the King, pleaded his age, and begged to be excused
from entering on a new reign. The King told him he could not part
with him. Fortified with this gracious and comfortable command, he
next consulted his friends. It was not their interest to point out to
him the ridicule of thinking to rule in the Cabinet of a third George,
almost a boy. Four days more determined the Duke to take a new
court-lease of folly.

The Duke of Devonshire, though greatly younger, might not have
been without difficulties too, if he had pleased to remember them.
He had been ill-treated in the late reign by the Prince and Princess
Dowager, hated the Favourite, and had declared he would quit whenever the new reign should commence; but he thought better of it.

The Princess Dowager and Lord Bute

The Princess, whose ambition yielded to none, was desirous to figure in the new era, and demanded to be declared *Princess-Mother*. Precedents were searched for in vain; and she missed even this shadow of compensation for the loss of the appellation of *Queen*—a loss which she showed a little afterwards she could not digest.

The Earl of Bute seemed to act with more moderation. His credit was manifest; but he allotted himself no ministerial office, contenting himself for the present with the post of Groom of the Stole, which he had filled under the Prince, and for which room was prepared by removing the Earl of Rochford with a large pension. Lord Bute's agents gave out that he would upon no account interfere or break with Mr. Pitt. The latter, however, did not trust to these vague assurances, but endeavoured to maintain the preceding system: talked to the King of the Duke of Newcastle as First Minister, and as wishing him to continue so; and said he had never chosen any other channel for his addresses or demands to the late King—an intimation that he would make none through Lord Bute. For himself, he had meddled with nothing but the war, and he wished his Majesty to give some mark that he approved the measures of the late reign.

The other ministers were not less attentive to their own views. The Duke of Bedford insisted on returning to the Government of Ireland, and that Lord Gower should remain Master of the Horse; but the latter point was accommodated by the removal of Sir Thomas Robinson (with a pension) from the Great Wardrobe, which was bestowed on Lord Gower; and Lord Huntingdon continued in the post he had enjoyed under the Prince. Mr. Mackenzie, the Favourite's brother, was destined to be Master of the Robes, but was forced to give way to the Duke of Newcastle, who obtained it for Mr. Brudenel; for, though bent on making his court, his Grace as often marred his own policy as promoted it.

Yet this seeming union of Pitt and Newcastle, on which the influence of the former in some measure depended, disgusted the City. They said that Mr. Pitt had temporised with Newcastle before from necessity, but now it was matter of election. Yet by the intervention of Mr Pitt's agents, the City of London recommended to the King to be advised by his grandfather's ministers; and they even hinted at the loss the

King of Prussia would suffer by the death of his uncle. Their attachment to their idol did not stop there. The first stone of the new bridge at Blackfriars was laid by the Lord Mayor a few days after the King's accession, and on it was engraved so bombast an inscription in honour of Mr. Pitt, and drawn up in such bad Latin, that it furnished ample matter of ridicule to his enemies.

The Favourite, though traversed in his views by the power of these two predominant men, had not patience to be wholly a cypher, but gave many lesser and indirect marks of his designs. A separate standard was to be erected. Lord George Sackville had leave to pay his duty to the King, and was well received; which gave such offence to Mr. Pitt, that Lord George was privately instructed to discontinue his attendance. Lady Mary Stuart, daughter of the Favourite, and Lady Susan Stuart, daughter of the Earl of Galloway, a notorious and intemperate Jacobite, were named of the Bedchamber to the Lady Augusta, the King's eldest sister; and Sir Henry Erskine was restored to his rank, and gratified with an old regiment. The Earl of Lichfield, Sir Walter Bagot, and the principal Jacobites, went to Court, which George Selwyn, a celebrated wit, accounted for from the number of Stuarts that were now at St. James's.

The countenance shown to the Tories, and to their citadel, the University of Oxford, was at first supposed by those who stood at distance from the penetralia, the measure of Mr. Pitt, as consonant to his known desire of uniting, that was, breaking, all parties. But the Tories, who were qualified for nothing above a secret, could not keep even that. They came to Court, it is true; but they came with all their old prejudices. They abjured their ancient master, but retained their principles; and seemed to have exchanged nothing but their badge, *the White Rose* for *the White Horse. Prerogative* became a fashionable word; and the language of the times was altered before the Favourite dared to make any variation in the Ministry.

These steps did not pass unnoticed: nor was the nation without jealousy, even in the first dawn of the reign. Papers were stuck up at the Royal Exchange and in Westminster Hall, with these words, *No Petticoat Government; no Scotch Favourite.* An intemperance which proceeded so far afterwards, that, as the King passed in his chair to visit his mother in an evening, the mob asked him if he was going to suck? The Princess herself was obliged to discontinue frequenting the theatres, so gross and insulting were the apostrophes with which she was saluted from the galleries.

The views of the Court were so fully manifested afterwards, that no doubt can be made but a plan had been early formed of carrying the prerogative to very unusual heights. The Princess was ardently fond of power, and all its appanages of observance, rank, and wealth. The deepest secrecy and dissimulation guarded every avenue of her passions; and close retirement was adapted to these purposes. She could not appear in public (after the arrival of the Queen) as the first woman of the kingdom: her unpopularity made her pride tremble; and privacy shrouded such hours as were not calculated to draw esteem; and it contracted her expenses. After the King's marriage she appeared seldom or never at St. James's, nor deigned to accompany the ceremony of the Coronation. The attendance of her ladies was dispensed with except on Drawing-room days; and by degrees even her Maids of Honour and Women of the Bedchamber were removed from her palace, where she lived in a solitude that would have passed for the perfection of Christian humility in the ages of monkish ignorance. Jealousy of her credit over her son made her impose almost as strict laws of retirement on him. He was accessible to none of his Court but at the stated hours of business and ceremony: nor was any man but the Favourite, and the creatures with whom he had garrisoned the palace, allowed to converse with the King. Affection had no share in this management.

The Princess, who was never supposed to disclose her mind with freedom, but on the single topic of her own children, had often mentioned her eldest son with contempt; and during the life of her husband had given into all his partiality for the Duke of York. When her views of governing by her husband were cut off, she applied to the untutored inexperience of his heir: and the first step towards the influence she meditated was by filling his mind with suspicions and ill impressions of all mankind. His uncle, the Duke of Cumberland, was made another instrument. The young Prince had a great appetite: he was asked if he wished to be as gross as his uncle? Every vice, every condescension was imputed to the Duke, that the Prince might be stimulated to avoid them.

The Favourite, who had notions of honour, and was ostentatious, endeavoured to give a loftier cast to the disposition of his pupil, though not to the disparagement of the vassalage in which he was to be kept. Lord Bute had a little reading, and affected learning. Men of genius, the arts and artists, were to be countenanced. The arts might amuse the young King's solitary hours: authors might defend the measures of the Government, and were sure to pay for their pensions with incense, both to their passive and active protectors. The pedantry and artifice of these shallow views served but to produce ridicule. Augustus fell asleep over drawings and medals, which were pushed before him every evening; and Maecenas had so little knowledge, and so little taste, that his own letters grew a proverb for want of orthography; and the scribblers he countenanced were too destitute of talents to raise his character or their own. The coins of the King were the worst that had appeared for above a century; and the revenues of the Crown were so soon squandered in purchasing dependents, that architecture, the darling art of Lord Bute, was contracted from the erection of a new palace to altering a single door-case in the drawing-room at St. James's. Yet his emissaries, the Scotch, were indefatigable in coining popular sayings and sentences for the King. It was given out that he would suffer no money to be spent on elections. Circumstances that recoiled with force, when every one of those aphorisms were contracted by practice.

But the chief engine to conciliate favour was the King's piety. The Princess, no doubt, intended it should be real, for she lived in dread of a mistress. But mankind was not inclined to think that her morals could have imprinted much devotion on the mind of her son: nor was any man the dupe of those professions but Secker, the Archbishop, who, for the first days of the reign, flattered himself with the idea of becoming First Minister in a Court that hoisted the standard of religion. He was unwearied in attendance at St. James's, and in presenting bodies of clergy; and his assiduity was so bustling and assuming that, having pushed aside the Duke of Cumberland to get at the King, his Royal Highness reprimanded him with a bitter taunt. The prelate soon discovered his mistake. Nor were the Princess or the Favourite inclined to trust the King in the hands of a churchman, whom they knew so well, and whose sanctity was as equivocal as their own.

As far as could be discerned of the King's natural disposition it was humane and benevolent. If flowing courtesy to all men was the habit of his dissimulation, at least it was so suited to his temper that no gust of passion, no words of bitterness, were ever known to break from him. He accepted services with grace and appearance of feeling: and if he forgot them with an unrestrained facility, yet he never marked his displeasure with harshness. Silence served him to bear with unwelcome ministers, or to part with them. His childhood was tinctured with obstinacy: it was adopted at the beginning of his reign, and called firmness, but did not prove to be his complexion. In truth, it would be difficult to draw his character in positive colours. He had neither passions nor activity. He resigned himself obsequiously to the government of his mother and Lord Bute: learned, and even entered with art into the lessons they inspired, but added nothing of his own. When the task was done, he relapsed into indifference and indolence till roused to the next day's part.

The Dukes of Richmond and Grafton

The Duke of Richmond, haughty and young, was offended that his cousin, Colonel Keppel, was removed from Gentleman of the Horse, which the King destined for one of his own servants. The Duke asked an audience; but began it with objecting to the distinction paid to Sir Henry Erskine. This so much disgusted, that the King would not hear the Duke on the subject of Keppel. On cooler thoughts, Lord Bute was sent to the Duke to offer him to be of the King's Bedchamber. He accepted it on condition that Keppel should remain Gentleman of the Horse, which was likewise granted. But this pacification lasted few days. Lord Fitzmaurice, a favourite of Lord Bute, was made Equerry to the King, though inferior in military rank to Lord George Lenox and Charles Fitzroy, brothers of the Dukes of Richmond and Grafton. The latter had been of the Bedchamber to the King, when Prince, but had quitted it from dislike of Court attendance, and disgusted with the haughty stateliness affected by Lord Bute. Richmond and Grafton were much of an age; each regarded himself as Prince of the Blood; and emulation soon created a sort of rivalship between them. The Duke of Richmond's figure was noble, and his countenance singularly handsome. The Duke of Grafton was low, but manly, and with much grace in his address. The passions of both were strong; but of the first, ardent; of the latter, slow and inflexible. His temper was not happy; but the Duke of Richmond's, which was thought worse, because more impetuous, was pliant, and uncommonly easy and accommodating in his family and society. Both were thought avaricious; but the latter very unjustly, generally approaching nearer to the opposite extreme of profusion. His parts, too, were quicker and more subtle than Grafton's, and more capable of application, though his elocution was much inferior. The Duke of Grafton had a grace and dignity in his utterance that commanded attention, and dazzled in lieu of matter; and his temper being shy and reserved, he was supposed to be endued with more steadiness than his subsequent conduct displayed. Neither of them wanted obstinacy; but their obstinacy not flowing from system, it was in both a torrent more impetuous in its course than in its duration.

The Duke of Grafton made a decent representation to the King, on the wrong done to his brother, and demanded rank for him. The other Duke carried a violent memorial, and commented on it in a manner which, some years afterwards, he found had never been forgotten or forgiven. The next day he resigned the Bedchamber, but not his regiment. In a few days he repented this step, and went to Lord Bute to explain away his resignation, which, he said, might not be known. Lord Bute replied all the world knew it. The Duke, thinking this coldness proceeded from a suspicion that he was influenced by Fox, his brother-in-law, disclaimed all connection with him, and said he had never approved his sister's marriage. Lord Bute, who even then probably had views of Fox's support as a counter-balance to Pitt, replied that Mr. Fox's alliance could be a disgrace to no man; as he must always be of great use and weight in this country. Yet the Duke's youth and frankness made him avow what he had said to Fox himself, in the presence of Lord Albemarle, who, though not much older, had far more worldly cunning, and no doubt reported the conversation to his master, the Duke of Cumberland; for Richmond and Albemarle, though first cousins, were no friends; and the latter possessed all the arts of a court. The Duke, rebuffed by the Favourite, next consulted the Duke of Cumberland, who told him prudently that he was sorry the Duke of Richmond, at twenty-three, had quarrelled with the King at twenty-two; and advised him to retire into the country, which he did.

1761

Lord Bute

The new year opened with promotions. The Lord Keeper Henley was made Lord Chancellor. Lord Denbigh, a creature of the Favourite, Master of the Harriers; and George Grenville was called to the Cabinet Council. Pitt had ever treated him with contempt, and little expected to find him vain or daring enough to enter the lists against him. Grenville's conceit of himself was by no means measured by the standard of modesty. His ambition was equal to Pitt's; and his plodding, methodic genius made him take the spirit of detail for ability. Avarice, which he possessed in no less proportion than his other passions, concurred to lead him from a master who browbeat and treated him superciliously to worship the rising sun. Lord Bute was in want of tools; and it was a double prize to acquire them from his rival's shop.

But Fortune, had he known how to use her gifts, was kinder to the Favourite than his own politics. His wife's father, old Wortley Montagu, died at this time, and left to her and her second son a fortune that, at four per cent., was estimated at one million three hundred and forty thousand pounds. This was the third death within twelve months that happened to aggrandize Lord Bute. The decease of his uncle, the Duke of Argyle, left Scotland open to his power; and that of the late King put the Crown itself into his hands. The estate of his father-in-law was all he was qualified to enjoy. What could be expected from a boy locked up from the converse of mankind, governed by a mother still more retired, who was under the influence of a man that had passed his life in solitude, and was too haughty to admit to his familiarity but half a dozen silly authors and flatterers? Sir Henry Erskine, a military poet, Home, a tragedy-writing parson, and Worseley, a rider of the great horse and architect, were his principal confidants. The nation was soon governed accordingly. And yet it was not the nation's fault if it did not receive the yoke even from this Junto!

Lord Talbot

But a phenomenon that for some time occasioned more speculation than even the credit of the Favourite, was the staff of Lord Steward being put into the hands of Lord Talbot, with the addition of an earldom. As neither gravity, rank, interest, abilities, or morals could be adduced to countenance this strange exaltation, no wonder it caused very unfavourable comments. This Lord had long affected a very free-spoken kind of patriotism on all occasions. He had some wit, and a little tincture of a disordered understanding; but was better known as a boxer and man of pleasure, than in the light of a statesman. The Duchess of Beaufort had been publicly divorced from her lord on his account; and was not the only woman of fashion who had lived with him openly as his mistress. He was strong, well made, and very comely; but with no air, nor with the manners of a man of quality. No wonder the promotion of such a Minister, in a reign that advertised piety was believed to have issued from that Sanctum Sanctorum of the Court, where the mysteries of the Bona Dea were not supposed to be celebrated. It grew more comic still, when the new statesman appeared to be a reformer too. As the Court knew that the measures it had in contemplation could only be carried by money, every stratagem was invented to curtail the common expenses of the Palace. As these fell under the province of the Lord Steward, nothing was heard of but cooks cashiered, and kitchens shut up. Even the Maids of Honour, who did not expect rigours from a great officer of Lord Talbot's complexion, were reduced to complain of the abridgement of their allowance for breakfast. The public joined in the cry, and the shops teemed with scandalous prints against the reformer and his patroness.

Miss Vansittart

Not to return to this Atalantis-kind of anecdote again (though too much agitated, and productive of too many consequences not to make an essential part in the history of this reign) it remained an indissoluble problem, what was the real secret of the interior of the Princess Dowager's Court. There was a Miss Vansittart, of a Jacobite family, who had suddenly been promoted by Lord Bute to be Maid of Honour. She had been pretty, but was past her bloom before the public ever heard her name. The Earl for several years visited her regularly every evening at seven for at least two hours. His wife, a very prudent and sensible woman, not apt to hazard an éclat, had given some marks of jealousy on this connection. But what surprized much more, was that Miss Vansittart grew the sole female intimate of the Princess, and passed as many hours alone with her Royal Highness in a morning, as she did with the Earl in an evening. The Princess often went to her house. They who justified her from any improper correspondence with Lord Bute, affirmed that the Princess, who was infinitely distempered, saw her surgeons at Miss Vansittart's apartment. But the royal chair and servants standing in the street was an affair of much

less secrecy, than it could be to be visited by surgeons at her own
uninhabited palace. On the other hand, if Miss Vansittart was the
Favourite's mistress, it did not seem to recommend her to the favour
of a greater mistress: nor did the Earl's age, turned of fifty, promise
to be able to keep pace between two rivals. The junction of Lord
Talbot to this singular trio did not make the mystery more explicable.
Of one use it was believed Miss Vansittart was to the Princess, of
being her agent for the sale of honours: Sir John Gibbon owned that
he had purchased a red ribband through that channel.

Speaker Onslow

The last day of the session, March 18th, was fixed for returning
the thanks of the House of Commons to Mr. Onslow, their Speaker,
who had filled the chair with unblemished integrity during the whole
long reign of George the Second, and who had the prudence to quit
the scene before his years and growing infirmities made him a burthen
to himself and the public. No man had ever supported with more
firmness the privileges of the House, nor sustained the dignity of his
office with more authority. His knowledge of the Constitution equalled
his attachment to it. To the Crown he behaved with all the decorum
of respect, without sacrificing his freedom of speech. Against encroachments of the House of Peers he was an inflexible champion. His disinterested virtue supported him through all his pretensions; and though
to conciliate popular favour he affected an impartiality that by turns
led him to the borders of insincerity and contradiction—and though
he was so minutely attached to forms that it often made him troublesome in affairs of higher moment, it will be difficult to find a subject
whom gravity will so well become, whose knowledge will be so useful
and so accurate, and whose fidelity to his trust will prove so unshaken.

George III and Lady Sarah Lenox

While the attention of mankind hung on the negotiation, the King's
messengers were suddenly sent forth to all Privy Councillors to meet
at one o'clock, at St. James's, July 8th, on urgent and important
business. The business itself was an absolute secret. Everybody concluded that so solemn and unusual a summons of the Council was

to give fuller sanction to peace. How great was the general surprise when they heard his Majesty had convened this assembly to notify his intended marriage with the Princess of Mecklenberg Strelitz! A resolution taken and conducted with so much mystery, that till that hour perhaps not six men in England knew such a Princess existed.

It has been mentioned with what aversion the Princess Dowager had opposed a marriage projected by the late King between his heir-apparent and a very accomplished Princess of Brunswick. A wife for her son, not chosen by herself nor obliged to her, by no means suited the views of the Princess. Could she have chained up his body, as she fettered his mind, it is probable she would have preferred his remaining single. But though his chastity had hitherto remained to all appearance inviolate notwithstanding his age and sanguine complexion, it was not to be expected such a fast could be much longer observed. A mistress would have been more tremendous than a wife. The next brother, the Duke of York, was not equally tractable, had expressed little reverence for his mother, and much antipathy to her favourite. If the King should die and leave even an infant, a minority did not deprive the Princess of all prospect of protracting her rule.

But there had happened circumstances still more pressing, more alarming. The King was fallen in love with Lady Sarah Lenox, sister of the Duke of Richmond; a very young lady of the most blooming beauty, and shining with all the graces of unaffected, but animated nature. What concurred to make her formidable to the Mother and Favourite, was, her being under the tutorage of Mr. Fox, her eldest sister's husband; and in truth, he and her family spared no assiduity to fix the young monarch's heart. And though Fox would probably not have been scrupulous or delicate on the terms of cementing that union, the King's overtures were so encouraging, that Fox's views extended even to placing the young lady on the throne. Early in the winter, the King told Lady Susan Strangways, Mr. Fox's niece, and the *confidante* of Lady Sarah, that he hoped she (Lady Susan) would not go out of town soon. She said, she should. 'But,' replied the King, 'you will return in summer, for the Coronation.' Lady Susan answered, 'I do not know; I hope so.' 'But', said the King again, 'they talk of a wedding. There have been many proposals; but I think an English match would do better than a foreign one. Pray tell Lady Sarah Lenox I say so.' The next time Lady Sarah went to Court (and her family took care that should not be seldom) the King said, he hoped Lady Susan had told her his last conversation.

The Junto was not blind to these whispers and dialogues. Lady Bute was instructed to endeavour to place herself in the circle, and prevent them. And the Princess Augusta marked her observation of what was going forward to Lady Sarah herself, laughing in her face, and trying to affront her. But Fox was not to be so rebuffed. Though he went himself to bathe in the sea (possibly to disguise his intrigues), he left Lady Sarah at Holland House, where she appeared every morning in a field close to the great road (where the King passed on horseback) in a fancied habit, making hay.

Such mutual propensity fixed the resolution of the Princess. One Colonel Graeme was dispatched in the most private manner as a traveller, and vested with no character, to visit various little Protestant Courts, and make report of the qualifications of the several unmarried princesses. Beauty, and still less, talents, were not, it is likely, the first object of his instructions. On the testimony of this man, the golden apple was given to the Princess of Mecklenburg; and the marriage precipitately concluded. The ambassador was too remarkable not to be farther mentioned. This Graeme, then, was a notorious Jacobite, and had been engaged in the late rebellion. On a visit he made to Scotland, his native country, after this embassy, David Hume, the historian, said to him, 'Colonel Graeme, I congratulate you on having exchanged the dangerous employment of making Kings, for the more lucrative province of making Queens.'

So complete was the King's deference to the will of his mother, that he blindly accepted the bride she had chosen for him; though, to the very day of the council, he carried on his courtship to Lady Sarah; and she did not doubt of receiving the crown from him, till she heard the public declaration of its being designed for another. Yet, in confirmation of the trust he had reposed in Lady Susan Strangways, himself appointed Lady Sarah to be one of the bride-maids to the Queen. Yet Lord Bute's friends affected to give another turn to the story, and insisted that the King had never thought of Lady Sarah but for his mistress. All, they affirmed, he had said to Lady Susan was, to bid her ask Lady Sarah if she should like a place in the family of the new Queen; that she had accepted it, and that the King had destined her to be Mistress of the Robes. Her surprise and disappointment, however, were too strongly marked to make this legend credible. Lady Susan adhered to the truth of what she had reported, in various examinations by her father and uncle. And the resentment Lady Sarah expressed, and which caused, as the Court said, her not being placed about the new Queen, was proof enough on which side the truth lay. The Junto persuaded the King she was a bad young woman; but if she was, what hindered her becoming his mistress? Was it criminal to propose being his wife rather than his mistress? And what became of the King's boasted piety, if he intended to place his mistress about his wife? Some coquet attempts, which Lady Sarah afterwards made to recover his notice, and her stooping to bear the Queen's train as bride-maid, did her more prejudice than all that was invented against her. Pique and extreme youth might excuse both; and her soon after preferring a clergyman's son to several great matches, gave evidence that ambition was not a rooted passion in her. Her rash conduct some few years afterwards showed how little she was formed to make herself or others happy.

In my own opinion, the King had thoughts of her as a wife; but wanted resolution to oppose his mother and Lord Bute. Fortunately, no doubt, in this instance; for the daughter of a subject, and the sister-in-law of so ambitious and exceptionable a man as Fox, would probably have been productive of most serious consequences. To avoid returning to this topic, I will only remember that, during the wedding-service, on mention of Abraham and Sarah, the King could not conceal his confusion. And the day following, when everybody was presented to the Queen, Lord Westmoreland, old and dimsighted, seeing Lady Sarah in the rich habit of bride-maid, mistook her for Queen and was going to kneel and kiss her hand.

The Queen (Charlotte of Mecklenburg-Strelitz)

She had been educated in that strict course of piety which in Germany reaches to superstition; a habit in which she was encouraged to such a degree, that when the King visited his mother, which he soon, at the desire of the Princess, began to do, without the Queen, she was afraid of staying alone, and retired to her two German women; her English ladies not being suffered to keep her company. Yet this weakness seemed solely the result of a bad education. Her temper appeared to be lively, and her understanding sensible and quick. Great good-nature, set off by much grace in her manner, recommended all she said. Her person was small, and very lean, but well made. Her face pale and homely, her nose something flat, her mouth very large. Her hair was of a fine brown, and her countenance pleasing.

When first she saw the palace she trembled. The Duchess of Hamilton smiled. The Queen said, 'You may laugh; you have been married twice; but it is no joke to me.' The King received her in the garden of St. James's; she would have kneeled, but he raised and embraced her, and led her to the Princess, where they and Lady Augusta dined together. Between nine and ten at night they went to chapel. The Duke of Cumberland gave her away, and after the ceremony they appeared for a few minutes in the Drawing-room, and then went to supper. She played and sung, for music was her passion, but she loved other amusements, too, and had been accustomed to them; but excepting her music, all the rest were retrenched, nor was she ever suffered to play at cards,[1] which she loved. While she was dressing, she was told the King liked some particular manner of dress. She said, 'Let him dress himself; I shall dress as I please.' They told her he liked early hours; she replied, she did not, and 'qu'elle ne vouloit pas se coucher avec les poules.' A few weeks taught her how little power she had acquired with a Crown. The affection she conceived for the King softened the rigour of her captivity. Yet now and then a sigh stole out, and now and then she attempted, though in vain, to enlarge her restraint. What must have penetrated deeper was that policy did not seem to be the sole motive of the mortifications she endured. At times there entered a little wantonness of power into the Princess's treatment of her. The King made her frequent presents of magnificent jewels; and, as if diamonds were empire, she was never allowed to appear in public without them. The first time she received the sacrament she begged not to wear them, one pious command of her mother having been not to use jewels at her first communion. The King indulged her; but Lady Augusta carrying this tale to her mother, the Princess obliged the King to insist on the jewels, and the poor young Queen's tears and terrors could not dispense with her obedience.

Lord Talbot

Here ended, almost as soon as it began, the credit of Lord Talbot. He was sometimes well, sometimes ill with Lord Bute, and though remaining in favour at Court, never seemed to have any influence there. A trifling circumstance, because it occasioned an event that made much noise afterwards, must be mentioned. As Lord Steward, Lord

[1] She did some years afterwards with the King, but quite in private. [H.W.]

Talbot composed part of that ridiculous pageant at the Coronation, the entry of the Champion. So fond was Lord Talbot of his share in this mummery, that he rehearsed his part on his steed in Westminster Hall, and carried his new Bishop of London to be witness of his feats. The Duke of York calling Hayter, who was lame, up to the *haut pas,* which he ascended with difficulty, the Bishop said, 'You see, sir, how hard it is for me to get a step.' When the day came, Lord Talbot piqued himself on not turning his back to the King, and produced a strange hubbub of laughter by trying to force his horse to retire backwards out of the hall. With the City, with the Knights of the Bath, and the Barons of the Cinque Ports, Lord Talbot had various squabbles, by retrenching their tables at the Coronation. Beckford told him it was hard if the citizens should have no dinner, when they were to give the King one, which would cost them ten thousand pounds. This menace prevailed. Sir William Stanhope, brother of Lord Chesterfield, a man of not less wit, and of more ill-nature than his elder, said, 'It was an affront to the Knights of the Bath; for *some* of us,' added he, 'are *gentlemen.*' It was a more bitter speech he made against the Scotch and their Protectress. 'He would not go to Court,' he said, 'for fear of the itch, which would reduce him to go to the Princess's Court for brimstone.' To the Barons of the Cinque Ports Lord Talbot said, 'If they came to him as Lord Steward, their request could not be granted; if, as Lord Talbot, he was a match for any of them.' This boisterous and absurd behaviour drew aside much odium from the Favourite; but as puppet-shows were not exhibited every day, the zany was forgotten, and the hisses of the mob soon fastened on the principal performer.

William Pitt

His hands tied, the nation affronted, and duped by the partial breaking off of the treaty with France, no proper resentment permitted against Spain, Mr. Pitt found he could do no farther good. His character had been lost by acquiescence; and nothing could rouse the nation, but his quitting the sphere of business, where he was so treacherously controlled. He had desired to enter his protest in the council-books against the temporising advice of his colleagues. He and Lord Temple delivered to the King their reasons and advice for a war with Spain; and October 2nd Mr. Pitt took leave of the Council, thanking the ministers of the late King for the support they had given to the war; and on the 5th he resigned the Seals. Lord Temple quitted on the 9th following.

It is difficult to say which exulted most on this occasion, France, Spain, or Lord Bute, for Mr. Pitt was the common enemy of all three. Newcastle, Hardwicke, Bedford, Devonshire, Mansfield, and Fox were not less pleased, for they had all concurred to thwart his plan. Lord Talbot alone, though of the same faction, seemed to see farther than any of them. He advised the Duke of Newcastle, 'not to die for joy on the Monday, nor for fear on the Tuesday.'

The nation was thunderstruck, alarmed, and indignant. The City of London proposed to address the King to know why Mr. Pitt was dismissed; but it being replied, that the King would tell them he had not dismissed Mr. Pitt, but had wished him to continue in employment, the motion dropped. Some proposed a general mourning; others, more reasonable, to thank Mr. Pitt for his services; but this too was damped; for the Favourite's agents were not idle, and insinuated that Mr. Pitt had acted with mischievous views; for they who were incapable of great views, were excellent in undermining. The King was advised to heap rewards on his late Minister. The Princess pressed it eagerly. A peerage, a vast pension, the government of Canada (as a mark that it was not to be restored at the peace), were offered to him. He had the frailty to accept a peerage for his wife, and a pension of three thousand a year for three lives!

Mrs. Anne Pitt

His own sister, Mrs. Anne Pitt, who was of the opposite faction, furnished his enemies with a severe sarcasm. She had been Maid of Honour to Queen Caroline, and was warmly attached to her brother, with whom she lived. On his promotion to the Pay-office, he had shaken her off in an unbecoming manner. She had excellent parts and strong passions. Lord Bolingbroke had recommended her to the late Prince, on whose death she had been made Privy-purse to the Princess; but being of an intriguing and most ambitious nature, she soon destroyed her own prospect by an impetuosity to govern her mistress, and by embarking in other Cabals at that Court. Her disgrace followed, but without dismission; on which she had retired to France. On her return, though she could never recover the favour of the

Princess, she so successfully cultivated the patronage of Lord and Lady Bute, that she kept her ground at Leicester Fields, and obtained a large pension. This she had notified by letter to her brother. He had coldly replied, that he congratulated her on the addition to her fortune, but was grieved to see the name of Pitt in a list of pensions. On his accepting one, she copied his own letter, turning it against himself; and though restrained by her friends from sending it to him, she repeated what she had done, till it became the common talk of the town.

William Pitt

The decency of Lord Temple's prelude to new opposition soon changed its hue in a manner more suited to his factious turbulence. On the 9th, the King and all the Royal family dined in the City with the Lord Mayor. Thither, too, went Mr. Pitt and Lord Temple in a chariot together—a step justly censured, and very near productive of fatal consequences. To *them* all acclamations were addressed; and the distinctions paid in the Guildhall to Mr. Pitt, to the total neglect of the King, bestowed all the honour of the triumph on the former. Little was wanting to turn the pageant into a tragedy. Riots ensued, and many persons were insulted. The Favourite had taken the precaution of having a guard of butchers and bruisers, and by the defence of that convoy alone, escaped mischief. Sir Samuel Fludyard, the Lord Mayor, caused diligent inquiry to be made into the proceedings of the day, and learned that Beckford himself had visited several public-houses over night, and had appointed ringleaders to different stations, and had been the first to raise the huzza in the hall on the entrance of Mr. Pitt. *His* joining himself to a pomp dedicated to a Court that he had just quitted, was not decent. The ambition of drawing to himself the homage of the people, was not modest. To offer himself as an incentive to civil tumult, and to how dangerous consequences he could not tell, was not a symptom of very innocent intentions.

Colonel Barré

Lord George was finishing his speech as I came into the House. My ear was struck with sounds I had little been accustomed to of late, virulent abuse on the last reign—and from a voice unknown to me.

I turned, and saw a face equally new; a black, robust man, of a military figure, rather hard-favoured than not young, with a peculiar distortion on one side of his face, which it seems was owing to a bullet lodged loosely in his cheek, and which gave a savage glare to one eye. What I less expected from his appearance was very classic and eloquent diction, and as determined boldness, as if accustomed to harangue in that place. He told the House that in the late King's reign we had been governed solely by Hanoverian measures and councils; and though called to order (in truth unparliamentarily), he proceeded with the same vociferous spirit to censure all ministers but Lord Bute; and for Mr. Pitt, who was not present, he received the appellation of a profligate minister, who had thrust himself into power on the shoulders of the mob. The present King, said this new Court-Tribune, was so English, that he did not believe he had looked into the map for Hanover; and he commiserated the present ministers, who were labouring through the dregs of German councils.

The reader must imagine the astonishment occasioned by this martial censor. He was a Colonel Barré, of French extraction, born at Dublin, and had served for some years in the war in America with reputation, prosecuting his studies with assiduity in the intervals of duty. With General Wolfe he had been intimately connected, both as an officer and penman; but had thought himself ill-used by Mr. Pitt, though the friends of the latter, and Lord Barrington, lately Secretary at War, bore witness that Mr. Pitt had made it a point to serve him. In his younger years he had acted plays with so much applause, that, it was said, Garrick had offered him a thousand pounds a year to come upon the stage.

This man, therefore, had been selected by Lord Fitzmaurice (become Earl of Shelburne by the death of his father) as a bravo to run down Mr. Pitt. Lord Shelburne held a little knot of young orators at his house; but Barré soon overtopped them; and Fox had pushed on the project of employing him to insult Pitt—to what extent was surmised by all the world.

1762

The Cock Lane Ghost

The facility which the Favourite found of mastering so great and victorious a kingdom, and of removing the man who had carried the glory of his country so high, was not the only evidence, that however enlightened an age may be, knavery and folly need never despair. The tares they sow will shoot amidst any harvest. Will it be credited that, while the Romish superstition was crumbling away even in Spain and Portugal, a set of enthusiastic rogues dared to exhibit in the very heart of London, a pantomime of imposture, which would hardly have been swallowed in a paltry village of Castile? The Methodists had endeavoured to establish in Warwickshire, not only the belief, but the actual existence, of ghosts. Being detected, they struck a bold stroke, and attempted to erect their system in the metropolis itself. A Methodist family, at first out of revenge, endeavoured to fasten on one Parsons the imputation of having debauched and murdered his wife's sister. A young girl was reported to be visited by the deceased, whom she called Fanny, and with whom she established a correspondence of question and answer—not by words, but by scratching. A certain number of scratches signified yes; another number, no. At first this farce, which was acted in Cock Lane, in the city, was confined to the mob of the neighbourhood. As the rumour spread, persons of all ranks thronged to the house. Two Methodist clergymen constantly attended the child, who lay in bed in a wretched chamber, with only a dim rushlight at one end. These worthy divines affected to cast an air of most serious import on the whole transaction, and by their interposition prompted Fanny and the girl on any dilemma. A servant wench commented and explained Fanny's oracle. The father would accept no money from the various visitants, for which he was promised an adequate recompense by the chiefs of the sect. When the story had gained a requisite footing, Fanny had the indiscreet confidence to declare that her body was not in the vault where it had been interred. Samuel Johnson, author of the Dictionary, was in the number of the deluded, and with some others as wise as himself, visited the vault, where, to the disappointment of their credulity, they found the body. Had the Apostles had the precaution of conveying it away, the fury of the people might have been actuated to strange lengths; for so much credit had the story gained, that Parsons, the accused, fearing a prosecution, began first. A regular trial instantly unravelled the cheat: the girl was detected of performing the scratchings herself, and one of the clergymen proved to be her abettor. Lord Chief Justice Mansfield tried the cause: the divine had the impudence to present a letter to him on the bench from the Archbishop of Canterbury, interceding on his behalf—for Secker had a fellow feeling for hypocritic enthusiasm. The Chief Justice put the letter into his pocket unopened, saying, it was impossible it could relate to the cause in question. Yet the punishment of these impostors was very moderate; whereas the same judge inflicted most severe penalties on one Anett, who published weekly papers against the book of Genesis. The Methodists did not take shame. They turned informers against profaners of the Sabbath, tried to establish great rigour on Good Friday and the fast-day, and to revive the superstition of holidays, when even the late Pope himself, Benedict XIV, had struck several out of the calendar. But the ritual of the Church of Rome was too rich in materials not to be copied by new zealots. They introduced into their service hymns sung in parts by children, as very captivating to the multitude; and the Countess of Huntingdon, the patronness of the rising Church, erected a chapel at Bath, and at other places of drinking waters; the sick and diseased being an obvious prey to Reformers. Hogarth exerted his last stroke of genius on the occasion above mentioned; the print he published on the Cock Lane Ghost had a mixture of humorous and sublime satire, that not only surpassed all his other performances, but which would alone immortalise his unequalled talents.

Bute and Newcastle

Both Houses thus complaisant and submissive, there wanted but the office of Prime Minister to glut the Favourite's ambition: and no wonder that he, who had dared to strike the name of the first monarch in military glory in Europe from the list of Great Britain's pensioners, only to gratify the feminine piques of the backstairs; and who had ventured successfully to remove Mr. Pitt from the command of that country which he had saved, restored, exalted;—no wonder, such a Phaeton should drive over a ridiculous old dotard, who had ever been in everybody's way, and whose feeble hands were still struggling for power, when the most he ought to have expected was, that his flattery and obsequiousness might have moved charity to leave him an appearance of credit. It was absurd for him to stay in place, insolent to attempt to stay there by force, and impudent to pretend to patriotism when driven out with contempt. Against his will he was preserved from having a share in the infamy of the ensuing peace.

May 14th, the Duke acquainted the King that he would resign, who answered coldly, 'Then, my Lord, I must fill up your place as well as I can.' Still Newcastle lingered; and, as he owned afterwards to the Duke of Cumberland, his friends had laboured to prevent the fatal blow. Lord Mansfield, he said, had *pleaded* with Lord Bute for above an hour, and could not extract from him a wish that the Duke should continue in the Treasury. Fox asked Lord Mansfield if this was true? He replied, 'Not an hour, for I soon saw it was to no purpose.'

Thus disgraced, and disgracing himself, on the 26th the Duke of Newcastle resigned: and he, who had begun the world with heading mobs against the ministers of Queen Anne; who had braved the Heir-apparent of the new family, and forced himself upon him as god-father to his son; who had recovered that Prince's favour, and pre-served power under him at the expense of every minister whom that Prince preferred; and who had been a victorious rival of another Prince of Wales; was now buffeted from a fourth Court by a very suitable competitor, and was reduced in his tottering old age to have recourse to those mobs and that popularity, which had raised him fifty years before: and as almost the individual crisis was revolved, with a scandalous treaty and a new prospect of arbitrary power, it looked as if Newcastle thought himself young again, because the times of his youth were returned, and he was obliged to act with boys!

Such pains, however, had been taken to disjoint his faction, that his exit from power was by no means attended with consolatory cir-cumstances. The Duke of Devonshire would not resign, though he declared he would seldom or never go to Council. Fox had warned him not to be too hasty in embarking in a party in which Pitt must be a principal actor; and remembering his Grace how large a share Pitt had had in planting the Tories at Court, and that, speaking of Legge, Pitt had said, 'I will have no more ear for Whig grievances.' The rest of Newcastle's friends were as little disposed to follow him: but that he might taste the full mortification of being deserted by those whom he had most obliged, whom he had most courted and most patronised, the clergy gave the most conspicuous example of ingratitude. For thirty years Newcastle had had the almost sole dis-posal of ecclesiastic preferments, and consequently had raised numbers of men from penury and the meanest birth to the highest honours and amplest incomes in their profession. At this very period there were not three bishops on the bench who did not owe their mitres to him. His first levee after his fall was attended but by one bishop, Cornwallis of Lichfield; who being a man of quality, and by his birth entitled to expect a greater rise, did but reflect the more shame on those who owed everything to favour, and scarce one of them anything to abilities.

The conduct of Lord Bute was not more wise than that of Newcastle. Instead of sheltering himself under that old man's name from whatever danger there might be in making peace, the Earl was driving together all those whom he ought to have kept divided; and really seemed jealous lest himself should not have the whole odium of sacrificing the glories and conquests of the war; an infatuation that so far excuses him, as he must have thought he did a service to his country in restoring peace—but what must his understanding have been if he could think that peace would be a benefit, let the terms be what they would! He supposed, too, that Newcastle, having in opposition to Pitt declared for peace, could not retract, and be against the peace. This was not knowing Newcastle or mankind. The situation, too, was materially changed: the weight of Russia was transferred from the hostile to the friendly scale; Martinico was fallen; and Europe could scarce amass the symptom of a fleet. A mind less versatile than Newcastle's could not want arguments against a precipitate treaty. Yet was it not Newcastle, nor a scandalous treaty, that shook the Favourite's power. It was his ignorance of the world; it was a head unadapted to government, and rendered still less proper for it by morose and recluse pride, and a heart that was not formed to bear up a weak head, that made him embark imprudently, and retreat as unadvisedly.

Sir Francis Dashwood

Lord Bute, on the resignation of the Duke of Newcastle, was immediately declared First Lord of the Treasury. George Grenville succeeded him as Secretary of State, and Sir Francis Dashwood was made his Chancellor of the Exchequer—a system that all the lustre of the Favourite's power could not guard from being ridiculous, though to himself mankind bowed with obsequious devotion. Grenville was ignorant of foreign affairs, and, though capable of out-talking the whole Corps Diplomatique, had no address, no manner, no insinuation, and had, least of all, the faculty of listening. The Favourite himself had never been in a single office of business, but for the few months that he had held the Seals: of the revenue he was in perfect ignorance, knew nothing of figures, and was a stranger to those Magi to the

East of Temple-Bar, who, though they flock to a new star, expect to be talked to in a more intelligible language than that of inspiration. When a Lord Treasurer or a First Lord of the Treasury is not master of his own province, it suffices if the Chancellor of the Exchequer is a man of business, and capable of conducting the revenue, of planning supplies, and of executing the mechanic duties of that high post. But in the new dispensation it was difficult to say which was the worst suited to his office, the Minister or his substitute. While the former shrouded his ignorance from vulgar eyes, and dropped but now and then from a cloud an oracular sentence; the deputy, with the familiarity and phrase of a fish-wife, introduced the humours of Wapping behind the veil of the Treasury. He had a coarse, blunt manner of speaking, that, looking like honesty, inclined men to hold his commonsense in higher esteem than it deserved. But, having neither knowledge nor dignity, his style, when he was to act as Minister, appeared naked, vulgar, and irreverent to an assembly that expects to be informed, and that generally chooses to reprehend, not to be reprehended. When a statesman ventures to be familiar, he must captivate his audience by uncommon graces, or win their good-will by a humane pleasantry that seems to flow from the heart, and to be the effusion of universal benevolence. This was the secret as well as character of Henry the Fourth of France. Even the semblance of it stood his grandson, our Charles the Second, in signal stead, and veiled his unfeeling heart, and selfish and remorseless insensibility.

Men were puzzled to guess at the motive of so improper a choice as this of Sir Francis Dashwood. The banner of religion was displayed at Court; and yet all the centurions were culled from the most profligate societies. Sir Francis had long been known by his singularities and some humour. In his early youth, accoutred like Charles the Twelfth, he had travelled to Russia in hopes of captivating the Czarina—but neither the character nor dress of Charles were well imagined to catch a *woman's* heart. In Italy, Sir Francis had given in to the most open profaneness; and, at his return, had assembled a society of young travellers, to which a taste for the arts and antiquity, or merely having travelled, were the recommendatory ingredients. Their pictures were drawn, ornamented with symbols and devices; and the founder, in the habit of St. Francis, and with a chalice in his hand, was represented at his devotions before a statue of the Venus of Medicis, a stream of glory beaming on him from behind her lower hand. These pictures were long exhibited in their club-room at a tavern in Palace Yard;

but of later years Saint Francis had instituted a more select order. He and some chosen friends had hired the ruins of Medenham Abbey, near Marlow, and refitted it in a conventual style. Thither at stated seasons they adjourned; had each their cell, a proper habit, a monastic name, and a refectory in common—besides a chapel, the decorations of which may well be supposed to have contained the quintessence of their mysteries, since it was impenetrable to any but the initiated. Whatever their doctrines were, their practice was rigorously pagan: Bacchus and Venus were the deities to whom they almost publicly sacrificed; and the nymphs and the hogsheads that were laid in against the festivals of this new church, sufficiently informed the neighbourhood of the complexion of those hermits. In truth, few of them were young enough to excuse such orgies. Old Lord Melcombe[1] was one of the Brotherhood. Yet their follies would have escaped the eye of the public, if Lord Bute from this seminary of piety and wisdom had not selected a Chancellor of the Exchequer. But politics had no sooner infused themselves amongst these rosy anchorites, than dissensions were kindled, and a false brother arose, who divulged the arcana, and exposed the good Prior, in order to ridicule him as Minister of the Finances.

John Wilkes

These successes and the tide of power swelled the weak bladder of the Favourite's mind to the highest pitch. His own style was haughty and distant; that of his creatures insolent. Many persons who had absented themselves from his levee were threatened with the loss of their own, or the places of their relations, and were obliged to bow the knee. But this sunshine drew up very malignant vapours. Scarce was the Earl seated but one step below the throne, when a most virulent weekly paper appeared, called *The North Briton*. Unawed by the prosecution of *The Monitor* (another opponent periodic satire, the author of which had been taken up for abusing favourites), and though combated by two Court papers called *The Briton* and *The Auditor* (the

[1] George Bubb Doddington, Lord Melcombe. However qualified by his wit to enliven any society, it cannot be supposed that between sixty and seventy he was more proper to partake of such revels than he had been in his youth. At that time having an assignation with a lady, and finding her lying on a couch, he endeavoured to avoid the conjuncture by crying, Oh! that I had you but in a wood! She replied, Well, what would you do? Would you rob me? [H.W.]

former written by Smollett, and the latter by Murphy, and both which the new champion fairly silenced in a few weeks), *The North Briton* proceeded with an acrimony, a spirit, and a licentiousness unheard of before even in this country. The highest names, whether of statesmen or magistrates, were printed at length, and the insinuations went still higher. In general, favouritism was the topic, and the partiality of the Court to the Scots. Every obsolete anecdote, every illiberal invective, was raked up and set forth in strong and witty colours against Scotland; while history was ransacked to furnish parallels of wanton dowagers and vigorous Prime Ministers. One of the first numbers was one of the most outrageous, the theme taken from the loves of Queen Isabella and Mortimer. No doubt but it lay open enough to prosecution, and the intention was to seize the author. But on reflection it was not thought advisable to enter on the discussion of such a subject in Westminster Hall; and as the daring audaciousness of the writer promised little decorum, it was held prudent to wait till he should furnish a less delicate handle to vengeance: a circumspection that deceived and fell heavy on the author, who, being advised to more caution in his compositions, replied, he had tried the temper of the Court by the paper on Mortimer, and found they did not dare to touch him.

This author, who must be so often mentioned in the following pages, was John Wilkes, member of Parliament for Ailesbury. He was of a plebeian[1] family, but inherited a tolerable fortune in Buckinghamshire, and had been bred at Oxford, where he distinguished himself by humorous attacks on whatever was esteemed most holy and respectable. Unrestrained either in his conduct or conversation, he was allowed to have more wit than in truth he possessed; and, living with rakes and second-rate authors, he had acquired fame, such as it was, in the middling sphere of life, before his name was so much as known to the public. His appearance as an orator had by no means conspired to make him more noticed. He spoke coldly and insipidly, though with impertinence; his manner was poor, and his countenance horrid. When his pen, which possessed an easy impudent style, had drawn the attention of mankind towards him, and it was asked, who this saucy writer was? Fame, that had adopted him, could furnish but scurvy anecdotes of his private life. He had married a woman of fortune, used her ill, and at last cruelly, to extort from her the provision he had made for her separate maintenance; he had debauched a maiden of family by an informal promise of marriage, and had been

[1] His father was a distiller. [H.W.]

guilty of other frauds and breaches of trust. Yet this man, bitter as he was in his political writings, was commonly not ill-natured or acrimonious. Wantonness, rather than ambition or vengeance, guided his hand; and, though he became the martyr of the best cause, there was nothing in his principles or morals that led him to care under what government he lived. To laugh and riot and scatter firebrands with him was liberty—Despotism will for ever reproach Freedom with the profligacy of such a saint!

Charles Churchill

Associated with Wilkes in pleasure and in the composition of *The North Briton* was a clergyman named Churchill, stepped out of obscurity about the same period, and as open a contemner of decency as Wilkes himself, but far his superior in the endowments of his mind. Adapted to the bear-garden by his athletic mould, Churchill had frequented no school so much as the theatres. He had existed by the lowest drudgery of his function, while poetry amused what leisure he could spare, or rather what leisure he *would* enjoy; for his Muse, and his whore, and his bottle were so essential to his constitution that his wife and his sermons had but the refuse of his time. Yet for some years his poetry had proved as indifferent as his lectures, till a cruel and ill-natured satire on the actors had, in the first year of this reign, handed him up to public regard. Having caught the taste of the town, he proceeded rapidly, and in a few more publications started forth a giant in numbers, approaching as nearly as possible to his model, Dryden, and flinging again on the wild neck of Pegasus the reins which Pope had held with so tight and cautious a hand. Imagination, harmony, wit, satire, strength, fire, and sense crowded on his compositions—and they were welcome for him—he neither sought nor invited their company. Careless of matter and manner, he added grace to sense, or beauty to nonsense, just as they came in his way; and could not help being sonorous, even when he was unintelligible. He advertised the titles of his poems, but neither planned nor began them, till his booksellers or his own want of money forced him to thrust out the crude but glorious sallies of his uncorrected fancy. This bacchanalian priest, now mouthing patriotism, and now venting libertinism, the scourge of bad men, and scarce better than the worst, debauching wives, and protecting his gown by the weight of his fist, engaged with Wilkes in his war on the Scots; and sometimes learning, and as often not knowing the characters he attacked, set himself up as the Hercules that was to cleanse the State, and punish its oppressors—and true it is, the storm that saved us was raised in the taverns and night-cellars; so much more effectual were the orgies of Churchill and Wilkes than the daggers of Cato and Brutus. The two former saved their country, while Catiline could not ruin his, a work to which such worthies seem much better adapted.

But while the wit and revelry of Wilkes and Churchill ran riot, and were diverted by their dissipation to other subjects of pleasantry or satire, they had a familiar at their ear, whose venom was never distilled at random, but each drop administered to some precious work of mischief. This was Earl Temple, who whispered them where they might find torches, but took care never to be seen to light one himself. Characters so rash and imprudent were proper vehicles of his spite; and he enjoyed the two points he preferred even to power, vengeance, and a whole skin.

This triumvirate has made me often reflect that nations are most commonly saved by the worst men in it. The virtuous are too scrupulous to go the lengths that are necessary to rouse the people against their tyrants.

Duc de Nivernois

His[1] counterpart, the Duc de Nivernois, had been long employed in negotiations at Rome and Berlin, but had not the good fortune to please at the latter Court, where the King even turned into ridicule his puny and emaciated little figure. His ill-health, the titles that had centred in his person, and had filled him with vanity (for he was Peer of France, Prince of the Empire, Grandee of Spain, and a Roman Baron), and his affection for polite learning, had disposed him to live in a retired circle of humble admirers, to whom he almost daily repeated his works both in prose and verse, but not without having attempted to soar higher. He had assumed devotion, in hopes of being Governor to the Dauphin—but, except in concluding the peace, which, consider-ing our eagerness, he could not avoid concluding, he had never met with brilliant success in any of his pursuits; being, as the celebrated Madame Geoffrin said of him, 'Guerrier manqué, politique manqué,

[1] The Duke of Bedford, Ambassador to France.

bel esprit manqué, enfin manqué partout.' To England he bore no good-will; and though, till the Treaty was signed, he concealed, as much as peevishness would let him, the disgust he took to this country, and was profuse in attentions to all, and in assiduity of court to the Favourite and his faction, yet, though he remained here a very little time after the signature, his nature broke forth, and scarce was enough good breeding left to skin over the sore reluctance of a momentary stay.

Henry Fox

When Fox thus stooped to be the Favourite's agent, he gratified many more passions than he could be supposed to mortify. In truth, except his pride, which had seldom restrained him, what views could he have but this step would gratify? To ravish the glories of the war from his rival, Mr. Pitt, to sacrifice them, and to be selected to defend that sacrifice, glutted his spirit of competition. Favourite he could not be, for the Princess hated, and Lord Bute feared him: but to be necessary to both was worth ambition, and the surest means of gratifying it; and to be master of the secret of the negotiation promised that superabundance of wealth—which by that secret he acquired. Should he succeed in carrying through the peace, he would have the first weight in the House of Commons (for what harmony there was between these *rival friends* may readily be conjectured); should he fail, it were but the loss of the Paymaster's place, inconsiderable in peace compared with its produce in time of war: for it must be noted that he would not accept the Seals, and thus stood in no responsible light— a strain of prudence that might have administered alarm to the Favourite himself!

Thus in the space of four months were the Princess and Lord Bute by their rash and ill-digested measures reduced to lean for support on Fox, whom they had most dreaded as the minister of the Duke of Cumberland; and who would add his own unpopularity to that of Lord Bute, and would necessarily determine Pitt to oppose with increased resentment.

Fox had embraced this invitation with such alacrity that he had signed the treaty with Lord Bute without consulting any of his friends; concluding, as over-refined politicians are apt to do, that he could bring them to his lure; and while he paid too high compliments to his own abilities, setting too slight estimation on theirs. His first application was to the Duke of Cumberland. That haughty and sensible Prince received him with scorn, reproached him warmly with lending himself to support a tottering administration, and bitterly with his former declarations of having given up all ambitious views. The next trial made by Fox was on Lord Waldegrave, to whom he urged that his Lordship had so much ridiculed the Princess and Lord Bute, that they had more to complain of than he had; and he endeavoured to enclose the Earl in his treaty with the Court, by asking him, if it should be proposed to call his Lordship to the Cabinet Council, whether he should like it? The Earl, who had been bred a courtier, who was of too gentle manners for opposition, and too shrewd not to see that the power of the Crown was predominant, desired time to consider, and went to Windsor to consult the Duke of Cumberland. His Royal Highness acknowledged the attention with many thanks, but would give no advice. The Earl, who wanted not to be told, that not advising him to make his court when he was disposed to it, was advising him against it, was not courtier enough to quit a Prince, his friend, for a Court that he himself despised and hated, and immediately wrote to Fox to desire the proposal might not be made to him. The Duke of Devonshire was in like manner endeavoured to be softened by Fox, who wished to wear the credit of reconciling his own friends to the peace, and bringing their support to the administration. But here again he was foiled. The Duke gave him a civil answer, assured him of his personal good wishes, but declined any connection with him as Minister.

Abandoned by his highest and most showy friends, Fox felt the mortification of discredit both with his patron and the public, and the keenest appetite for revenge. As a politician, his credit was saved by his industry and success; and by his arts his vengeance was soon gratified on two of those that thus cast him off. But now were the seeds sown, which, though slowly, produced such bitter crops in subsequent years. Detested by the public, Fox could never recover from the stain contracted at this period. . . .

Charles Townshend

Their greatest difficulty was with Charles Townshend who slipped through their fingers at every turn, and could be held down to no decision. He refused to be First Lord of Trade with the same power over the Colonies as had been granted to Lord Halifax. At the same time he was loth to resign, though in that quarter the needle rested at last: a mark of that want of judgment that was conspicuous in all his actions; for, having fluctuated from uncertainty of the issue, he chose the losing side but the very day before the great victory of the Court on the preliminaries. His post of Secretary at War was soon after given to Ellis. Townshend's bons-mots wounded where his conduct could not. It being reported, to justify the treatment of the Duke of Devonshire, that the King complained he had been kept prisoner; 'True,' said Townshend, 'he is a prisoner, but he mistakes his jailor.' Another of his sayings had not only proved a prophecy, but was often applied in the following years. He had said of the last arrangement before Fox was set at the head, that 'it was a pretty lutestring administration which would do very well for summer wear.'

Horace Walpole

After so many considerable names, it will look perhaps, like vain presumption in me to name myself as one whom it was thought necessary to manage. But, as it proves how low the arts and attention of Fox could descend; and as my answer (at least, I have always suspected so) contributed to an event of much consequence afterwards, I shall be excused by the candid for giving some account of it. I had soon after my appearance in the world, lived in much intimacy with Fox, had warmly espoused his side when persecuted by the Duke and Duchess of Richmond, and had happened to have conferred some other little favours on him. I had carefully avoided receiving the smallest or the greatest from him. As his character opened more to the world, I declined any connection with him in politics, though determining never to have a quarrel with him, as I well knew his vindictive nature. When he united with the Duke of Newcastle, he had offered, in truth slightly enough, to procure the reversion of a considerable place, which I hold only for my brother's life, to be confirmed for my own, provided I would be upon good terms with the Duke. I had ever in the most open manner spoken of that Minister with contempt: and having never to this hour received a favour from any Minister, I shall be believed that I never would accept one from Fox. I answered accordingly with much scorn, 'I will not accept that reversion from the Duke.' Fox knowing this spirit, and knowing too that I had declared to Lord Bute that I would receive no favour from Court, had no hope of fixing me to his measures by any offers he could make. Nor yet had he had reason to know I was averse to the preliminaries, on which I had kept silent. The truth was, I had been civilly treated on the King's accession, and had so much disliked Newcastle and Hardwicke, that few men were better pleased than myself to see a new Administration; and had not the standard of Prerogative been hoisted, and disgrace brought on this triumphant country, I should probably have remained a satisfied and indifferent spectator. Yet was I not so steeled by the glories of the war as to be insensible to the yearnings of humanity; and therefore, ignominious as the articles were, my conscience would not suffer me to speak against a treaty that would stop such effusion of blood. Sentiments, I confess, most unheroic: yet I blush not to own that they divided my sensations, and forbade my voting *against* the preliminaries, though I was too much an Englishman to vote *for* them, and accordingly left the House before the putting of the question.

1763

Lord Granville

John Earl Granville, the antagonist of one Prime Minister, Prime Minister himself, and then assistant to every succeeding Prime Minister, died on the second day of the new year. The rhodomontade, to which he was addicted, was set off by parts and wit, or forgiven to his good-humour. It was very unlike the presumptuous ascendant of Pitt, or the lofty ignorance of Lord Bute. Pitt, unsociable and muffled in clouds, was adored from the terror imprinted by his lightnings. Bute thought distance and obscurity sufficient characteristics of divinity; but Granville, like Bacchus, rattled his car among men, and was but the more admired the more he familiarized himself with mortals. He had fallen unpitied but unhated; and sunk in rank without sinking in esteem, his fall having lessened him less than his exaltation. He seemed so proper for every part, that in him it did not seem mean to be second, after commanding.

Norton

Norton, Solicitor General, as bold and as blunt, but never as honest as Lord Northington, being consulted to the same point, advised to take away the places, and then see if the law would restore them. This man now rose from obscure infamy to that infamous fame which long will stick by him. It was known that in private causes he took money from both parties, and availed himself against one or other of them of the lights they had communicated to him. Yet his abilities were so good, and his knowledge so great, that no man had more extensive practice in Westminster Hall. In Parliament he had for some years been disregarded; but his foul-tongued and causidical boldness, his clearness in argument or facility in assertion, his attachment to Lord Mansfield, and his total alienation from all principle, offered him as a proper tool to a Court, that was to wade through the letter of the law to the demolition of the spirit. Yet his authority alone could not encourage such a violation of justice as had now been in agitation. The Favourite, too, and the Favourite's favourites, might think it more eligible to leave patent-places unmolested; they must have coveted them more than they could wish, to render them precarious.

Sir Francis Dashwood

We must now quit Fox, to make room for a doughty hero of more comic cast, the Chancellor of the Exchequer. Hitherto he had but just acted enough as Minister, to show that he neither was one nor was fit to be one. The time was now come for *opening the Budget*, when it was incumbent on him to state the finances, debts, and calls of Government; and to chalk out a plan of proper supplies. All this he performed so awkwardly, with so little intelligence or clearness, in so vulgar a tone, and in such mean language, that he who had been esteemed a plain country gentleman of good sense, said himself afterwards, 'People will point at me, and cry, *There goes the worst Chancellor of the Exchequer that ever appeared!*' His famous measure was the tax on cider; and whoever would know more of his ability in conducting that business, will find it amply detailed in the *North Britons*; a coarse and satiric picture; yet but little exaggerated. The tax itself deserves far more than the author of it to live in the memory of English history, for the crisis it occasioned or drove on.

Lord Bute Resigns

Few political clouds seemed less big with mischief than this storm, unnaturally conjured up, and little likely to last; for what principle of union could there be in common between the City of London and two or three distant counties whose apples were to be taxed? The spell, *excise,* was pronounced, but had lost its terrors. They who sounded loudest the alarm, neither were alarmed, nor expected to breathe much dread into others. But there was a frame of nerves more easily thrown into disorder. Fear seized on the Favourite; he said, 'We shall have thirty thousand men come down to St. James's!' The assault that had been made on him the first day of the session had left a lasting impression; and he had showed early in the reign that fortitude was not a ruling ingredient in his composition. He had appointed himself a guard of bruisers the day of his attending the King into the City in 1761, when Mr. Pitt made his insolent parade thither at the same time. Now, bating the slight distemperature occasioned by the cider-tax, England seemed to be willingly and submissively prostrate at the Favourite's feet. Would she have rebelled for a partial tax, after acquiescing in the peace? Fear does not calculate, but lumps apprehensions in the gross. The panic was taken, and on the seventh of April, to the surprise of mankind, it was notified that Lord Bute intended to resign the next day, and to retire for his health, not being able to go through the fatigue of business.

It is true, that he had at times declared that as soon as he had made the peace, he would quit his post—but few had heard the declaration, and fewer believed it. The ministers knew nothing of his intention till the day before it was publicly notified; and Fox was so entirely out of the secret that he reproached the Earl bitterly for leaving him in that ignorance and dilemma,—the Favourite's own speeches in Parliament expressing a wish of retirement had rather confirmed men in the opinion that he had no thoughts of it. No one act had had the least air of his giving up his power; nor had any measures been taken to replace him or carry on the present system. But the best comment on his behaviour at that moment was his subsequent conduct. The fondness he retained for power, his intrigues to preserve it, the confusion he helped to throw into almost every succeeding system, and his impotent and dark attempts to hang on the wheels of Government, which he only clogged, and to which he dreaded even being suspected of recommending drivers, all proved that neither virtue nor philosophy had the honour of dictating his retreat; but that fear, and fear only, was the immediate, inconsiderate, and precipitate cause of his resignation.

Yet let me not be thought to lament this weak man's pusillanimity. I am condemning his want of policy, but rejoice at it. Had he been firm to himself, there was an end of the Constitution! The hearts of Englishmen were corrupt and sold, and the best heads amongst them toiled in the cause of Despotism. A happy panic blew up the system of absolute power when it had lasted but five months; and a trifling Opposition overturned in a fortnight the work of that majority which a fortnight had purchased. Yet the struggle was not over. The rod fell into abler and more resolute hands; the mercenaries were not disbanded, though the commander-in-chief ran away. Fortunately he became incompatible with his successors; and liberty owed its salvation not to its friends, but to discord among the conspirators.

The Duchess of Bedford

The Bedford faction were not to be contented with empty honours or slight emoluments. They sent for their Duke from France, who, to grasp the more by seeming moderation, resigned the Privy-seal—as most men thought, with views on the Treasury itself. At least his squadron vaunted that they had two or three administrations in readiness before the King should be obliged to employ the Opposition. The Favourite from the first moment of his power had made it a point to gratify nay, to outrun the Duke of Bedford's largest wishes. Nothing he had asked, nothing his creatures were immodest enough to demand, had been denied—yet Lord Bute was balked in his hopes of purchasing the attachment of that connection—not from their usual perfidy. He had lost them before they suspected the smallest diminution of his omnipotence. He had not gratified the ambition of the Duchess. She had marked for herself the first post in the Queen's family: but with more attention to her pride than to her interest, had forborn to ask it, concluding it must be offered to her. The Princess and Lord Bute, either not suspecting, or glad to be ignorant of her views, were far

enough from seeking to place so dangerous a woman in the very
heart of the Palace. This neglect the Duchess deeply resented and
never forgave. She was even so weak as to declare that inveteracy in
a letter to her sister Lady Elizabeth Waldegrave from Paris, which
Lord Bute intercepting, there first learned what an aspic was lodged
near his bosom. I have it from good authority from friends of Lord
Bute, that a deeper affront rankled in her Grace's breast; a neglect
of a tenderer kind; her Grace having, said they, made overtures of
her favours to the Earl, as soon as she perceived with what puissance
he ruled the Court. Gallantry, it is true, reigned as fiercely in the
Duchess's composition as ambition; but could she expect or wish the
very sacrifice that would have defeated the latter? Or could she think
that the Earl between forty and fifty could deceive one experienced
matron, and content another, when nothing upon earth was less
tempting than either? I therefore do not warrant this anecdote. I do
the former of the Duchess's letter, which Lord Bute himself told to
Fox, from whom I heard it. The Earl assigned it as the reason why
he had not received but once returned the frequent visits of the Duke
of Bedford on his coming back from France.

Lord Bute and Horace Walpole

My place of Usher of the Exchequer was granted in reversion to
Samuel Martin; and a place in the Custom-house, held by my brother,
but the far greater share of which had been bequeathed to me by my
father for my brother's life, was also granted in reversion to Jenkinson.
I was, I confess, much provoked at this last grant, and took occasion
of fomenting the ill-humour against the Favourite, who thus excluded
me from the possibility of obtaining the continuance of that place to
myself in case of my brother's death. But in truth, except in the want
of that attention, I had no reason to complain. I had refused to accept
the grant from Fox, and I had in terms told Lord Bute that I would
accept no favour from him, though with great civility, and without
acting in any shape as hostile to him. Thus my resentment kept no
deep root: and I can say with the utmost truth, that as I afterwards,
though never connected with him, was on many occasions friendly
to that great Favourite, so no word in these Memoires to his prejudice has been dictated by a vindictive spirit; but the whole narrative
is faithfully the representation of what I knew and heard of him.

Infinite ill has he occasioned to this country; in which light only it is my intention to pass sentence on his character. In other respects, the meanness of his abilities and the poorness of his spirit place him below resentment. His private virtues, the long and bitter persecution he has undergone, and many domestic misfortunes, would extract every sting which exact or necessary justice did not sharpen. The last trans- action I am going to mention flowing notoriously from his dispensa- tion was of a nature not to be palliated or forgotten. To see it in its full force of indignity offered to so mighty a country, the reader must place himself at the moment when England, triumphant over France and Spain, had annihilated their navies and sat sole arbitress of peace and war, absolutely secure that Europe combined could not wrench her conquests from her, and sure of proving her moderation by con- senting to peace on almost whatever terms she should please to dictate.

At that moment did a pusillanimous Favourite not only make peace, relinquishing the greater and most valuable part of our acquisitions, but (what never entered into the imagination of distress and slavery itself), he purchased that scandalous peace of the envoy of a little prince who was not even a party in the war! In short, it now came out, that a pension on Ireland of one thousand pounds a year for thirty-one years to Count Virri, the Sardinian Minister, through whose hands the real negotiation had passed, was the price and tribute of that shame which Lord Bute, by the treaty of Paris, heaped on Great Britain!

Lord Waldegrave

The very day on which the Favourite resigned the reins of govern- ment died the man who, of all England, would perhaps have rejoiced the most to behold that event. James, Earl Waldegrave, was carried off by the small-pox, April 8th. With unbounded benevolence, and of the most flowing courtesy to all men, Lord Waldegrave, whose pene- tration no weakness could escape, nor art impose upon, though vice he overlooked, and only abstained sometimes from connecting with black and bad men, Lord Waldegrave, I say, had been so thoroughly fatigued with the insipidity of his pupil the King, and so harrassed and unworthily treated by the Princess and Lord Bute, that no one of the most inflammable vengeance, or of the coolest resentment, could harbour more bitter hatred and contempt than he did for the King's mother and Favourite. This aversion carried him to what I scarce believed my eyes when he first showed me, severe satires against them. He has left behind him, too, some Memoires of the few years in which he was governor to the Prince, that will corroborate many things I have asserted, and will not tend to make these anecdotes be reckoned unjust and unmerciful.

Lord Waldegrave died most unseasonably for his own honour. He stood so high in the esteem of mankind for probity, abilities, and temper, that, if any man could, he might have accomplished a coalition of parties, or thrown sense into that party, which, though acting for the cause of liberty, rather wounded than served it, so ill were they formed for counsel or conduct. Had he lived still longer he must, by the deaths of the chiefs, have been placed incontestably at the head of that party himself. Indeed, but just before his illness, he was much looked up to by very different sets. Lord Bute himself had thought of him for a considerable share on his own retreat; and, but the day before Lord Waldegrave was seized with the small-pox, he had been offered the Embassy to France or Lord-Lieutenancy of Ireland, both of which he peremptorily declined. And yet, after his death, the Court boasted they had gained him: a report much resented and eagerly contradicted by his friend the Duke of Cumberland.

George Grenville, Lord Egremont, and Lord Halifax

Mr. Grenville had hitherto been known but as a fatiguing orator and indefatigable drudge; more likely to disgust than offend. Beneath this useful unpromising outside lay lurking great abilities; courage so confounded with obstinacy that there was no drawing the line betwixt them; good intentions to the public, without one great view; much economy for that public, which in truth was the whole amount of his good intentions; excessive rapaciousness and parsimony in himself; infinite self-conceit, which produced impossibility of instructing, convincing, or setting him right; implacability in his temper and a total want of principles in his political conduct; for, having long professed himself uncommonly bigotted to the doctrines of liberty, he became the staunchest champion of unwarrantable power. As all his passions were expressed by one livid smile, he never blushed at the variations in his behaviour. His ingratitude to his benefactor, Lord Bute, and his reproaching Mr. Pitt with the profusion of a war which he had

sometimes actively supported, and always tacitly approved, while holding a beneficial place, were but too often paralleled by the crimes
of other men; but scarce any man ever wore in his face such outward
and visible marks of the hollow, cruel, and rotten heart within.

Lord Egremont was a composition of pride, ill-nature, avarice, and
strict good-breeding; with such infirmity in his frame, that he could
not speak truth on the most trivial occasion. He had humour, and
did not want sense, but had neither knowledge of business, nor the
smallest share of parliamentary abilities.

Of the three, Lord Halifax was by far the weakest, and at the
same time the most amiable man. His pride, like Lord Egremont's,
taught him much civility. He spoke readily and agreeably, and only
wanted matter and argument. His profusion in building, planting, and
on a favourite mistress, had brought him into great straits, from which
he sought to extricate himself by uncreditable means. He aimed at
virtues he could not support; and was rather carried away by his vices
than sensible of them.

John Wilkes

After a week's deliberation Wilkes was seized, April 30th, by three
messengers, on a *general warrant,* signed by Lord Halifax. They had
been ordered to apprehend him at midnight, but abstained till noon
of the 30th. Churchill, his friend, then with him, slipped out of the
house, either to secure himself or to give the alarm. Mr. Wood, the
Under-Secretary, and Philip Carteret Webbe, a most villainous tool and
agent in any iniquity, seized his papers, though he had received intimation time enough to convey away the most material. He was conducted
to Lord Halifax's, where he behaved with much firmness and confidence, and grievously wounded the haughty dignity attempted to be
assumed by Lord Egremont. They committed him close prisoner to
the Tower—a severity rarely, and never fit to be practised but in cases
of most dangerous treason. This treatment served but to increase
Wilkes's spirit and wit. He desired to be confined in the same room
where Sir William Windham, Lord Egremont's father, had been kept
on a charge of Jacobitism; and said he hoped, if there could be found
such a chamber in the Tower, that he might not be lodged where any
Scotchman had been prisoner.

About the same time, being told of the reasons alleged by the King of Spain for setting aside his eldest son, two of which were, that the Prince squinted, and did not believe the mysteries of our holy religion; then said Wilkes, 'I can never be King of Spain, for I squint, and believe none of those mysteries.'

The rigour of the commitment gave serious alarm. But the very day on which it happened, Wilkes's friends applied to the Court of Common Pleas for his habeas corpus, expecting it from Lord Chief Justice Pratt, and scorning or despairing of it from Lord Mansfield.

Lord Temple instantly resorted to the Tower, but was denied admittance to the prisoner; a restraint the ministers found the very next day they must take off. Lord Temple then returned to visit Wilkes, as did the Duke of Grafton and some few others of rank; but, in general, the prisoner's character was so bad, and his conduct so rash and unguarded, that few, who were either decent or cautious cared to be concerned with him.

The habeas corpus being granted, Wilkes was carried to the Court of Common Pleas, May 3rd. He spoke for an hour, said 'attempts had been made to corrupt him, now to persecute him; he had been worse treated than any rebel Scot.' The crowd in Westminster Hall gave a great shout! The Chief Justice, with great dignity, reproved them. The judges took time to deliberate. The people were profuse of their acclamations to the sufferer.

On the 5th, he wrote a letter to his daughter (a child whom he had placed in a convent in France for her education), and sent it open to Lord Halifax; it congratulated her on living in a *free* country. He was the same day turned out of his commission in the militia.

On the 6th being again conveyed from the Tower to Westminster Hall, Pratt and the other Judges of the Common Pleas unanimously discharged him from his confinement; the Chief Justice delivering their opinions, and dismissing him on his Parliamentary privilege, 'because, though privilege of Parliament does not hold against a breach of the peace, it does against what only *tends* to a breach of the peace'. The case of the Seven Bishops was quoted: the Judges Wright, Holloway, and Allibone had been against them. Allibone, said Pratt, was a papist; Wright and Holloway had been appointed for the occasion; but Powel, an honest man, had declared for the Bishops. On the other hand he quoted a recent case of Lord Tankerville, who having been arrested on a prosecution for bribery in the election for Windsor, the Lords had declared it a breach of privilege—we shall find how much less tender the Commons were of *their* privileges. The Chief Justice had no sooner

granted the enlargement of Wilkes, than two of the King's serjeants
presented letters to the Court from the Attorney and Solicitor Generals,
demanding to be admitted into the Court, as the case concerned the
King's interest. The Attorney, it is said, has a right of interfering in
any court where the King's interest is agitated: it is doubted whether
the Solicitor has the same prerogative. To both Pratt answered that
they had applied too late. Now did the Court feel the consequence of
having forced Pratt to be Chief Justice against his will.

This triumph quite overset the little discretion of which Wilkes had
been master. He seemed to put himself into the situation of a King,
who not content with the outworks with which the law has surrounded
his person, attempts to employ the law as offensive artillery. Affecting
to have been robbed of moveables, when his papers were seized, Wilkes
entered into a virulent controversy by letter with the Secretaries of State;
and even endeavoured, though in vain, to obtain warrants for searching
their houses. This wild conduct did not help his cause. His next step fell
more perniciously on his own head. He erected a printing-press in his
own house; and against the remonstrances of Lord Temple, who never
wanted fear where there was room for it, and who had no taste for
anything that did not lead directly home to faction, indulged himself in
realizing those sallies of his humour and intemperance, which are scarce
excusable when transient and confined to the jollity of intoxicated
moments at table. The Court regarding Lord Temple as the instigator,
not as the Socrates of this Alcibiades, removed him from the Lord-
Lieutenancy of the county of Buckingham. The printers, who had been
vexed in their business by the orders of the Secretaries of State, and
encouraged by the victory of Wilkes, prosecuted the messengers, and
obtained damages to the value of £300.

Comte de Guerchy

The Comte de Guerchy was an amiable soldier; not to be named
for parts, but far better qualified for his situation than his own Court
believed, having a good knowledge of the world, a perpetual attention
to his employment, consummate discretion, much natural ease in his
behaviour, with either no impertinence, or with thorough mastery
of it, and a complaisance so properly applied, that he was agreeable
to all parties, and yet always well with the reigning ministry here.

It gave him a ridicule at home, that he was enslaved to a penurious and deformed wife; but that dominion of Madame de Guerchy was his greatest felicity. She had an excellent understanding and a talent for learning the tempers, humours, and connections of England; her constant application to which, and the necessary curiosity in consequence, were concealed by the natural coldness and reserve of her disposition. Nor did her attention to their fortune ever disgrace her husband, nor throw even an air of economy on his table. At Paris her devotion and domestic retirement had passed for insipid virtues that prevented her good sense from being so much as suspected. At the Count's first audience, he told the King, with pleasant candour, *that it was a proof of his master's intentions to preserve the peace, that he was sent over, who was no man of talents or intrigue.*

Thus formed to succeed and never to offend, no man was more unfortunate than this ambassador; and it required not only dexterity, but the simplicity of his conduct to surmount the most cruel and disagreeable ideas, first carelessly dropped, and then maliciously dispersed to his prejudice. The Duc de Nivernois had brought over and left here to manage the affairs of their Court till M. de Guerchy's arrival, the Chevalier d'Eon, a military man, but who had been much employed in secret negotiations in Russia, for which he had been largely praised and very ill paid. The man had notable parts, great appearance of bashful merit, and learning enough to charm the superficial pedantry of the Duke, who had treated him with a fondness and intimacy that was ridiculous; and that, by being over kind, proved cruel; for having to serve him made d'Eon the courier of the peace, the Duke went farther, and procured him to be styled plenipotentiary during the absence of the ambassador. Vigils and vanity turned the poor young man's head, which was by no means ballasted by a good heart. He mistook the road of fortune for fortune itself, and thought that high-sounding titles lifted him to a level with those that conferred them. He forgot his modesty, and learned to talk loftily, or, as his masters thought, arrogantly. Under this unhappy intoxication he was thunderstruck with a declaration from the Duc de Nivernois, that on the ambassador's arrival he was to sink into his pristine insignificance. To laugh this off, the Duke had familiarly pictured him to himself as sometimes a plenipotentiary and sometimes a tool of office. Other accidents concurred to aggravate this mortifying notice. He could obtain no arrears; and having made free with the remittances of his new master to give dignity to his own mission, he received a very humiliating reprimand from Monsieur de Guerchy. To crown all, Wilkes's writings had breathed a spirit of independence into a poor brain born to crouch at a desk or to rise by servility. The ambassador was no sooner arrived, than the Chevalier behaved in a manner to which French ministers are little accustomed from their inferiors. At the same time d'Eon took it into his fancy that one Treyssac de Vergy, an adventurer, was brought over to assassinate him; and on this belief broke out so outrageously against the Count after dinner at Lord Halifax's, that the Earl, at M. de Guerchy's desire, was obliged to send for Justice Fielding, and put d'Eon under arrest; and next day Vergy swore the peace against him.

Wilkes and Lord Sandwich

As soon as the Address was voted, Lord Sandwich produced a poem, called an *Essay on Woman,* with notes pretended to be written by Bishop Warburton. It was a performance bawdy and blasphemous to the last degree, being a parody of Pope's *Essay on Man,* and of other pieces, adapted to the grossest ideas, or to the most profane. Wilkes and Potter, son of the late Archbishop of Canterbury, had formerly composed this indecent patchwork in some of their bacchanalian hours; and Wilkes, not content with provoking the vengeance of the King, of the Princess, of the Favourite, of twenty subaltern ministers, and of the whole Scottish nation, had, for the amusement of his idle hours, consigned this *innocent* rhapsody to his own printing-press—a folly unparalleled, though he had intended to restrain the edition to twelve copies. However, as he could not commit a wanton imprudence, without giving birth to some villainy or tyranny in others, this very poem was now laid before the House of Lords in consequence of a train of both kinds. One of the copies had been seized among his papers by that caitiff Philip Carteret Webbe. Still was even that ministry ashamed to accuse Wilkes on evidence which had fallen into their hands by such illegal means—unanswerable proof that they were conscious of their guilt, and knew they could not justify their proceedings. But the bloodhounds having thus fallen on the scent, were not to be turned aside by delicacies. Could they procure another copy the business would be effected—and effected it was. Carteret Webbe set his tools to work, for even hangmen have deputies. There was one Kidgell, a dainty priggish parson, much in vogue among the old

ladies for his gossiping and quaint sermons, and chaplain to the
Scotch Earl of March. This fellow got at a proof-sheet; and by the
treachery of one of Wilkes's printers, who thought himself ill-used,
and by the encouragement of his patron, who consulted Lord Bute and
Lord Sandwich, and was egged on by them to proceed, Kidgell
and Webbe purchased the whole poem: and now did Sandwich, who
had hugged this mischief for months in his breast, lay open the precious
poem before his brother Lords in strains of more hypocrisy than would
have been tolerable even in a professed Methodist. Parts of it were read.
Fanny Murray, a noted girl of the town, was declared in it a better
piece than the Virgin Mary for never having borne a child; and the
ass that *had* been a noble animal was proclaimed to be disgraced for
having carried the Messiah into Jerusalem. The pious Lord Lyttelton
groaned in spirit, and begged they might hear no more. Bishop
Warburton, who had not the luck, like Lord Lyttelton, to have his
conversion believed by any one, foamed with the violence of a Saint
Dominic; vaunted that he had combated infidelity, and laid it under
his feet; and said, the blackest fiends in hell would not keep company
with Wilkes, and then begged Satan's pardon for comparing them
together.

Lord Temple had got no intelligence of this bomb, and knew little
what to say; but concluding justly that the piece had been found
among Wilkes's papers, condemned the means by which it was
obtained. It was instantly voted blasphemous, and a breach of privilege
against the person of the Bishop of Gloucester. Lord Sandwich then
moved that Wilkes should be voted the author; but even Lord Mansfield condemned so hasty and arbitrary a course; and said it was pre-
viously necessary to hear the accused person in his own defence; on
which the proceeding was adjourned to the next day but one. I was
in a division in the lobby of the House of Commons, when I heard
what was passing in the other House, and immediately informed Mr.
Pitt. He replied with indignation, 'Why do not they search the Bishop
of Gloucester's study for heresy?'

Events now thickened so fast, that, to avoid confusion, I will here
say a little more on this head. The plot so hopefully laid to blow
up Wilkes, and ruin him in the estimation of all the decent and grave,
had, at least in the latter respect, scarce any effect at all. The treachery
was so gross and scandalous, so revengeful, and so totally unconnected
with the political conduct of Wilkes; and the instruments so despicable,
odious, or in whom any pretensions to decency, sanctimony, or faith

were so preposterous that losing all sight of the scandal contained in the poem, the whole world almost united in crying out against the informers. Sandwich, in opening the discovery, had canted till his own friends could not keep their countenances. Sir Francis Dashwood was not more notorious for singing profane and lewd catches; and what aggravated the hypocrisy, scarce a fortnight had passed since this holy Secretary of State himself had been present with Wilkes at a weekly club to which both belonged, held at the top of Covent Garden Theatre, and composed of players and the loosest revellers of the age. Warburton's part was only ridiculous, and was heightened by its being known that Potter, his wife's gallant, had had the chief hand in the composition of the verses. However, an intimacy commenced between the Bishop and Sandwich, and some jovial dinners and libations of champagne cemented their friendship. Kidgell, the jackal, published so precise, affected, and hypocritic an account of the transaction, that he, who might have escaped in the gloom of the treachery, completely blasted his own reputation; and falling into debt, was according to the fate of inferior tools, abandoned by his masters, and forced to fly his country. Though the rank and fortune of Sandwich saved him from disgrace of that kind, he had little reason to exult in his machination. He brought a stigma on himself that counterworked many of his own views and arts; and Churchill the poet has branded his name on this account with lasting colours. The public indignation went so far, that the Beggar's Opera being performed at Covent Garden Theatre soon after this event, the whole audience, when Macheath says, 'That Jemmy Twitcher should peach me, I own surprises me,' burst out into an applause of application; and the nickname of *Jemmy Twitcher* stuck by the Earl so as almost to occasion the disuse of his title.

1764

Princess Augusta

So early as in the late reign there had been thoughts of a double alliance with the ducal house of Brunswick; but when the jealousy of the Princess Dowager had prevented the marriage of her son with a princess of that line, there had remained no great propensity in the Court of Brunswick to the other match between the hereditary

Prince and Lady Augusta. It had, however, been treated of from time to time; and in 1762 had been agreed, but was abruptly broken off by the influence of the King of Prussia. Lady Augusta was lively, and much inclined to meddle in the private politics of the Court. As none of her children but the King had, or had reason to have, much affection for their mother, she justly apprehended Lady Augusta's instilling their disgusts into the Queen. She could not forbid her daughter's frequent visits at Buckingham House, but to prevent any ill consequence from them, often accompanied her thither. This, however, was an attendance and constraint the Princess of Wales could not support. Her exceeding indolence, her more excessive love of privacy, and the subjection of being frequently with the Queen, whose higher rank was a never-ceasing mortification, all concurred to make her resolve at any rate to deliver herself from her daughter. To attain this end, profusion of favours to the hated House of Brunswick was not thought too much. The hereditary Prince was prevailed on to accept Lady Augusta's hand, with fourscore thousand pounds, an annuity of £5000 a year on Ireland, and £3000 a year on Hanover. Fourscore thousand pounds were given with the late Princess Royal to the Prince of Orange, but she was a King's daughter. The Princesses Mary and Louisa had but forty thousand each.

Lady Augusta was not handsome, but tall enough, and not ill-made; with the German whiteness of hair and complexion, so glaring in the Royal Family, and with their precipitate, yet thick, Westphalian accent. She had little grace or softness in her manner: yet with more attractions she might have failed to gain a heart that was not inclined to part with its liberty, and least of all to one of her family. The Prince arrived on the twelfth of January; and, as if to prejudice him against his bride, the plan was formed to disgust him as much in order to send him away as soon as possible. He was lodged at Somerset House: no guards were stationed there. The Lord Steward chose the company that should dine with him; and every art was used to prevent his seeing Mr. Pitt, or the chiefs of the Opposition. At the wedding, which was on the 16th, the servants of the King and Queen were ordered not to appear in new clothes. But though these little artifices had the desired effect of affronting the Prince, they only drew mortifications on the Court. The people, enchanted with novelty, and a hero, were unbounded in their exultations wherever he appeared; and as the behaviour of the Court got wind, took pleasure, when he attended the King to the theatres, to mark their joy at the presence of the Prince, and to show the coldest neglect of their Sovereign. Nor was the Prince less assiduous to intimate his dissatisfaction, even to ill-breeding, turning his back on the King, as he stood over against him in the box at the Opera; and even going away during half the representation. To the Duke of Newcastle and others in disgrace, he was full of attentions; dined twice with the Duke of Cumberland, and affectedly lingered there, though the King and Queen waited for him to a ball; and, as he found *that* step would be the most offensive, though indeed due from him to one so partial to his family, he made a visit to Mr. Pitt at Hayes. These little hostilities were carried on with such vigour on both sides, that, notwithstanding all his curiosity and desires expressed of a longer stay, the King forced him and his bride to depart on the 25th—only thirteen days after his arrival. They were overtaken in a great storm at sea, and in extreme danger of being lost; but escaped, not only with good fortune to themselves, but to the Court of England, who would have appeared as guilty to the people in driving them out at such a season, as if they had raised the tempest by sorcery.

Sir William Meredith and Sir George Saville

Sir William Meredith and Sir George Saville were both men of character, and both singular in different ways. The first was a convert from Jacobitism; inflexibly serious, and of no clear head: yet practice formed him to a manner of speaking that had weight and was worth attending to by those who had patience for it. He was, I believe, an honest man, though not without personal views, which a little sharpened his scorn of those who had the like views, and were not equally honest.

Sir George Saville had a head as acutely argumentative as if it had been made by a German logician for a model. Could ministers have been found acting by the advice of casuists and confessors, Sir George would still have started distinctions to hamper their consciences; but though *they* walk *not* in such ruled paths, his want of ambition carried him so seldom to the House, that they were not often troubled with his subtleties. He had a large fortune, and a larger mind; and though his reason was sharp, his soul was candid, having none of the acrimony or vengeance of party; thence was he of greater credit than service to that in which he listed.

Jeremiah Dyson

Jeremiah Dyson was made one of the Lords of Trade. Of this man it is necessary to say a few more words. He was a tailor's son, had risen under Nicholas Hardinge from a subaltern clerk of the House of Commons, to succeed him as first Clerk; and by education and principle was thought, and had conversed as a staunch Republican. In that employment he had comported himself with singular decency and intelligence. In truth, his parts were excellent; he was quick, subtle, shrewd, clear, both in conception and delivery, and was master of argumentative eloquence, though void of every ornamental part of it. Being of an unhealthy complexion, and very fretful temper, he had quitted his laborious post, and was now come into Parliament, secretly sold to the Favourite; but from his behaviour as their Clerk, having conciliated much goodwill to himself among the Members, he was for some time heard with great favour and satisfaction, an indulgence he lost afterwards, when his warmth made them recollect he had once been their servant. He now appeared as devoted to George Grenville; and indeed was excellently useful from his parts and great knowledge of parliamentary business, to all who employed him. But proving both slippery to his friends as fast as they fell, and vexatious to his enemies, few men became equally unpopular. Having deserted Grenville on a change of times, and happening to convert his tied wig into a bag, Lord Gower being asked the reason, said 'It is because no *Tye* will hold him.'

The Earl and the Countess of Northumberland

Lord Northumberland had an advantageous figure and much courtesy in his address, which being supported by the most expensive magnificence, made him exceedingly popular with the meaner sort. They who viewed him nearer were not the dupes of his affability or pretensions. The old Nobility beheld his pride with envy and anger; and thence were the less disposed to overlook the littleness of his temper, or the slender portion he possessed of abilities; for his expense was a mere sacrifice to vanity, as appeared by his sordid and illiberal behaviour at play. Nor were his talents more solid than his generosity. With

'The State Quack'

'He's a braw Doctor & has ta'en his Degrees at Edinburgh': Bute
purveys his cures while the Princess of Wales performs on the tight rope

From a print of September 1760

John Wilkes

Detail of a group portrait
by Richard Houston,
about 1768

George III

Detail of a portrait from
the studio of Allan Ramsay,
about 1767

mechanic application to every branch of knowledge, he possessed none beyond the surface; and having an unbounded propensity to discussion, he disgusted his hearers without informing them. Yet his equals were but ill-grounded in their contempt of him. Very few of them knew so much; and there were still fewer that had not more noxious vices, and as ungenerous hearts. Lord Northumberland's foibles ought to have passed almost for virtues in an age so destitute of intrinsic merit.

The Countess of Northumberland was a jovial heap of contradictions. The blood of all the Percies and Seymours swelled in her veins and in her fancy; while her person was more vulgar than anything but her conversation, which was larded indiscriminately with stories of her ancestors and her footmen. Show, and crowds, and junketting were her endless pursuits. She was familiar with the mob, while stifled with diamonds; and yet was attentive to the most minute privileges of her rank, while almost shaking hands with a cobbler. Nothing was more mean than her assiduity about the King and Queen, whom she termed her *Master* and *Mistress*; and yet, though indirectly reprimanded by the latter, she persisted in following her Majesty to the theatres with a longer retinue of domestics than waited on the Queen herself. She had revived the drummers and pipers and obsolete minstrels of her family; and her own buxom countenance at the tail of such a procession gave it all the air of an antiquated pageant or mumming. She was mischievous under the appearance of frankness; generous and friendly without delicacy or sentiment; and a fond wife without curbing her Lord's amours, or her own.

Mr. Legge

Mr. Legge, after languishing some months, died August 23rd. A blow considerable to our party, as he was the only man in it proper on a change to have been placed at the head of the House of Commons. His abilities were known and respected: his timidity and time-serving had not been much remarked but by the few he had been most conversant with; for, being supple and cheerful and never offensive, he had always seemed to loiter behind his party, rather than to desert it. He met death with more manliness and unconcern than could have been expected, as he was not old, was happy, rich, and above the affectation of heroism or philosophy. An old friend, visiting him the day before he died, Legge said to him, 'Brother sportsman, I used to laugh at your being too heavy for a chase, but now you are come in at the death.' It was not equally sensible and unaffected, that he sent to Mr. Pitt to acquaint him with his own approaching dissolution, and to exhort him to do his utmost to remove the present Ministers. Legge ought to have known how little Pitt would regard the death-bed admonition of a man for whom living he had little veneration. Legge left behind him, with orders for publication, a relation of his quarrel with Lord Bute, relating to an election for the County of Hampshire. This piece neither hurt the Favourite, nor reflected honour on the deceased. That the former should have meddled in an election, even before his master's accession to the Crown, could not surprise nor seriously shock any man: nor, though the narrative was not to appear till after his death, had Legge worked it up with a spirit to do himself honour. His obsequiousness pierced through the veil of hostility, and everybody saw that, without other views, he would not have encountered a rising Minister; nor, by Legge's own account, had the Favourite mitigated the scorn with which he treated him. I have said that Lord Bath loved money so much that he thought a paltry sum, though given after his death, considerable bounty. It was much the same with Legge: he was so naturally compliant and inoffensive that his daring to order the publication of a tame and posthumous satire seemed to him an effort of prodigious vengeance.

The Cavendish Family

To give the finishing blow to the hopes and credit of the Opposition, the Duke of Devonshire who had gone to Spa at the end of August for a paralytic disorder, died there in the vigour of his age. He was by no means an able or enterprizing man, but enjoyed a character uncommonly respected; and was universally regretted by all the Whigs as Head of their party. . . .

The young Duke was but sixteen, was awkward and full of the sheepish bashfulness of his race. He was entirely in the hands of his three uncles, the Lords George, Frederic, and John, all warm Whigs, enthusiasts to the memory of their father and brother, of characters eminently unstained, and not a little persuaded that their family was, and ought to be, the most distinguished in the kingdom. Their property was enormous, their credit great, and reputation truly honourable; but the talents of the race had never borne any proportion to their other advantages. The first Duke, besides being the finest gentleman of the age, had succeeded to the merits of his friend Lord Russell's martyrdom. Since that period the family had affected to drop all polish, and to wear the manners of plain English gentlemen, under an outside that covered considerable pride. Sir Robert Walpole had made advantage of their popularity, and having strongly attached the second and third Dukes to himself, he had placed them before himself as the leaders of the Whig party, and cried up their unembellished good sense, though the second Duke had no sense at all, and the third a very dubious portion. William, the fourth and late Duke, with something more of the manners of a Court, had less abilities than his father. His brother Lord George had none at all. Lord Frederic was lively, and having lived in courts and camps, a favourite of the Duke of Cumberland, was by far the most agreeable, and possessed the most useful sense of the whole family. Lord John, the youngest, was hitherto little known. I shall have occasion to mention him frequently hereafter. He had read a good deal, and his eyes saw not faster than his memory retained. He was accurate in repeating words, sentences, nay volumes, if he pleased; nor was he defective in quickness or reasoning. Under the appearance of virgin modesty he had a confidence in himself that nothing could equal, and a thirst of dominion that was still more extraordinary. It consisted solely in governing those with whom he was connected, without views either of interest or power. To be first, in however small a circle, was his wish—but in that circle he must be absolute: and he was as ready to sacrifice the interests and fortunes of those his friends and slaves, as he was of his own. His plan seemed to be the tyranny of a moral philosopher. He was a kind of Heresiarch that sought to be adored by his enthusiastic disciples, without a view of extending his sect beyond that circle. His fair little person, and the quaintness with which he untreasured as by rote the stores of his memory, occasioned George Selwyn to call him *the learned Canary-bird*.

Charles Churchill

On the first of November the sentence of outlawry was pronounced against Wilkes; and on the fourth died that bacchanalian bard, his friend Churchill. He was on a visit to his friend Wilkes at Boulogne, where his excesses threw him into a fever, and where he died in a few days with Epicurean indifference—a meteor that had shone but four years; and never so brightly as he might have done. He had wished, he said, for an opportunity of satirizing Mr. Pitt and Charles Townshend, who had not yet entirely listed themselves with the Court, the moment for which Churchill waited impatiently; yet writing as he did at random, it was a chance whether he would have touched or not the true blemishes and characteristic marks of men so compounded of defects and exquisite ingredients. Churchill could hew out a block that would brave time and last to posterity, but stood not near enough to seize the lineaments and shades that distinguish a portrait, and exhibit a resemblance to the eyes of cotemporaries.

Archbishop Stone

On the 19th [of November] died Stone, the famous Primate of Ireland, aged fifty-seven, having ruined his constitution by indulgence to the style of luxury and drinking established in Ireland, and by conforming to which he had found the means of surmounting the most grievous prejudices and of gaining popularity, ascendant, power; an instance of abilities seldom to be matched. He was aided too by several virtues; he was generous and charitable, and of a soul above revenge. When Lord Chesterfield held the government of Ireland, he told the Primate, 'My Lord, you must govern this kingdom, for you have the best parts in it; but you want one thing; you must take orders;' alluding to the irregularity of his life. But Stone had greater parts than Lord Chesterfield imagined, for he *did* govern that kingdom without conforming to the decencies of his profession.

Stone was survived but a few days by his ancient competitor, the Earl of Shannon; a more common character, he having sold his patriotism for a peerage; and maintaining by hypocrisy an influence that Stone had supported with the boldness of a statesman, and with scorn of the little knavery that he might have borrowed from his rank of Archbishop.

1765

Sir William Pynsent

About the same time happened the following extraordinary event. Sir William Pynsent, a baronet of Somersetshire, died and left his whole fortune to Mr. Pitt, no ways related nor personally known to him. Nor, as it appeared, was this great legacy so much the reward of his illustrious services as of his opposition to General Warrants. Sir William Pynsent, at his death, was aged eighty-six, had formerly served in Parliament, and had voted against the Treaty of Utrecht; his principles being zealously and unalterably Whig. He was said to have had parts and humour, not many scruples; living to her death with his own only daughter in pretty notorious incest. Lord North had married his next relation, had courted him, and stood fair to be his heir; till, having voted for the tax on cider, Sir William, who had long lived retired upon his estate, had not only quarrelled with his cousin North, but had encouraged the mob to burn him in effigy. He then became enamoured of Mr. Pitt; is said to have cast some inconstant glances towards Wilkes, and, immediately before his death, had indubitably given orders to his lawyer to draw a new will entirely in the favour of General Conway; but it was not prepared in time. Mr. Pitt, therefore, found himself in possession of real and personal estates worth above forty thousand pounds, without the regret of losing a friend, without the imputation of having flattered his bene-factor, for he had never seen him, without injuring a family, for Sir William had no very near relation, and not one that expected his fortune; and with the satisfaction of owing such a public mark of esteem to his own virtue or merits.

Dr. John Brown

So triumphant was the Administration that the very creatures of Mr. Pitt were forward to chant their praises and stigmatize their opponents. Besides a sermon against libels, preached on the 30th of January by Dr. Lyttelton, Bishop of Carlisle, there was at this time a servile tract against Faction, published by Dr. Browne, who, a few years before had written a thing, called *An Estimate,* which, not-withstanding its pert and silly positions had met with unaccountable success. In that piece Mr. Pitt had been his hero. This Browne, the ape of Pope, and who had written some poems, not without merit, had afterwards produced two very indifferent tragedies; and, lastly, an absurd treatise on Music, which he pretended to apply to the formation of a visionary government. He ended his life deplorably by his own hand in a fit of illness and madness, having been invited to Russia to assist the Czarina in some of her ostentatious projects on legislation, and being oppressed, either with imaginary glory, or despondence of supporting his reputation.

The King's Illness

It was too notorious to be concealed that the Princess Dowager had brought into the royal blood a humour which occasioned the deaths of several of her children, and at length her own. The late King in his resentment of her conduct and ingratitude, often mentioned it in bitter terms, and vaunted with truth how pure his own blood had been from any infection. In their childhood the present King and the Princess of Brunswick were thought free from that unhappy disorder: but some time before his marriage the King's face was full of pimples. These had so entirely disappeared, that it was apprehended he had made use of external remedies to repel them. It is certain that from that time he frequently laboured with disorders on his breast, particularly during the Queen's first pregnancy. He was now again seized with a cough and fever, for which he was repeatedly blooded four times, and was apprehended to be in much danger. So critical a situation made men take notice that, to secrete him from all intercourse with his Court, Lord Bute had placed the King at Buckingham House, a damp unwholesome spot, and rendered more perilous by the neighbourhood of two infectious hospitals. The vigour of his age and his sanguine constitution seemed to require more exercise and air than he enjoyed in that sauntering and domestic life. It was even said that Dr. Duncan, advising his Majesty to have one of his palaces in the country fitted up, and to live there for some time, Lord Bute harshly reprimanded the physician, and asked him what he had to do to advise beyond his line?—a question which reason could easily have answered, though awe might not.

Bishop Warburton

Bishop Warburton, who thought the persecution he had suffered from Wilkes and Churchill, his devotion to the Ministry, and his great pre-eminence in learning over his brethren on the Bench, had entitled him to one of the most considerable mitres, resented so much the promotion of Terrick to the See of London that, during the King's illness, in the King's own chapel, he preached on neglected merit, and, with the same modesty that shines through his writings, drew pictures of himself and his rival under the distinctions of merit and demerit.

The Duke of Newcastle

With regard to the Duke of Newcastle, whom I had always despised, and with whom a common cause had obliged me to act, I did find how well grounded my contempt of him had been, and to how little purpose it was to act with him. He was always eager, but never ready: delighting in talking over measures, but knew not how to begin or pursue them; and was as happy in seeming to lead an in-effectual party, as he had been in governing the nation. He thought he possessed secrets if he did but whisper, or was whispered. Attendance on him was his supreme joy; and if two of the party came to him on the same business, he made one of them wait, to wear an air of mystery to both. There never was a man who loved power so much, and who could enjoy the shadow with the same content, when the substance was gone. Nor is it less remarkable, that though favour at Court was the object of his life, he began it with insulting the Prince of Wales (George II), and concluded it with affronting the Princess Dowager.

The Mob

But though the Ministers had been forced to make atonement, the sacrifice was by no means accepted. The King treated them with every mark of estrangement and aversion; and it was visible to every eye that their fall was determined. Previous to their dismission, they tasted of the horror in which they were held by the people. The very day on which the Regency-bill passed, the Lords read another bill sent from the Commons, for imposing as high duties on Italian silks as are paid on those of France, on this foundation, that the French sent their silks to Genoa and Leghorn, and then entered them as Italian merchandize. This bill had passed the Commons with little notice, all attention having been engrossed by the plan of the Regency. When it was read by the Lords, the Duke of Bedford alone spoke against it; nobody said a word for it, and it was thrown out. It happened that the silk manufacture was at a low ebb, and many weavers in Spitalfields were unemployed. The next day about three or four thousand of those poor men went very quietly and unarmed to Richmond, to petition the King for redress. The Queen was walking in the paddock, and was alarmed by their numbers, but they gave no offence, and followed the King in the same peaceable manner to Wimbledon, whither he was gone to a review. The King told them he would do all that lay in his power to relieve them, and they returned pleased and orderly.

But the next day, May 15th, whether they distinguished between the assurances given by his Majesty and the rejection of the Bill by the Lords; or whether, as is more probable, they had been instigated underhand, they went to the House of Lords in great bodies, behaving in the most riotous manner, abusing the Peers, and applauding the Commons, who had passed their Bill. The Chancellor's coach they stopped, and asked him if he had been against the Bill? He stoutly replied, Yes. They were abashed at his firmness, and said they hoped he would do justice. He replied, 'Always, and everywhere; and whoever did, need fear nothing.' When the Duke of Bedford appeared, they hissed and pelted him; and one of the mob taking up a large stone for the new pavement, dashed it into the chariot: the Duke broke the force of the blow by holding up his arm, but it cut his hand, and bruised him on the temple; so narrowly he escaped with his life. They then followed him to his own house, where with great temper he admitted two of the ringleaders to a parley, and they went away seemingly appeased.

The next day the House of Lords issued out orders for preservation of the peace; but the weavers continued to parade the streets and the Park, though without committing any violence.

On the Friday, the Lords sent for Justice Fielding, who said the weavers had done no mischief. The Chancellor, who had been trusted by the Ministers with none of their late extraordinary measures, and who probably foresaw their downfall, was sullen, and would take no part. Few lords attended, and everything announced to the Ministers their approaching disgrace. About dinner-time, the Duke of Bedford received intelligence that his house would be assaulted at night, on which he sent away his jewels and papers, and demanded a party of horse; the Duchess persisting in remaining with him in the house. His friends and dependents, and several officers, garrisoned it; and, as was foreseen, the rioters in prodigious numbers assaulted the house in the evening, and began to pull down the wall of the court; but the great gates being thrown open, the party of horse appeared, and sallying out, while the Riot Act was read, rode round Bloomsbury-square, slashing and trampling on the mob, and dispersing them; yet not till two or three of the guards had been wounded. In the meantime a party of the rioters had passed to the back of the house, and were forcing their way through the garden, when fortunately fifty more horse arriving in the very critical instant, the house was saved, and perhaps the lives of all that were in it. The Duke, however, and his company kept watch all night; and the coffee-houses were filled with curious and idle people, who sent with great indifference every hour to learn how the siege went on. The disappointed populace vented their rage on the house of Carr, a fashionable mercer who dealt in French silks, and demolished the windows. All Saturday they remained peaceable; and though another attack was threatened, no further mischief ensued.

On Sunday evening I went to compliment the Duke and Duchess, as most of their acquaintances did, on their escape. I found the square crowded, but chiefly with persons led by curiosity. As my chariot had no coronets, I was received with huzzas; but when the horses turned to enter the court, dirt and stones were thrown at it. When the gates opened, I was surprised with the most martial appearance. The horse-guards were drawn up in the court, and many officers and gentlemen were walking about as on the platform of a regular citadel. The whole house was open, and knots of the same kind were in every room. When I came to the Duchess, and lamented the insult they had suffered, she replied, with warmth and acrimony, that the mob had been set on by Lord Bute. I was not much inclined to believe *that*, nor thought a mob a tool with which Lord Bute would choose to amuse himself. Immediately after, came in the Earl and Countess of Northumberland. Words cannot describe the disdainful manner in which they were received.[1] The Duke of Bedford left the room; the Earl was not asked to sit, nor spoken to; but was treated with such visible marks of neglect and aversion, that Lord Waldegrave said to another of the family, 'Faith! this is too much.' In my own opinion, the mob was blown up by Humphrey Cotes, and the friends of Wilkes. Almon, the friend and printer of the latter, owned to me, that they were directed by four or five gentlemen in disguise, who were not suspected; and

[1] Their son was married to one of Lord Bute's daughters. [H.W.]

seemed willing to disclose the secret to me. I said, 'Name no names to me, I will not hear them.' He gave me a print published by Cotes against Lord Bute and Lord Holland; and talked of risings that would be all over England. I said, 'I should be sorry to have the mob rise: it would occasion the army being quartered in London, and then we should be enslaved.'

Perhaps I have dwelt too minutely on this episode; perhaps I have done so on many other points equally unimportant. But it must be remembered that I am painting a portrait of the times, rather than writing history. The events, too, of this time were so linked together, that trifles gave birth to serious eras; and unless it be detailed with the circumstantial exactness which I shall use, and which I stood in a situation to know more thoroughly than most men, from my intimacy or connection with many of the actors, the history of this reign will be very imperfectly understood; and posterity would see sudden and extraordinary changes, without being able to account for them from the public appearances of things. When it is known, it will be easy to compose a more compendious account; and my narrative, that may serve for the scaffolding, may be thrown by as no longer of use.

Mr. Conway and Lord Rockingham

In the first draught of the new settlement it was proposed that Mr. Conway should be Chancellor of the Exchequer; and for some time Lord Rockingham refused to accept without that assistance. Conway's inclination was to be Secretary at War; his resolution not to quit the military line. I, who knew his unacquaintance with the business of the Treasury, the disgusting coldness of his manner, which would revolt those he ought to court, and who foresaw (though not to the degree I found afterwards) how little he was made to ingratiate himself with strangers, and consequently to conduct the House of Commons, earnestly dissuaded him from undertaking that post. My opinion concurring with his own sentiments, though at first he had been staggered, he set himself to refuse that employment with a vehemence much beyond his natural temper. For Secretary of State he was excellently fitted, and no man ever applied himself to the business of his office with such unrelaxed industry. Unluckily, the department he refused was bestowed on Dowdeswell, who was so suited to the drudgery of the office, as far as it depends on arithmetic, that he was fit for nothing else. Heavy, slow, methodical without clearness, a butt for ridicule, unversed in every graceful art, and a stranger to men and courts, he was only esteemed by the few to whom he was personally known.

The Marquis of Rockingham was almost the reverse. More childish in his deportment than in his age, he was totally void of all information. Ambitious, with excessive indolence; fond of talking business, but dilatory in the execution, his single talent lay in attracting dependents; yet, though proud and self-sufficient, he had almost as many governors as dependents. To this unpromising disposition, he had so weak a frame of person and nerves, that no exigence could surmount his timidity of speaking in public; and having been only known to that public by his passion for horse-races, men could not be cured of their surprise at seeing him First Minister, as he never could give them an opportunity of knowing whether he had any other talents. A silent First Minister was a phenomenon unknown since Parliaments had borne so great a share in the revolutions of government. His personal character was blameless—unfortunately, the times required something more than negative qualities!

Horace Walpole and Mr. Conway

The dissolution of our Opposition now afforded me that opportunity of retreating from those who had composed it, for which I had so eagerly longed; nor was I dilatory in executing my resolution. Many new reasons concurred to make me adhere to the plan I had formed. It was against my opinion that my friends had accepted the Administration; and though I would not peremptorily advise Mr. Conway to decline taking part, when he told me he thought himself obliged in honour to obey the King's and Duke's commands; still I saw so much weakness both in the leaders and the numbers, that I entertained no hopes of the permanence of their power. Chiefs who could not conduct a party with sense, seemed little qualified to govern a nation. I had given notice, that if ever they attained power, I would have nothing further to do with them. They had attained it now, but with so little prospect of maintaining their ground, that nothing was so probable as their being soon driven to opposition again. In that I was determined to engage with them no more. If I quitted them triumphant, they would have no right to call on me should they again be defeated by their own want of skill. I had fully satisfied my honour and my engagements; and had anybody cause to complain, it was myself—but I chose to part with them on good terms; nor would I, where I was really hurt, condescend to utter a reproach. This topic truth demands that I should explain. I had entered into Opposition on the view of the violent measures, and still more violent designs of the Court. Personal dislike to the Bedford faction had inflamed my natural warmth, and the oppression exercised on Mr. Conway had fixed in me an unalterable desire of overturning that Administration. Not the smallest view of self-interest had entered into my imagination. On the contrary I risked an easy ample fortune with which I was thoroughly contented. When I found unjust power exerted to wrong me, I am not ashamed to say I flattered myself that, if ever our party was successful, I should obtain to have the payments of my place settled on some foundation that should not expose me to the caprice or wanton tyranny of every succeeding Minister; for court I was resolved to make to none, whether friend or foe, a haughtiness I maintained throughout my life, never once condescending to go to the levee of any First Minister. My wish of making this independence perfectly easy I had hinted to Mr. Conway during our opposition. He received it with silence. It was not in my nature to repeat such a hint. As disinterestedness was my ruling passion, I did hope that on the change some considerable employment would be offered to me, which my vanity would have been gratified in refusing. It was mortifying enough to me, when Mr. Conway (for I have said that during the last negotiation I was confined in bed with the gout) reported to me the proposed arrangement of places, to find that my name had not been so much as mentioned. That I would take no place was well known, I had frequently declared it. From the Duke of Cumberland, to whom I had never paid court; from the Duke of Newcastle, whom I had constantly ridiculed; from Lord Rockingham and the Cavendishes, whom I had treated with a very moderate share of regard, I had no reason to expect much attention: and though some notice is due to all men who are respected in a party, *they* were excusable in proposing nothing for me, when they found nothing demanded for me by my own intimate friend and near relation. He must be supposed to know my mind best: if he was silent, what called on them to be more solicitous for my interest? But what could excuse this neglect in Mr. Conway? For him I had sacrificed everything; for him I had been injured, oppressed, calumniated. The foundation of his own fortune, and almost every step of his fortune, he owed solely to me. How thoroughly soever he knew my sentiments, was a compliment at least not due to me? Whatever was due to me, much or little, he totally forgot it; and so far from once endeavouring to secure my independence, in his whole life after he never once mentioned it. I had too much spirit to remind him of it, though he has since frequently vaunted to me his own independence. Such failure of friendship, or, to call it by its truer name, such insensibility, could not but shock a heart at once so tender and so proud as mine. His ensuing conduct completely opened my eyes. When I saw him eager and anxious to exalt his brother Hertford to the Vice-Royalty of Ireland, and his brother-in-law Lorn to a regiment; and when he omitted no occasion of serving them and the Duke of Argyle and Lord Frederic Campbell—all four, men who had abandoned him to persecution without a pang, I saw clearly into his nature. He thought it noble, he thought it would be fame, to pardon the neglect he had met with; and that the world would applaud his generous return of their ungenerous and interested behaviour. No glory would have accrued from his serving me, as it would have been natural and no more than was expected. His heart was so cold that it wanted all the beams of popular applause to kindle it into action. I had command enough of myself not to drop a word of reproach on a friendship so frozen; but, without a murmur, and with my wonted cheerfulness, as soon as my strength was tolerably recruited, I declared my intention of making a visit to Lord Hertford, at Paris, before he quitted his embassy. I acted with the same unconcern to the whole party, for I would neither suffer them nor my enemies to know that I had any cause to be dissatisfied with Mr. Conway. When I scorned to open myself, even to him, it was not likely I should be more communicative to others. As disgust with my friends did not, as most commonly happens, reconcile me to my enemies, I foresaw that I might still have occasion to make use of my power with Mr. Conway to the annoyance of the latter; for though Mr. Conway had none of the warmth of friendship, yet he had more confidence in me, and knew he might have, than in any man living; and, notwithstanding the indifference I have described, he frequently trusted me afterwards with secrets that he reserved from his wife and his brother.

He no sooner discovered that my intention was to remain in France much longer than he expected, than he broke out into complaints, entreaties, and reproaches: and, as if he had satisfied all the duties of friendship, and I had violated them, he tried with angry words to divert me from my purpose, urged the occasion he should have for my advice, and called my retreat desertion of my friends. Satisfied with making him feel the want of me, and now hardened against the calls of friend-ship, I treated the matter lightly, civilly, and desultorily. I reminded him of the declaration I had often made of quitting the party as soon as they should be successful, which he could not deny; and, with a little mixture of conscious scorn, I said I knew the obligations the party had had to me; I knew none I had to them. Vexed, and his pride hurt, he employed Lady Ailesbury to tell me in his presence that he looked upon my behaviour as deserting him; and himself dropped many peevish accents. Fixed in the plan I had laid down to myself, nothing could provoke me to be serious; I carried off all with good humour; and, above owing to a retort of reproaches which I ought to have owed to his sentiments, I parted with him with such inflexible, and consequently mysterious, cheerfulness, that he knew not what interpretation to put on my behaviour—if he did guess, he was more blameable than I suspected. His insensibility had made me insensible; his ingratitude would have given me stronger sensations. But it is justice to him to say, that I think he was incapable of ingratitude: his soul was good, virtuous, sincere; but his temper was chill, his mind absent; and he was so accus-tomed to my suggesting to him whatever I thought it was right for him to do, that he had no notion of my concealing a thought from him; and as I had too much delicacy to mention even my own security, I am persuaded it never came into his conception. His temper hurt me, but I forgave his virtue, of which I am confident, and know it was superior to my own. We have continued to this day on an easy and confidential footing; but conscious that I would not again devote myself for him, I have taken strict care never to give him decisive advice, when it might lead him to a precipice. Before I set out, and as a mark that I meant no breach with him, at the same time to serve another friend, and to wear an air of interest with the Administration which might disguise my dissatisfaction, I desired Mr. Conway to raise Sir Horace Mann, the resident at Florence, to the rank of envoy; which was immediately done. The Bedfords, however, knew me enough to surmise that my retreat was the effect of some dislike I had conceived to the new system; and at my return to England, near eight months afterwards officiously threw out civilities that might draw me to their connection. I soon let them see that whatever my dislikes were, nothing had happened to soften my conduct, or change my opinion of them and their principles. Nor was it much longer before they found that I had lost neither inclination nor power to bar their return to Court by the weight I retained with Mr. Conway.

The Duke of Cumberland

On the 30th of October his Royal Highness was playing at picquet with General Hodgson. He grew confused, and mistook the cards. The next day he was recovered enough to appear at Court; but after dinner was seized with a suffocation, and ordered the window to be opened. One of his *valets-de-chambre*, who was accustomed to bleed him, was called, and prepared to tie up his arm; but the Duke said, 'It is too late!—it is all over!'—and expired.

I have spoken so much of his Royal Highness's character in the beginning and in various parts of these Memoires, that little addition is necessary. His haughtiness and severity had made him most obnoxious in the early parts of his life. His profound understanding had taught him to profit of his mortifications; and though he never condescended to make himself amiable but to very few, he became as much respected, though deprived of power, as if his heroism had been victorious. Whether his good sense would have resisted prosperity with equal temper, I much doubt. He would have made a great King, but probably too great a King for so corrupt a country. His indifference to death, which he had so long and so frequently had in prospect in the last years of his life, and which he seemed to invite, was, I believe, less owing to the solidity of his courage, which was intrepid, than to the unhappiness of his situation. His bodily infirmities, though borne without complaint or impatience, were grievous. His mind had been more sensibly afflicted. Born with a martial spirit and fond of command, he had not only been unsuccessful in every battle, except that of Culloden, but had been forced by cruel circumstances from the favourite profession of his soul; in civil life he was kept, by the temper of his father and the aversion of the Princess Dowager, in a state of neglect and disgrace. Fox, who he had a right to expect should stickle for his power, had betrayed and abandoned him; Pitt had made it a point to bar him from all influence; and the two Pelhams, after leaning on him for a while, had sacrificed him to the Princess and to their own ambition or jealousy of credit. His mind had not been formed for idleness, and could ill digest an exclusion from all military and all civil counsels; and was too lofty and too unpliant to feed on trifling amusements. It had the great, but none of the little powers of philosophy; could bear misfortune, but could not compensate to itself for the want of its object. He used books rather than liked or valued them, and cared for none of the arts. His principles restrained him from going any considerable lengths against the Crown; nor could he stoop to bestow those caresses that are necessary to form extensive connections. He dealt his smiles to those who followed him, like a King that rewards, not like the head of a party, who has farther to go. The dignity of his conduct and behaviour gave his Court the air of a dethroned monarch's, but had nothing of a Prince whom his nephew's Court had suspected of having views on the Crown.

The French Royal Family

I will close the account of this remarkable year with a few observations I made in France.

Louis the Fifteenth did not want sense, and had as much humanity as was consistent with insensibility and indolence. The first prevented him from suspecting evils that did not immediately fall under his eye; and the latter from inquiring what oppressions his people suffered. He was more shy than reserved, and all these qualities tended to make him the slave of habit. He hated new faces rather than loved old servants. Being free from ambition, having no appetite for glory of any kind, and impressed with sentiments of devotion, he preferred peace, and listened to any overtures of treaty, whether victorious or vanquished. To the Queen he had been for many years strictly constant; was always a civil husband, and, in her last illness, a tender one. To his children he was most affectionate. To his mistresses profuse, but capable of harshness whenever he quitted them. Cardinal Fleury governed him with unbounded authority; Madame de Pompadour by art, and at last by complaisance in procuring other women for him, engrossed him entirely, but with no hold on his affections, for her death made not the slightest impression on him. The Duc de Choiseul having been placed by her, succeeded to the ascendant that habit gives, and thence excluded other favourites, rather than became one himself. The King's life was regulated by the most mechanic sameness. An hour or two he could not deny to his Ministers: hunting took up the rest of daylight. Women amused his private hours: cards and a supper, with a select company, concluded the evening. All the flattery of that vain and obsequious nation, who love themselves in their kings, gave him no pleasure. It was a negative kind of nature that could neither be totally spoiled nor amended. But the true picture of him was an anecdote, that I learned

Henry Pelham

From an engraving by Paton Thomson after Richard Bentley and an unknown artist; a plate in the 1822 edition of the 'Memoires of the last ten years of the reign of George II'

William Pitt,
Earl of Chatham

*Detail of a portrait from
the studio of Richard
Brompton*

The Duke of Argyll

*Detail of a portrait by
Allan Ramsay*

from good authority. A sensible confidant of Cardinal Fleury reproached him with not making the King apply to business. This was the answer of that wise Minister: 'I have often endeavoured what you recommend; and one day went so far as to tell the King that there had been kings dethroned in France for their *fainéantise*. It seemed to strike him deeply. He made no reply: but two days afterwards said to me, "I have been reflecting on what you told me of some of my predecessors being deposed —pray resolve me: when the nation deposed them, were they allotted large pensions?" From that moment,' said the Cardinal, 'I saw it was in vain to labour at making him a great King.'

The Queen was not only a pious but a good woman. Indifferent to the gallantries of her husband, and free from ambition, she lived well with him, his mistresses, and ministers. Fond of talking and universally obliging, the nation thought her void of any particular attachment; yet she showed an unalterable friendship to the Duchesse de Luynes: and her affection to her father, King Stanislas, and the loss of her son the Dauphin undoubtedly hastened her death. Though she could not prevent the expulsion of the Jesuits, the King's esteem for her mitigated their fall. It was to the honour of both that, though the daughters of Stanislas and Augustus, the Queen and the Dauphiness lived in uninterrupted harmony.

The Dauphin, who died while I was in France, was totally unknown till his death. His caution of not giving jealousy to his father, and his respectable fear of not alarming the bigotry of his mother and wife, had made him conceal both his good sense and the freedom of his sentiments with such care, that the former was not suspected; and the latter was so unknown, that the nation, now running with their usual vehemence into any new opinion, and, consequently growing Freethinkers, believed and hated him as an Enthusiast. Yet he had a good understanding, had carefully though secretly cultivated it, and was a modern Philosopher in the largest sense of that term. During his illness, which continued many weeks, he seemed neither to regret his youth nor hopes; was patient, complaisant, and indulgent; and a few days before his death gave proof of his good sense and good nature. A man of quality that attended him had the brutal absurdity to solicit him to ask some favour, on his behalf, of the King, 'who', said the person, 'can refuse your Royal Highness nothing in your present condition.' The Dauphin laughed at the indelicacy, but would not divulge the name of the man. To please his family, the Prince went through all the ceremonies of the Church, but showed to his attendance, after they were over, how vain and ridiculous he thought them. Many expressions he dropped in his last hours that spoke the freedom of his opinions; and to the Duc de Nivernois he said he was glad to leave behind him such a book as Mr. Hume's Essays.

The Dauphiness, with whom he lived on the best terms, he had, however, no fondness for: his first wife had been far more dear to him. The second was morose and ungracious; and, dying in a year after her husband, was not at all regretted. In her last moments, having sharply reprimanded the Duchesse de Lauragais, the latter, turning to another lady, said, 'Cette Princesse est si bonne, qu'elle veut que personne ne la regrette.'

The Duc de Choiseul, the Prime Minister, was a man of excellent parts, but of a levity and indiscretion, which most of that nation divest themselves of before his age, or when they enter into business. Except the hours which he spent with the King, the rest of his life was dissipation, pleasure, profuseness, and *bons mots*. Rash, daring, and presumptuous; good-humoured, but neither good nor ill-natured; frank, gay, and thoughtless, he seemed the Sovereign more than the Minister of a mighty kingdom. Scorning, rather than fearing, his enemies, he seldom undermined and seldomer punished them. He dissipated the nation's wealth and his own; but did not repair the latter by plunder of the former. Mr. Pitt's superiority he could never digest or forgive; and though he was incapable of little mischief in his own country, great crimes had rather a charm for him. He excited the war between the Russians and Turks, to be revenged on the Czarina; and I saw him exult childishly in his own house on her first defeats. At last he descended to the mean and cruel oppression of Corsica, for the sake of gathering a diminutive laurel, after being baffled in the large war. Gallantry without delicacy was his constant pursuit. His wife, the most perfect character of her sex, loved him to idolatry; but, though a civil husband, he spared her no mortification that his carelessness could inflict. His sister, the Duchesse de Grammont, too openly connected with him by more ties than of blood, had absolute influence over him, and exerted it cruelly and grossly to insult the Duchesse de Choiseul, who more than once was on the point of retiring into a convent, though without the least belief of the doctrines held there. Madame de Grammont, who had none of the accomplishments that graced the small but harmonious figure of the Duchesse de Choiseul, had masculine sense, and almost masculine manners. She was wonderfully agreeable when she pleased, a vehement friend, a rude and insolent enemy. The nation revered and neglected the wife; detested and bowed to the sister. The Minister had crushed the Jesuits, for he loved sudden strokes of éclat; and, to carry that measure, had countenanced the Parliaments till they grew almost too ungovernable. But as he seldom acted on deep system, he sometimes took up a tone of authority, and as quickly relaxed it—a conduct that confounded the nation and a little the Parliaments; but that war from thoughtlessness, or to ruin a rival, the Duc d'Aiguillon, he chiefly left to the latter; and he could not have left it to worse hands. Proud, ambitious, vindictive, and void of honour or principle, the Duc d'Aiguillon, with very moderate parts, aimed at power with the Crown, by being the Minister of its tyranny. The infamous oppression exercised on that undaunted man, M. de la Chalotais, flowed from the revenge of this Duke, who to carry his point lent himself even to the exploded Jesuits; and though that connection could be no secret to the Duc de Choiseul, he suffered rather than encouraged a plan that clashed so much with the service he had rendered to his country by abolishing the Order. Nor was it to his honour that shame and the outcry of mankind rescued M. de la Chalotais, rather than the justice of the Prime Minister.

1766

The Pretender and His Sons

On the first day of the year died at Albano that sport of fortune, the Chevalier de St. George, better known by the appellation of the Old Pretender. He had not only outlived his hopes, but almost all those who had given him any hopes. His party was dwindled to scarce any but Catholics; and though he left two sons, his line was verging to extinction. The second son was actually a Cardinal; the elder, sunk in drunkenness, despair, and neglect at Bouillon. His father's death seemed a little to reanimate him: but that revival was but waking to new mortifications. The Court of France did not even put on mourning for the father; and when Prince Charles determined to set out for Rome, the Pope despatched a courier to prevent him. The Roman nobility were not fond of being preceded even by a phantom of royalty; and both they and the College of Cardinals were apprehensive of the sottishness and rashness of the young man. The Pope dreaded the resentment of England, and feared an order to prohibit English travellers from visiting Rome; a mighty source of wealth to that city. And he, who had so obstinately protected the Jesuits against the threats of France and Spain, and who at last sacrificed part of his dominions to his zeal for the Order, had the timidity to renounce the most meritorious martyr of the Church, rather than expose himself to the very uncertain vengeance of a heretic Court. The Young Pretender persisted in his journey: the Pope as pertinaciously refused to acknowledge him for King of England; yet with the additional absurdity of continuing to style him Prince of Wales—though he could not be the latter without becoming the former. To such complete humiliation was reduced that ever unfortunate house of Stuart, now at last denied that empty sound of royalty by that Church and Court for which they had sacrificed three kingdoms! Pathetically might the Prince have exclaimed,

'Hic pietatis honos! sic nos in sceptra reponis!'

The Cardinal of York ceded to his brother the annuity he received from the Pope, whose only bounty, whose only grace, was restricted to the allowance of that exchange!

Edmund Burke

There appeared in this debate a new speaker, whose fame for eloquence soon rose high above the ordinary pitch. His name was Edmund Burke (whom I have just mentioned), an Irishman, of a Roman Catholic family, and actually married to one of that persuasion. He had been known to the public for a few years by his *Essay on the Sublime and Beautiful*, and other ingenious works; but the narrowness of his fortune had kept him down, and his best revenue had arisen from writing for booksellers. Lord Rockingham, on being raised to the head of the Treasury, had taken Burke for his private Secretary, as Mr. Conway had his cousin William. Edmund immediately proved a bitter scourge to George Grenville, whose tedious harangues he ridiculed with infinite wit, and answered with equal argument. Grenville himself was not more copious; but, with inexhausted fertility, Burke had an imagination that poured out new ideas, metaphors and allusions, which came forth ready dressed in the most ornamental and yet the most correct language. In truth, he was so fond of flowers, that he snatched them, if they presented themselves, even from Ovid's *Metamorphoses*. His wit, though prepared, seldom failed him; his judgment often. Aiming always at the brilliant, and rarely concise, it appeared that he felt nothing really but the lust of applause. His knowledge was infinite, but vanity had the only key to it; and though no doubt he aspired highly, he seemed content when he had satisfied the glory of the day, whatever proved the event of the debate. This kind of eloquence contented himself, and often his party; but the House grew weary at length of so many essays. Having come too late into public life, and being too conceited to study men whom he thought his inferiors in ability, he proved a very indifferent politician—the case of many men I have known, who have dealt too much in books or a profession: they apply their knowledge to objects to which it does not belong, and think it as easy to govern men, when they rise above them, as they found when themselves were lower and led their superiors by flattery. It is perhaps more expedient for a man of mean birth to be humble after his exaltation than before. Insolence is more easily tolerated in an inferior, than in an inferior mounted above his superiors.

William Burke, the cousin of Edmund, wrote with ingenuity and sharpness; and both of them were serviceable to the new Administration, by party-papers. But William, as an orator, had neither manner nor talents, and yet wanted little of his cousin's presumption. Edmund, though the idol of his party, had nothing of the pathetic and imposing dignity of Pitt, though possessed of far more knowledge, and more reasoning abilities. But Pitt could awe those whom he could no longer lead, and never seemed greater than when abandoned by all. Charles Townshend, who had studied nothing accurately or with attention, had parts that embraced all knowledge with such quickness, that he seemed to create knowledge instead of searching for it; and, ready as Burke's wit was, it appeared artificial when set by that of Charles Townshend, which was so abundant, that in him it seemed a loss of time to think. He had but to speak, and all he said was new, natural, and yet uncommon. If Burke replied extempore, his very answers that sprang from what had been said by others, were so painted and artfully arranged, that they wore the appearance of study and preparation. Like beautiful translations, they seemed to want the soul of the original author. Townshend's speeches, like the Satires of Pope, had a thousand times more sense and meaning than the majestic blank verse of Pitt; and yet, the latter, like Milton, stalked with a conscious dignity of pre-eminence, and fascinated his audience with that respect which always attends the pompous but often hollow idea of the Sublime.

The Earl of Chatham

The glory with which the late Ministers retired was half of it plucked from the laurels of the new Earl of Chatham. That fatal title blasted all the affection which his country had borne to him, and which he had deserved so well. Had he been as sordid as Lord Northington, he could not have sunk lower in the public esteem. The people, though he had done no act to occasion to reproach, thought he had sold them for a title, and, as words fascinate or enrage them, their idol Mr. Pitt was forgotten in their detestation of the Lord Chatham. He was paralleled with Lord Bath, and became the object at which were shot all the arrows of calumny. He had borne his head above the obloquy that attended his former pension—not a mouth was opened now in defence of his title; as innocent as his pension, since neither betrayed him into any deed of servility to prerogative and despotism. Both were injudicious; the last irrecoverably so. The blow was more ruinous to his country than to himself. While he held the love of the people, nothing was so formidable in Europe as his name. The talons of the lion were drawn, when he was no longer awful in his own forests.

The City of London had intended to celebrate Mr. Pitt's return to employment, and lamps for an illumination had been placed round the Monument. But no sooner did they hear of his new dignity, than the festival was counter-ordered. The great engine of this dissatisfaction was Lord Temple, who was so shameless as to publish the history of their breach, in which he betrayed every private passage that Mr. Pitt had dropped in their negotiation and quarrel which could tend to inflame the public or private persons against him. This malignant man worked in the mines of successive factions for near thirty years together. To relate them is writing his life. . . .

Like oracles and groves, whose sanctity depended on the fears of the devout, and whose mysterious and holy gloom vanished as soon as men dared to think and walk through them, Lord Chatham's authority ceased with his popularity; and his godhead, when he had affronted his priests.

In all his actions was discernible an imitation of his model, Ximenes; a model ill-suited to a free government, and worse to a man whose situation and necessities were totally different. Was the poor monk thwarted or disgraced, the asylum of his convent was open; and a cardinal, who was clothed in a hair-cloth at Court, missed no fine linen, no luxury, in his cloister. Lord Chatham was as abstemious in his diet; but mixed Persian grandeur with herbs and roots. His equipages and train were too expensive for his highest zenith of wealth, and he maintained them out of place and overwhelmed with debts. A wife and children were strange impediments to a Ximenes. Grandeur, show, and a pension, could not wrestle with an opulent and independent nobility, nor could he buy them, though he had sold himself. His services to his country were far above those of Ximenes, who trampled on Castilian pride but to sacrifice it to the monarch of Castile. Lord Chatham had recalled the spirit of a brave nation, had given it victory and glory; and victory secured its liberty. As Ximenes had no such objects, the inflexibility of Ximenes was below the imitation of Camillus. It was mean ambition to stoop from humbling the crowned heads of France and Spain, to contend with proud individuals and the arrogance of factions—at least, would a real great man have doated on a coronet, who prided himself in lowering the peerage? Lord Chatham had been the arbiter of Europe; he affected to be the master of the English nobility; he failed, and remained with a train of domestics whom he could not pay. More like Nicolas Rienzi than Ximenes, the lord of Rome became ridiculous by apeing the tawdry pageant of a triumph. Yet, as what is here said is the voice of truth, not the hiss of satire, British posterity will ever remember that, as Lord Chatham's first Administration obtained and secured the most real and substantial benefits to his country, the puerilities of his second could not efface their lustre. The man was lessened, not his merits. Even the shameful peace of Paris, concluded in defiance of him, could not rob the nation of all he had acquired; nor could George the Third resign so much as Pitt had gained for George the Second. Half the empire of Indostan conquered under his administration by the spirit he had infused, still pours its treasures into the Thames. Canada was subdued by his councils, and Spain and France, that yet dread his name, attest the reality of his services. The memory of his eloquence, which effected all these wonders, will remain when the neglect of his cotemporaries, and my criticisms, will be forgotten. Yet it was the duty of an annalist, and of a painter of nature, to exhibit the varying features of his portrait. The lights and shades of a great character are a moral lesson. Philosophy loves to study the man more than the hero or the statesman; and whether his qualities were real or fictitious, his actions were so illustrious, that few names in the registers of Time will excite more curiosity than that of William Pitt.

1767
The Marquis of Tavistock

A melancholy event relaxed a little the assiduity of the Opposition.
The Marquis of Tavistock, only son of the Duke of Bedford, was
thrown from his horse as he was hunting, and received a kick that
fractured his skull. He languished about a fortnight, and died at the
age of twenty-seven. If there was a perfectly amiable and unblemished
character in an age so full of censure and so much deserving it, the
universal esteem in which the virtues of that young Lord were held,
seemed to allow that he was the person. His gentleness, generosity and
strict integrity made all the world or love or admire him. Full of
spirit and martial ardour, which he suppressed in deference to a father
to whom his life was so important, he had the genuine bashfulness
of youth, and the humility of the lowest fortune. His large fortune
he shared with his cotemporary friends, assisting them in purchasing
commissions. Yet he had taste for those arts whose excellence and
splendour became the house of so great an heir, and indulged himself
in them when they did not interfere with his more favourite liberality.
His parts were neither shining nor contemptible; and his virtue assisted
his understanding in preserving both from being biassed or seduced.
To observers, it was clear that he much disapproved the want of principle in the relations and dependents of his parents; yet so respectful
was his duty to his father, and so attentive his tenderness to his mother,
and so artfully had she impressed it, that Lord Tavistock's repugnance
to their connections and politics was only observable by his shunning
Parliament, and by withdrawing himself from their society to hunting
and country sports. It was from the same piety towards his parents
that, contrary to his inclination, he had accepted the hand of an amiable
young lady,[1] chosen for her passive demeanour by the Duchess, to
whom however he proved an affectionate husband. Yet as his youthful
passions were very strong, he had been captivated by another fair
lady,[2] who was brutally treated by her Lord, and whose virtue was

[1] Lady Elizabeth Keppel, youngest daughter of William Anne Earl of Albemarle.
[H.W.]
[2] Lady Elizabeth Spenser, wife of Henry Herbert Earl of Pembroke, and younger
sister of George Duke of Marlborough, who had married Lady Caroline Russell,
sister of Lord Tavistock.   [H.W.]

proved by the following circumstance, as her lover was reduced to so difficult an undertaking to gain her, and without success: Lord Tavistock applied himself to an ardent study of the Law for six months, to learn by his own knowledge if there was not a possibility of procuring a divorce for a wife on the notorious adultery of her husband. His own widow, who doated on so excellent a young man, survived him not two years. The indecent indifference with which such a catastrophe was felt by the faction of the family, spoke but too plainly that Lord Tavistock had lived a reproach and terror to them. The Duke, his father, for a few days almost lost his senses—and recovered them too soon. The Duchess was less blameable, and retained the impression longer. But while all mankind who ever heard the name of Lord Tavistock were profuse in lamenting such a national calamity, it gave universal scandal when, in a little fortnight after his death, they beheld his father, the Duke, carried by his creatures to the India House to vote on a factious question. This unexampled insensibility was bitterly pressed home on the Duke two years afterwards in a public libel. Yet, surely, it was savage wantonness to taunt a parent with such a misfortune; and of flint must the heart have been that could think such a domestic stroke a proper subject for insult, however inadequate to the wound the anguish appeared: how steeled the nature that could wish to recall the feelings of a father on such a misfortune! In Borgia's age they stabbed with daggers; in ours with the pen!

Chatham

Lord Chatham himself either was not, or would not be, in a condition to strike any great stroke. Though he still continued to take the air publicly, his spirits and nerves were said to be in the lowest and most shattered condition. Added to the phrenzy of his conduct, a new circumstance raised general suspicion of there being more of madness in his case, than mere caprice and impracticable haughtiness. He had put himself into the hands of Dr. Addington, a regular physician it is true, but originally a mad-doctor, innovating enough in his practice to be justly deemed a quack. The physician, it was supposed, was selected as proper to the disease; whereas, if all was not a farce, I should think that the physician rather caused the disease, Addington having kept off the gout, and possibly dispersed it through his nerves, or even driven it up to his head; so long did Lord Chatham remain without a fit of the gout, and so childish and agitated was his whole frame, if a word of business was mentioned to him: tears and trembling immediately succeeded to cheerful indifferent conversation. Some passages too, which I shall specify hereafter, indicated a fond kind of dotage. Yet do I very much doubt whether the whole scene was not imposition, and the dictates of disappointment, inability and pride, rather than the fruits of a brain extraordinarily distempered. A slave to his passions, a master dissembler, and no profound statesman, his conduct was more likely to be extravagant by design, than from the loss of his senses. As he reappeared in the world, and yet governed his domestic affairs with the same wild wantonness and prodigality, it is probable that there was not more folly in his secession from business, than could be accounted for in so eccentric a composition. If it was nothing but singularity and passion, Lord Chatham was certainly the first man who ever retired from business into the post of Prime Minister.

Charles Townshend

It was on that day and on that occasion that Charles Townshend displayed in a latitude beyond belief the amazing powers of his capacity, and the no less amazing incongruities of his character. He had taken on himself early in the day, the examination of the Company's conduct; and in a very cool sensible speech on that occasion, and with a becoming consciousness of his own levity, had told the House that he hoped he had atoned for the inconsideration of his past life by the care he had taken of that business. He had scarcely uttered this speech, but, as if to atone for that (however false) atonement, he left the House and went home to dinner, not concerning himself with Dyson's motion that was to follow. As that motion was, however, of a novel nature, it produced suspicion, objection and difficulties. Conway being pressed, and not caring to be the sole champion of an invidious measure, that was in reality not only in Townshend's province, but which he had had a principal hand in framing, sent for him back to the House. He returned about eight in the evening, half-drunk with champagne, and more intoxicated with spirits. He rose to speak without giving himself time to learn, and without caring what had been in agitation, except that the motion had given an alarm. The first thing he did, was to call God to witness that he had not been consulted on the motion—a confession implying that he was not consulted on a business in his own department; and the more marvellous, as the disgrace of which he seemed to complain or boast of, was absolutely false. There were sitting round him twelve persons who had been in consultation with him that very morning, and with his assistance had drawn the motion on his own table, and who were petrified at his most unparalleled effrontery, and causeless want of truth. When he sat down again, Conway asked him softly, how he could affirm so gross a falsehood? He replied carelessly, 'I thought it would be better to say so'—but before he sat down, he had poured forth a torrent of wit, parts, humour, knowledge, absurdity, vanity and fiction, heightened by all the graces of comedy, the happiness of allusion and quotation, and the buffoonery of farce. To the purpose of the question he said not a syllable. It was a descant on the times, a picture of parties, of their leaders, of their hopes and defects. It was an encomium and a satire on himself; and while he painted the pretensions of birth, riches, connections, favour, titles; while he affected to praise Lord Rockingham, and that faction, and yet insinuated that nothing but parts like his own were qualified to preside; and while he less covertly arraigned the wild incapacity of Lord Chatham, he excited such murmurs of wonder, admiration, applause, laughter, pity and scorn, that nothing was so true as the sentence with which he concluded, when speaking of Government; he said, it was become what he himself had often been called, a weathercock.

Such was the wit, abundance, and impropriety of this speech, that for some days men could talk or inquire of nothing else. 'Did you hear Charles Townshend's champagne speech?' was the universal question. For myself, I protest it was the most singular pleasure of the kind I ever tasted. The bacchanalian enthusiasm of Pindar flowed in torrents less rapid and less eloquent, and inspires less delight than Townshend's imagery, which conveyed meaning in every sentence. It was Garrick writing and acting extempore scenes of Congreve. A light circumstance increased the mirth of the audience. In the fervour of speaking Townshend rubbed off the patch from his eye, which he had represented as grievously cut three days before: no mark was discernible, but to the nearest spectators a scratch so slight, that he might have made, and perhaps had made it himself with a pin. To me the entertainment of the day was complete. He went to supper with us at Mr. Conway's, where, the flood of his gaiety not being exhausted, he kept the table in a roar till two in the morning, by various sallies and pictures, the last of which was a scene in which he mimicked inimitably his own wife and another great lady with whom he fancied himself in love, and both whose foibles and manner he counterfeited to the life. Mere lassitude closed his lips at last, not the want of wit and new ideas.

To solve the contrast of such parts and absurdity in the same composition, one is almost tempted to have recourse to that system of fairy Manicheism, wherein no sooner has one benevolent being endowed the hero of the tale with supernatural excellence, but a spiteful hag of equal omnipotence dashes the irrevocable gift with some counter qualification, which serves to render the accomplished prince a monster of contradictions.

It was not less worth reflection, that, while this phenomenon of genius was, perniciously to himself and uselessly to his country, lavishing an unexampled profusion of parts on wanton buffoonery, only to excite transient and barren applause; the restorer of his country was lurking in darkness and shrouding a haughty sterility of talents from the public eye, under the veil of phrenzy or untractable obstinacy. The simplicity of a great character was wanting both to Lord Chatham and Townshend.

Chatham

At this period came to my knowledge a transaction, at which I have already hinted, and which in truth at that time persuaded me of the reality of Lord Chatham's madness. When he inherited Sir William Pynsent's estate, he removed to it and sold his house and grounds at Hayes, a place on which he had wasted prodigious sums, and, which yet retained small traces of expense, great part having been consumed in purchasing contiguous tenements to free himself from all neighbourhood. Much had gone in doing and undoing, and not a little portion in planting by torch-light, as his peremptory and impatient temper could brook no delay. Nor were these the sole circumstances that marked his caprice. His children he could not bear under the same roof, nor communications from room to room, nor whatever he thought promoted noise. A winding passage between his house and children was built with the same view. When at the beginning of this his second Administration, he fixed at North End by Hampstead, he took four or five houses successively, as fast as Mr. Dingley, his landlord, went into them, still, as he said, to ward off the noises of neighbourhood. His inconsiderate promptitude was not less remarkable at Pynsent. A bleak hill bounded his view; he ordered his gardener to have it planted with evergreens; the man asked, 'With what sorts?' He replied, 'With cedars and cypresses.' 'Bless me, my lord!' replied the gardener, 'all the nurseries in this county (Somersetshire) would not furnish a hundredth part.' 'No matter; send for them from London;' and they were fetched by land-carriage. Yet were these follies committed when no suspicion was had of his disorder. But by these and other caprices he had already consumed more than half of the legacy of Pynsent. His very domestic and abstemious privacy bore a considerable article in his housekeeping. His sickly and uncertain appetite was never regular, and his temper could put up with no defect. Thence a succession of chickens were boiling and roasting at every hour to be ready whenever he should call. He now, as if his attention to business demanded his vicinity to town, bent his fancy to the repossession of Hayes, which he had sold to my cousin, Mr. Thomas Walpole. The latter, under great inquietude, showed me letters he had received from Lady Chatham, begging in the most pathetic terms that he would sell them Hayes again. She urged that it would save her children from destruction; and that her children's children would be bound to pray for him; requesting that he would take some days to consider before he refused. He did; and then wrote to her that he was very averse from parting with the place, on which he had laid out much money; but if the air of Hayes was the object, Lord Chatham was welcome to go thither directly for a month, or for the whole summer; that he would immediately remove his family, who were there, and Lord Chatham would find it well aired. This she declined accepting. Mr. Walpole then sent Nuthall to her. She, who had never appeared to have a will or thought of her own, but to act with submission at her Lord's nod, now received Nuthall alone, and besought him not to own to her Lord that she had yet received any letter from Mr. Walpole, but to deliver it as just arrived, if Lord Chatham should ask for the answer—and then carried him to her Lord. He seemed in health and reasonable; but asking if Nuthall knew anything about Hayes, and being told the contents of the letter, he said, with a sigh, 'That might have saved me!' Lady Chatham, seeming to be alarmed, said, 'My Lord, I was talking to Mr. Nuthall on that subject; we will go and finish our discourse;' and carried him out of the room. She then told him they had agreed to sell the Wilt-shire estate (part of Pynsent's), and with part of the produce re-purchase Hayes, which, however, they must mortgage, for they owed as much as the sale would amount to. Mr. Walpole, distressed between un-willingness to part with Hayes, and apprehension that Lord Chatham's ill-health would be imputed to him, as that air might have been a remedy, consulted the Chancellor. The latter on hearing the story, said, 'Then he is mad,' and sent for James Grenville. Asking when he had seen Lord Chatham, Grenville replied, the day before, and had found him much better. Lord Camden said, 'Did he mention Hayes?' 'Yes', said Grenville, 'and then his discourse grew very ferocious'. No doubt there was something in these words of Grenville that had the air of a part acted: one can scarce believe a brother-in-law would have been so frank, had there been no concerted plan in the phrenzy; yet what wonder if anything seemed more credible than the fictitious madness of a First Minister in no difficult situation? From this period the few reports of the few who had access to him concurred in representing him as sedate, conversable, even cheerful, till any mention was made of politics: then he started, fell into tremblings, and the conversation was broken off. When the Session was closed, these reports wore away; and as he remained above a year in close confinement at Hayes, unconsulting, and by degrees unconsulted, he and his lunacy were totally forgotten; till new interests threatened his reappearance, which after many delays at length happened, though with no solution given by any friend of so long a suspension of sense or common sense. Mr. Walpole had yielded Hayes.

The Duke of Grafton

As times show men, the fluctuation and difficulties of those I am describing brought forth some symptoms, though not so fully as it appeared afterwards, of the singular cast of the Duke of Grafton's mind. Hitherto he had passed for a man of much obstinacy and firmness, of strict honour, devoid of ambition, and though reserved, more diffident than designing. He retained so much of this character, as to justify those who had mistaken the rest. If he precipitated himself into the most sudden and inextricable contradictions, at least he pursued the object of the moment with inflexible ardour. If he abandoned himself to total negligence of business in pursuit of his sports and pleasures, the love of power never quitted him; and when his will was disputed, no man was more imperiously arbitrary. If his designs were not deeply laid, at least they were conducted in profound silence. He rarely pardoned those who did not guess his inclination: it was necessary to guess, so rare was any instance of his unbosoming himself to either friends or confidants. Why his honour had been so highly rated, I can less account; except that he had advertised it, and that obstinate young men are apt to have high notions before they have practised the world and assayed their own virtue.

The King

In all my experience of the King or knowledge of his measures, he never interfered with his Ministers, scarce took any part in his own business (I speak of the past years of his reign), unless when he was to undo an Administration. Whether hating or liking the persons he employed, the moment he took them, he seemed to resign himself entirely to their conduct for the time. If what they proposed was very disagreeable to him, at most he avoided it by delay. How far he had entered into his mother's and Lord Bute's plans while they were all-powerful at the beginning of his reign, cannot be known. Afterwards he had, undoubtedly, confidence in none of his Ministers; which according with his extreme indolence and indifference to all men, his Ministers found little obstruction to their views from the closet, till the greater indolence of the Duke of Grafton and Lord North taught his Majesty to act on his own judgment, assisted by the secret Junto of the creatures of Lord Bute. The sensible disgrace that fell on the Crown from so frequent a change of Ministries had at last alarmed the King and made a lasting impression. And yet the ruling principle of the reign, which had been, by breaking and dividing all parties, to draw attention and dependence only to the King himself, had succeeded so happily, that even these storms tended to strengthen the unbounded influence at which the King aspired, and which he pursued invariably on every returning calm. The ductility and congenial indolence of the Duke of Grafton, accompanied with much respect and good breeding, fixed his Majesty in preferring him to all the men whom he *could* employ: and though the Duke not long afterwards fell into a connection of very ill-odour at Court, yet the tedious tyranny of Grenville, and the inveteracy of Rockingham to Bute, were so much more dreaded, that Grafton did not cease to be almost a favourite; with the additional comfort to the King, that if forced to sacrifice him, it would be the loss of an useful tool, rather than of a Minister for whom he had any fondness.

Charles Townshend

On the 4th of September died Charles Townshend, of a neglected fever, in, I think, the forty-second year of his age. He met his approaching fate with a good humour that never forsook him, and with an equanimity that he had never shown on the most trifling occasions. Though cut off so immaturely, it is a question whether he had not lived long enough for his character. His genius could have received no accession of brightness; his faults only promised multiplication. He had almost every great talent, and every little quality. His vanity exceeded even his abilities, and his suspicions seemed to make him doubt whether he had any. With such a capacity he must have been the greatest man of this age, and perhaps inferior to no man in any age, had his faults been only in a moderate proportion; in short, if he had had but common truth, common sincerity, common honesty, common modesty, common steadiness, common courage and common sense.

Comte de Guerchy

On the 17th of the same month [September] died at Paris the Comte de Guerchy, their Ambassador to England. His death was occasioned by a former ill-cured complaint, but hastened by the various mortifications he had received from d'Eon, and the recent neglect and ill-usage of his own Court. He had been a lover of the Duchesse de Grammont, the Prime Minister's sister, who, aspiring at rank, had fixed on the Duc de Grammont as a man suited to her purposes. It was said that having consulted Monsieur de Guerchy, he without considering that her resolution was probably taken, inveighed with too much sincerity against the choice of so contemptible a man; and was never forgiven. Certain it is, that his embassy being finished, he found nothing but coldness at home, and no hopes of reward or recompense of his services or mortifications. This cruelty being censured, pensions were granted to his widow and son.

The Duke of York

On the very same day [17 September] departed, at Monaco, Edward, Duke of York, next brother of the King. His immoderate pursuit of pleasure and unremitted fatigues in travelling beyond his strength, succeeded without interruption by balls and entertainments, had thrown his blood, naturally distempered and full of humours, into a state that brought on a putrid and irresistible fever. He suffered considerably, but with a heroism becoming a great Prince. Before he died, he wrote a penitential letter to the King (though, in truth, he had no faults but what his youth made very pardonable), and tenderly recommended his servants to him. The Prince of Monaco, though his favourite child was then under inoculation at Paris, remained with and waited on him to his last breath, omitting nothing that tenderness could supply or his royal birth demand. The Duke of York had lately passed some time in the French Court, and by the quickness of his replies, by his easy frankness, and (in him) unusual propriety of conduct, had won much on the affection of the King of France, and on the rest of the Court, though his loose and perpetually rolling eyes, his short sight, and the singular whiteness of his hair, which the French said resembled feathers, by no means bespoke prejudice in his favour. His temper was good, his generosity royal, and his parts not defective: but his inarticulate loquacity and the levity of his conduct, unsupported by any countenance from the King, his brother, had conspired to place him but low in the estimation of his countrymen. As he could obtain no credit from the King's unfeeling nature, he was in a situation to do little good; as he had been gained by the Opposition, he might have done hurt—at least so much to the King that his death was little lamented. Nor can we judge whether more years and experience would have corrected his understanding or corrupted his heart, nor whether, which is most probable, they would not have done both.

The Duke of Gloucester

The Duke of Gloucester, of as fair complexion, as short-sighted, of worse health, but of a more manly form, was a Prince of a very different disposition. Reserved, serious, pious, of the most decent and sober deportment, and possessing a plain understanding though of no brilliancy, he was of all his family the King's favourite, though admitted to no confidence, intimacy, or credit. An honourable amour which totally engrossed him, and of which I shall have occasion to speak hereafter, preserved him from the irregularities into which his brothers Edward and Henry fell, and which the severity of confinement in which they were held by their mother till they attained the age of twenty-one, did much excuse.

Henry, Duke of Cumberland

Henry, Duke of Cumberland, though not tall, did not want beauty, but with the babbling disposition of his brother York, he had neither the parts nor the condescension of the latter; familiarizing himself with bad company, and yet presuming on a rank which he degraded, and, notwithstanding, made an annoyance. His youth had all its faults, and gave no better promises.

Lord North

In the room of Charles Townshend, Lord North, son of the Earl of Guildford, was appointed Chancellor of the Exchequer. He had sound parts, wit, and, it was thought, industry; an ungracious manner, a voice untuneable, and a total want of polish in his behaviour. He had been an active and ready agent in the whole cause against Wilkes, and was not a man that the friends of the Constitution could regard with partiality: but there were so few upright, that it was become almost eligible to select the exceptionable, in order to lessen confederacies amongst those whose union would be formidable should they return to power in a body. Lord North's (supposed) application and facility of access repaired in some degree the negligence and disgusting coldness of the Duke of Grafton.

Lord Townshend

Trifling as this first success was, it was the greatest service which the Lord-Lieutenant rendered to the Government. Obstinate against advice, thirsting for low popularity, and void even of decorum, he soon lost all consideration. Drunkenness and buffoonery, unsupported by parts or policy, rendered him the scorn even of the populace. That he might exempt himself from the reproach of whatever in his instructions was disagreeable to the Irish, he spoke of himself as entrusted with no power; and giving a loose to his own turn for caricature, he drew ridiculous pictures of himself in ignominious attitudes with his hands tied behind him; thus shunning opposition by meriting contempt.

Lord Weymouth

... There was nothing in Weymouth's character that recommended his morality. He was a prompt and graceful speaker of a few apt sentences, which, coming from a young and handsome figure attracted more applause than they merited. Yet, considering the life he led, his parts must naturally have been very good; for sitting up nightly, gaming and drinking till six in the morning, and rising thus heated after noon, it was extraordinary that he was master of himself, or of what little he knew. His great fortune he had damaged by such profuse play, that his house was often full of bailiffs; and he had exposed himself to receive such pressing letters and in such reproachful terms, that his spirit was as much doubted, as what is called his point of honour among gentlemen gamesters. He was in private a close and sound reasoner, and good-humoured, under a considerable appearance of pride; but having risen on such slender merit, he seemed to think he possessed a sufficient stock, and continued his course of life to the total neglect of the affairs of his office, the business of which was managed, as much as it could be, by Mr. Wood, his under-secretary.

1768

Dunning aud other Lawyers

On the 14th of January the House of Commons met. Dunning was declared Solicitor-General in the room of Willes, who was made a Judge to make room for him. This was an extraordinary promotion, as Dunning was connected with Lord Shelburne, and was to be brought by him into the ensuing Parliament. The affair indeed had been agitated before the accession of the Bedfords, who wished to raise Wedderburne to the Solicitor's place; but the great reputation of Dunning decided it in his favour. He was the most shining pleader then at the bar, and being a zealous Whig, had distinguished himself greatly as counsel for Wilkes. The fame of his eloquence sunk entirely and at once in the House of Commons, so different is the oratory of the Bar and of Parliament. Lord Mansfield, Hume Campbell, and Lord Camden, maintained a superior reputation in both kinds. Wedderburne shone brightest in the House. Norton had at first disappointed the expectation entertained of him when he came into Parliament; yet his strong parts, that glowed through all the coarseness of his language and brutality of his manner, recovered his weight, and [he] was much distinguished. But Sir Dudley Rider, the soundest lawyer, and Charles Yorke, one of the most reputed pleaders, talked themselves out of all consideration in Parliament—the former by laying too great stress on every part of his diffusive knowledge, the latter by the sterility of his materials.

Some Authors

It may not be amiss, by way of appendix, to say a few words on the state of literature during the period I have been describing. It will be the less improper as the controversies and politics of the age gave the principal, almost the whole tone to letters at that time. I do not mean to send the reader to the gross and virulent libels of Wilkes and his still coarser imitators. As a writer, Wilkes's chief merit was an easy style, the vehicle of little knowledge, of not much more wit, and of extreme boldness. He was so far an original as being the first who dared to print the most respected names at full length. In imitation of him, the daily and evening newspapers printed every outrageous libel that was sent to them. Till that time the abuse of the week was generally confined to essays in the journals on Saturdays. Bolingbroke and Pulteney were content with battering the Administration once in seven days . . .

Two other poets of great merit arose, who meddled not with politics; Dr. Goldsmith, the correct author of *The Traveller*; and Mr. Anstey, who produced as original a poem as *Hudibras* itself, the *New Bath-guide*. The easiest wit, the most genuine humour, the most inoffensive satire, the happiest parodies, the most unaffected poetry, and the most harmonious melody in every kind of metre, distinguish that poem by their assemblage from the works of all other men. It was a melancholy proof of how little an author can judge of the merit of his own

compositions, when he afterwards produced *The Patriot*, in which nobody could discover his meaning, or whether he had any meaning; and
in which, amidst various but unsuccessful attempts at humour, nothing
remained but his sonorous numbers. He afterwards sunk to no kind of
merit at all.

I do not know whether this period may not be said to have *given
birth* to another original poem; for notwithstanding its boasted antiquity,
and the singularity of the style, it remains a doubt with me and many
others, whether *Fingal* was not formed in this age from scraps, perhaps
not modern, but of no very early date. Its sterility of ideas, the insipid
sameness that reigns throughout, and the timidity with which it
anxiously avoids every image that might affix it to any specific age,
country or religion, are far from bespeaking a savage bard, who the
more he was original, the more he would naturally have availed himself
of the images and opinions around him. Few barbarous authors write
with the fear of criticism before their eyes. The moon, a storm, the
troubled ocean, a blasted heath, a single tree, a waterfall, and a ghost;
take these away and Cadmus's warriors, who started out of the earth,
and killed one another before they had time to conceive an idea, were
as proper heroes for an epic poem as Fingal and his captains.

I will mention but two other authors of this period, Dr. Robertson,
and Mrs. Macaulay. The first as sagacious and penetrating as Tacitus,
with the perspicuity of Livy, and without the partialities of his own
countryman, Hume, gave a perfect model of history in that of Scotland.
In biography, his method and style were still preserved, though his
Charles the Fifth fell far short of his other work. The female historian,
as partial in the cause of liberty as bigots to the Church and royalists to
tyranny, exerted manly strength with the gravity of a philosopher. Too
prejudiced to dive into causes, she imputes everything to tyrannic views,
nothing to passions, weakness, error, prejudice, and still less to what
operates oftenest, and her ignorance of which qualified her yet less for
an historian, to accident and little motives. She seems to think men have
acted from no views but those of establishing a despotism or a republic.

Horace Walpole and the Memoires

As I had rather disparage these Memoires than disappoint the reader
by promising him more satisfaction than he will find, let me remind
him that I had now quitted my seat in Parliament; and consequently,

what traces of debates shall appear hereafter must be mutilated and imperfect, as being received by hearsay from others, or taken from notes communicated to me. As I had detached myself, too, from all parties, I was in the secrets of none: and though I had curiosity enough to fathom some opportunities of learning others, and made observations on what was passing, in which I was assisted by the clue of what I had formerly known; yet it will doubtless be perceived that my information was often incomplete, and that the mysterious springs of several events never came to my knowledge. In those situations I shall be far from decisive—yet that very ignorance may guide future historians to the search after authentic papers; and my doubts may lead to some certainty. It may yet be asked why I choose, under these impediments, to continue my narrative, while I allow that it must fall short of the preceding parts? The honestest answer is the best: it amuses me. I like to give my opinion on what I have seen: I wish to warn posterity (however vain such zeal!) against the folly and corruption and profligacy of the times I have lived in; and I think that, with all its defects, the story I shall tell will be more complete than if I had stopped at the end of the foregoing Parliament, which was no era of anything but of my own dereliction of politics; and not having been the hero of my own tale, I am desirous at least of bringing it down to the termination of the political life of some of the principal actors in the foregoing pages. I propose to carry the work down to the pacification with Spain in 1771, when not only all our foreign quarrels were terminated, but when the Court had surmounted every domestic difficulty, had pacified the Colonies and Ireland; and by the aid of Fortune and by the folly of Opposition, had little to disturb them but their own indiscretion, and the restless, though timid desires of ascertaining and extending a prerogative which the King enjoyed effectually by less obnoxious, though less dangerous, means than force. Whether I shall live to complete this plan, or whether, if I do, I shall not again be tempted to prosecute it further, I am equally ignorant. The reader, that is amused, may perhaps be glad if I proceed. If I am tedious, the most delicate of my readers will always have that facile remedy in his power, of ceasing to read me the moment he is tired. To such, therefore, I make no apology. To please the other sort, if I can, at least to employ some vacant hours, I continue my journal.

John Wilkes

The Parliament having been dissolved on the 11th of March, 1768, and the writs issued for the general election of another, the memorable John Wilkes, who had resided for some time at Paris, and had fallen almost into oblivion, came suddenly over, and declared himself a candidate to represent the City of London. His first step, indeed, was to write a submissive letter to the King, imploring pardon; but his Majesty refusing to read the letter, Wilkes, bold from his desperate situation, and fond of extraordinary daring, opened his new campaign by this attack on the Metropolis itself, though an outlaw, and subject to be sent to prison on his former sentence. Men wondered at the inactivity of a Government that had by no means shown itself indifferent to the persecution of so audacious a criminal, and expected every day to hear he was taken up. But whether the Court looked with contempt on a measure that promised so little success, or whether, which I believe was their true motive, they feared that new severity would enhance the merits of the martyr in the eyes of the people, neither the Government nor the Courts of Law interposed to check his career. Alderman Sir William Baker was the only citizen of note and fortune that countenanced his pretensions; yet Wilkes persisted, appeared openly on the hustings, and contested a seat with the most popular of the City's magistrates. The lower people embraced his cause with ardour; and he soon appeared to have so many partisans, that his fortune became combined with that national phrenzy, stock-jobbing. Bets on his success were turned into stock; and in the phrase of the times, *he was done*, like other wagers on the funds. The credit of the candidate Alderman was, however, too firmly established to be shaken so suddenly. Wilkes was every day the lowest on the poll, and the very first evening as he left the court, he was arrested for debt—probably by the underhand direction of the Ministry; but his attorney answered for his appearance; and preferring to be a prisoner to the Government, as more likely to create pity, than to lie in prison for debt, Wilkes acquainted the Solicitor of the Treasury, that he intended to surrender himself to his outlawry. He returned each day to the hustings, but lost his election; Harley, the Lord Mayor, Sir Robert Ladbrook, Beckford, and Trecothick, being elected; the last, a West India merchant, who at the time of the Stamp Act, had signalized himself by procuring petitions against it from

Bristol, Liverpool, and other commercial towns. Sir Richard Glynn, Paterson, the unpopular creature of Lord Holland, and Wilkes, being thrown out. During the struggle, Beckford and Trecothick behaved towards Wilkes with much civility; the Lord Mayor with sullen coldness, and occasionally with spirited resistance.

Far from dismayed, Wilkes, like an able general, rallied his forces, and declared himself a candidate for the county of Middlesex; nay, threatened to stand for Surrey, too, in opposition to George Onslow, one of his deserting friends; yet hitherto he had no eminent patronage. Lord Temple, linked with Grenville, abandoned him. Humphrey Cotes, an old ally, but who in his absence, it was said, had cheated him of some money, made amends by warm activity; and the Duke of Portland, incensed by his late affair with Sir James Lowther, on Wilkes's pretensions to Middlesex espoused his cause. Lord Mansfield, equally revengeful, timorous, and subtle, pretended that it was the office of the Chancellor to bring this outlaw to justice; but the Chancellor and the Duke of Grafton did not care to increase their unpopularity by adding persecution to the complaints Wilkes had already made of their giving him up. Still less was Lord Camden solicitous to save Lord Mansfield from danger and odium. The Chancellor went to Bath, and the Duke with his mistress to Newmarket.

On the 28th of March the election began at Brentford; and while the irresolution of the Court and the carelessness of the Prime Minister, Grafton, caused a neglect of all precautions, the zeal of the populace had heated itself to a pitch of fury. They possessed themselves of all the turnpikes and avenues leading to the place of election by break of day, and would suffer no man to pass who bore not in his hat a blue cockade inscribed with the name of Wilkes and Number 45, or written on paper. The other candidates were Sir William Beauchamp Proctor and Mr. Cooke, the former Members. Cooke was confined with the gout: a relation who appeared for him was roughly handled at Hyde Park Corner, and Sir William's carriage was demolished. At Brentford the mob was more peaceable, but had poured in such numbers, that on the first day's poll the votes for Wilkes were 1200, for Proctor 700, for Cooke 500. At night the people grew outrageous; though when Wilkes first arrived in town, I had seen him pass before my windows in a hackney chair, attended but by a dozen children and women; now all Westminster was in a riot. It was not safe to pass through Piccadilly; and every family was forced to put out lights: the windows of every unilluminated house were demolished. The coach-glasses of such as did not huzza for *Wilkes and Liberty* were broken, and many chariots and coaches were spoiled by the mob scratching them with the favourite 45. Lord Weymouth, Secretary of State, sent orders to Justice Fielding to have constables kept in readiness. He begged his Lordship not to tell it, but there was not a constable in London; all had been sent for to Brentford. On this the guards were drawn out. Lord Bute's house was attacked, but the mob could not force an entrance, nor at Lord Egmont's in Pall Mall. The Duke of Northumberland the mob obliged to appear and to give them liquor, and to drink with them to Wilkes's success. Some ladies of rank were taken out of their chairs, and ordered to join the popular cry; and to Lady Holderness they cried, 'No King! No regal Government!' In the City they attacked the Mansion House and broke the windows. The Lord Mayor, a zealous anti-Wilkite, sent for the trained bands, but they were not sufficient to disperse the tumult. Six thousand weavers had risen in behalf of Wilkes, and were the principal actors. Some of the regimental drummers beat their drums for Wilkes, who finding his election secure, dismissed the weavers, and by the next morning all was quiet, but the poll was at an end. Wilkes was too triumphant to be resisted; and, master to act as he pleased, he threw his supernumerary votes in to Cooke, who was elected with him.

The second night was less tumultuous; but the Scots, sullenly persisting in not celebrating their enemy's triumph by illuminations, had their windows broken. The Dowager Duchess of Hamilton, one of the beautiful Gunnings, though born in Ireland, had contracted such hatred to Wilkes from her two Scotch marriages, that though with child, and though her husband, Lord Lorn, was in Scotland, and all her young children by both matches were in the house with her, she resolutely forbade her house to be lighted up. The mob assaulted it, broke down the outward gates with iron crows, tore up the pavement of the street, and battered the doors and shutters for three hours, but could not surmount her courage. The Count de Seilern, the Austrian Ambassador, the most stately and ceremonious of men, they took out of his coach, and chalked 45 on the sole of his shoe. He complained in form of the insult; it was as difficult for the Ministers to help laughing as to give him redress.

The Methodists

The Methodists endeavoured to draw notice to themselves, but were disappointed. Lord Baltimore was prosecuted for a rape on a loose girl, who had stayed in his house for some days under many opportunities of escaping, but was acquitted on his trial, notwithstanding the hypocrites had much incensed the populace against him. Six young Methodists were expelled from Oxford, but their party could raise no clamour on this supposed persecution. Whitfield, their archpriest, attending one Gibson, who was hanged for forgery, to the gallows, and preaching his funeral sermon, assured the audience that he was gone to heaven; and that a fellow executed at the same time was probably in the same paradise, having had the happiness of touching Gibson's garment. But these impieties and martyrdoms were drowned in the lustre of St. Wilkes's glory, and for once the barefaced libertine carried away the vulgar from the holy knaves.

The Duke of Grafton and Nancy Parsons

The funeral of the Princess Louisa opened a scene to the public eye, which explained much of that ambiguity and incoherent conduct of the Duke of Grafton, which we who were connected with him had long known and felt, and which I deferred unfolding to the reader, till I could state the whole in one comprehensive picture. The Earl of Hertford, married to the Duke's aunt,[1] was Lord Chamberlain. It was of his office to select a chief mourner. The Duchess of Norfolk[2] as a Catholic could not officiate. The Duchess of Somerset,[3] a widow, was old and retired. The next was the Duchess of Richmond,[4] who as daughter-in-law of Mr. Conway, Lord Hertford would have wished to name; but the Duke of Richmond being warmly in opposition, it was apprehended that they would not like the compliment, and as the Duke did not love Lord Hertford, the latter thought it not impossible but the answer might be couched in no very civil terms, though as the Duke was one of the best bred men alive, I think the notion was groundless; and it is more probable that the King, who must have been consulted, had chosen to have this slight put on the Duke, or that Lord Hertford himself had affected the difficulty, in order to pay a compliment to the Prime Minister, who was at the same time his wife's nephew; a compli-

[1] Lady Elizabeth Fitzroy, youngest daughter of Charles 2nd Duke of Grafton. [H.W.]
[2] Mary Blount, wife of Edward Duke of Norfolk. [H.W.]
[3] Lady Charlotte Finch, daughter of Daniel Earl of Nottingham and Winchelsea, second wife and widow of Charles Duke of Somerset. [H.W.]
[4] Lady Mary Bruce, youngest daughter of the last Earl of Ailesbury, whose widow married General Conway. [H.W.]

ment in which, however, he was much disappointed. Passing over therefore the three first Duchesses he chose the next, the Duchess of Grafton,[1]
for though she was parted from her Lord, the Duke had desired his
relations and friends to treat her with the same respect as before,
declaring he had no complaint against her but the disagreement of their
tempers. The Duchess, a woman of commanding figure though no
regular beauty, graceful, full of dignity and of art too, fond of admiration, unbending to the Duke's temper, which, had she tried, it had been
difficult to please, had thought to govern him by spirit, and had lost him
before she was aware; nor could her tears prevent the separation or the
most recluse life for a year recover his affection. Finding all solicitation
ineffectual, and provoked by his affronting her in public places whither
he openly attended his mistress, one Nancy Parsons,[2] a girl distinguished
by an uncommon degree of prostitution; the Duchess, whose passions
had never been warm, had of late relaxed her reserve, had encouraged a
lover, and undoubtedly was desirous of procuring a divorce even at the
expense of her character—at least the Duke's éclat on the funeral
precipitated the discovery.

No sooner did the Duke learn the designation of his wife for the
chief mourner, than he wrote to Lady Hertford in the most angry style,
desiring to know, *if it was intended to insult him, that a woman from
whom he was parted, was set up to figure at a public ceremony?* Lady
Hertford went to him and assured him the step he disapproved, had
been taken out of respect to him, and that her Lord had offended the
Richmonds by the preference. Grafton was outrageous, and said if he
had known it two hours sooner, when he was with the King, he would
have resigned. He suspected very absurdly that there was a formed
design of setting up the Duchess against him; taxed Lady Hertford,
who had never liked her, of favouring the Duchess, and owned that all
his ill-usage of his own brother Colonel Fitzroy, which in truth had been
shocking, had flowed from a like motive, though Mr. and Mrs. Fitzroy
had never seen the Duchess, but as form and the Duke's own request
had exacted. When he could not contest these truths, he at last confessed
he knew that the Duchess was with child by Lord Ossory.[3] This was

[1] Anne Liddel, only child of Henry Lord Ravensworth. [H.W.]
[2] Nancy Parsons had been a Figurante at the Opera, and had boasted of having
raised an hundred guineas in one week from different lovers at a guinea a head. She
then married a Mr. Haughton of Jamaica, from whence she was just returned a
widow. [H.W.]
[3] John Fitzpatrick, 2nd Earl of Upper Ossory, nephew of the Duke of Bedford
and Lord Gower. [H.W.]

sufficient to deter Lord Hertford to set her aside; he acquainted her with the Duke's disapprobation; she received the notice sensibly and with submission and the Duke pretended to be pacified.

But though hatred of his wife had been the motive of much of the Duke's past conduct, and of other rash steps he afterwards took, a deeper mine had been laid, and fired with notable success. Nancy Parsons or Mrs. Haughton,[1] though voluptuous and prone to sacrifice to her passions at any expense,[2] could not at first resist the flattering prospect of becoming the Duchess of Grafton. She had caused the Duchess to be watched, and the mistress of a First Minister could not want syncophants to flatter her with hopes, as soon as the Duchess's frailty was discovered. But she had abler counsellors than her own passions. In the list of her former lovers had been Rigby. He hated me and all the house of Conway, and knew the General and I had great weight with the Duke of Grafton. It was easy however to shake our credit. Conway, as cold as the Duke, loved to be flattered more than to flatter; I still more easily disgusted, and having no particular point in view, had addressed myself of late less to the Duke than to the Duchess, who was far more agreeable, and through whom I had first become acquainted with her husband. As my assiduity about her was open and undisguised, the mistress was instructed not only to sound it in the Duke's ear, but to involve Mr. Conway, the Hertfords and the Fitzroys in the same charge, and the Duke believed all, because my part was true. It was this pique had carried away the Duke so easily from Conway to the Bedfords. Conway, Fitzroy and I had totally neglected the favourite Sultana, and Rigby paid her zealous homage. Bradshaw too, the favourite Secretary of the Treasury, and formerly a notorious pimp, was Rigby's agent both with the Duke and the mistress; such a Cabal was fitted for low mischief; and it required less parts than they had to prejudice so weak and passionate a man as the Duke of Grafton against friends, who in truth gave themselves no trouble to secure his favour. I had abruptly dropped him the moment I had discovered his unworthy treatment of Conway, but the latter who had a real friendship for and obligations to him, could not digest his coldness. Authorized by what

[1] She was called so from her husband justly, but till the dignity of mistress of Prime Minister made her treated with more respect, she had only been known to the public by her former name of Nancy Parsons. [H.W.]

[2] She was very far from being faithful to the Duke, as was well known during his attachment to her. It was more extraordinary that a woman of her vocation should have sacrificed so brilliant a post, and a prospect still greater, to a real inclination, as will appear; for though the rank of the rivals was equal, the fortune and power of the Duke of Grafton were out of comparison superior to his successors. [H.W.]

the Duke had confessed to Lady Hertford, Conway remonstrated to him on his unjust suspicions and estranged behaviour. The Duke shuffled off the accusation, on which Conway complained to the King, who offered to mediate betwixt them, the Court dreading to lose the Duke, who now stood unconnected, and consequently dependent, and whom they especially wanted to the defence of Sir James Lowther against the Duke of Portland—a cause in which Grafton had made himself a principal. This detail was essential not only to elucidate past events, but others more important that are to follow.

Character of an Anonymous Hero

Of all the tumults, the fiercest and most memorable was the following. A dispute having arisen between the coalworkers and the coalheavers, the latter of whom were chiefly Irish, nay, some of them Whiteboys, an Act of Parliament had passed the last year, subjecting the coalheavers to the jurisdiction of the alderman of the ward, an office had been erected, and one Green, who kept an alehouse, had been constituted their agent. Houston, a man who wanted to supplant Green, had incensed the coalheavers against him, and they threatened his destruction. Apprised of their design, he every night removed his wife and children out of his house. One evening he received notice that the coalheavers were coming to attack him. He had nobody with him but a maid-servant and a sailor, who by accident was drinking in the house. Green asked the sailor if he would assist him? 'Yes', answered the generous tar, 'I will defend any man in distress.' At eight the rioters appeared, and fired on the house, lodging in one room above two hundred bullets; and when their ammunition was spent, they bought pewter pots, cut them to pieces, and fired them as ball. At length with an axe they broke out the bottom of the door; but that breach the sailor defended singly; while Green and his maid kept up a constant fire, and killed eighteen of the besiegers. Their powder and ball being at last wasted, Green said he must make his escape: 'for you,' said he to the friendly sailor, 'they will not hurt you.' Green retiring from the back room of his house, got into a carpenter's yard, and was concealed in a saw-pit, over which the mob passed in their pursuit of him, being told he was gone forwards. I should scarce have ventured this narrative, had not all the circumstances been proved in a court of justice. Yet how many reflections must the whole story create in minds not conversant in a vast capital, free, ungoverned, unpoliced, and indifferent to everything but its pleasures and factions! Who will believe that such a scene of outrage could happen in the residence of Government? that the siege lasted nine hours, and that no guards were sent to the relief of the besieged till five in the morning? Who will believe that while such anarchy reigned at one end of the Metropolis, it made so little impression at the Court end that it was scarce mentioned? Though in London myself, all I heard was, that a man had been attacked in his house, and had killed three of the rioters. Nor were the circumstances attended to, till the trial of Green for murder, of which he was honourably acquitted, divulged his, his maid's, and the sailor's heroism. Yet did not the fury of the colliers cease, though seven of them were taken and executed. Green was forced to conceal himself from their rage; but his sister, giving a supper to her friends for joy of her brother's safety, her house was attacked by those assassins, their faces covered with black crape, who tore her into the street, and murdered her. Yet, perhaps, of all the circumstances of this tragedy, not one was so singular, from the display of so great a mind, as the indifference of the sailor, who never owned himself, never claimed honour or recompense for his generous gallantry. As brave as the Cocles of fabulous Rome, his virtue was satisfied with defending a man oppressed; and he knew not that an Alexander deserved less fame than he, who seemed not to think that he deserved any.

The Duke of Grafton

The Duke of Grafton being assured that the Duchess was with child, resolved to acquaint her that he knew, and was determined to prove it. This notification he pressed both Lord Hertford and Mr. Conway to carry to her; both declined an office so unworthy of a gentleman (for he had couched his letter in the harshest terms) and did not improve their favour with him by the refusal. He then pressed the task on his secretary Mr. Stonehewer, who being not less reluctant, the Duke said brutally with an oath, 'I did not propose it to you as a party of pleasure.' A footman was at last forced to be the messenger.

Lord Bute

On the 2nd of August, the Favourite Earl of Bute, whom foolish conduct, and the odium attending it, had thrown into a real, imaginary, or pretended ill state of health, set out for the waters of Barège. His mortifications were, in truth, sufficient to break a firmer spirit; nor had his fortune or wealth contributed but to his unhappiness, his domestic griefs being as poignant as his unpopularity. His eldest daughter, an amiable woman, was wedded to a capital brute, Sir James Lowther. His third daughter, whom the Northumberlands had obtained for their son, was discontent with her husband, and was confined by his family to the country under pretence of a gallant disposition, though the world suspected that the fall of her father had made the Duke and Duchess wish to get rid of the daughter. Lord Bute's second son, the heir of his mother's vast riches, had married ill, grew to hate his wife for having drawn him into marriage, and would not live with her, though his father forgave her, and solicited their reconciliation. It was perhaps not the least of the Earl's sorrows, that though, by the interest of the Princess, Lord Bute and his Cabal retained the chief power in the secret councils, the King was not sorry to be delivered from the thraldom in which the Earl had held him. At least, it was known that his Majesty dreaded of being suspected of retaining too great partiality to the Favourite, though he had resolution enough to avow or discountenance him entirely.

Archbishop Secker

On the 3rd [of August] died Secker, Archbishop of Canterbury, whose character I have given at large before. His early life had shown his versatility; his latter time, his ambition; but hypocrisy not being parts, he rose in the Church without ever making a figure in the State. Dr. Frederic Cornwallis, Bishop of Lichfield and Coventry, a prelate of inconsiderable talents, but a most amiable, gentle, and humane man, was preferred to the primacy by the Duke of Grafton, who had a friendship for the Bishop's nephew, Earl Cornwallis. Terrick of London, the most time-serving of the clergy, was sorely disappointed in missing the first mitre of England.

King Christian of Denmark

In the midst of these disorders arrived Christian VII King of Denmark, his Majesty's brother-in-law. This young prince had left his dominions some months before, intending to visit the chief nations of

Europe; and having great curiosity to see England, had proposed this visit. The English monarch, who had no taste for show or amusements, and who every day sunk more and more into privacy and lifeless solitude, had waived the offer on pretence of the national confusions: but Christian, who had both the obstinacy and caprices of youth and royalty, had persisted, and came. George, as childish and sullen as Christian was wrongheaded, seemed to make a point of affronting a Prince his equal, his brother, and first cousin. Not a single nobleman, not a single equipage was sent on the road to receive, escort, or convey the Danish King. He arrived at St. James's in a hired carriage. The only attention paid to him was, that an apartment was new furnished, gilt plate brought from the Tower, and an expensive table kept for him and his suite. Neither the King nor Queen were at St. James's to receive him; and the King even arrived there to his levee an hour later than usual. He then saw his Ministers, and the King of Denmark was at dinner before King George would admit Lord Hertford, his own Lord Chamberlain, who brought a message from the Dane, who had had the attention of ordering his own Lords to wait on the King at his levee. It is scarce to be credited that though Christian was in his palace, he neither went to him, nor received him there, but coldly sent him word he would see him at the Queen's palace at half an hour after five. When common decency was thus neglected, it is not wonderful that national interest was forgotten. Christian at that time was a pensioner of France, and it imported us to win him out of their hands. When he went afterwards to Paris, he found every mark of respect, every instance of magnificence and liberality that a great Court, attentive to its interest or glory, knew how to bestow.

This Danish King was in truth an insipid boy, and there appeared no cause for his expensive ramble, though to support it he had laid a tax on all his placemen and pensioners. He took notice of nothing, took pleasure in nothing, and hurried post through most parts of England without attention, dining and supping at seats on the road, without giving himself time enough to remark so much of their beauties as would flatter the great Lords who treated him. This indifference was excused in a whisper by Bernsdorffe his Prime Minister, who attributed it to his Majesty's extreme shortsight, which Bernsdorffe confessed was the great secret of the State. Yet the King's manner was very civil, and though his person was diminutive and delicate, he did not want graceful dignity. He had taken an early dislike to his Queen, and had disgraced his cousin the Prince of Hesse for espousing her interest. Himself was then influenced by the Russians, Bernsdorffe and the Russian Minister governing him entirely; the latter even with rudeness to the Queen. But the King had a Favourite, who had still more power over him, Baron Holke, a handsome young man, who attended him in his travels.

Princess Amalie, who felt the dishonourable treatment of her nephew, and who did not dislike to mark it to the public, made a ball and great entertainment for him at Gunnersbury. The King and the Princess Dowager then paid him the same civilities; but to show how much they disliked the precedent, left Princess Amalie out of their entertainments. In France, whither he went next, the litterati cried up this young Monarch as a pattern of a Patriot King; and it was probably from their praises he imbibed so much merit, that at his return to his kingdom he granted to his subjects free liberty of the Press—the idea was certainly not instilled into him here by the King or the Princess Dowager!

Madame du Barry

Old Marshal Richelieu, who had preserved none of his faculties but that last talent of a decayed Frenchman, a spirit of backstairs intrigue, had contrived to give to his master at near sixty, what at twenty the King would not take from his recommendation, a new mistress. On the death of Madame de Pompadour his Majesty had declared that he was grown too old to expect love to his person, and therefore would have no more a favourite sultana. But, as if men only declare they know what is sensible in order to mark their folly in stronger colours, he now ran headlong into an amour that every circumstance attending it stamped with ridicule. The nymph was past twenty-six, and her charms, which were not striking, had lost more than their bloom; and the life she had led made those slender remains dangerous. Nor had she ever risen to any distinction in her profession, but ranked with those wretched women who are the sport of the loosest debauchees, and the objects of the most casual amours. She had been entertained, not for his own pleasure, but to draw to his house young travelling Englishmen, by a Comte du Barry, who kept a gaming table, and who had exercised the same laudable industry in taverns here. Mademoiselle Lange was pitched upon by the Cabal of Choiseul's enemies as the instrument of their plot, and of his downfall. To dignify this Helen with a title, for du Barry was a man of quality, his brother was ordered to marry her, and the other, from having been a pimp to Richelieu, ascended to be his associate in politics. Belle, first *valet-de-chambre* to the King, and who exercised the same function for his master as du Barry for Richelieu, was prevailed on or bribed to present the new Countess to the Monarch, who having passed the season of sentiment, was charmed with an Abishag, whose birth demanded no degree of attention, and whose knowledge of her profession furnished her with a fund of those indelicate secrets that promote the pleasures of love in antiquated Davids. David's surgeon was alarmed at a connection that endangered the sacred health of his Sovereign and reprimanded Belle for his imprudence. The poor man was so terrified at what he had done that it struck him to the heart and carried him off. His Majesty's health escaped; but his glory, his peace, his Minister, and what remained of liberty in his kingdom, were the victims of this intrigue. I shall return to the subject, as I had opportunities of knowing it from the most indisputable authority.

The Duke of Newcastle

On the 17th of November died the Duke of Newcastle at the age of seventy five. He had had a stroke of palsy some months before; and then, and not till then, had totally abandoned politics. His life had been a proof that even in a free country great abilities are not necessary to govern it. Industry, perseverance, and intrigue gave him that duration of power which shining talents and the favour of the Crown could not secure to Lord Granville, nor the first rank in eloquence and the most brilliant services to Lord Chatham. Adventitious cunning repaired Newcastle's folly; rashness overset Lord Granville's parts; and presumptuous impracticability Lord Chatham.

James Townshend, Sawbridge and George Onslow

James Townshend and Sawbridge becoming considerable actors in the scenes that followed, it is necessary to give some brief account of them. The father of the former had been all his life a venal retainer of the Court. The son, inheriting an easy fortune from a relation, and being of a fiery constitution, and not void of parts, had entered into the politics and following of the Earl of Shelburne, and had a mind assorted to violent and determined counsels. Sawbridge was brother of the celebrated historian, Mrs. Macaulay. He had quitted the army on marrying a lady of large fortune. Independence and his sister's republicanism had thrown him into enthusiastic attachment to liberty. His soul was all integrity, and his private virtues all great and amiable. His capacity, though not deficient, was not bright, nor his eloquence adapted to popularity. Consequently he was more respected in his party than followed; his honesty restraining the dictates of his zeal, and his bigotry being founded in principle, not on doctrines and creeds.

A man differently constituted began now to distinguish himself on the other side. This was Colonel George Onslow, nephew of the late Speaker. He had been known as one of those burlesque orators who are favoured in all public assemblies, and to whom one or two happy sallies of impudence secure a constant attention, though their voice and manner are often their only patents, and who, by being laughed at for absurdity as frequently as for humour, obtain a licence for saying what they please. This man, who was short, round, quick, successful in jokes, and of a bold and resolute nature, had gone warmly into Opposition with Lord Rockingham and the old Whigs; but now with his cousin, the elder George Onslow, had enlisted under the Duke of Grafton, and followed the banners of the Court; incensed particularly at Wilkes for exposing the correspondence of his cousin, lately one of Wilkes's passionate admirers. The Colonel, seeing a man in the street pasting up a speech of Oliver Cromwell, ordering the people to pull the members out of the House, Onslow seized the fellow in spite of the mob, and complained of him to the House. This act was applauded, and the prisoner ordered to attend. He accused a milkman of having incited him, and the latter was committed to Newgate.

The Duke of Portland and Sir James Lowther

The other House had been engaged in hearing the contested election for Cumberland, which, under the names of the candidates comprehended the great rivalship between the Duke of Portland and Sir James Lowther. The Duke was a proud, though bashful, man, but of an unexceptionable character, which was illuminated by the hard measure he had so recently received from the Treasury, who had wrested an estate from him in favour of Sir James for the purposes of this very election. To the unpopularity of being son-in-law of the Favourite, Sir James united many odious arbitrary qualities, and was equally unamiable in public and private. The countenance of the Crown itself could not serve him against those prejudices. Even in *that* House of Commons he lost his cause by 247 to 95, the Scots, the Princess's Cabal, and a few more, alone supporting him. The Duke of Grafton, affecting candour to repair the injury he had done to the Duke of Portland, took no part till the two last days, and then, though acting zeal for Sir James, sending only the two Secretaries of the Treasury to his assistance. The Bedfords, resenting the disappointment of Lord Waldegrave by the promotion of the Duke of Beaufort, deserted Sir James Lowther, though professing to wish well to his cause, some of them staying away, others voting against him in compliment to Lord Weymouth, who had married the Duke of Portland's sister; and Lord George Sackville, who had hung so long on Lord Bute to no purpose, spoke strongly against Sir James, to show his discontent; on which Sir James said to him, 'My lord, you ought to have remembered that you have been on your trial too':—nor was Sir James satisfied with this rebuke, as will be seen hereafter.

John Wilkes

I have been as brief as possible on the several stages of Wilkes's history, detailed in so many publications; yet the subject must be tedious to future readers not interested in so ridiculous a war. Yet, were the steps omitted, who could conceive how the affairs of a great nation could stand still, while all the attention of the nation and of the public hung on such a motley character? He was dignified by the asperity of the Court; but not the vengeance of the Princess, the connivance, nay, and passion of the King, or the rancour of the Scotch, could raise his importance so high, as to excuse or palliate their employing their thoughts, time, and power to crush a personage that was fitter to be the Merry Andrew than the martyr of one of the most formidable Courts in Europe.

1769

The Douglas Case

About this time was heard decisively the great cause between the Houses of Douglas and Hamilton, by appeal to the Lords: a cause as singular and as ambiguous as perhaps ever came before a court of judicature. The last Duke of Douglas, a kind of lunatic, had at various periods made different wills; at first in favour of the Hamiltons, the nearest males of his race; but latterly he had substituted as his heir the son of his sister, who having offended him by marrying a poor, elderly gentleman, had retired to France, and there, though herself past fifty, had been, or pretended to have been, delivered of two boys, of whom one only survived. A cloud of circumstances concurred to make the Hamiltons suspect that both children were supposititious, and purchased of different peasants. The Duchess of Douglas, a woman of bold and masculine spirit, and herself a Douglas, who had artfully procured to get married to the Duke after the death of his sister, whom she had never seen, espoused the cause of Lady Jane's children, and prevailed on the Duke, in his last days, to restore the inheritance to his rejected nephew. The widow Duchess of Hamilton, one of the beautiful Gunnings, and of a spirit equally proud and pertinacious, though of the most delicate frame and form and outward softness, as obstinately defended the cause of her sons, particularly of the youngest, who had been named the former heir; and being incited by one Andrew Stuart, an artful and very able young man, and one of the trustees of her children, she, at immense expense to the Duke, her son, had pursued the disquisition into the births of Lady Jane's children; and by the books of the police at Paris, had, at the distance of near twenty years, and by the industry of Stuart, collected such a mass of circumstantial evidence, that it seemed to many men to prove that Lady Jane had never been with child, nor ever resided long enough in one place to give even an air of probability that she had lain in; to which should be added, that Lady Jane could never fix on any consistent account of the person in whose house, or of the house in which she had been delivered, and in which she allowed she had not stayed above three or four days. Much proof appeared of Lady Jane's art and hypocrisy: on the other side, little or none that she had acted like a mother, having neglected the younger child entirely for a year; and the survivor proving to have all probable appearance of a swarthy French peasant, and no ways resembling his pretended parents, who were fair and sandy, like most Scots. The Duke, Lady Jane's brother, had till near his death been persuaded of the imposture; and the cause coming before the Lords of Session in Scotland, had, after the fullest discussion, been determined in favour of the Hamiltons. Mankind grew wonderfully divided in their opinions, when the cause was now brought before the English Peers. Though the cheat, if one, had its foundation and almost its detection in France, the French inclined to the legitimacy of the children; so did the generality in Scotland: and, above all, the compassion excited in favour of infants avowed by both parents, though, in truth, very equivocally by Lady Jane on her death-bed, carried the current in favour of young Douglas. He was not less eagerly patronised by the Duke and Duchess of Queensberry: the Duke was his guardian; and the Duchess, no less celebrated formerly by Prior, Pope and Swift, than the Duchess of Hamilton in the times of which I write, was still more singular and persevering than the two other dames of the same rank,—circumstances that contributed powerfully to attract the attention of the public. Much perjury appeared on both sides, certain proof on neither; the want of which decided the suit at last in favour of the compassionate part of the question.

After a hearing of many and long days, with an attendance scarce ever known there on a cause, the House of Lords reversed the decree in favour of the Hamiltons, and restored the Douglas. The Lord Advocate Montgomery spoke for thirteen hours in three days, and with applause. Mr. Charles Yorke was the least admired. The Duchess Douglas thought she had retained him; but hearing he was gone over to the other side, sent for him, and questioned him home. He could not deny that he had engaged himself to the House of Hamilton—'Then, sir,' said she, 'in the next world whose will you be, for we have all had you?' Mr. Alexander Wedderburne (for the Hamiltons too), spoke with greater applause than was almost ever known. Dunning, on the same side, and Norton for the Douglas, made no great figure. The Duke of Bedford, Lord Sandwich, and Lord Gower, were the most zealous for the Hamiltons. Lord Mansfield, it had long been discovered, favoured the Douglas; but the Chancellor Camden, with dignity and decency, had concealed his opinion to the very day of the decision. The debate was opened by the Duke of Newcastle, and very poorly. He was answered by Lord Sandwich, who spoke for three hours with much humour, and scandalised the bishops, having, with his usual industry, studied even the midwifery of the case, which he retailed, with very little decency. The Chancellor then rose, and with becoming authority and infinite applause, told the Lords that he must now declare he thought the whole plea of the Hamiltonians a tissue of perjury, woven by Mr. Andrew Stuart; and that were he sitting as judge in any other court, he would order the jury to find for Mr. Douglas; and that what that jury ought to do on their oaths, their Lordships ought to do on their honours. He then went through the heads of the whole case, and without notes recapitulated even the dates of so involved a story; adding, that he was sorry to bear hard on Mr. Stuart, but justice obliged him. This speech, in which it was allowed he outshone Lord Mansfield, had the most decisive effect. The latter, with still more personal severity to Stuart, spoke till he fainted with the heat and fatigue; and, at ten at night, the decree was reversed without a division,—a sentence, I think, conformable to equity, as the child was owned by both parents, and the imposture not absolutely proved; yet, in my opinion, not awarded in favour of truth—a declaration I should not be so arrogant as to make, if many very able men were not as much persuaded as I am of the child being supposititious. Nor was the cause terminated at last without a duel between Andrew Stuart and Thurloe, who had poured out torrents of abuse on his antagonist in the course of the pleadings; but no mischief was done. This curious trial was set forth by each party in such ample volumes, that it is unnecessary to give a larger detail of it here; but a few concomitant and subsequent circumstances require a place.

The Duke of Bedford, the Earls of Sandwich, Bristol, and Dunmore, and Lord Milton protested against the decision in favour of Mr. Douglas, for that he was not proved to be the son of Lady Jane, and for that they thought it had been proved that he was not so. The next morning Mr. Andrew Stuart found on his table a bond for four hundred pounds a year for his life, a present from Mr. Johnston Pulteney, his friend, in consideration of the cruel treatment he had met with. When the news arrived at Edinburgh that the Douglas had carried his cause, the mob rose and almost killed the President of the Session who had been against him. They broke into Holyrood House, plundered the apartments of the Hamiltons, and made it dangerous for their friends to remain in the town. The sedition lasted two days, nor was put an end to but by the Guards. Mr. Andrew Stuart, some considerable time after, printed and gave away a tract on the case, and more particularly in his own defence against Lord Mansfield. It was a prodigy of abilities, reasoning and severity, yet observing a show of tenderness and decorum, that did not abate the edge of the satire. Some circumstances too, corroborating the question he supported, had abated since the trial; and at last the principal evidence for the Douglas was convicted of perjury in another cause in France. Lord Mansfield, agreeably to his cowardice and implacable character, answered the book only by preventing Stuart from being sent to India in a very lucrative employment.

Norton and Dundas

Amongst these notorious personages, notice must be taken of Sir Fletcher Norton. He had been purchased for this business (for even his attachment to Lord Mansfield and the Court were not sufficient to secure his zeal, though the cause was so bad) by the place of Chief Justice in Eyre and a pension of £3000 a year. It was stipulated that Norton should quit the Law, and be chief manager in the House of Commons; but no sooner was the bargain struck and the pension secured, than Norton, not caring to give up £7000 a year, which he got by his profession, pleaded that he could not *in honour* abandon his clients. His next *point of honour* was trying to prove by construction that Wilkes had been condemned of more than he had been condemned. Another acquisition to the Court was Sir Laurence Dundas, the rich commissary, a friend of Grenville, and now seduced from him by Rigby, another late friend of Grenville. Dundas commanded the votes of nine members. He demanded a peerage for himself, having acquired above eight hundred thousand pounds in less than four years of the late war— so far fairly that he had executed the commission on cheaper terms than anyone else had offered. He was, besides, nobly generous; yet it would have been gross indeed to have raised such an upstart to the peerage on no other foundation than the money he had gained from the public. It was known too, that Prince Ferdinand had been on the point of hanging him on part of his contract not being furnished so soon as he had engaged it should be.

Some Republicans

Wilkes was no sooner expelled, than he again presented himself as candidate for the county of Middlesex, and in the *North Briton* published a very bold address to the freeholders, in which, under the title of *The Administration*, he severely lashed the House of Commons. There was at this time an avowed though very small Republican party, the chiefs of which were Mrs. Macaulay, the historian, her brother Sawbridge, his brother-in-law Stephenson, a rich merchant, and Thomas Hollis, a gentleman of strict honour and good fortune, a virtuoso, and so bigotted to his principles, that, though a humane and good man, he would scarce converse with any man who did not entirely agree with his opinions. He had no parts, but spent large sums on publishing prints and editions of all the heroes and works on his own side of the question; but he was formed to adorn a pure republic, not to shine in a depraved monarchy.

Edmund Burke

Mr. Grenville, though dipped with them in Opposition, had never forgiven Lord Rockingham and his friends for succeeding him in power, and for repealing the Stamp Act, nor had ceased pelting them in pamphlets. Just before the Parliament met, he had written, or assisted in writing, a tract called *The State of the Nation*, in which they had been bitterly treated. Hoping union with him, at least willing to act with him in Opposition, they had borne all former provocations. They now at last replied in a large quarto called *Observations on the State of the Nation.* It was drawn up by Edmund Burke, and did more honour to his talents as a writer than as a politician. The book solidly confuted Grenville, exposed him, and exploded his pretensions to skill in finance; but then it made all approach to him impossible, notwithstanding Lord Temple's endeavours to unite them. It almost as explicitly abjured Lord Bute; a step the party two years after tried as injudiciously to recover, when it was too late. If the work did honour to the author and to his party's principles, yet it showed that that party was composed of impracticable men; and what was worse for their cause, it declared inviolable attachment to the Marquis of Rockingham, a weak, childish, and ignorant man, by no means fit for the head of Administration. Burke had far more shining abilities than solid conduct, and, being dazzled by his own wit and eloquence, expected that those talents would have the same effect on others. His ambition built airy castles, and would not attend to those parts of policy that make no immediate show. One quotation in his book was singularly happy, and in one line drew the portrait of Grenville,—

Vixque tenet lachrymas quia nil lachrymabile cernit. It was in truth Grenville's character to weep over woes that he wished to exterminate by rigour.

Colonel Luttrell

It required a man of the firmest virtue, or a ruffian of dauntless prostitution, to undertake the office of opposing Wilkes in the decisive contest for the county of Middlesex. There was a young officer, called Colonel Luttrell, whose father, Lord Irnham, was devoted to Lord Bute. They were descended of a good Irish family, who had been attached to and had betrayed King James the Second; and the morals and characters of both father and son, especially of the former, were in no good estimation. The father had parts, wit, and boldness: the son affected to be a bravo, too, but supported it ill. The son was pitched upon by the Junto for candidate for Middlesex; and Lord Holland and his sons openly espoused him. This last circumstance, and the zeal of the Scots, crowned his unpopularity; and lest it should not, Wilkes gave out that Luttrell was to be rewarded with a daughter of Lord Bute. One of the race, not long after, attained a far more elevated match![1]

So desperate did Luttrell's cause appear, that great bets were made on his life; and at Loyd's coffee-house, it was insured for a month. A third candidate soon appeared, one Captain Roache, another duelling Irishman, supposed to be selected by Wilkes, as a proper antagonist to Luttrell.

The Duke of Grafton

It is now time to cast an eye on the conduct of the Prime Minister, the Duke of Grafton. Though in the plenitude of power he had rather acquiesced in the measures of the Cabinet than directed them, and in the heat of Luttrell's affair, had gone to amuse himself at Newmarket. While his divorce was in agitation, he had proposed to his brother Colonel Fitzroy to change his security of a large annuity on the estate at Euston for one on the estate in Northamptonshire. This was construed into an intention of furnishing a jointure for his mistress, whom it was now universally supposed he would marry. His flatterers already treated her as Duchess of Grafton, and indeed the Duke himself to one of them

[1] See p. 243, Duke of Cumberland and Mrs. Horton.

declared he *could* marry no other woman while Mrs. Haughton (or Nancy Parsons) was alive. Fitzroy thought the offered exchange dangerous and refused it. The brothers grew warm, and the Duke with his usual insolence threatened that he would have an Act of Parliament to force his brother's acquiescence. This passed in the public rooms at St. James's; Lord Hertford and Mr. Conway interposed, and showed the Duke the impossibility of carrying so violent a measure. Fitzroy complained to the King, and the matter was hushed up. The divorce being now terminated, the Session was no sooner at an end than the Duke astonished mankind by a step more unforeseen than any of his foregoing precipitancies, but equally flowing from his sullen and revengeful passions. He suddenly declared his intention of marrying Miss Elizabeth Wrottesley, one of the Duchess of Bedford's nieces, and brought up by her. The cloud of reasons that spoke against the match, while no ostensible one could possibly be alleged in favour of it, marked it out as counselled solely by his own unforgiving temper. The young lady was uncommonly void of beauty, grace, or insinuation. She had no fortune; her father Sir Richard Wrottesley, who had turned parson from a mad fondness for preaching, was to the last degree debauched and disreputable, and treated his wife inhumanly. The Duke of Grafton had declaimed against the arts and morals of the Duchess of Bedford and Lord Gower, the young lady's nearest relations; and what crowned all objections, she herself was first cousin of Lord Ossory, who the day after the divorce had married the repudiated Duchess—but this, which seemed the greatest impediment, was the real motive of Grafton's choice[1]: he knew the Duchess of Bedford enough to be sure that the hopes of governing the First Minister through his new wife would effectually prevent her from countenancing his late wife; and he judged so well, that having made a visit to the new Lady Ossory, now her niece, the Duchess of Bedford had the meanness to excuse that visit to the Queen, pleading her affection to her nephew Lord Ossory.

But not only private reasons might have combatted this match; it was equally repugnant to his political interests. The King had adopted him as a man totally unconnected, and detached from all factions, the

[1] He carried his revenge so far and so meanly, that after Lord Ossory had married his repudiated wife, he was the cause that Lord Ossory could not obtain the Embassy to Spain, which he ambitioned, and which Lady Ossory wished from unwillingness to appear any more in public in England, in which she persisted living retired in the country, and when it was remonstrated to her that so recluse a life was a prejudice to Lord Ossory, she consented to come to town in winter, but would not go to public places. [H.W.]

favourite qualification in the present reign! On that foot unlimited
power was thrown into his hands; what would be the consequence of
his new alliance? It was not only casting himself on the most unpopular
set of men in England, and who he knew had betrayed him, but it was
planting them in the Court, and determining to rule by that faction
alone, more obnoxious if possible to the King, the Princess, and Lord
Bute, than they were to the nation. Instead of governing by his absolute
dependence on the King, he seemed to be strengthening himself in a
manner that might enable him to dictate; and by increasing his importance he was sure of losing his only tenure of favour. His own family
foresaw a new source of division, and his creatures shuddered at seeing
him throw himself into more artful hands. Some of them, who had paid
the most servile court to his late favourite Sultana beheld with horror
the success of a plot they had assisted in against her. She had gone to
France under pretence of ill health; and this artifice, which she had
practised before with advantage, was believed to be a playful method of
increasing his passion. It appeared that this last journey had other views,
not commonly found in dames of her experience. The glare of a Ducal
Coronet, at last within her reach, and the rank of wife to the First
Minister had not been able to surmount her dislike of his person; and
the charms of the young Duke of Dorset had made impressions that
seldom disturb the reason of professed courtezans. He was unusually
handsome, was well made, and had an air of sentimental melancholy,
which more than atoned with women for his want of sense. His silence
had the air of amorous absence, and he looked so ready to sigh that it
served him instead of sighing; it seeming charity to afford him that pity
which he was formed to repay so delightfully. Mrs. Haughton probably
made only the substantial part of these reflections; yet she sacrificed more
to him than many women would have done, who with as little virtue
perhaps in their hearts, would have preferred the power of the one Duke
to the possession of the other's person. The fact is, Grafton's spies
intercepted Mrs. Haughton's letters to Dorset[1] and discovered them to
their patron, and though she returned as soon as his new match was
avowed, he refused to see her, insisted on her restoring his letters and
obtained them and totally dismissed her with a precarious pension of
£400 a year. To her when he notified his intended marriage to his aunt

[1] She lived with the Duke of Dorset to the summer of 1776, and was thought to
be married to him; but the Duke then engaging in new amours, she left him for
the young Lord Maynard whom she still had charms or art enough to captivate, and
had hopes of marrying and actually did marry before the end of the year. [H.W.]

Lady Hertford, he imputed his quarrels with his family: but his past and subsequent variations were the sallies of a temper in which gloomy obstinacy, and vindictive inconstancy predominated by turns.

If the Duchess of Bedford, who now looked on herself as a kind of Queen Mother, was transported with the match, it was by no means equally grateful to the rest of her family. Lord Gower hungered and thirsted after power and favour. He had meditated giving his own eldest daughter for a wife to the Duke of Grafton, and was by no means contented with the succedaneum of his niece, and the influence of his sister over her. Neither ensured his credit with the Duke, and yet should the Duke fall, Lord Gower knew that he might now be involved in the same ruin. To avoid that catastrophe he thought supplanting the Duke would be the safest as well as pleasantest precaution. Their sister Lady Waldegrave, not less jealous of the Duchess of Bedford, was ready to join in the plot, and their ally Lord Weymouth had too much unprincipled indolence to refuse his assistance to a league which required no more fatigue than assent to treachery

General Paoli

The first advantages gained there [Corsica] by the French had been solemnized in a ridiculous manner by ostentatious inscriptions, that were soon followed by defeats; but hosts continually poured in on the abandoned islanders; and the deficience in military skill in Pascal Paoli, the Dictator of the aspiring Republic, and even his want of valour, as the French themselves asserted, reduced Corsica beneath their yoke. Paoli, who aspired to power, not to the fame of virtue, distinguished between his country and his hopes, and not having fallen like Leonidas, did not despair like Cato. He made his escape and arrived in England, where his character had been so advantageously exaggerated by Mr. Boswell's enthusiastic and entertaining account of him, that the Opposition were ready to receive and incorporate him in the list of popular tribunes. The Court artfully intercepted the project; and deeming patriots of all nations equally corruptible, bestowed a pension of £1000 a year on the unheroic fugitive. Themistocles accepted the gold of Xerxes, and excused himself from receiving a visit from Mrs. Macaulay, who had given him printed advice for settling a republic. I saw him soon after his arrival, dangling at Court. He was a man of decent deportment, vacant of all melancholy reflection, with as much ease as suited prudence, that seemed the utmost effort of a wary understanding, and so void of anything remarkable in his aspect, that being asked if I knew who it was, I judged him a Scottish officer (for he was sandy-complexioned and in regimentals) who was cautiously awaiting the moment of promotion. All his heroism consisted in bearing with composure the accounts of his friends being tortured and butchered, while he was sunk into a pensioner of that very Court that had proclaimed his valiant countrymen and associates rebels!

The Duke of Grafton

The Duke of Grafton, who had been honoured with the Garter, and elected Chancellor of the University of Cambridge, could not bear the thoughts of business. He diverted himself in the country, coming to town but once a week or once a fortnight to sign papers at the Treasury; and as seldom to the King. I could but reflect how different had been the application of Sir Robert Walpole, my father, who, with relaxation but for two fortnights in the year, found it difficult enough to govern the kingdom and keep Opposition at bay, though secure of the King, secure of peace with France by meeting as pacific dispositions in Cardinal Fleury, void of alarms from Ireland and America, that were as quiet as his own county of Norfolk, and called on for no attention to a new empire that had now accrued to us at the eastern boundary of the world. The consequences were such as might be expected. Walpole maintained the equilibrium; under Grafton everything fell into confusion. Were any representations made to him, he threatened to resign, affirming that he only retained his power, because his quitting at that crisis would produce a dissolution of Parliament, from which he foresaw the worst consequences. The only step he took was to advise with the Chancellor, who told him surlily, that his Grace had consulted him but twice last session, and then had acted directly contrary to his advice.

Lord Chatham

As the Session approached, Lord Chatham engaged with new warmth in promoting petitions. He asked Mr. Cholmondeley, Member for Cheshire, why his county had not petitioned? and told him he himself would move for dissolution of the Parliament; and if not able to stand on his legs, 'I will speak,' said he, as he lay on his couch, 'in this horizontal posture.'[1]

Junius

These many essays towards an insurrection were crowned by the unparalleled remonstrance of Junius to the King, the most daring insult ever offered to a Prince but in times of open rebellion; and aggravated by the many truths it contained. Nothing could exceed the singularity of this satire, but the impossibility of discovering the author. Three men were especially suspected, Wilkes, Edmund Burke, and William Gerard Hamilton.[2]

The desperate hardiness of the author in attacking men so great, so powerful, and some so brave, was reconcileable only to the situation of Wilkes; but the masterly talents that appeared in those writings were deemed superior to his abilities. Yet in many of Junius's letters an inequality was observed; and even in this remonstrance different hands seemed to have been employed. The laborious flow of style, and fertility of matter, made Burke believed the real Junius: yet he had not only constantly and solemnly denied any hand in those performances, but was not a man addicted to bitterness; nor could any one account for such indiscriminate attacks on men of such various descriptions and professions. Hamilton was most generally suspected. He, too, denied it— but his truth was not renowned. The quick intelligence of facts, and the researches into the arcana of every office, were far more uncommon than the invectives; and men wondered how any one possessed of such talents, could have the forbearance to write in a manner so desperate as to prevent his ever receiving personal applause for his writings: the venom was too black not to disgrace even his ashes.

[1] Mrs. Anne Pitt asking Lord Chesterfield if he would not go and hear her brother speak *in his horizontal posture*, he replied, he would, if he were not deaf, for the most agreeable things he had ever heard had been from persons in a horizontal posture. He was then seventy-four. [H.W.]

[2] Mr. Hamilton having on his first appearance in Parliament, and of a family little known, made a very fine speech, and never but one more in the English Parliament, though he afterwards made a figure, when Secretary to the Lord Lieutenant of Ireland, in that House of Commons, was generally distinguished from all the other Hamiltons by the name of *Singlespeech*, on which George Selwyn applied to him the old riddle on a fart,

> Fatherless and motherless, and born without a skin,
> Speaks when it comes in the world, and never speaks again. [H.W.]

The Duke of Gloucester and Lady Waldegrave

A *North Briton*, of very inferior or no merit, followed this remonstrance, and spared the two royal brothers no more than Junius had
palliated the errors of the King. The Duke of Cumberland, a weak and
debauched boy, was censured for an intrigue with Lady Grosvenor,
which became of public notoriety, and will be mentioned hereafter. The
Duke of Gloucester, a virtuous, discreet, and unexceptionable Prince, had
involved himself in a more serious affair; of which, as I can, I must give
a more particular account than was known to others.

Maria Walpole, second natural daughter of my brother Sir Edward,
and one of the most beautiful of women, had been married, solely by
my means, to James, late Earl of Waldegrave, Governor to the King and
Duke of York, an excellent man, but as old again as she was, and of no
agreeable figure. Her passions were ambition and expense: she accepted
his hand with pleasure, and by an effort less common, proved a meritorious wife. When after her year of widowhood she appeared again in
the full lustre of her beauty, she was courted by the Duke of Portland;
but the young Duke of Gloucester, who had gazed on her with desire
during her husband's life, now openly showing himself her admirer, she
slighted the subject, and aspired to the brother of the Crown. Her
obligations to me, and my fondness for her, authorized me to interpose
my advice, which was kindly but unwillingly received. I did not desist;
but pointing out the improbabilities of marriage on one side, on the
other the distemper in the royal blood so apparent in the Prince, the
little likelihood of the King's consent, and the chance of being sent to
Hanover separated from her children, on whom she doated, the last
reason alone prevailed on the fond mother, and she yielded to copy a
letter I wrote for her to the Duke of Gloucester, in which she renounced
his acquaintance in the no new terms of not being of rank to be his wife,
and too considerable to be his mistress. A short fortnight baffled all my
prudence. The Prince renewed his visits with more assiduity after that
little interval, and Lady Waldegrave received them without disguise.
My part was soon taken. I had done my duty—a second attempt had
been hopeless folly. Though often pressed to sup with her, when I knew
the Duke was to be there, I steadily refused, and never once mentioned
his name to her afterwards, though as their union grew more serious,
she affectedly named him to me, called him *the Duke*, and related to

me private anecdotes of the Royal Family, which she could have received but from him. It was in vain; I studiously avoided him. She brought him to see my house, but I happened not to be at home; he came again, alone: I left the house. He then desisted, for I never stayed for his court, which followed the Princess Dowager's, but retired as soon as she had spoken to me. This, as may be supposed, cooled my niece's affection for me; but being determined not to have the air of being convenient to her from flattery, if she was not married, and having no authority to ask her the question on which she had refused to satisfy her father, I preferred my honour to her favour, and left her to her own conduct. Indeed my own father's obligations to the Royal Family forbade me to endeavour to place a natural daughter of our house so near the Throne. To my brother the Duke was profuse of civilities, which I pressed him to decline; and even advised him not to see his daughter, unless she would own her marriage, which might oblige the Duke, in vindication of her character, to avow her for his wife. Married, I had no doubt they were. Both the Duke and she were remarkably religious; and neither of them dissolute enough to live, as they did at last, with all the liberties of marriage. The King and Queen denied their legal union, yet the respect with which they treated her spoke the contrary; and the homage which all men and all women paid her by a fortune singular to her, assured the opinion of her virtue, and made it believed that the King, privy to their secret, had exacted a promise of their not divulging it. By degrees her situation became still less problematic; and both the Duke and she affectedly took all occasions of intimating it but by a formal declaration. At first she had houses, or lodgings, in the palaces nearest to his residence; and the latter were furnished from the royal wardrobe without limitation. She changed her liveries to a compound of the royal, was covered with jewels, the Duke's gentlemen and equerries handed her to her chair in public, his equipages were despatched for her, his sister, the Queen of Denmark, sent her presents by him, and she quitted all assemblies at nine at night, saying, 'You know I must go.' At St. Leonard's Hill, in Windsor Forest, near his own lodge at Cranbourn, he built her a palace, and lay there every night: his picture and Lord Waldegrave's she showed in her bedchamber. These were not the symptoms of a dissoluble connection!

The French Court

As the interior of the Court of France is scarce known in this country, a short account of the intrigues at the time I am describing, may be at present not unacceptable to posterity. I passed many months at Paris in four different years, had very intimate connections there with persons of the first rank, and of various factions; and I spent five evenings in a week with the Duchesse de Choiseul and her select friends in the summer of 1769. The Duke was often of the party; and his levity and her anxiety on his account let me into many secrets, and explained enough of the rest to make me sufficiently master of the critical situation of the Minister at that time. I must take up his story a little further back to make it perfectly intelligible.

Madame de Pompadour, who to the end of her life governed Louis XV by habit, by which he was always governed, had established the Duc de Choiseul in the Ministry, and left him in possession of the chief share of power. Cardinal de Fleury and she had been successively absolute: but the King had never resigned himself entirely to anybody else. The Duc de Choiseul had quick parts, and despatched business with the same rapidity that he conceived it. His ambition was boundless, his insolence ungoverned, his discretion unrestrained, his love of pleasure and dissipation predominant even over his ambition. He was both an open enemy and a generous one, and had more joy in attacking his foes than in punishing them. Whether from gaiety or presumption, he never was dismayed. His vanity made him always depend on the success of his plans; and his spirits made him soon forget the miscarriage of them. He had no idea of national or domestic economy, which, being a quality of prudence and providence, could not enter into so audacious a mind. He would project and determine the ruin of a country, but could not meditate a little mischief, or a narrow benefit. In private his sallies and good humour were pleasing, and would have been more pleasing if his manner had not been overbearing and self-sufficient. The latter created him enemies; the former, friends. Among the first were the Maréchal de Richelieu and the Duc D'Aiguillon. To the impertinence of a fashionable old beau, Richelieu added all the intrigues and treacheries of a Court, having tried every method but merit to raise himself to the first post. At past seventy he still flattered himself with the vision of pleasing women and governing the King, because the King at near sixty had not done being pleased with women. The Duc D'Aiguillon was universally abhorred. His abominable tyranny and villainy in his government of Bretagne had made him dreaded; and his ambition being much superior to his abilities, he had betrayed the badness of his heart before he had reached the object to which he aspired. The Duc de Choiseul despised Richelieu, and had kept down D'Aiguillon. They were connected before; their resentments and views united them more intimately, but it was the contemptible one that shook their antagonist's power.[1]

At first a sort of mystery was observed. But the fair one gained ground rapidly, and Solomon soon began to chant the perfections of his beloved. The Court was shocked to hear to what an idol of clay they were to address their homage. They were accustomed to bow down before a mistress—but took it into their heads that the disgrace consisted in her being a common girl of the town. The King's daughters, who had borne the ascendant of Madame de Pompadour in their mother's life, grew outrageous, though she was dead, at the new favourite for being of the lowest class of her profession; and instead of regarding this amour as only ridiculous, treated it with a serious air of disobedience, that would have offended any man but so indulgent and weak a father, or a very wise one. The poor King blushed, and by turns hesitated and exalted his mistress. In private the scene was childish; his aged Majesty and his indelicate concubine romped, pelted each other with sugar-plums, and were much oftener silly than amorous. The Faction did not sleep: the next point was that Madame du Barry should be presented publicly. The King promised: her clothes and liveries were made.

Instead of attempting to remove or buy the new mistress, the Duc de Choiseul's conduct was as imprudent and rash as the King's was pitiful. He spoke of Madame du Barry publicly, without decency or management; which being quickly carried to her, and she complaining of it, he said at his own table, before a large company:—'Madame du Barry est très mal informée; on ne parle pas de catins chez moi.' The King's irresolution and the Minister's insolence suspended the abjection of the courtiers. Even the men avoided the mistress; and when the King proposed to carry any of them to her, they excused themselves, slipped away, or were silent. Had they never been mean, such conduct had been noble.

[1] H.W. here repeats his account of Mme du Barry; see above, p. 201–2.

In this suspense, inquiry was made for some lady of great rank to present the new Countess. Not one could be found that would stoop to that office. Marshal Richelieu was forced to fetch an obscure lady from Bordeaux. The presentation, however, was delayed. Madame, the eldest of the King's daughters, took to her bed, and protested she would not receive the mistress. This stopped it for some time. The Duc de la Vauguion, Governor of the Dauphin, a great bigot and partisan of the Jesuits, went to Madame, and advised her to be civil to the Countess. She asked him if he came by the King's orders? He said, no, but as a well-wisher to her Royal Highness. She bade him instantly quit the room; and the hypocrite reaped nothing but the shame of having prostituted himself to so scandalous an office for the good of the Church— the zealot party hoping everything from the rising Cabal—and, in fact, as despotism soon took such strides under the new influence, enthusiasm had reason to flatter itself with a restoration, too, under a doating Prince, a common strumpet, and old debauchee, and a pimp-sharper, aided by such adjuncts as the Head of the Law and D'Aiguillon, who breathed the very spirit of the Inquisition. This Junto soon called a female saint to their counsels, the Carmelite Louisa, the King's youngest daughter; and the poor Monarch divided his leisure between Capreae and Mount Carmel.

In the meantime the Duc de Choiseul went so far as to talk of resigning, if the presentation took place. Arrogant as he was, this bravery was not solely of his own growth, but inspired by the women of his connection. Of all human kind, there were not two beings so insolent as his own sister, the Duchess of Grammont, and her friend, the Princess of Beauvau. These amazons took it into their heads to brave the King and his mistress; and, though the creatures of favour, were so transported by this imaginary heroism, that they urged the Duke to resign in defiance. This impertinence in Madame de Grammont was absurd beyond measure. Subsisting but by her brother's power, abhorred for her haughtiness, suspected of many gallantries, and notorious for one that ought to have been the most secret, her intrigue with her brother, what could she expect from his fall, but universal neglect? The Princess, no Penelope, was hurried on by equal impetuosity, and by rancour, to another person, whom I shall mention presently: yet, divested of their passions, both these viragos had uncommonly good understandings. There was a third person, who it was more surprising took the same line, though regulated by the same decency that governed all her actions. This was the Duchess of Choiseul, a woman in whom industrious malice could not find an imperfection, unless that charming one of *studying* to be a complete character. She was too virtuous to fear reproach or contagion from civilities to the mistress, and should have left it to the Duchess and Princess to be disdainful prudes. Yet in a quiet style she was not less earnest than they in soliciting her husband not to bend to the ignominy of the hour. The King, who, by a singular situation, opened all letters, having the chief postmaster his own creature and not the Minister's, read the Duchess's importunities with her husband; and as he had expected more duty from her, resented her behaviour more than that of the two other dames.

After an anxious suspense of three months, and when the public began to think the presentation warded off, it suddenly took place. The King returning from hunting, found (no doubt by concert) Marshal Richelieu, who was in waiting in the outward room with a letter in his hand. The King asked what it was? 'Sire,' said the Duke, 'it is from Madame du Barry, who desires the honour of being presented to your Majesty.' 'With all my heart,' replied the King; 'she may come tomorrow, if she pleases.' This was said aloud. The Duc de Choiseul and Versailles learnt the news at the same moment. Next day all Paris was there to see the ceremony.

1770

Charles Yorke

The wanton insolence of the Court on the first day's victory was well nigh costing them a total defeat. They had dismissed the Chancellor without being provided with a successor. Mr Conway acquainted me in the greatest secrecy that the Duke of Grafton, dismayed at Yorke's refusal of the Great Seal, would give up the Administration. Not a lawyer could be found able enough—or if able, bold enough—or if bold, decent enough—to fill the employment. Norton had all the requisites of knowledge and capacity, but wanted even the semblance of integrity, though for that reason was probably the secret wish of the Court. He was enraged at the preference given to Yorke; yet nobody dared to propose him, even when Yorke had refused. Sir Eardley Wilmot had character and abilities, but wanted health. The Attorney-General, De Grey, wanted health and weight, and yet asked too extravagant terms. Dunning, the Solicitor-General, had taken the same part as his friends Lord Camden and Lord Shelburne. Hussey, so far from being inclined to accept the office, determined to resign with his old friend Lord Camden, though earnest against the dissolution of the Parliament. Of Lord Mansfield, there could be no question; when the post was dangerous, his cowardice was too well known to give hopes he could be pressed to defend it. In this exigence, Grafton's courage was not more conspicuous. His first thought, without consulting the King's inclination, was to offer the Administration to Lord Chatham or Lord Rockingham; but inclining to the latter. He had desired Mr. Conway to come to him in the evening and meet Lord Gower, Lord Weymouth and Lord North in the most private manner for consultation. Conway went away in haste to Court, promising to return and dine with me, that he might consider what advice he would give to the Duke at night; but what was my astonishment when in two hours Mr. Onslow came and told me that Mr. Yorke had accepted the Seals! He had been with the King overnight (without the knowledge of the Duke of Grafton) and had again declined; but being pressed to reconsider, and returning in the morning, the King had so overwhelmed him with flatteries, entreaties, prayers, and at last with commands and threats, of never giving him the post if not accepted now, that the poor man sunk under the importunity, though he had given a solemn promise to his brother, Lord Hardwicke, and Lord Rockingham, that he would not yield. He betrayed, however, none of the rapaciousness of the times, nor exacted but one condition, the grant of which fixed his irresolution. The Chancellor must of necessity be a Peer, or cannot sit in the House of Lords. The Coronet was announced to Yorke; but he slighted it as of no consequence to his eldest son, who would probably succeed his uncle Lord Hardwicke, the latter having been long married and having only two daughters. But Mr Yorke himself had a second wife, a very beautiful woman, and by her had another son. She, it is supposed, urged him to accept the Chancery, as the King offered or consented that the new peerage should descend to her son and not to the eldest—the rest of his story was indeed melancholy, and his fate so rapid as to intercept the completion of his elevation.

He kissed the King's hand on the Thursday; and from Court drove to his brother, Lord Hardwicke's—the precise steps of the tragedy have never been ascertained. Lord Rockingham was with the Earl. By some it was affirmed, that both the Marquis and the Earl received the unhappy renegade with bitter reproaches. Others, whom I rather believe, maintained that the Marquis left the house directly; and that Lord Hardwicke refused to hear his brother's excuses, and retiring from the

222

room, shut himself into another chamber, obdurately denying Mr. Yorke an audience. At night it was whispered that the agitation of his mind, working on a most sanguine habit of body, inflamed of late by excessive indulgence both in meats and wine, had occasioned the bursting of a blood-vessel; and the attendance of surgeons was accounted for, by the necessity of bleeding him four times on Friday. Certain it is that he expired on the Saturday between four and six in the evening. His servants in the first confusion had dropped too much to leave it in the family's power to stifle the truth: and though they endeavoured to colour over the catastrophe by declaring the accident natural, the want of evidence and of the testimony of surgeons to colour the tale given out, and which they never took any public method of authenticating, convinced everybody that he had fallen by his own hand—whether on his sword, or by a razor, was uncertain.

Yorke's speeches in Parliament had for some time, though not so soon as they ought, fallen into total disesteem. At the Bar, his practice had declined from a habit of gluttony and intemperance, as I have mentioned. Yet, as a lawyer, his opinion had been in so high repute, that he was reported to have received an hundred thousand guineas in fees. In truth, his chief practice had flourished while his father was not only Lord Chancellor, but a very powerful Minister. Yorke's parts were by no means shining. His manner was precise and yet diffuse, and his matter more sententious than instructive. His conduct was timid, irresolute, often influenced by his profession, oftener by his interest. He sacrificed his character to his ambition of the Great Seal, and his life to his repentance of having attained it.

The Duke of Grafton

Such was the conclusion of the Duke of Grafton's Administration, which had lasted two years, and when he was but thirty-four years of age. His fall was universally ascribed to his pusillanimity; but whether betrayed by his fears or his friends, he had certainly been the chief author of his own disgrace. His haughtiness, indolence, reserve, and improvidence, had conjured up the storm; but his obstinacy and fickleness always relaying each other, and always *mal à propos*, were the radical causes of all the numerous absurdities that discoloured his conduct and exposed him to deserved reproaches; nor had he a depth of understanding to counterbalance the defects of his temper. The power of the Crown and the weakness of the Opposition, would have maintained him in his post, though he was unfit for it, as immediately appeared by the Court's recovering its ascendant the moment the Duke retired; for though Lord North had far better parts, yet his indolence proved as great as Grafton's; but having as much good humour as the Duke wanted, it was plain that the Parliament were willing to be slaves, provided they could be treated with decency. Grafton had quitted the King's service, when Prince, disgusted with Lord Bute: had been captivated by Lord Chatham, yet came into place without him; then quitted for him Lord Rockingham and the Whigs. He then declared against a place of business; then gave himself up to Lord Chatham, and was made his first Lord of the Treasury; grew as violently partial to Mr. Conway, yet was with difficulty persuaded to stay in place even with him—then would act with nobody but him: as abruptly and lightly consented to let him retire to make way for the Bedfords; and after a life of early decorum, dipped with every indecency into the most public and abject attachment to a common courtezan; gave himself up to Lord Bute's influence; rushed into an alliance with the Bedfords whom he hated, against his interest; and at last permitted them to betray him, not without suspecting, but without resenting it.

The detail of his conduct was as weak and preposterous as the great lines of it. His intrusion of Luttrell, his neglecting to call the Parliament before the petitions spread, his wasting his time at Euston and Newmarket though the tempest raged, his disgusting the Chancellor, and when he had disgusted him, not turning him out before the Parliament met, but leaving him to avail himself of the merit of martyrdom by being turned out for his speech and vote; and then turning him out when it was both too late and too soon, because no successor had been prepared in time; these wild and inconsistent steps plunged him into difficulties which yet he might have surmounted, if his inconstancy had been art, his rashness courage, or his obstinacy firmness.

He was the fourth Prime Minister in seven years who fell by his own fault. Lord Bute was seized with a panic and ran away from his own victory. Grenville was undone by his insolence, by joining in the insult on the Princess, and by his persecution of Lord Bute and Mackenzie. Lord Rockingham's incapacity overturned him; and now the Duke of Grafton, by a complication of passions and defect of system, destroyed a power that it had depended on himself to make as permanent as he could desire.

Lord North

Frederic, Lord North, eldest son of the Earl of Guildford, was now in the thirty-eighth year of his age. Nothing could be more coarse or clumsy or ungracious than his outside. Two large prominent eyes that rolled about to no purpose (for he was utterly short-sighted), a wide mouth, thick lips and inflated visage, gave him the air of a blind trumpeter. A deep untuneable voice, which, instead of modulating, he enforced with unnecessary pomp, a total neglect of his person, and ignorance of every civil attention, disgusted all who judge by appearance, or withhold their approbation till it is courted. But within that rude casket were enclosed many useful talents. He had much wit, good-humour, strong natural sense, assurance and promptness, both of conception and elocution. His ambition had seemed to aspire to the height, yet he was not very ambitious. He was thought interested, yet was not avaricious. What he did, he did without a mask, and was not delicate in choosing his means. He had lent himself readily to all the violences of Mr. Grenville against Wilkes, had seized the moment of advancement by accepting the post of Chancellor of the Exchequer (after a very short opposition) when the Court wanted a person to oppose to the same Mr. Grenville; and with equal alacrity had served under the Duke of Grafton. When the first post became vacant by the Duke's strange retreat, no man so ready to place himself in the gap as Lord North. It was in true worth his ambition, though he should rule but a day, to attain the rank of Prime Minister. He had knowledge, and though fond of his amusement, seemed to have all necessary activity till he reached the summit. Yet that industry ceased when it became most requisite. He had neither system, nor principles nor shame; sought neither the favour of the Crown or of the people, but enjoyed the good luck of fortune with a gluttonous Epicurism that was equally careless of glory and disgrace. His indolence prevented his forming any plan. His indifference made him leap from one extreme to another; and his insensibility to reproach reconciled him to any contradiction. He proved as indolent as the Duke of Grafton, but his temper being as good as the Duke's was bad, he was less hurt at capital disgraces than the Duke had been at trifling difficulties. Lord North's conduct in the American war displayed all these features. He engaged in it against his opinion, and yet without reluctance. He managed it without foresight or address, and was neither ashamed when it miscarried, nor dispirited when the Crown itself became endangered by the additional war with France. His good-humour could not be good-nature, for at the beginning of the war he stuck at no cruelty, but laughed at barbarities with which all Europe rung. It could not be good sense, for in the progress he blushed at none of the mischiefs he had occasioned, at none of the reproaches he had incurred. Like the Duke of Grafton, he was always affecting a disposition to retire, yet never did. Unlike the Duke, who secured no emoluments to himself, Lord North engrossed whatever fell in his way, and sometimes was bribed by the Crown to promote Acts, against which he pretended his conscience reclaimed—but it never was delicate when profit was in the opposite scale. If he had ambition, it was of very mean complexion, for he stooped to be but nominal Prime Minister, and suffered the King's private Junto to enjoy the whole credit of favour, while between submission and laziness, Lord North himself was seldom the author of the measures in which he bore the principal part. This passive and inglorious tractability, and his being connected with no faction, made him welcome to the King; his having no predominant fault or vice recommended him to the nation, and his good-humour and wit to everybody, but to the few whom his want of good breeding and attention offended. One singularity came out in his character, which was, that no man was more ready for extremes under the administration of others, no man more temperate than Lord North during his own. In effect, he was a man whom few hated, fewer could esteem. As a Minister he had no foresight, no consistence, no firmness, no spirit. He miscarried in all he undertook in America, was more improvident than unfortunate, less unfortunate than he deserved to be. If he was free from vices, he was as void of virtues; and it is a paltry eulogium of a Prime Minister of a great country, yet the best that can be allotted to Lord North, that though his country was ruined under his Administration, he preserved his good-humour, and neither felt for his country or for himself. Yet is true, too, that he was the least odious of the Ministers with whom he acted; and though servile in obedience to a Prince who meant so ill, there was reason to think that Lord North neither stimulated, nor was more than the passive instrument of the black designs of the Court.

The other chief Ministers were Lord Dartmouth, Lord Suffolk, Lord Gower, Lord Weymouth, Lord Sandwich, Lord Rochford, and afterwards Lord George Germain, besides two, who, though not ostensible Ministers, had more weight with the King than Lord North himself.

Of those, Lord Dartmouth only stayed long enough to prostitute his character and authenticate his hypocrisy. The Chancellor, Bathurst, was too poor a creature to have any weight; and Lord Rochford, though more employed, had still less claim to sense, and none at all to knowledge. Lord Suffolk's soul was harrowed by ambition, and as he had not parts to gratify it, he sought the despotism of the Crown as means of gratifying his own pride. Lord Gower, Lord Weymouth, and Lord Sandwich, all had parts, and never used them to any good or creditable purpose. The first had spirit enough to attempt any crime; the other two, though notorious cowards, were equally fitted to serve a prosperous Court; and Sandwich had a predilection to guilt if he could couple it with artifice and treachery. Lord George Germain was proud, haughty, and desperate. Success by any means was necessary to restore his credit; and a Court that was capable of adopting him, was sure he would not boggle at anything to maintain himself. Lord Mansfield was by birth, education, principle, cowardice, and revenge for the public odium, a bigot to tyranny. He would have sacrificed the universe, and everything but his personal safety, to overturn the constitution and freedom of England. But in the blindness of that rage, and from not daring to open the attempt where the danger to himself would have been imminent, he was the author of the liberty of America, and the instrument of Providence to bless a whole continent, whose destruction he sought to involve with that of his country. Jenkinson had, and deserved, no marked character; he was the tool of the King and Lord Mansfield, and had just parts enough to make his servility inexcusable. Wedderburne, Sir Gilbert Elliot, and Dyson were also much implicated in the following councils—but the two latter died early in the American War. Thurlowe, Rigby, and Ellis bore their part in kindling that fatal flame—but I am anticipating what did not appear till three or four years later—though it was both necessary to specify the chief incendiaries of the ensuing calamities, and to account for Lord North's escaping capital hatred for seeming to bear so capital a part in so criminal a scene; but as not one of the set I have recapitulated had recommended himself to the favour of the public, Lord North, by his good-humour, easily drew most good-will to himself, and did not, like most of the rest, push it from him by insolence and avowed profligacy.

The King and his Ministers

Let it be observed, however, that, when I impute to the King and his mother little more than a formed design of reducing the usurped authority of the great Lords, I am far from meaning that there were not deeper designs at bottom. Lord Mansfield was by principle a tyrant; Lord Holland was bred in a monarchic school, was cruel, revengeful, daring, and subtle. Grenville, though in principle a republican, was bold, proud, dictatorial, and so self-willed that he would have expected Liberty herself should be his first slave. The Bedford-faction, except the Duke himself, were void of honour, honesty and virtue; and the Scotch were whatever their masters wished them to be, and too envious of the English, and became too much provoked by them, not to lend all their mischievous abilities towards the ruin of a constitution, whose benefits the English had imparted to them, but did not like they should engross. All these individuals or factions, I do not doubt, accepted and fomented the disposition they found predominant in the Cabinet, as they had severally access to it; and the contradictions which the King suffered in his ill-advised measures, rivetted in him a thirst of delivering himself from control, and to be above control he must be absolute. Thus on the innate desire of unbounded power in all princes, was engrafted a hate to the freedom of the subject, and therefore, whether the King set out with a plan of extending his prerogative, or adopted it, his subsequent measures, as often as he had an opportunity of directing them himself, tended to the sole object of acting by his own will. Frequent convulsions did that pursuit occasion, and heavy mortifications to himself. On the nation it heaped disgrace, and brought it to the brink of ruin; and should the event be consonant to the King's wishes of establishing the royal authority at home, it is more sure that the country will be so lowered, that the Sovereign will become as subject to the mandates of France, as any little potentate in Europe.

William Beckford

This was the last public incident in the life of William Beckford, Lord Mayor of London, he dying three weeks afterwards of a violent fever contracted, as supposed, from the agitation into which his violence had thrown his blood, and from sudden cold caught in the country, whither he had retired for a little repose. He died on the 21st of June, aged sixty-two. He had boldness, promptness, spirit, a heap of confused knowledge, displayed with the usual ostentation of his temper, and so uncorrected by judgment, that his absurdities were made but more conspicuous by his vanity. Under a jovial style of good humour, he was tyrannic in Jamaica his native country, and under an appearance of prodigality, interested. On the other side, the excesses of his factious behaviour were founded neither on principle nor on rancour. Vainglory seemed to be the real motive of all his actions.[1] His death was one of the heaviest blows Lord Chatham could receive, cutting off all his influence in the City; and it was another cause of the Opposition's ensuing humiliation, the turbulence of Beckford, his imposing noise, and his great wealth, concurring to his authority. His successors in the party were utterly contemptible, except Trecothick, who was a decent man. This last was chosen Mayor for the rest of the year. A statue was voted to Beckford's memory, and ordered to be placed in Guildhall, with the words he had ventured to speak to the King engraven on the pedestal,—so strong was the party as yet in the City. Lord Chatham, the day before Beckford's death, forced himself into his house, and got away all the letters he had written to that demagogue.

The Princess Dowager

Another journey excited uncommon curiosity. The Princess Dowager of Wales, after an uninterrupted residence of thirty-four years in this country, and after having secluded herself in a manner from the world during the last nine years, set out for Germany, under pretence of visiting her brother the Duke of Saxe Gotha, and her daughters the Queen of Denmark and the Princess of Brunswick. As mystery and policy were imputed to all her actions, her declarations were not believed, merely because she made them. The people concluded she went to meet Lord Bute; others expected that some stroke would be

[1] When Beckford received an account of the magnificent seat he had built at Fonthill being burnt down, he only wrote to his steward, 'Let it be rebuilt.' Lord Holland's youngest son being ill, and Beckford inquiring after him, Lord Holland said he had sent him to Richmond for the air—Beckford cried out, 'Oh! Richmond is the worst air in the world; I lost twelve natural children there last year!' [H.W.]

struck during her absence to which she might plead not having been privy. As she carried the Duke of Gloucester with her, some believed that it was a trial to break his connection with Lady Waldegrave; some that she was displeased at the increasing power of the Queen; and a few, though perhaps not the worst guessers, that she went to secure her wealth in Germany. That the Princess of Brunswick was included in the motives of that journey is most probable. It was settled that the Princess and her husband, the hereditary Prince, should come to England the next year; and it is as certain that the Queen prevailed on the King to forbid their coming. The Princess of Wales, who had so cordially hated both her daughter and son-in-law, had taken much affection to them, not only from the court they paid to her, but from the use she found in her daughter. The Princess Dowager, having lost much of her influence over the King, was often refused favours that she asked of him. This her haughty spirit could not brook. Princess Augusta had no such reserve. Her intimacy coeval with the King had given her entire familiarity with him; and she would take no denials: her mother employed her in teasing the King till he granted whatever she asked. The ease and gaiety of the Princess Dowager during her residence abroad showed how much share her unpopularity, fear and sullen pride had in her recluse system—fear, not without cause: as she passed through Canterbury she was hissed and insulted—yet at Dover she met with no affronts; nor were there any illuminations or bonfires in London for joy of her departure, as had been expected. She had a slight interview with her daughter of Denmark, an extraordinary Princess! Christian the Seventh had conceived an instantaneous aversion to her on their marriage; and had even disgraced his favourite cousin, the Prince of Hesse, for taking her part. While her husband was in England, the Russian Minister treated her disrespectfully; but though the Czarina governed the Danish King, the Queen with proper spirit commanded the insolent foreigner to quit the kingdom. Her resolution continued after her husband's return; and at last gained the ascendant. Bernsdorffe, Prime Minister and creature of Russia, was disgraced; so was young Holke, the King's favourite. Thus far her Majesty acted with reputation—but when the public beheld the King's physician engross all favour, and when that physician seemed equally dear to both King and Queen, the wildest conjectures were let loose—certain it is that the Queen showed a lofty spirit as well as singular manners. She was grown to enormous fatness; yet when she met her mother on the frontiers, she was accoutred in a man's habit with breeches of buckskin; and when the Princess of Wales lamented the disgrace of Bernsdorffe, the ancient Minister of the family, the Queen of Denmark said abruptly, 'Pray, Madam, let me govern my own kingdom as I please.'

The Duke of Cumberland

During the absence of her Royal Highness was decided against her youngest son the Duke of Cumberland, the suit of Lord Grosvenor for adultery. Lady Grosvenor, a vain young woman, of a good person, moderate beauty, and no understanding, had already given handle to scandal by too much intimacy with the late Duke of York. Still more indiscreet with the Duke of Cumberland, their letters were intercepted by the husband; and never was the public regaled with a collection of greater folly. Yet to the lady's honour be it said, that, bating a few oaths, which sounded more masculine than tender, the advantage in grammar, spelling, and style was all in her favour. His Royal Highness's diction and learning scarce exceeded that of a cabin-boy, as those eloquent epistles, existing in print, may testify. Some being penned on board of ship were literal verification of Lord Dorset's ballad,—

> 'To you, fair ladies, now at land,
>   We men at sea do write;
> But first would have you understand,
>   How hard 'tis to indite.'

Grievous censure fell on his governor and preceptor, Mr. Legrand and Mr. Charles, and not less on the Princess herself, so totally had his education been neglected. He had been locked up with his brother the Duke of Gloucester till the age of twenty-one, and thence had sallied into a life of brothels and drunkenness, whence the decency of the elder, and his early connection with Lady Waldegrave, preserved the Duke of Gloucester. The younger was pert, insolent, sense-less, and not unwillingly brutal. So little care taken of a Prince of the Blood did but confirm the opinion of the public, that the plan of the Princess, Lord Bute, and the King had been to keep down and discredit the King's brothers as much as possible. The Duke of Cumberland, at least, did not disappoint the scheme, as will hereafter appear. As a dozen years afterwards it was evident that no greater

care, though with still more rigorous confinement, had been taken
of the morals and style of the Prince of Wales, who issued from that
palace of supposed purity, the Queen's house, as if he had been
educated in a night-cellar, it gave but too much ground for suspecting
that, undeterred by what had happened to his brother, the jealousy
of his heir had not been less predominant in the King than it had
been in the neglect of his brothers.

The Marquis of Granby

While discord and interest thus tore in pieces the Opposition, Fate
was preparing to deprive them of their most important centurions.
Beckford was already gone. The next was the Marquis of Granby,
the idol of the army and of the populace. He died at Scarborough,
October 20th: in so few months did Lord Chatham lose his Tribune
and his General, and was reduced to his ill-content friend Chancellor
Camden, his ill-connected brother Lord Temple, and his worse-recon-
ciled brother Mr. Grenville!

Were there any reality in the idea that noble blood diffuses an air
of superior excellence over the outward form, and refines the qualities
of the mind; and were that idea not refuted by the majority of
examples to the contrary, Lord Granby would have appeared a shining
instance of both effects. His large and open countenance, its manly
and pure colours glowing with health, his robust and commanding
person, and a proportion of florid beauty so great that the baldness of
his head, which he carried totally bare, was rather an addition to
its comely roundness than a defect, and a singularity more than an
affectation; all distinguished him without any extrinsic ornament,
and pointed out his rank when he walked without attendance, and
was mixed with the lowest people, who followed him to beg his
charity, or to bless him for it. His mind was as rich in the qualities
that became his elevated situation. Intrepidity, sincerity, humanity, and
generosity, were not only innate in his breast, but were never corrupted
there. His courage and his tenderness were never disunited. He was
dauntless on every occasion, but when it was necessary to surmount
his bashfulness. His nerves trembled like a woman's, when it was
requisite that he should speak in public. His modesty was incapable
of ostentation. His rank, his services, and the idolatry of the people
could inspire him with no pride, a sensation his nature knew not.

Of money he seemed to conceive no use but in giving it away: but that profusion was so indiscriminate, that compassion or solicitation, and consequently imposture, were equally the masters of his purse. Thus his benevolence checked itself, and wasted on unworthy objects the sums he often wanted to bestow on real distress. Nor was it less fatal to his own honour, but plunged him in difficulties from which some discretion in his bounty would have secured him. As his understanding was by no means proportioned to his virtues, he was always obnoxious to the interested designs of those who governed him; and between his own want of judgment and the ascendant of those who hampered him in their toils by supplying his necessities with money at exorbitant interest, he was bought and sold by successive Administrations and different parties; and generally, when the former fell, he abandoned those he had attached himself and been obliged to, and lent himself to measures which his principles disapproved, and then reverted to those principles against his inclination. No man meant to feel more patriotism, or to be more warmly attached to the constitution of his country; yet his unsuspicious nature suffered him to be easily made the tool of its enemies; and when he sacrificed his darling command of the army in a convulsion of integrity, he neither acted with grace nor firmness, nor showed a knowledge of the question for which he devoted himself, nor made the stand so soon as he ought to have done; and, what was worse, he was forced upon the step he took unwillingly by a man who had not the reputation of common honesty, or pretended to be actuated by any principle but self-interest and revenge.

In an age more simple, Lord Granby had been a perfect hero. In a rude age he would probably have been a successful general from his own valour, and the enthusiasm of attachment which his soldiers felt for him; but in times wherein military knowledge is so much improved, it was perhaps fortunate for his country that the sole command was never entrusted to him on any capital emergency. Yet they must have been the many solid virtues which he possessed, that could make him so greatly respected in a corrupt age, when talents are more esteemed than merit, or when hypocrisy alone runs away with the character and rewards of virtue.

His domestic qualities were all of the amiable kind. His only remarkable vice proved fatal to him: his constant excesses in wine inflaming his sanguine complexion, hurrying him out of the world at forty-nine!

George Grenville

The second event hinted at was the death of Mr. George Grenville. He had been dangerously ill in the summer, had recovered in some degree, relapsed, and had been brought to town in October for advice, where he soon fell into a desperate state, followed by a delirium that lasted to his death, which happened the very morning the Parliament met. His body being opened, his case appeared most singularly uncommon: his ribs were carious or quite worn away, and his skull as thin as paper. This extraordinary malady was imputed to a disorder in his blood, which had penetrated to the blood-vessels of his bones, and had corroded them.

Mr. Grenville was, confessedly, the ablest man of business in the House of Commons, and, though not popular, of great authority there from his spirit, knowledge, and gravity of character. His faults, however, had been capital, and to himself most afflicting. His injudicious Stamp Act had exposed us to the risk of seeing all our Colonies revolt; and his resentment of the repeal had prevented him from ever forgiving Lord Chatham and Lord Rockingham, a sincere junction with whom might have driven the Court to restore him to power. His rash and ungrateful provocation of the Favourite, his indecently taking part with the Bedfords in their violent insult to the Princess on the Regency Bill, his forcing the King to break his word and turn out Mr. Mackenzie, and his silly parsimony in stinting the King's expense in trifles, were crimes that had never been forgiven, the King, the Princess, and the Favourite being as weak in not pardoning him, as he had been in offending.

Lord George Sackville Germain

The next day [14 December] Lord George Sackville Germain, and Lord George Cavendish, moved that no messages should be sent to the other House but by the eldest sons of peers, who alone would not be in danger of being insulted there; and that such eldest sons should be restrained from going thither on any other occasion. Colonel Onslow, alluding to the two Lords, said, the motion ought to have been that no message should be sent but by the younger sons of peers;

and alluding to Lord George Sackville, that the motion seemed to imply timidity. Governor Johnstone went much further, and said, he did not conceive *that any man was proper to take care of the honour of that House, who had forfeited his own ho iour*. The motion was rejected by about 130 to 40.

So gross an insult as Johnstone's called for chastisement, and did prove how much the world and he had mistaken Lord George Sackville. The latter with temper that became the courage he showed, took four days to settle his affairs and to make provision for an infant of which his wife was just delivered; behaving at the same time with a cheerful indifference that deceived her and his whole family. He then, taking T. Townshend for his second, challenged Johnstone, and met him in Hyde Park. The latter was accompanied by Sir James Lowther. Each fired two pistols; Johnstone's first struck off the butt-end of Lord George's. They fired again; both missed, and the affair ended, exceedingly to the honour of Lord George's coolness and intrepidity. The brutality of Johnstone shocked everybody, especially as his character had as much of the bully as the bravo in it; and as it was presumed he had depended on Lord George's supposed want of spirit, or trusted to the publicity of the affront for any consequences being prevented, which is always dishonourable in the aggressor. His boisterous reputation, and a vague anonymous challenge given out in the newspapers to the author of a *North Briton* on the Scotch, had recommended him for this service to his patron, Sir James Lowther, who, in resentment for Lord George's deserting him on the Cumberland election, had brooded over it till now that he excited that ruffian's assault. But so odious was Sir James from the whole tenor of his life, that Johnstone seemed the less hateful of the two, especially as Sir James appeared to glut his eyes with revenge.

The King

Such was the complexion of the King's whole conduct. By aiming at power which he did not dare to exert, he was forced to court the most servile, and buy dear the most worthless, never conceiving that the firmest authority is that founded on character, and on the respect paid to virtue. He bought temporary slaves, who had the power of manumitting themselves the moment they wished to be bought over again. He lost his dominions in America, his authority over

Ireland, and all influence in Europe, by aiming at despotism in England; and exposed himself to more mortifications and humiliations than can happen to a quiet Doge of Venice. Another feature in his character was that he could seem to forgive any injury or insult when the offender could be of use to him; he never remembered any service when the performer could be of none.

Lord Weymouth

The secret motives of Lord Weymouth's resignation were these:— at the beginning of Spain's hostilities, the King, who began to affect a military turn, had been eager for war, and Lord Weymouth, whose ambition aspired to the lead in Administration, had gone eagerly into the royal views. On that plan, and encouraged by Wood's awe of Lord Chatham, they had thrown every damp on the negotiation, and involved themselves in repeated declarations of the war being unavoidable. Lord North, of pacific mould, and the Scottish Junto as apprehensive as Wood that a war would bring back Lord Chatham, had taken a contrary course, and had brought back the King from his martial system. Lord Weymouth, who would not have hesitated to change his language had he thought peace could be effected, chose rather to waive his ambition than his security, and adhered to war. Nor was this all. His extreme indolence and drunkenness made it impossible that he should execute the duties of his office in time of war. He seldom went to bed till five or six in the morning, nor rose next day till twelve or one. His parts must have been great, for in that besotted state he was still able to express himself in the House of Lords with elegance, quickness, and some knowledge, in a few short sentences; not indeed deserving all the applause bestowed on them by his faction. A few reflections on his character and on the time may be useful; as it will seem extraordinary hereafter that a man so improperly compounded for a minister, should in a government partly popular have been the hinge on which so important a crisis turned.

Whether it is owing to the variations of our climate, or to the uncertainty and fluctuations of our government; whether to the independence that our freedom suggests; or whatever else be the cause, it is certain that no other country produces so many singular and discriminate characters as England. And as the nature of our Government excludes no man from attaining a share in it; and as the licence of opposition and of the press suffers the most severe scrutiny even into the private life of all men in power, it is not surprising that there should be a greater variety in the actors, and a larger harvest of anecdotes relating to them than to the Ministers of other nations. Here, too the character of the man influences his conduct. In monarchies, the temper and disposition of the Prince gives the tone to his subjects and servants. When ministers and factions awe the Sovereign, *their* passions, not *his,* prescribe their conduct. Never was this truth so elucidated as in the first years of George the Third. Having no predominant passion of his own, but hypocrisy enough to seem to approve whatever his Ministers for the time being willed, almost every year of his reign wore a different stamp. It began with popularity under Lord Bute, but veered as suddenly to Majesty at home. Lord Chatham, had he had time, would have dictated to Europe. Fox, Lord Holland, established universal corruption and revenge. Grenville exercised rigour and economy. With Lord Rockingham entered redress and relaxation. Lord Chatham's second Administration was an interregnum of inexplicable confusion. The Duke of Grafton did as little, without being out of his senses. The people almost seized the reins next, and the Ministers, to save themselves, were content to secure the doors of the Cabinet and of the House of Commons from being stormed, while both the King and the Parliament were vilified and insulted. His Majesty seemed almost as contented to let the populace brave him, as he had been to let Lord Bute, Lord Holland, and Grenville trample on them.

Among men of such various complexion, Lord Weymouth was not the least singular. He was tall, handsome, and from a German education, solemn and formal in his outward deportment. His look spoke absence, and nothing in his ostensible appearance discovered a symptom of the quickness, cunning, and dissoluteness within. A perfect insensibility produced constant and facile good humour; yet his bent brow and constitutional pride indicated no pleasantry or social mirth. His parts were strong, his conception ready, his reasoning acute, his delivery short and perspicuous. His parts must have been very strong to be capable of emerging from his constant drunkenness and dissipation; for though he had been well instructed, had a retentive memory, and a head admirably turned to astronomy and mechanics, he abandoned all improvement so entirely, that it was wonderful how he had gleaned so much common knowledge of politics as embellished his short speeches, and for a quarter of an hour in every debate infused into him aptness and propriety. The becoming decency and dignity of his appearance was all the homage he paid to public opinion. He neither had nor affected any solid virtue. He was too proud to court the people, and too mean not to choose to owe his preferments to the favour of the Court or the cabals of faction. He wasted the whole night in drinking, and the morning in sleep, even when Secretary of State. No kind of principle entered into his plan or practice; nor shame for want of it. He ruined his tradesmen without remorse, and, if that was an excuse, without thought; and with equal indifference frequently saw bailiffs in his house: for pride is a constitutional stoicism, independent of circumstances. With as little sense of fashionable as of real honour, he had often received letters with demands of gaming debts, written in a style that even such gentlemen seldom endure without resentment. Taciturnity, except with his bacchanalian companions, was his favourite habit, because it harmonized with his prodigious indolence; and ambition, though his only passion, could not surmount his laziness; though his vanity made him trust that his abilities, by making him necessary, could reconcile intrigue and inactivity. His timidity was womanish, and the only thing he did not fear was the ill opinion of mankind.

1771

Doctor Samuel Johnson

Our Ministers, however, triumphing in having avoided a war, set forth an exultation written by Dr. Samuel Johnson, and very abusive on the Opposition, the Bill of Rights, Lord Chatham, Junius, and the Lord Mayor, with most of their names at length,—the very kind of grievance of which the Court complained. With a lumber of learning and some strong parts, Johnson was an odious and mean character. By principle a Jacobite, arrogant, self-sufficient, and over-bearing by nature, ungrateful through pride and of *feminine bigotry*, he had prostituted his pen to party even in a dictionary, and had afterwards for a pension, contradicted his own definitions. His manners were sordid, supercilious, and brutal, his style ridiculously bombast and vicious; and, in one word, with all the pedantry he had all the gigantic littleness of a country schoolmaster.

Charles James Fox

March 31. 1771.—Charles Fox was one of those vigorous exuberancies of genius, which this country, where nothing restrains or contracts the mind, pushes forth from time to time. They seem to be born at full manhood, and to expand all the powers of their understanding at their first appearance. Such were the second Duke of Buckingham, Lord Rochester, the Duke of Wharton, Lord Bolingbroke and Charles Townshend, to the last but one of whom Charles Fox bore the greatest resemblance. Their ambition was equal, their argumentative faculties alike, and politics their only real passion. Neither had any wit, nor affected it. Rochester, Buckingham and Wharton were the slaves of every vice, every whim and every frolic, and as much libertines in practice as in theory. Their sallies and wit palliated and even threw graces into their debauchery; nor could the perfidy and crime of the two latter extinguish the memory of their agreeable intemperance. Bolingbroke's art reconciled many who detested his character. The fickleness and pusillanimity of Townshend debased more variety of powers, genius and wit, than had fallen to the share of all the others, and though he had few or inconsiderable vices, and had not dipped into any crimes, he was no more esteemed than Buckingham or Wharton. The latter was the model which Charles Fox set himself to copy, thinking that excess of vice and libertinism would give a relief to his excellent parts, by proving how brightly they could emerge from the most dissolute indulgences, and how little they wanted application and industry. He drank hard, because it was a vice, gamed to attain a name from the excess of his losses, and followed women but little because nature had not distinguished him from other young men by superior potency in love.

The faculties of his mind were genuine, strong and mature. He conceived, digested and replied at once. His reasoning and elocution were equally impetuous. He seemed to have thought on all manly subjects, by the time he could write 'man,' and was the reverse of all other youths, for his vices were affected, and his solidity natural. Such an amazing burst of parts, that wanted no ripening and anticipated instruction, produced as rapid effects; in others admiration and envy; in himself excess of vanity and presumption, beyond what even flattery and intoxication could warrant. Bold, spirited and confident, he behaved as if already in possession of all the triumphs he aspired to, and familiarized himself with pre-eminence, before he was known enough to have published even his pretensions. Thus at twenty-two he acted and was hated as a leader of a party; his arrogance, loquacity and intemperance raising him the enemies of a Minister before he had acquired the power of one. The very youngest men alone were attached to his fortunes, and hoped to share those premature honours which he already engrossed in idea. As he was goodhumoured, well-bred and profuse, they did not feel themselves humbled by his superiority as older men did, on whose pride and position he trampled and encroached. He was as agreeable as strong sense divested of graces and wit, could make him; and as little disagreeable as such overbearing presumption could allow.

His education had certainly been formed in no moral school, nor did any gleam of virtue engage that he would degenerate from his father's system of unprincipled libertinism. Nature had not given him discretion, nor could it give him experience before the time: and when decency, candour and modesty were cast off, it is no wonder that he entered on the public stage with almost as much unpopularity as his father had left it. Both had the same arbitrary notions, but avarice, that had tempered the violence of the one, had not yet taught the other to moderate any impulse of his complexion. The son lived but for fame and for himself, and was impetuous to crowd into the first months of his life all enjoyments, all glory. At once copying and neglecting his father, such hasty renown, such prodigality, and want of attention to him overwhelmed Lord Holland with the confused pangs of pride and mortification.

Mr. Smelt

The care of the Prince of Wales was a trust no less important. Two points only were looked to in his education. The first was, that he should not be trusted to anything but a ductile cypher; the other, that he should be brought up with due affection for regal power; in other words, he was to be the slave of his father, and the tyrant of his people. Praise is due even to those who execute ably their own views, let those views be ever so bad. The governors selected for the Prince were chosen very suitably to the plan I have mentioned. The King pitched upon Lord Holderness to officiate as the solemn phantom or governor; Lord Mansfield recommended Dr. Markham, the Master of Westminster

School, a creature of his own, sprung out of the true prerogative seminary at Christchurch, Oxford; a pert arrogant man, to fill the post of preceptor; and thus was the heir of the Crown not likely to degenerate. Lord North, the nominal First Minister, had the mortification of finding that he was rather a necessary than agreeable tool, for he knew nothing of these designations till they were ready to be notified to the public.

This arrangement had nothing in it but what was to be expected. That a man, the very reverse of all those who were in favour at Court, should have been admitted into this Junto, was real matter of surprise; and can only be accounted for by the security of the King and his Cabal, in having blocked up the chief avenues to the Prince. One Jackson, an ingenious young man, recommended by Lady Charlotte Finch, governess of the royal children, was named sub-preceptor; but the person at whom I hinted, and who was appointed sub-governor, was Mr. Leonard Smelt, whose singular virtues and character deserve to be recorded independently of his office. He was younger son of a gentleman in Yorkshire, and had a commission in the Office of Ordnance, which he threw up, finding no attention paid by his superiors to his representation of many abuses there. He fell in love with the niece of General Guest in Scotland, but retired thence to avoid her, as he had not fortune sufficient to maintain her. Another young lady, heiress to great wealth, conceived a passion for him, and obtained her father's consent before she acquainted Mr. Smelt with her passion, which he had not suspected. So far from it, he swooned away with surprise and concern, when the father offered him his daughter. Mr. Smelt confessed his former engagement, refused the lady, and again retired. Soon after this his father died, and disinheriting his elder son, who had disobliged him, bequeathed his whole fortune to Leonard. The first act of this excellent young man was to marry his beloved first mistress; the second to settle half his fortune on his brother's children. His principles in public life were as generous as in private; a steady friend to the constitution of his country, he had signed the Yorkshire remonstrance to the King against the intrusion of Luttrell into the House of Commons. His next introduction to his Majesty was as sub-preceptor to his son: happy for the Prince had he had no other governor—at least, no other director of his morals and opinions of government. But Mr. Smelt had neither authority to instruct his pupil in matters of State, nor perhaps discernment enough to baffle the insidious lessons of his associates, for he was ignorant of the world as well as of its depravity. Being a neighbour of Lord Holderness, the latter introduced him, and he was received, notwithstanding his disqualification as a patriot.

Chevalier d'Eon

The Chevalier d'Eon, of whom I have given an account, occasioned at this period much and strange discourse. A notion had for some time prevailed that he was a woman in man's habit. The Duc de Choiseul believed it from the report of a female English spy who pretended to be certain of it from having washed his linen; and as the report spread, it gained further credit from assertions that he never dressed himself before any witness, nor could any of his comrades recollect an instance of his amours. His beard though black was inconsiderable; and though he was strong and an excellent fencer, his legs had a feminine turn. At first he pretended to resent the report but afterwards spoke and wrote so dubiously on his sex, that the most judicious suspected him for author of the fable from interested views. Sometimes he disappeared and returned again, till by the usual discrepancy of opinion, very great sums were wagered on the question, and he, though he denied the charge in print, was taxed with encouraging those bets in order to share the spoil, according as he should pronounce on his own gender: but the question came to no issue and was forgotten like other legends of the day.[1]

The Princess Dowager

... But these were piddling consolations. The Court was predominant at home; Wilkes was fallen, the City was recovering from the dominion of the popular Tribunes, the Rockingham-party was crest-fallen, and now came news that Spain had actually restored to us Falkland's Isle, which it had been doubted she never would surrender. Thus was the King at peace both at home and abroad, after a vexatious and ignominious struggle for near eleven years. It seemed an additional promise of tranquillity to him, that his mother, who by the bad education she had given him, and the bias which she impressed by her creatures on his councils, was now known to be dying, and though she had lost much of her influence, she retained enough over his awe of her, to perplex his measures and throw uncertainty over the duration of

[1] D'Eon was afterwards allowed to be a woman and assumed the habit. [H.W.]

his Ministries. At this very period such a storm of private calamities burst on his head, as few kings ever experienced at once. Part of them touched his pride, and accordingly penetrated deep; he had a happy insensibility that surmounted the rest without an effort.

The malignant humour in the blood of the Princess Dowager had fallen on her throat, and though her fortitude was invincible and her secrecy and reserve invariable, the disorder could no longer be concealed. She could swallow but with great difficulty and not enough to maintain life long. At times the disease oozed too plentifully from her mouth to be disguised, and her sufferings, and her struggles to hide them, were so much beyond her strength, that she frequently fainted and was thought dead. Yet would she not allow she was ill, even to her children; nor would she suffer a single physician or surgeon to inspect her throat, trusting herself solely to a German page, who had some medical know-ledge; and going out to take the air, long after it was expected that she would die in her coach. Her danger was publicly known by the be-ginning of November, on the fifth of which month, when her death was hourly expected, an express arrived from Leghorn, that her son the Duke of Gloucester was at the point of death there, and it was concluded by that time dead. He had gone to a warmer climate in hopes of palliating the same terrible distemper of which his mother was dying and which she had transmitted to most of her children. The Duke had passed by sea from Genoa to Leghorn, where landing, he had fallen into a diarrhoea, attended by every bad symptom.

The Duke of Cumberland and Mrs. Horton

The very next day it became public that the Duke of Cumberland had, on the first of [November], retired to Calais with a widow, Mrs. Horton, whom he had married, and had notified his wedding to the King. What was the astonishment of mankind, what the mortifica-tion of the King and Princess, and what the triumph of Wilkes, when it came out that this new Princess of the Blood was own sister of the famous Colonel Luttrell, the tool thrust by the Court into Wilkes's seat for Middlesex! Could punishment be more severe than to be thus scourged by their own instrument? And how singular the fate of Wilkes, that new revenge always presented itself to him when he was sunk to the lowest ebb!

The Duke of Cumberland, after having been exposed to the derision of mankind by his foolish letters to Lady Grosvenor, by his absurd conduct in that intrigue, and by his pusillanimity on the detection, had added perfidy to ridicule, and abandoned the lady to her shame. He had next engaged openly in an intrigue with another married woman, a Mrs. Bailey, a very handsome wife of a timber-merchant; and it was uncertain which was most proud of the honour, the husband or the wife. But they had not long displayed their triumph in all public places, before the restless Duke, seeking new diversions, was made a more substantial conquest of at Brighthelmstone by Mrs. Horton, who had for many months been dallying with his passion, till she had fixed him to more serious views than he had intended.

She was the daughter of Simon Luttrell, Lord Irnham, and had married a gentleman of fortune, with whom she had been in love; and had the misfortune of losing an only child, an infant daughter, and her husband within a fortnight of each other, still covering her grief for the first to conceal the misfortune from the last. She was rather pretty than handsome, and had more the air of a woman of pleasure than of a woman of quality, though she was well made, was graceful, and unexceptionable in her conduct and behaviour. But there was something so bewitching in her languishing eyes, which she could animate to enchantment if she pleased, and her coquetry was so active, so varied, and yet so habitual, that it was difficult not to see through it, and yet as difficult to resist it. She danced divinely, and had a great deal of wit, but of the satiric kind; and, as she had haughtiness before her rise, no wonder she claimed all the observance due to her rank after she became Duchess of Cumberland. It had been believed that she would marry General Smith, a very handsome well-built young man; but glory was her passion, and she sacrificed her lover to it, as she had never sacrificed her virtue to her lover. Thus in herself she was unexceptionable, at least superior to the frailty of her sex, if not above its little ambition. From her family, though ancient, she drew many disadvantages. Her ancestors had been noted and long odious in Ireland for treachery, villainy, and arrogance. Her father did not retrieve the honour of his blood, and though very brave in his person, and tolerably brutal, had every other failure of his race. Nor was he happier in his own issue. Not intending to return to his native country, Ireland, he had given up his house there to his son, but changing his mind, went thither. His son shut both his father and mother out of the mansion-house, and was countenanced by his brothers and sisters,—a scene of vexation that pierced the mother's heart, and threw her into religious melancholy.

But to the King the most grievous part of the affliction was the connection with Colonel Luttrell, and the satisfaction it must give to the friends of the Constitution to see the invasion of their privileges punished by the same hand by which they had been attacked; for it was soon known that Mrs. Horton's brothers had been privy to the matrimonial transaction between the Duke and their sister. The Duke's flight to Calais with his bride spoke as little heroism as he had exerted at St. Albans,[1] and showed how little consultation he had held on the validity of his marriage; yet it proved indissoluble, the Royal Family being expressly excepted out of the late Lord Hardwicke's Marriage Act. That proud legislator had indeed inserted them; but the late Duke of Cumberland and Lord Holland, in order to traverse Hardwicke, had represented to the late King that it was an indignity to the Princes of the Blood to be levelled with the mass of his subjects, and the haughty Monarch had ordered them to be erased out of the Bill, saying, 'I will not have my family laid under those restraints.'

The Princess Dowager

In the meantime came more favourable accounts of the Duke of Gloucester. He recovered, though the hiccup and symptoms of death had appeared on him; and as soon as his strength was a little recruited, he sailed to Naples, the voyage whither again brought on a return of his flux; but he once more mastered it; and the English physicians were of opinion that the discharge might for some time relieve the virulence of his complaint, though no man flattered himself with a long duration of the Duke's life. On his return he visited Rome, and the Stuarts had once more the mortification of seeing a Prince of the rival Blood and a Protestant, distinguished with peculiar honours by a Pope, who even conversed with him.

This was the last gleam of comfort to the dying Princess: but this reprieve of her son was bitterly dashed by the shame and misery that fell on her daughter, the Queen of Denmark, of which, as she languished till the beginning of the next year, she lived long enough to hear, and but just long enough to die with the anxiety of dreading a fatal conclusion to that daughter.

She now beheld the wretched consequences of the wretched education she had given her children. The Queen of Denmark had been kept in

[1] Where he was caught with Lady Grosvenor. [H.W.]

her nursery till sent to Copenhagen; had had no company but servants, and could have seen nothing but an intimacy with Lord Bute, which all the Princess's children spoke of with disgust; and could have heard nothing but passionate lamentations from the Princess on the impotence of power possessed by English Sovereigns,—lessons that seem to have made but too deep impression on the inexperienced young Queen, when she came to have a lover, and be mistress of absolute power. The Duke of Gloucester, the Princess of Wales had always loved the least, though the most meritorious of her children. She thought him insuperably dull, nor was he bright: one day in his childhood she ridiculed him before his brothers and sisters, and bade them laugh at the fool. He sat silent and thoughtful. She said, 'What! now you are sullen.' He replied, No, he was thinking.—'Thinking!' replied his mother, with scorn; 'and pray, what was you thinking of?' He answered, 'I was thinking what I should feel if I had a son as unhappy as you make me!'

This unfortunate mother's fate is a speaking lesson to princes. Had the credit and happiness of her children been her object, her own life might, except in those she lost, have been prosperous and renowned. Her own ambition, and the desire of making her son more powerful than the laws allowed, led her and him into disgraces, mortifications, humiliations. Reviled, traduced, hated, she scarce dared to appear out of her palace; her Favourite she saw driven from his country, and his life frequently endangered. Her younger children disgraced her; and the eldest, as well as herself, missed the despotism she sought for both, and obtained only that triste pre-eminence of Turkish sultans, being shut up with mutes in their own seraglio.

END OF MEMOIRES 1771

APPENDIX

Character of George the Third

There were but four leading characteristic marks in the King's composition. He was unfeeling, insincere, cunning and trifling. Nature had given him the first quality and the last. His mother had taught him the second, and practice the third. He was rather silly than a fool; for what sense he had was employed to deceive others, generally to his own prejudice, and yet so servile and interested were his subjects, and self-love made them so vain of being countenanced by him, that though all the world knew his insincerity, and everybody saw how indiscriminate his notice and his smiles were, he found they were still captivating, and lost nothing of their effect, though so promiscuously prostituted.

The Princess Dowager, to concentre all his attachment to herself, had early given him a bad impression of all mankind, and mankind took no pains to efface those prejudices. She too had inculcated into him a desire of extending his prerogative; she had laboured to instil firmness into him, and proclaimed it as his predominant characteristic. But he was more fond of his will than of his prerogative; and all his firmness was reducible to perseverance; for he was flexible on any emergency, and contented himself with waiting for an opportunity of cancelling his concessions. Thus would he yield to part with any minister, or to accept any, but was determined to sacrifice those he had been forced to accept, though not so constant in recalling those that had been torn from him, for he forgot services, but not offences. Having no vices but those of the heart, the flattery of the Court had proclaimed him pious—he was not, for except his regular appearance at Chapel, himself affected neither in his practice or conversation the tone of devotion, so that he was really no hypocrite farther than liking to be thought what he took no trouble to be.

His constancy to the Queen was owing to his pride, suspicion, and a very governable constitution, not to affection for her. He feared the influence of a mistress and her connections, and when he was far from having entire confidence in the only woman he conversed with amorously, he was not likely to unbosom himself in social pleasures.

247

Not one of his various Ministers ever had his perfect confidence, and though he prated eternally and often imprudently, he always reserved his chief secrets to himself. His extreme temperance was no more a virtue than his chastity. The malignant humour in his blood could only be kept down by the abstemiousness of a hermit, and none of his passions were strong enough not to yield to his care of his person.

His subservience to his mother was made a reproach to him almost as unjustly as piety and virtue were ascribed to him, for he hated her and Bute even before he attained the Crown; mortified her early and the Earl often. He affected to love his brother Gloucester, but never gave any proofs of it, though many of indifference and cruelty. Of his children he was excessively fond while they remained infants, an affection which as they grew up, moulted to no more than familiarity, and never ripened to any gratification of their inclinations. His eldest son he detested early, and abhorred Charles Fox, as supposed his favourite, though he never was, though he advised the Prince prudently and soon ceased to be in his favour.

Portrait of Lord Mansfield

Parts bright, quick and solid; eloquence clear or subtle; facility in quoting or in forging quotations; application never deviating from its point, but by fear, and always returning 'when the danger subsided; equally minute in his attention to great or little objects, when they tended to promote his sole plan: these were the qualities, these the defects that made Lord Mansfield the ablest man of his time, and the most detestable; for the destruction of the Constitution was the sole incentive to his aspiring. Other men are capable of the worst actions to gratify their ambition; he was ambitious to glut his lust of promoting despotism. He had no personal vices, but principles that are commendable in others tainted his heart with every bad affection. They gave him envy, jealousy, avarice, revenge and treachery. He hated the best men, if they were attached to their country, and promoted the worst, because such alone were capable of seconding his views. That he added cruelty to the black catalogue must not be imputed to the same cause. Cowards are always sanguinary, and Lord Mansfield's cowardice was more constitutional than even his love of tyranny. It disgraced every period of his life, and yet was the only quality that abated the malignity of his principles. He neither dared to be Chancellor nor Prime Minister, though the ablest man on the Bench or in the Cabinet, because he never had spirit enough to dictate the arbitrary measures that he was incessantly and secretly suggesting. He was always whispering daggers, always afraid of grasping them, unless he could find out a chicane in law, for he never consulted the Code but to pervert or undermine it. As he had all the mischievous qualities of a woman, even to the alacrity of uttering the grossest untruths, he hated juries with a feminine animosity; and though he preferred every sinister method of promoting his views to the open and honest, his malevolence to those landmarks of liberty broke out as frequently as the lewdness of a prude. His partiality in causes was so notorious that his decrees were treated as wilful deviations from the plainest letter of the law; and while he copied Jefferies in cruelty and subservience to prerogative, his authority as Chief Justice sunk to the level of a quibbling attorney. He shuffled before Lord Camden, faltered before Lord Chatham, and dreaded Norton, who he knew had betrayed him. The King admired him as a tool, and despised him as a coward. All men reverenced his abilities, feared his art, abhorred the blackness of his soul, and derided his pusillanimity. He served the House of Hanover on Jacobite principles. He did much hurt by the law, more to the law; and was an enemy to human nature by reflection and meditation. He wished to be the instrument of enslaving England, provided he were dead first and in no danger from its resentment for having forged its chains.

NOTES ON THE TEXT

A = 'First Copy', or rough draft, Waldegrave MSS.
B = 'Second Copy', or fair copy, Waldegrave MSS.
ed. = (1) for '*George II*' (1751–60), Lord Holland;
     (2) for '*George III*' (1760–71), Sir Denis le Marchant;
     (3) for '*Last Journals*' (1772–83), Dr. Doran.

Page 1, line 1   It had been much expected ... President of the Council [first extract, not in B].

p. 3, l. 9   unfashionable [ed.], fashionable [A, B].

p. 4, l. 13   [... refuse the gift] But of all the various productions, which if he did not father, he at least did not disown, I could never trace anything certainly up to his manufacture. [A, not in B].

p. 5, l. 4   and if ... holy wedlock [A and British Museum fragment; excision from B].

p. 6, l. 4   and if he ... than a monster [A, excision from B].

p. 14, l. 4   With the most heroic ... that it gratifies [B, added on opposite page, not in A; in its place in A and, erased, in B as follows] It is uncertain whether his inordinate passion for war proceeded from brutal courage, from love of rule, or from love of blood; for he was as cruel as if he had been a coward; it is certain that it ...

p. 28, l. 23   his Duchess ... Burlington's daughter [A, excision from B].

p. 32, l. 34   [... *Dunciad*] Was there no glory in directing the council and operations of such men as Sir William Windham, Lord Bath and Lord Granville? Was it having no address to have succeeded, as he has done in his letters, if not in vindicating the exploded Treaty of Utrecht, yet at least in proving that the Whigs had been still more blameable in refusing the glorious and advantageous terms that had been offered by France? On the other hand ... [A, not in B].

p. 34, l. 32   A f.91 *ends* ... take leave of the reader &c/Finis/ finished May 1752. 'Comparison of Pelham and Walpole', not in A.

p. 37, l. 32   ... steal an opportunity from [end of B, the rest of the extract is taken from the printed text].

p. 38, l. 31   [Osborn] Osborn, Oldmixon [A].

p. 42, l. 5   [... of his Purple] as a young squire in England, who has been prohibited too great familiarity with his huntsman [not in B, deleted in A].

pp. 45–46	(*Mr. Pelham*) [A, missing from B].
p. 50	(*Lord Gower and Lord Albemarle*) [A, missing from B].
p. 51, l. 22	... let those who hear [B ends, the rest is from A and ed.].
p. 53, l. 28	[... popular assembly] Murray was a sophist, Fox an inquisitor, Pitt an executioner [A].
p. 55, l. 1	veins in the calf of [A, B deleted] beauty [B].
p. 55, ll. 3–4	who maliciously ... roundness [A, B deleted].
p. 76, l. 25	and Mason ... his own merit [B] and Mason was too sedulous a copyist of Gray's march to tread a step beyond the print of his buskin [A].
p. 78, l. 37	but his passion ... benefitting individuals [B, not in A].
p. 88, l. 7	though it is questionable ... lofty ideas [B, not in A]; 'From this passage, as well as others, it is clear that our author revised his work many years after he wrote it. To this chapter, in a copy fairly transcribed, he has subjoined Oct. 28th. 1763; but in the same copy, the concluding sentence of the paragraph in text does not occur.' [ed.]
p. 96, l. 11	compromised [B], composed [A].
p. 97, l. 2	Amalie [B], Emily [A]. Walpole's spelling of this Princess's name is inconsistent throughout.
p. 98, l. 20	... disposal of his Ministers] At first he contented himself with fifty thousand annually but for several years two thousand pounds were regularly paid to him every Monday morning [A, deleted].
p. 99, n.	'Note to the end of reign of George II' [B, not in A].
pp. 114–15	Not in printed text. [*Miss Vansittart*]
p. 128	Henry 4th ... Charles 2nd ... Charles 12th. [A, B].
p. 130, l. 22	He was of a plebeian family but inherited a [B], He was a gentleman of [A].
p. 136, l. 10	triumphant [B], indifferent [A].
p. 140, l. 2	This neglect the Duchess ... heard it [B, deleted].
p. 140, l. 17	The Earl assigned ... for France [excision from B, supplied from A].
p. 148, l. 10	Fanny Murray ... Jerusalem [B, deleted].
p. 166, l. 16	But it is justice ... superior to my own [B, added in A in smaller handwriting between the lines].
p. 166, l. 38	Nor was it ... Conway [B, added in A in smaller handwriting between the lines].
p. 156, l. 39	weight [B], influence [A].
p. 170, l. 28	Mr Pitt's superiority ... the large war [B, not in A].
p. 172, l. 32	*Metamorphoses* [ed.], Metamorphosis [A, B].
p. 175, l. 27	nor could George the Third ... Second [B, not in A].
p. 177, l. 33	whereas it all ... the disease [B, not in A].
p. 183, l. 22	till the greater ... creatures of Lord Bute [B, not in A].

p. 183, l. 28   And yet the ruling . . . returning calm [B, not in A].

p. 189, l. 33   Memoirs/ of the Reign/ of King George the Third/ from the beginning of his second Parliament [A and B, heading].

p. 192, l. 13   incensed by . . . James Lowther [B, not in A].

p. 192, l. 21   with his mistress [A, deleted in B].

pp. 194–97   Not in printed text; erased in B, but still legible. [*Duke of Grafton*]

p. 196, l. 27   and formerly a notorious pimp [doubly erased in B].

p. 196, l. 28   and the Mistress [doubly erased in B].

p. 198, ll. 23–31   Not printed in text; excision from B.

p. 199, l. 7   [. . . gallant disposition] to which her lord was but ill suited [B, deleted].

p. 210, l. 13   Not in printed text; excision from B but evidently of a shortened version. [*Duke of Grafton*]

pp. 216–17   Many small changes made between A and B; whole passage carefully rewritten.

p. 216, l. 3   weak, insolent and debauched [A].

p. 216, l. 11   Governor to the King and Duke of York [not in A].

p. 216, l. 14   with pleasure [not in A].

p. 216, l. 15   after her year of widowhood [not in A].

p. 216, l. 30   The Prince grew more assiduous and Lady Waldegrave without disguise received his visits [A].

p. 216, l. 33   hopeless [not in A].

p. 217, l. 1   Royal [not in A].

p. 217, l. 3   but I was not at home [A].

p. 218, l. 11   Not in A. A f.39 ends . . . perfectly intelligible./ Here to come in the history of Mme du Barry.

p. 223, l. 35   nor had he a depth . . . treated with decency [not in A].

p. 224, l. 32   fourth [B], fifth [A].

p. 224, l. 36   [. . . overturned him]; Lord Chatham's absurdity, and want of conduct, was madness, or reduced him to act madness [A, not in B].

p. 224, l. 35   Mackenzie [ed.], Mackinsy [A, B].

p. 225, l. 25   till he reached the summit . . . attention offended [B]; A (deleted) reads:
To the Court he was agreeable from being connected with no party, and from having no glaring fault or vice, was not unwelcome to the nation. He appeared in no light but in that of a useful minister: yet one great singularity came out in his character, which was that no man was more ready for violent extremes under the Administration of others, no man was more temperate than Lord North during his own. [last sentence occurs later in B; rest of passage in B only].

p. 226, l. 11   reclaimed [B], recoiled [ed.].

p. 227, l. 12   Germaine . . . Germain [A, B].

p. 231, l. 34   As a dozen years afterwards . . . his brothers [B, not in A].

pp. 232–233   Were there any reality . . . at forty-nine [B; on inserted sheets in A, headed 'Character of Lord Granby'].

p. 235, l. 2   Johnstone [ed.], Johnson [A and B, *passim*].

pp. 235–36   Such was the complexion . . . could be of none [not in A].

pp. 236–38   Whether it is owing to . . . opinion of mankind [B; on inserted sheets in A, headed 'Character of Lord Weymouth', with several minor changes in B].

p. 238, ll. 2–5   He neither had nor . . . cabals of faction [not in A].

p. 238, ll. 10–11   for pride is . . . of circumstances [not in A].

p. 238, ll. 21ff. not in A; A ends at end of 1770.

p.239, l. 1–p.   on inserted sheets in B, the last of which is mutilated, after
240 l. 26   [. . . pride and mortification].

p. 246, l. 15   think me [A, B], make me [ed.].

p. 247   *Appendix*: 'Portrait of Lord Mansfield', from an unpublished MS in the possession of Mr W. S. Lewis.

p. 248   *Appendix*: 'Character of King George III', from an unpublished MS in the possession of Mr W. S. Lewis.

EXPLANATORY NOTES

THE ROYAL FAMILY

(Dates are given only where significant for the *Memoirs*)

George II (1727–60) married Caroline of Anspach (1683–1737); their children included:

1 Frederick, Prince of Wales (1707–51), married Augusta of Saxe-Gotha, 'Princess Dowager', (died 1772);
2 Anne, Princess Royal (1709–59), married William IV of Orange;
3 Amelia;
4 William, Duke of Cumberland (1721–65);
5 Mary, married Frederick II of Hesse-Cassel;
6 Louisa, married Frederick V of Denmark (1746–66).

The children of Frederick Prince of Wales included:

1 Augusta, born 1737, married 1764 Charles William Ferdinand, Duke of Brunswick;
2 George III (1760–1820), born 1738, married 1761 Charlotte of Mecklenburg-Strelitz;
3 Edward Augustus, Duke of York (1739–67);
4 William, Duke of Gloucester (1743–1805), married secretly 1766 Maria, Dowager Countess Waldegrave;
5 Henry, Duke of Cumberland (1745–90), married secretly 1771 Mrs Horton;
6 Caroline Matilda (1751–75), married Christian VII of Denmark (cousin).

The children of George III included:

1 Prince of Wales, later George IV, born 1762;
2 Frederick, Duke of York, born 1763;
3 William IV (1830–37), born 1765;
4 Charlotte, born 1766;
5 Edward, Duke of Kent, born 1767; and ten others.

THE WALPOLE FAMILY

1 Sir Robert Walpole (1676–1745); Prime Minister 1721–42, created first Earl of Orford 1742; his younger brother was
2 Horatio Walpole (1678–1757), first Baron Walpole of Wolterton; whose son was

254

3 Horatio Walpole, second Baron Walpole, and Earl of Orford, second creation.

Sir Robert Walpole's sons were:

4 Robert (ca. 1701–51), second Earl of Orford;
5 Sir Edward (1706–84), who had three illegitimate daughters, the second of whom, Maria, married the second Earl Waldegrave, and after his death the Duke of Gloucester;
6 Horatio, or Horace Walpole (1717–97), author of the *Memoirs*; fourth Earl of Orford;

Robert Walpole's son was

7 George (1730–91), third Earl of Orford.

THE WALDEGRAVE FAMILY (IN THIS PERIOD)

1 James, first Earl Waldegrave (1685–1741), succeeded by his son
2 James, second Earl (1715–63); Lord of the Bedchamber, chief confidant of George II, governor of the Prince of Wales (afterwards George III); married 1759 Maria, illegitimate daughter of Sir Edward Walpole; three daughters; succeeded by his brother
3 John, third Earl, distinguished soldier, Lt.-General, died 1784; succeeded by his son
4 George, fourth Earl (1751–89), Colonel 14th Regt; married his cousin, Elizabeth Laura, daughter of second Earl Waldegrave; succeeded by eldest son
5 George, fifth Earl (1784–94), accidentally drowned at Eton; succeeded by his brother
6 John James, sixth Earl, Lt.-Colonel, who became owner of Horace Walpole's box containing the *Memoirs*; died 1835 at Strawberry Hill.

Page 1	The first extract concerns the state of the Ministry at the beginning of 1751, as a prologue to detailed accounts of Parliamentary Debates, here omitted.
p. 1, ll. 8, 14	[the Duke] of Cumberland, second son of George II, commander of the Army in Flanders.
p. 3	[Conway] H.W.'s cousin, exemplar of virtue, and probable source of many of the confidential details that follow.
pp. 6–10	[*The Prince of Wales*] cf. H.W. letter to Sir Horace Mann, 21 March 1751.
p. 10	[*Prince George's Governor*] cf. H.W. letter to Mann, 1 April 1751.
p. 16, l. 3 f.b.	[Middleton] Conyers Middleton, *A Free Enquiry into the Miraculous Powers*, 1749.
p. 17, l. 1	[Archbishop] Thomas Herring.

p. 17, l. 9   [Durham] Joseph Butler, author of the *Analogy of Religion*.

p. 22, l. 11   [forgery] Paul Wells, executed at Oxford, 1749.

p. 27, l. 22   [Lord Gower] 'John Leveson Gower, Baron Gower, was elected President of the Board (the Jacobite meeting) in 1742, on the death of the Earl of Lichfield, while he was Lord Privy Seal, which he resigned soon after; but came into the same place again on the coalition, and was some time after created an Earl.' [H.W.]

p. 29, l. 18   [hideous humour] disease.

pp. 30, 32   [*The Craftsman*] anti-Walpole periodical.

p. 47, l. 12   [our present Minister] the Duke of Newcastle. This was written in 1756. [H.W.]

p. 49   [*George Washington*] cf. H.W. letter to Mann, 6 October 1754.

p. 50   [*Parliamentary Orators*] cf. H.W. letters to Conway 15 November 1755, to Bentley 16 November 1755.

p. 60, l. 18   [vailing to] yielding to.

p. 60 ff.   [*Admiral Byng*] cf. H.W. letters to Mann, 14 June 1756 and subsequently.

p. 60, last line   [vent] sale.

p. 69, l. 9   [The fatal morning] 14 March 1757. Cf. H.W. letter to Mann, 17 March.

p. 70, l. 6   [devoted] condemned.

p. 70   [*General Conway and others*] This concerns the expedition to surprise Rochfort, and the Fleet off the Isle of Oleron.

p. 81, l. 6   [the Bill] 'Pratt prepared a Bill for explaining and extending the Habeas Corpus, and ascertaining its full operation.' [H.W.]

p. 84   [*William Pitt and General Wolfe*] cf. H.W. letters to Mann 9 February and 16 October; to Conway, 18 October; and to William Pitt, 19 November 1759.

p. 87   [*Lord Granby and Lord Sackville*] cf. H.W. letter to Conway, 14 August 1759.

p. 88   [*General Waldegrave*] The battle was Minden, 1 August 1759. John, younger brother of James, second Earl, whom he succeeded in the title in 1763.

p. 92, l. 1   [this affair] the court-martial of Lord George Sackville.

p. 94   [*Lord Ferrers*] cf. H.W. letter to Montagu, 6 May 1760.

p. 96 ff.   [*George the Second*] cf. H.W. letter to Montagu, 25 October 1760.

p. 101   [*Accession of George the Third*] cf. H.W. letters to Montagu, 31 October and 24 November 1760.

pp. 119–120   [*Lord Talbot*] For an account of the Coronation, see H.W. letter to Montagu, 24 September 1761.

p. 123   [*The Cock Lane Ghost*] cf. H.W. letter to Montagu, 2 February 1762.

p. 134, l. 3 f.b.   [their greatest difficulty] the Court party's.

p. 138   [*Lord Bute Resigns*] cf. H.W. letter to Montagu, 8 April 1763.

p. 141   [*Lord Waldegrave*] cf. H.W. letter to Mann, 10 April 1763.

p. 147   [*Wilkes and Lord Sandwich*] cf. H.W. letters to Mann, 17 November, and to the Earl of Hertford, 9 December 1763.

p. 152   [*The Earl and the Countess of Northumberland*] 'Sir Hugh Smithson, of a very recent family, had married Lady Elizabeth Seymour, only daughter of Algernon Duke of Somerset, whose mother was an heiress of the Percies Earls of Northumberland; on which foundation Hugh and Elizabeth were created Earl and Countess of Northumberland.' [H.W.]

p. 157   [*Dr. John Brown*] author of *Estimate of the Manners and Principles of the Times* (1757).

p. 167, l. 21   [his bodily infirmities] 'He was enormously fat, had lost one eye, and saw but ill with the other; was asthmatic and had had a stroke of the palsy, besides the wound in his leg that had not healed.' [H.W.]

p. 171, l. 3 f.b.   [the Pope] Clement XIII.

p. 172, l. 17   [in this debate] 'On the 27th of January, Mr Cooke of Middlesex presented a petition from some of the North-American provinces assembled in Congress, against the Stamp Act.' [H.W.]

p. 174, l. 5 f.b.   [Ximenes] Cardinal, bishop of Toledo, and Prime Minister of Spain, (1437–1517); greatly extended the Kingdom of Castile.

p. 175, l. 19   [Rienzi] tribune of Rome, died 1354.

p. 178, l. 17   [on that day] 8 May, 1767: there had been a debate on the East India Company.

p. 186, l. 3 f.b.   [Trifling as this first success was] 'Lord Townshend, the new Lord-Lieutenant, was favourably received in Ireland. He carried with him the consent of the King that the Judges there should hold their places, as in England, *quamdiu se bene gesserint*.' [H.W.]

p. 188, l. 7 f.b.   [Anstey] Christopher Anstey, author of *New Bath Guide* (1766).

p. 189, l. 9   [*Fingal*] 1762, part of the spurious Ossianic poetry of James MacPherson.

p. 191   [*John Wilkes*] cf. H.W. letter to Mann, 1 April 1768.

pp. 194–97 [*The Duke of Grafton and Nancy Parsons*] Since this passage is now published for the first time, H.W.'s footnotes are given in full; also on pp. 198 and 210–13, where the narrative is continued.

p. 197 [*Character of an Anonymous Hero*] cf. H.W. letter to Mann, 12 May 1768.

p. 197, l. 13 [Whiteboys] Irish revolutionary organisation.

p. 206, l. 25 [restored the Douglas] 'The Douglas cause began in 1762. The judges in the Court of Session were divided—being seven to seven. The casting vote of the Lord President gave the decision to the Hamiltons. This judgment was reversed in the Lords on Feb. the 27th, 1769.' (ed.)

p. 208, l. 9 [this business] measures against Wilkes, which culminated in his expulsion from the House of Commons.

p. 210 [*Colonel Luttrell*] cf. H.W letter to Mann, 14 April 1769.

p. 215 [*Junius*] 'Letters of Junius' (1768–73) are now generally believed to have been written by Sir Philip Francis.

p. 221 [*Charles Yorke*] Charles Pratt, Lord Camden, who was opposed to the American policy of the Court party, remained Lord Chancellor until the Great Seal was taken from him in January 1770. 'After struggling with all the convulsions of ambition, interest, fear, honour, dread of abuse, and above all with the difficulty of refusing the object of his whole life's wishes, and with the despair of recovering the instant if once suffered to escape, Charles Yorke, having taken three days to consider, refused to accept the Seals of Chancellor.' [H.W.]

p. 225 [*Lord North*] cf. H.W. letter to Mann, 30 January 1770.

p. 228, l. 3 f.b. [potentate in Europe] H.W. continues: 'This is my impartial opinion of the reign of George the Third, from the death of his grandfather to the end of the year 1771, when I wrote these annals; and the subsequent transactions to the commencement of the new Parliament in 1784 have but corroborated my ideas.'

pp. 228–29 [*William Beckford*] Beckford 'presented an address to the king complaining of a false return made at the Middlesex election, 1770, and replied to the king's curt answer with an impromptu speech, which was subsequently inscribed on a monument erected in his honour in Guildhall.' (D.N.B.)

p. 230, l. 36   [Denmark, an extraordinary Princess!] Caroline Matilda, believed to be mistress of the King's physician, John Frederick Struensee; for this she was imprisoned, divorced and exiled in 1772.

p. 242   [*Chevalier d'Eon*] 'discovered to be a man at his death, 1810' [D.N.B.].

pp. 247–49   [Appendix] These two drafts have not yet been dated but are considerably later than 1771.

INDEX

Addington, Dr Henry (1713–90), 177
Aiguillon, A.-V. Duc d' (1720–98), 171, 218, 220
Ailesbury, Lady, 166
Albemarle, William Anne Keppel, 2nd Earl (1702–54), 50, 176
American War of Independence, xviii, xix, xxi, 227
Anett, Peter Deist (1693–1769), 125
Anne, Princess Royal (1709–59), d. of George II, m. William IV of Orange, 31, 150
Anson, Lord (1697–1762), First Lord of the Admiralty, 1751, 27, 60, 61, 68, 74
Anstey, Christopher (1724–1805), poet, author of *The New Bath Guide*, 188
Argyll, John, 2nd Duke of (1678–1743), 40
Argyll, Archibald Campbell, Earl of Islay and 3rd Duke of (1682–1761), 23, 40, 113, 165
Ashburton, John, 1st Baron, *see* Dunning, John
Asturias, Prince of, 90
Atterbury, Francis (1662–1732), Bishop, 97
Augusta, Princess of Saxe-Gotha, m. Frederick, Prince of Wales; mother of George III, also known as The Princess Dowager (d. 1772), xvii, 7–9, 19, 54–56, 70, 73, 103, 104, 106, 107, 114–16, 118–21, 133, 134, 139, 141, 147, 149, 150, 158, 159, 167, 183, 199, 201, 212, 217, 228, 229–31, 234, 242–3, 245–6, 247
Augusta, Princess, d. of Frederick, Prince of Wales, m. Duke of Brunswick (1737–64), 55, 150, 229
d'Ayen, Duc, 65

Bagot, Sir Walter, 108
Bailey, Mrs (friend of the Duke of Cumberland), 244
Baltimore, Frederick, 6th Baron (1731–71), 11, 193, 194
Barré, Colonel Isaac (1726–1802), 122, 123
Barrington, William Wildman, 2nd Viscount (1713–93), Secretary of War (1765–78), 51, 123
Barry, Mme du (mistress of Louis XV), xvii, 201, 219–21
Bath, William Pulteney, Earl of (1684–1764), 12, 15, 16, 28, 30, 32, 154, 188
Bath, Thomas Thynne, 3rd Viscount Weymouth and 1st Marquis of (1734–96), 187, 213, 222, 226, 236
Beaufort, Duchess of, 114
Beaufort, Duke of, 204
Beauvau, Princesse de, 220
Beckford, William (1709–70), M.P., 51, 120, 122, 191, 192, 228, 229
Bedford, Duchess of, 139, 140, 161, 213
Bedford, John, 4th Duke of (1710–71), xvii, 20, 25; character, 1, 26, 28, 39, 40, 41, 107, 121, 132, 159, 160, 161, 176, 177, 204, 206
Belle (valet de chambre to Louis XV), 202
Benedict XIV, Pope, 64, 125
Bentley, Richard (1708–82), xxvii, xxx
Bernsdorff (Russian Minister), 201, 230
Berry, the Misses, xi, xxx
Blackburne, Lancelot, Archbp. of York (1658–1742), 10, 23
Blakeney, General William (1672–1761), 57, 58

Bolingbroke, Henry St. John, Viscount (1678–1751), 7, 16, 22; character, 32–34, 43, 121, 188, 239
Boswell, James (1740–95), 213
Bower, Archibald (1686–1766), historian, Jesuit, 80
Braddock, Major-General Edward (1695–1755), 50
Bristol, George William Hervey, 2nd Earl of (1721–75), 207
Brown, Dr John (1715–66), author of *The Estimate*, 157
Brunswick, Prince of, *see* Ferdinand
Duchess of, *see* Augusta
Princess of, 116
Buckingham, George Villiers, 2nd Duke of, 239
Burke, Edmund (1729–97), 172, 209, 215
Burke, William (cousin of Edmund), 172, 173
Burnet, Gilbert, *History of his own Times*, xv
Bute, John Stuart, 3rd Earl of (1713–92), also known as The Favourite, First Lord of Treasury (1762–63), xviii, 54–55, 103, 105, 106, 107–13, 114, 115, 117, 119, 120–23, 125–27, 129, 130, 133, 136–42, 147, 148, 152, 154, 158, 161, 162, 183, 198–99, 204, 209, 210, 212, 224, 229, 231, 234, 237, 246
Byng, Hon. John, Admiral (1704–57), x, xii, xiii, 58–61, 66–70, 82

Calabria, Duke of (Spanish heir-apparent), 89
Camden, Charles Pratt, 1st Earl (1714–90), 144, 182, 188, 192, 206, 221, 249
Cameron, Dr Archibald (1707–53), 45
Cameron, Donald ('The Gentle Lochiel'), Jacobite (1695–1758), 45
Campbell, Alexander Hume, 51, 52, 188
Carhampton, Henry Luttrell, 2nd Earl of (1743–1821), 210, 224, 241, 243, 245
Carlos, Don, 89
Caroline of Anspach, Queen of George II, (1683–1737), 4, 5, 7, 8, 18, 19, 23–25, 29, 32, 34, 70, 76, 100, 121
Caroline, Princess (Elizabeth-Caroline), unmarried d. of George II (1713–57), 76, 77
Caroline Matilda, Princess (d. of Frederick, Prince of Wales), m. King Christian VII of Denmark, divorced 1772 (1751–75), 34, 229, 245
Carteret, John, *see* Granville, Earl
Catherine II, Czarina, 158, 230
Cavendish, Lord Frederic, 154, 164
Lord George, 154, 164, 234
Lord John (1732–96), 154, 164
see also Devonshire, Duke of
Chalotais, M. de la, 171
Charles Edward, Prince (the Young Pretender (1720–88), 43, 171
Charlotte of Mecklenburg-Strelitz, Queen of George III (1744–1818), 109, 116, 117, 118, 119, 139, 153, 200, 217, 230
Chateauroux, Duchesse de (mistress of Louis XV), 44, 57
Chesterfield, Philip Stanhope, 4th Earl of (1694–1773), 3, 4, 5, 7, 20, 53, 120, 156, 215

Choiseul, Duc de (1719–85), 168, 170, 218–21, 242
  Duchesse de, 170, 218, 220, 221
Christian VII, King of Denmark, 72; visits George
  III, 199–201
Churchill, Charles (1731–64), poet, 131, 132, 149, 155,
  156
Cibber, Colley (1671–1757), actor and poet, 76
Clanrickard, Earl of, 95
Clarendon, Edward Hyde, Lord (1609–71), xiii, xiv,
  xv, 38
Clayton, Dr Robert, Bp. of Clogher (1695–1758), 79
Cock Lane Ghost Affair, xii, 123–125
Conway, Francis Seymour, see Hertford
Conway, Hon. Henry Seymour (1721–95), Field
  Marshal, brother of Earl of Hertford, cousin of
  H. Walpole, 3, 51, 52, 71, 157, 162, 163, 172, 179,
  194, 211, 222
Cooke, Mr (M.P.), 192, 193
Cornwallis, Charles, 2nd Earl (1738–1803), 71, 199
Cornwallis, Frederick (1713–83), Bp. of Lichfield,
  later Archbp. of Canterbury, 126, 199
Cotes, Humphrey, 161, 192
Critical Review, 93
Cumberland, Henry, Duke of (son of Frederick,
  Prince of Wales) (1745–90), 186, 216, 231
Cumberland, William Augustus, Duke of, son of
  George II (1721–65), xii, xxi, 1, 3, 13–15, 25, 39,
  41, 60, 72–76, 77, 78, 83, 85, 95, 98, 99, 104, 109,
  110, 112, 119, 133, 134, 142, 151, 155, 163, 164,
  167–68
Czarina, see Catherine and Elizabeth

Damiens, 65, 66
Darlington, Countess (George I's mistress), 100
Dartmouth, William, 2nd Earl of (1731–1801), 226,
  227
Dashwood, Sir Francis, 1st Baron Despencer (1708–
  81), Chancellor of Exchequer, 51, 52, 127–29,
  137, 149
Dauphin of France, death and character of, 169
Dauphiness, the, 170
Deffand, Mme du, xvii
Denmark, King and Queen of, see Caroline and
  Christian
Devonshire, William Cavendish, 3rd Duke of (1699–
  1755), 28
  William, 4th Duke of (1720–64), Lord Lieut. of
  Ireland, First Lord of Treasury 1756–7, xxvi,
  xxx, 28, 74, 76, 77, 83, 95, 106, 121, 126; death
  of, 154, 164
Devonshire, 5th Duke of, 154
Dodington, George Bubb (Lord Melcombe) (1691–
  1762), 7, 8, 11, 51, 129
Doran, Dr John, xxvii, xxxi
Dorset, Lionel Cranfield Sackville, 1st Duke of
  (1688–1765), Lord Lieut. of Ireland, 2, 13
Dorset, Charles Sackville, Lord Middlesex, 2nd Duke
  of (1711–69), 13
Dorset, John Frederick, 3rd Duke of (1745–99), 212
Douglas, Duchess of, 205
  last Duke of, 205
  Lady Jane, 205, 206
Douglas Legitimacy lawsuit, 205ff.
Dowdeswell, William (1721–75), Chancellor of
  Exchequer, 162
Dryden, John (1631–1700), 97, 131
Dunmore, John Murray, 4th Earl (1732–1809), 207
Duncan, Dr (George III's physician), 158
Dundas, Sir Laurence, 208
Dunning, John, 1st Baron Ashburton (1731–83),
  Solicitor General, 187, 206, 221
Dyson, Jeremiah (1722–76), politician, 152, 178, 227

Echard, Laurence, *History of England*, xv, 38
Edward, Prince, 2nd son of Prince of Wales, see York,
  Duke of
Egmont, John Perceval, 2nd Earl of (1711–70), 51, 193
Egremont, Charles Wyndham, 2nd Earl of (1710–63),
  29, 142, 143
Elizabeth, Lady (2nd daughter of Prince of Wales),
  55, 91
Elizabeth, Czarina (d. 1762), 62, 128, 170
Elliot, Sir Gilbert, 51, 68, 227
Ellis, Welbore, 1st Baron Mendip (1713–1802), 135,
  227
Emily, (Amelie) Princess (unmarried d. of George
  II), xxvi, 7–9, 18, 73, 77, 98, 99, 100, 103, 104;
  character, 25, 201
Eon, Chevalier d', 146, 147, 184, 242
Erskine, Sir Henry (d. 1765), 108, 111, 113

Ferdinand, King of Spain, 88
Ferdinand, Prince of Brunswick, 86, 87, 150, 208, 230
Ferrers, Laurence Shirley, 4th Earl (1720–60), 92, 94,
  95
Fielding, Mr Justice, 160, 193
Fitzroy, Lord Charles, 87, 111
Fitzwalter, Lady, mother of 4th Earl of Holderness,
  29
Fleury, Cardinal, 44, 168, 214, 218
Fowke, General, 61
Fox, Charles James (1749–1806), xxv, 239, 240, 248
Fox, Henry, see Holland, Lord
Frederick Louis, Prince of Wales (1707–51), m.
  Augusta of Saxe-Gotha, father of George III,
  xvii, 2, 6, 19, 34, 54, 55, 91, 106, 126; death and
  character, 7ff., 9, 10, 11, 12, 13, 56

Galloway, Earl of (Jacobite), 108
George I (1660–1727), 5, 19, 33, 97, 99, 100
George II (1683–1760), m. Caroline of Anspach, xi,
  xvii, 1, 2, 3, 5, 7–10, 13, 16, 18, 19, 21, 25–27,
  31–34, 39, 40, 56, 60, 61, 66, 68, 69–70, 72, 73–77,
  83, 87, 96–100, 102, 104, 107, 115, 123, 159, 175;
  character, 22–24
George III (1738–1820), m. Charlotte of Mecklenburg-Strelitz, xi, xviii, 10, 55, 102–106, 109, 110,
  111, 112, 115, 116, 117, 119, 120, 121, 123, 126,
  139, 145, 150, 153, 158, 159, 160, 163, 168, 175,
  183–84, 185, 190, 191, 194, 197, 199, 200, 201,
  211, 212, 215, 216, 217, 222, 224, 226, 227, 228,
  234, 235–36, 237, 240, 241, 242, 243, 245;
  character, 247
George IV (1762–1830), Prince of Wales, 232, 240
Germaine, see Sackville
Gilbert, John, Bp. of Salisbury and Archbp. of York
  (1757), 70
Gloucester, Maria, Duchess of (former Countess
  Waldegrave), 216, 217, 230
Gloucester, William Henry, Duke of (1743–1805),
  185, 216, 230, 245
Goldsmith, Oliver (1728–1774), 188
Gower, Granville Leveson-Gower, 2nd Earl (1721–
  1803), 27, 105, 107, 152, 206, 211, 213, 222, 226
Graeme, Colonel, 117
Grafton, Ann (born Liddell), Duchess of, 195, 198
Grafton, Charles Fitzroy, 2nd Duke of (1683–1757),
  Walpole's godfather, ix, 24
Grafton, Augustus Henry Fitzroy, 3rd Duke of
  (1735–1811), xvi, xviii, xxii, xxv, 111, 144, 182,
  194–7, 198, 204, 210–13, 214, 221, 223, 224, 237
Grammont, Duchesse de, 170, 184, 220

Granby, John Manners, Marquis of (1721–70), 87, 88, 232

Granville, John Carteret, Earl (1690–1763), Lord Pres. of the Council, 4, 8, 12, 20; character, 21, 32, 41, 59, 74, 78, 79, 202; Lord Lieut. of Ireland, 19; death, 136

Gray, Thomas (1716–71), x, xi, 76

Green, Matthew, xv

Grenville, Hon. George (1712–70), xvi, xviii, 51, 52, 112, 152, 172, 182, 183, 192, 208, 224, 225, 232, 237; apptd. Secy. of State, 127; character, 142; death, 234

Grenville, Richard Temple, see Temple, Earl

Grey, William de, 1st Baron Walsingham (1719–81), Attorney-General, 221

Grosvenor, Lady, 216, 231, 244, 245

Guerchy, Comte de, French Ambass., 145–7, 184

Hales, Dr Stephen (1677–1761), physiologist and inventor, 97

Halifax, George Montagu Dunk, 2nd Earl (1716–71), 26, 68, 142, 143, 147

Hamilton, Duchess of, 119, 193, 205ff.

Hamilton, William Gerard (1729–96), suspected of being author of Letters of Junius, 215

Harcourt, Simon Harcourt, 1st Earl (1714–77), 10

Hardwicke, Philip Yorke, Earl of (1690–1764), Lord Chancellor, 17, 68, 73, 74, 81, 83, 121, 245

Hardwicke, Philip Yorke, 2nd Earl (1720–90), 222

Harley, Thomas (1730–1804), Lord Mayor, 191–3

Harrington, William Stanhope, 1st Earl of (1690–1756), Lord Lieut. of Ireland, 2, 8

Hartington, Lord, xxvi, 10, 28

Haughton, Mrs, see Parsons, Nancy

Hawkins, Surgeon to Pr. of Wales, 6

Hay, Dr, 51, 68

Hayter, Thomas (1702–62), Bp. of Norwich, 10, 120

Henley, Sir Robert (1708–72), Lord Keeper, 93; appd. Lord Chancellor, 112

Herring, Thomas (1693–1757), Archbp. of Canterbury, 17, 70

Hertford, Elizabeth (Fitzroy), Countess of, 194, 195

Hertford, Francis Conway, 1st Earl of (1719–94), nephew of Sir Robert Walpole, 72, 165, 194, 198, 200, 211

Hervey, John, Lord (1696–1743), xvi, 8, 30, 76

Hesse, Prince of, 200, 230

Hoadley, Benjamin (1676–1761), Bp. of Winchester and writer, 17

Hogarth, William (1697–1764), 80, 125

Holderness, Robert D'Arcy, 4th Earl of (1718–78), Ambass. to Holland and Secy of State, xxvi, 29, 31, 39, 240, 241

Holke, Baron (favourite of Christian VII of Denmark), 201, 230

Holland, Henry Fox, 1st Baron (1705–74), xvi, xx, xxi, xxvii, 12, 13, 51, 53, 59, 60, 73, 74, 82, 83, 86, 104, 112, 116, 121, 123, 133, 134, 135, 137, 138, 162, 210, 228, 229, 237, 240, 245

Holland, Henry Richard, 3rd Baron (1773–1840), xxv, xxvii

Hollis, Thomas (Republican), 209

Horton, Mrs (sister of Col. Luttrell), m. Duke of Cumberland, 210, 243–5

Howe, William, 5th Viscount (1729–1814), 71

Hume, David (1711–76), philosopher and historian, 117, 170, 189

Huntingdon, Countess of, 95, 125

Huntingdon, Earl of (Master of the Horse), 105, 107

Hussey, Mr, 30, 222

Hutton, Matthew (1693–1758), Archbp. of York, and later of Canterbury, 17, 70

Ilchester, 6th Earl of, xxiv, xxviii, xxix

Ilchester, 7th Earl of, xxv, xxviii, xxix

Inverness, John, titular Earl of (supporter of Old Pretender) (1691–1746), 42

Irnham, Simon Luttrell, Lord, 210, 244

James (III), Old Pretender (1688–1766), 41–43; death, 171

Jenkinson, see Liverpool, Earl of

Johnson, Dr Samuel (1709–84), xiii, 124; character, 238

Johnstone, Governor, 235

Junius, author of Letters, xviii, 215

Kendal, Ehrengard von Schulemburg, Duchess of (1667–1743), Geo. I's mistress, 5, 33, 100

Kent, Duke of, 6

Keppel, Colonel (cousin of Duke of Richmond, appointed Gentleman of the Horse), 111

Keppel, William, see Albemarle

Kidgell, John, 147–49

Königsmark, Count, 99–100

Lee, Dr Sir George (1700–58), lawyer and politician, 9, 12, 55

Legge, Hon. Henry Bilson (1708–64), 4th son of Earl of Dartmouth, Chancellor of the Exchequer, 27, 28, 51, 52, 55, 56, 73, 126, 153–4

Lennox, Lady Sarah, 115–18

Lennox, Lord George (brother of Duke of Richmond), 111

Lewis, Mr W. S., xi, xiii, xvi–xvii, xix, xxi, xxix

Ligonier, John (Jean-Louis), 1st Earl (1680–1770), Field Marshal, 15

Lincoln, Henry Fiennes, 9th Earl of (1720–94), 9; succeeds uncle as 2nd Duke of Newcastle-under-Lyme, 63

Liverpool, Charles Jenkinson, 1st Earl of (1727–1808), 140, 227

Lorn, Lord (brother-in-law of Conway), 165, 193

Louis XV (1710–74), 64–66; character, 168, 218–21

Lowther, Sir James, later Earl of Lonsdale (1736–1802), 192, 197, 199, 203, 204, 235

Luttrell, Henry Lawes, see Carhampton

Lyttelton, Charles, Bp. of Carlisle (1714–68), 157

Lyttelton, George, Lord (1709–73), 2, 7, 29, 30, 51, 52, 63, 93, 148

Lyttelton, Col. Sir Richard, 2

Macaulay, Mrs (1731–91), historian, 189, 209, 213

Mailly, Mme de (Louis XV's mistress), 44

Mann, Sir Horace (1701–86), envoy at Florence, xii, xiii, 166

Mansfield, William Murray, 1st Earl of (1705–93), Lord Chief Justice, 53, 78, 79, 80, 81, 105, 121, 124, 126, 137, 144, 148, 188, 192, 206–8, 222, 228; character, 248–9

Marie, Princess (1723–72), daughter of Geo. II, m. Frederick of Hesse-Cassel, 98, 150

Mason, William (1724–97), poet, 76

Melcombe, Lord, see Dodington, George

Meredith, Sir William, M.P. (d. 1790), 151

Middlesex, Lady (mistress of Prince of Wales), 8

Middlesex, Lord, see Dorset, 2nd Duke

Middleton, Dr Conyers (1683–1750), 16

Miner, Dorothy, xxxi

Montagu, George, ix, xi

Montagu, John, see Sandwich, Earl of

Mordaunt, General Sir John (1697–1780), 71

Munchausen, Baron, 73, 75, 98
Murray, see Mansfield

Newcastle, Thomas Pelham-Holles, Duke of (1693–1768), xi, xii, xviii, 1, 10, 12, 13, 15, 17, 20, 24–26, 29, 38, 39, 55, 58, 59, 60, 62, 74, 81, 82, 83, 91, 98, 107, 121, 135, 136, 159, 164, 202; character and career, 18, 19, 63, 86, 105, 106, 125, 126, 127
Nivernois, Duc de, 132, 146
North, Frederick, 2nd Earl of Guildford and later Lord North (1732–92), xviii, xx, xxi, 9, 10, 157, 183, 186, 224, 225–7, 241
North Briton, The, 129, 131, 208, 216, 235
Northey, Sir Edward (Attorney General) (1652–1723), 51, 52
Northington, Robert Henley, 1st Earl of (1708–72), 137, 174
Northumberland, Earl and Countess of, 152–3, 161
Norton, Sir Fletcher (1716–89), later Lord Grantley, Speaker of Commons, 137, 188, 206, 208, 249
Nugent, Robert Nugent, Earl (1702–88), 51, 52

Onslow, Arthur (Speaker) (1691–1768), 15, 98, 115
Onslow, George, M.P., 192, 203
Onslow, Colonel George (Speaker's nephew), 203, 234
Orange, Prince of, 31, 34
    Princess of, see Anne
Orford, Earls of, see Walpole
Orléans, Duc d', 9
Ormond, Duke of, 4
Osborn (historian), 38
Ossory, John Fitzpatrick, 2nd Earl, 195, 211
    Countess of, xii, 211
Oxford, Earl of, 13

Paoli, Pascal (Corsican general) (1725–1807), 213–14
Parma, Duke of, 89
Parsons, Nancy (Mrs Haughton), mistress of Duke of Grafton, xxv, 194, 195, 196, 211, 212
Pelham, Hon. Henry (1695?–1754), bro. of Duke of Newcastle, 1st Lord of Treasury, xviii, 1, 10, 11, 19, 20, 21, 24, 27, 28, 34–38, 39, 45–46, 59, 83
Pelham, Thomas (cousin of Duke of Newcastle), 63
Pembroke, Henry Herbert, 10th Earl of (1734–94), 176
Pitt, Anne (William Pitt's sister), 121, 122, 215
Pitt, William (Earl of Chatham) (1708–78), Sec. of State (1756–61), Lord Privy Seal (1766–68), xiii, xviii, xxi, 8, 12, 13, 28, 51, 53, 66, 71, 73, 77–79, 82, 83, 84, 142, 157, 167, 170, 173, 202, 214, 222, 229, 237; character, 85ff., 105, 106, 107, 108, 113, 120–2, 174, 175, 177–8, 180–2
Pompadour, Mme de, 57, 168, 201, 218
Pope, Alexander (1688–1744), 131, 173
Portland, William Henry Cavendish-Bentinck, 3rd Duke of (1738–1809), 192, 197, 203, 204, 216
Potter, Thomas (1718–59), 51, 147
Powell, Sir John, judge (1633–96), 144
Powlett, Earl, 5
Pratt, Sir John, see Camden
Procter, Sir William Beauchamp, 192
Prussia, Frederick II, King of, 28, 73, 86, 108, 150
Pulteney, Johnston, 207
Pulteney, William, see Bath, Earl of
Pynsent, Sir William, 156–7, 180

Queen, the, see Charlotte and Caroline
Queensberry, Duchess of, 206
Queensbury, Charles, 3rd Duke of (1698–1778), 206

Richelieu, L. F.-A., Marquis de (1696–1788), 57, 68, 201, 218
Richmond, Mary, Duchess of, 135, 194
Richmond, Chas. Lennox, 3rd Duke of (1735–1806), 111, 112, 135, 194
Rigby, Richard (1722–88), Paymaster, Secy. to Duke of Devonshire, 96, 196, 208, 227
Roache, Captain, opposes Luttrell in Middlesex election, 210
Robertson, William (1721–93), 189
Robinson, Sir Thomas, later Lord Grantham (1695–1770), 107
Robyns, Mr, 5
Rochester, Earl of, 239
Rochford, William Zuylestein, 4th Earl of (1717–81), 107, 226
Rockingham, Charles Wentworth, 2nd Marquis of (1730–82), xviii, 162, 172, 203, 222, 237; character, 163, 209
Russell, Lady Caroline, 176
Russell, Lord, 155

Sackville, Charles, see Dorset
Sackville, Lord George (Germain), 1st Viscount Sackville (took name Germain in 1770) (1716–85), 51, 52, 87, 88, 108, 226, 227, 234, 235
St. George, Chevalier, see James, Old Pretender
Sandwich, John Montagu, 4th Earl of (1718–92), 1, 9, 26; character, 27, 28, 39, 147, 149, 206, 226
Saville, Sir George, 8th Bt. (d. 1784), 151
Sawbridge, John (1732–95), brother of Mrs Macaulay), 202, 203, 209
Secker, Thomas (1693–1768), Archbp. of Canterbury, 5–6, 17, 110, 124, 199
Selwyn, George Augustus (1719–91), wit and politician, 108, 155, 215
Shannon, Henry Boyle, Earl of (1682–1764), 156
Shelburne, Sir William Petty Fitzmaurice, 2nd Earl of (1737–1805), 1st Marquis of Lansdowne, 123, 187, 222
Shelley, Mr (nephew of Duke of Newcastle), 63
Smelt, Leonard (1719?–1800), Capt. in R.E. and sub-governor to George, Prince of Wales, 240–2
Smollett, Tobias (1721–71), novelist, 93–94, 130
Sobieski, Princess (wife of Old Pretender), 42
Somerset, Charlotte, Duchess of, 194
Spain, Royal Family of, 88
Spencer, Lady Elizabeth, 176
Stair, John, 2nd Earl of (1673–1747), 40
Stanhope, Earl, 9
Stephenson, Republican, 209
Stevens, Mr, mathematician, 5
Stone, Andrew (preceptor to Frederick, Prince of Wales), 10
Stone, Dr George, Primate of Ireland, 156
Stonehewer, Mr (Grafton's secretary), 198
Stormont, David Murray, 2nd Viscount (1727–96), with Old Pretender, 42
Strange, Lord, 51
Strangways, Lady Susan (Henry Fox's niece), 116–18
Stuart, Andrew, 205, 207
Stuart, Lady Mary (Bute's daughter), 108
Stuart, Lady Susan (Earl of Galloway's daughter), 108
Stuart, Mackenzie (brother of Bute), 107, 224, 234
Stuart, 2nd son of Bute, 199
Suffolk, Henrietta, Lady, George II's mistress, 4, 22, 23, 33, 41, 99, 100
Sunderland, Charles Spencer, 3rd Earl of (1674–1722), 9, 19

Talbot, Bishop, 5
Talbot, Earl (Lord Steward), xxvi, 113–14, 115, 119–20

Tankerville, Earl, 144
Tavistock, Marchioness of, 176
Tavistock, Marquis of (son of Duke of Bedford), death of (1767) and character, 176–7
Temple, Richard Temple Grenville, 1st Earl (1711–79), 68, 120, 132, 144, 145, 192, 232
Terrick, 199
Thomas, John (1696–1781), Bp. of Peterborough and preceptor to George, Prince of Wales, 70
Thurloe (Thurlow), Edward, 1st Baron (1731–1806), 207, 227
Townshend, Charles, 2nd Viscount (1674–1738), 2, 4, 19
Townshend, Hon. Charles (1725–67), son of 3rd Viscount, Sec. of War and Chancellor of Exchequer, 52, 134, 135, 173, 178, 184, 186, 239
Townshend, Hon. George, Marquis (1724–1807), eldest son of 3rd Viscount, 60, 85, 186
Townshend, Lady Etheldreda (wife of 3rd Viscount), ix, 3, 21
Trecothick, West India merchant, 191, 192, 229
Tweedale, John Hay, 4th Marquis of (d. 1762), 40

Vane, Miss (mistress of Frederick, Prince of Wales), 8
Vansittart, Miss (Maid of Honour to Princess Dowager), 114–15
Vauguion, Duc de (governor to the Dauphin), 220
Vergy, Treyssac de, 147
Vintimille, Mme de (Louis XV's mistress), 44
Virri, Count, Sardinian Minister, 141

Wake, William, Archbp. of Canterbury (1657–1737), 99
Waldegrave, Col. (m. daughter of Lord Gower), 27
Waldegrave, 1st Earl, xxiii, 99
Waldegrave, James, 2nd Earl (1715–63), xxiii, xxv, 56, 99, 104, 134, 216; death from smallpox, 141–2
Waldegrave, John, 3rd Earl (d. 1784), brother of 2nd Earl, 88, 161, 204
Waldegrave, 4th, 5th and 6th Earls, xxiii
Waldegrave, Lady Elizabeth (sister of Duchess of Bedford), 140, 213
Wales, Princes of, see Frederick and George III
Wales, Princess of, see Augusta
Walpole, Sir Edward (1706–84), Horace's brother and father of Duchess of Gloucester, 140, 216
Walpole, Horace, 4th Earl of Orford, author of the Memoires, his works, x; character, 82–84, 135–6, 140, 163–6, 189–90
Walpole, Horatio (Horace the Elder), 1st Baron Walpole (1678–1757), uncle of Horace, ix, 16

Walpole, Sir Robert, 1st Earl of Orford (1676–1745), father of Horace, Prime Minister (1721–42), ix, 4, 8, 11, 12, 17–21, 24, 25, 27, 28, 30, 32, 33, 34–38, 40, 43, 51, 52, 59, 78, 79, 82, 100, 214
Walpole, Thomas (Horace's cousin), 181–2
Warburton, William, Bp. of Gloucester (1698–1779), 91, 147–9, 158–9
Washington, George (1732–99), future President of the U.S.A., 49–50
Webbe, Philip Carteret (1700–1770), 143, 147, 148
Wedderburne, Alexander, 1st Earl of Rosslyn (1733–1805), 187, 206, 227
Weldon, Sir Anthony (d. 1649?), historian, 38
Wesley, John, 80
Westmoreland, Lord, 118
Weymouth, Viscount, see Bath, Marquis of
Wharton, Philip, Duke of (1698–1731), 239
Whitfield (or Whitefield), George, Methodist leader (1714–1770), 79, 80, 95, 194
Whithead (poet), 76
Wilkes, John (1727–97), xii, xv, xviii, xix, 129ff., 143, 144, 145, 147, 148, 155, 191, 192, 193, 204, 208, 215, 225, 243
Willes, Sir John (1685–1761), Chief Justice, 11, 22, 187
Williams, Sir Charles Hanbury (1708–59), 30
Wilmington, Spencer Compton, Earl of (1673–1743), 19, 24
Wilmot, Sir John Eardley (1709–92), 221
Winchelsea, Earl, 28
Windham, Sir William (1717–61), 32, 143
Winnington, Thomas (1696–1746), Lord of Admiralty, Paymaster and Privy Councillor, 21, 30
Winton, George, 5th Earl (d. 1759), 43
Wolfe, James, General (1727–59), 71, 84–85
Wolfenbuttel, Duke of, 75, 99
Wood, Robert, Under Secretary, 143, 187
Wrottesley, Miss Elizabeth, 211
Wrottesley, Sir Richard, 211

Yarmouth, Amalie Walmoden, Countess of (1704–65), mistress of Geo. I, 9, 22, 23, 72, 74, 98
York, Cardinal of (2nd son of Old Pretender), 41, 171, 172
York, Edward, Duke of (son of Prince of Wales) (1739–67), 7, 34, 55, 56, 74, 104, 105, 116; death and character, 185
Yorke, Charles, son of Lord Hardwicke, Lord Chancellor (d. 1770), 206, 221–3
Yorke, Sir P., see Hardwicke

Zinzendorff, Count (Head of Moravian Church), 79